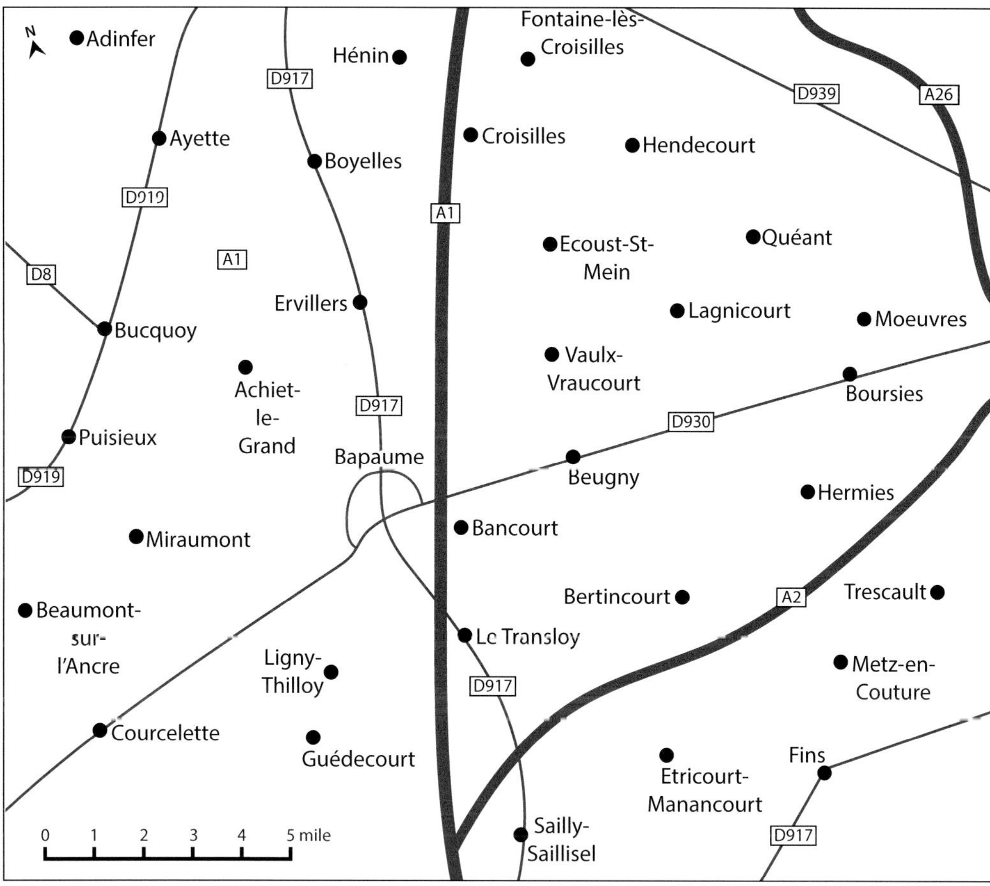

Map 1 The Northern Devastated Zone.

The Battles for the Wastelands

The British and Dominion Corps' engagements in the Northern Devastated Zone, March 1917–September 1918

K.W. Mitchinson

Helion & Company

Dedication

To J.B.

Again, to walk those verdant but once tortured acres …

Helion & Company Limited
Unit 8 Amherst Business Centre
Budbrooke Road
Warwick
CV34 5WE
England
Tel. 01926 499 619
Email: info@helion.co.uk
Website: www.helion.co.uk
Twitter: @helionbooks
Visit our blog at blog.helion.co.uk

Published by Helion & Company 2024
Designed and typeset by Mach 3 Solutions (www.mach3solutions.co.uk)
Cover designed by Paul Hewitt, Battlefield Design (www.battlefield-design.co.uk)

Front cover: September 1918. British lorries passing through the ruins of what was once the village of Ecoust-St-Mein. (With permission. Copyright IWM Q7294)
Back cover: A railway bridge over the Canal du Nord destroyed during the German withdrawal of March 1917. The southern portal of the tunnel near Ytres is in the background. (With permission. Copyright IWM Q46949)

ISBN 978-1-804514-28-3

British Library Cataloguing-in-Publication Data.
A catalogue record for this book is available from the British Library.

Contents

List of Illustrations vi
Introduction x

1 Advance to the Hindenburg Line: March-April 1917 13
2 Battles for the Outpost Villages: II, V, VIII Corps 22
3 Battles for the Outpost Villages: I ANZAC 30
4 Battles for the Outpost Villages: XV Corps 37
5 Hindenburg Line Reached: Conclusion 41
6 Losing the Wastelands: Introduction 43
7 Losing the Wastelands: VI Corps, March 1918 45
8 Losing the Wastelands: IV Corps, March 1918 59
9 Losing the Wastelands: V Corps, March 1918 85
10 Losing the Wastelands: Conclusion 121
11 Regaining the Wastelands: August–September 1918 130
12 Regaining the Wastelands: Conclusion 161

Tour 1: Le Transloy (43 miles) 167
Tour 2: Bapaume (36 miles) 174
Tour 3: Favreuil (45 miles) 181
Tour 4: Ervillers (33 miles) 189

Appendix 196

Maps 198

Index: People and Places 219
Index: Formations and Units 224

List of Illustrations

The area to the north-east of Mesnil-en-Arrouaise where the much dispersed troops of 141 Brigade and elements of 51 and 52 Brigades fought desperate delaying actions on 24 March 1918. 101

Taken from Four Winds Farm looking north-east over Five Points Cemetery (centre right), to Vallulart Wood and the site of the former Hayettes Wood beyond. The buildings comprising what is today known as Gare, close to the canal's southern portal, are on the right. 101

From Vallulart Wood above the southern portal of the canal east-south-east towards the area cut by Mouettes Trench. This was originally part of a German trench system and was used in turn by both sides. By September 1918 it was part of the system known to the British as the Ytres-Equancourt Line. 102

The present day remains of Dessart Wood from the D55 north of Fins are centre left. Dessart Ridge Switch ran right to left in front of the camera and then joined with Metz Switch a little further to the north. The March 1918 southern boundary of V Corps with VII Corps ran roughly parallel to the switch a few hundred yards further to its east. 102

Looking north-west on the D55 Equancourt – Neuville Bourjonval road from about where Neuville Switch joined the Green Line in March 1918. Ytres church is centre. The line of trees in the foreground marks where the northern end of Hayettes Wood once reached. 103

From the northern end of Dessart Switch to the east of Metz showing part of Winchester valley and Gouzeaucourt Wood. The D7 (which becomes the D29B east of the wood) is just visible in the centre. Metz Switch ran through the camera position, which is close to the communal and British cemeteries. In March 1918, 47th Division fought hard here in the switch to stem the enemy advance; in September the New Zealanders advanced across the area with 38th Division on their right. 103

The pre-war railway forked about 800 yards east-north-east of Delsaux Farm. The southern fork crossed the road here 1,200 yards west of Lebucquière and ran on down to beyond Ytres. The western edge of Vélu Wood can be seen in the centre. German troops debouching from the wood in March 1918 were cut down in swathes by machine guns on this slight ridge and by artillery in the Green Line to their rear. 104

The old railway embankment to the east of Vélu Wood. The original trestle bridge over the track was probably destroyed by the Germans during their withdrawal to the Hindenburg Line. Its stone replacement was constructed post-war. It was from the embankment that two companies of 7/A&SH fought their dogged rearguard in March and close to where both Captains James and Gribble won their Victoria Crosses. 104

The site of Bruno Mill, with Doignies church centre. On 21 March 1918 hundreds of Germans were killed as they advanced towards Hermies Switch by crews of a pair of machine guns of 25 Bn MGC positioned on the mill's ruins. 105

Spoil Heap on the west bank of the canal east of Hermies was a major German strong point both once the advance to the Hindenburg Line was halted and again in September 1918. Its garrisons caused significant Allied casualties during the offensives and the more routine life of trench warfare. 105

Yorkshire Bank was another of the canal's spoil heaps. Today is it cut by the A26 *péage*. From 1917 it was riddled with British dug outs and command posts. There are a few lumps of concrete on its surface but these appear to come from a date later than the Great War. 106

The north-west corner of Maricourt Wood in the valley running south-west from Lagnicourt- Marcel. The Wingate Memorial is behind the camera, with the position of the important Vaulx Trench, part of the March 1918 Battle Zone, running in front of the wood and across the valley to the site of the former Vaulx Wood. In this sector, Vaulx Wood Switch ran along the valley to link Lagnicourt village defences with Vaulx Trench. This trench crossed Vaulx Wood's northern face. Vaulx-Vraucourt lies in the lower ground beyond the ridge in the far distance. 106

Looking from about the position of Lark Post south-east to Boursies. The post marked the boundary between 6th and 51st Divisions on 21 March 1918. The Hindenburg Line south of Pronville lay about 1,800 yards to the north of the post. 107

Part of the complex of sunken lanes on the north side of the Hirondelle valley a few hundred yards east of Noreuil. On 2 September 1918, 2/Royal Scots and 1/RSF suffered heavily as they tried to clear enemy garrisons from the dugouts and posts lining the lanes. The track climbing the hill on the opposite side of the valley leads into Lagnicourt. 107

This partly sunken track runs south past Noreuil Australian Cemetery to join the D36 west of Lagnicourt. The area just north of the junction was known to the British as Dunelm. It was something of a strong point protecting the western exits from Lagnicourt and had a communication trench linking it with the important Lagnicourt Trench to the east. 108

The valley of the Hirondelle between Noreuil and Vaulx-Vraucourt. Vraucourt Copse is in the right distance. The pre-war broad gauge railway ran along the flat land just beneath the bank. In March 1918 the valley marked the boundary between 59th and 6th Divisions, and thus also the boundary between VI and IV Corps. 108

The Hirondelle west of Noreuil. Today this path offers a pleasant, shaded walk between Vaulx-Vraucourt and Noreuil. On 21 March 1918 it was the scene of confused and desperate fighting between the advancing Germans and troops of 6th Division. 109

The Hog's Back, with the shrouded church tower of Ecoust-St-Mein in the centre distance. On 21 March, hundreds of Germans were cut down on this plateau by machine guns and artillery of 59th Division. The ill-fated counter-attack by two battalions of 177 Brigade also crossed the area as they advanced over their division's Battle Zone towards Ecoust and Noreuil. 109

Frequently used as a brigade HQ and an assembly area, Judas Farm lies to the north side of the Sensée valley and west of St-Léger. Today's farm complex is significantly larger than the original but the route of the old railway and its embankment can still be seen to its north and east. 110

St-Léger Wood from the south. The TGV and the *péage* are off camera to the right. The lane goes under the two and connects with the track climbing from Croisilles British Cemetery. 110

With Favreuil church central, this shows the ground crossed in August 1918 by troops of 111 Brigade in the somewhat confusing attack on the trench west of the village. The tree on the extreme left lines the lane linking Sapignies to Favreuil down which 2/4th Dukes may also have advanced. 111

The land north-east of Ervillers as it begins to climb towards St-Léger. It was in this lower ground that troops of 34th and 40th Divisions tried to reorganise on 23-24 March, and from where 13/East Surrey assembled for its attack on Mory. Guardsmen of 4 Guards Brigade held the ground on the slope to the right. 111

The copse in the centre lies immediately north of the D36 linking Mory with Ervillers. The southern end of the latter village on the D917 is seen beyond the trees. The copse did not exist before the war and grows on what was then very heavily contested land during the March Offensive. Exhausted remnants of 31st and 40th Divisions garrisoned hastily dug slit trenches and shell holes on the slope immediately east of Ervillers. 112

Ervillers from the south. The lane was crossed by Bee Wood Trench and Bee Wood Support as they reached down towards Béhagnies. In March 1918 this area was defended by remnants of 40th and 41st Divisions and later by 125 and 126 Brigades of 42nd Division. 112

By German standards Sapignies cemetery is small. This sometimes untidy site contains the graves of 1,550 soldiers. Most of those troops interred in the mass grave died in March and April 1918. 113

The spire of Biefvillers church is left of centre. The photo looks across from the quarry close to the junction of the track running down from Sapignies to the D10E3. In March 1918 the fields here were cut by quickly dug trenches manned by units largely of 41st and 25th Divisions. In late August that year, troops of, 2nd, 37th and 62nd Division assembled in and around the village for their attacks on Sapignies and Favreuil. 113

The higher ground to the east of Bucquoy, with the dark mass of Logeast Wood in the left distance. This was the area held for a short time by 62nd Division on 25 March. Its defence allowed remnants of 41st Division to pass to the rear. The enemy poured out of Logeast Wood in hot pursuit. 114

The Cojuel valley from between Douchy and Ayette. On 28 March 2/Grenadier Guards of 4 Guards Brigade, 31st Division, halted an attack on Douchy by Germans advancing down the valley towards the camera. 114

From west of Courcelles looking north-east from the British position known as the Milk Work on the D12. Ridge Work was to the left on the ploughed field, with Coffee Redoubt further over and to the right. Moyenneville lies on the other side of the high ground on which the RFC established an airfield in 1917. 115

Railway Cutting Cemetery, west-south-west of Gomiécourt. The cemetery holds the graves of men of 2nd and 3rd Divisions killed in August 1918. The cutting was an important rallying point and command centre in March and August 1918. Its banks were mined for dugouts by both German and British forces. 115

Taken from the lower slope of the Gomiécourt ridge looking north by east towards Ervillers. The village church is central. This is the ground defended by battalions of 42nd Division in March 1918 and the scene of offensive actions by tanks and troops of 2nd and 3rd Division in August. Bee Wood was about in the centre of the photograph nestled on the bank which is marked by the broken line of trees running across the ground left to right. 116

Corps and Divisional Commanders

Lt Gen A. Haldane, VI Corps. 116
Lt Gen C. Shute, V Corps April-November 1918. 116
Lt Gen C. Jacob, II Corps. 117
Lt Gen E.A. Fanshawe, V Corps August 1916-April 1918 117
Lt Gen I. Maxse, XVIII Corps. 117
Lt Gen G. Harper, IV Corps. 117
Lt Gen Sir W. Birdwood, I ANZAC Corps. 118
Maj Gen C. Romer, 59th Division. 118
Maj Gen C.E. Lawrie, 63rd Royal Naval Division. 118
Maj Gen G. Gorringe, 47th Division. 118
Maj Gen G.P. Fielding, Guards Division. 119
Maj Gen C. Deverell, 3rd Division. 119
Maj Gen G. Jeffries, 19th Division. 119
Maj Gen G. Barrow, 7th Division. 119
Maj Gen G. Bainbridge, 25th Division. 120
Maj Gen T. Cubitt, 38th Division. 120
Maj Gen Sir J. Ponsonby, 40th Division. 120
Maj Gen W. Braithwaite, 62nd Division. 120

Tour Map 1 Le Transloy. 168
Tour Map 2 Bapaume 175
Tour Map 3 Favreuil. 182
Tour Map 4 Ervillers. 190

Introduction

Between the spring of 1917 and late summer of 1918, British and German armies fought their way backwards and forwards across a swathe of Picardy which had been deliberately and systematically devastated. The area concerned is that which lies roughly between Le Transloy and Bapaume in the south and Croisilles and Hénin-sur-Cojeul in the north; Bucquoy and Puisieux in the west to Gouzeaucourt and Villers-Plouich in the east. Within this zone in March 1917, British II, V, VII, and XV Corps, and I ANZAC followed the Germans as they withdrew to the Hindenburg Line. The same areas witnessed the sometimes chaotic retreat of IV, V, and VI Corps a year later and then also the semi-open warfare fought by the same three corps during the summer months of 1918.

Most of these mainly non set-piece actions have been considerably neglected by recent writers and historians. Similarly, many of the fields and villages where they took place have been largely ignored by guidebooks. The intent here is to provide a practical guide to visiting the areas and to explain the tactical encounters by which the British and Dominion corps captured, lost, and recaptured such villages as Achiet-le-Petit, Gomiécourt, Ervillers, Mory, Croisilles, Frémicourt, Ytres, Lebucquière, Beaumetz, Hermies, Metz-en-Couture, and Gouzeaucourt. The eastern areas of the 1916 Battle of the Somme and the 1917 Battles of Arras and Bullecourt will not be examined. These have been covered by other guides and volumes.

The area is one of undulating open fields, country roads, farm tracks, scattered copses, small villages, and the Canal du Nord. Many British battlefield tourists tend to think there is nothing worth seeing, and generally know little of what happened in the fields between Bapaume and the Hindenburg Line. There are few physical remains of fortifications but there several dozen CWGC cemeteries, many of which appear to receive no visitors for months at a time. It is hoped that with the assistance of this book the visitor will begin to appreciate the significance of those actions and of how they contributed to the operational and strategic conduct of the war.

The land is ideal for touring either by car, bike, or on foot. It is within very easy and short travelling distance from the places where most British visitors to the Somme and Arras stay. Access is easy and some of the larger villages have even retained cafes and fuel stations.

The usual suggestions apply as far as what to take with you. Above all, be aware of the current French regulations for foreign motorists. Avoid parking where you may well cause obstruction to farm traffic. Inevitably a tractor will appear and want to turn onto the track you think has not been used since 1918. There are often parking spaces outside the village *mairie* or church. If cycling, take a puncture repair kit, spare inner, tyre levers, allen keys, crash helmet, high viz jacket, etc. Do not forget to take a hat, sun cream, compass, and mono/binoculars. A camera and a note pad are always useful. The *Série Bleue* IGN 2407 SB

Bapaume, and the 2507 SB *Cambrai* maps will be particularly useful if walking or biking. They cover the area concerned.

As most tourists visit by car four circular tours, with their approximate mileage, are suggested as a means of exploring the areas. The routes are somewhat artificial and can easily be condensed, amalgamated, or extended. They try to draw attention to the sites and cemeteries scattered across the various battlefields. If using a bike, the *Série Bleue* maps will allow you to avoid the roads by riding farm tracks and field headlands which are suitable for tractors but less so for vehicles. Most of these lanes and tracks were originally sunken and have since been ploughed out but if exploring on foot or by bike these cross-country routes allow a more intimate knowledge and understanding of the terrain.

The sources used for the text are the army, corps, division, brigade, and unit war diaries. Some regimental and divisional histories have also been used but as many of these relied heavily on the war diaries for their content the diaries have been the first port of call. It was thought unnccessary to footnote every quotation but if the reader wishes to investigate further it is usually clear from the text from which unit of formation diary the quotation was taken.

Several of the smaller cemeteries do not possess the bronze boxes in which registers are normally kept. As most of them do hold an up-to-date register it has been decided not to give detailed accounts of when the cemetery was constructed and the numbers of known and unknown remains within. Some of the cemeteries have also been included in guidebooks covering the Bullecourt and Arras battles. The most comprehensive of these volumes is Peter Hughes' *Visiting the Fallen: Arras South* (Pen & Sword, 2015) The book has been remaindered and can normally be bought for a very reasonable £5. Most travellers these days will also have easy access to the Commonwealth War Graves Commission website through their smart phones (but beware of possible roaming charges). Details of cemeteries and those buried or remembered within them can easily be discovered online. The four car tours included in this account do contain some information for those cemeteries which are not so readily accessible in published volumes and for those which do not normally contain registers.

Maps

The simplified sketch maps are designed to display the relative position of villages and some of the defensive works in their neighbourhood. Because the terrain was fought over three times the maps would become too cluttered if the position of battalions and brigades were shown for each of the three occasions. It is suggested that when exploring the battlefields the index and text are used in conjunction with the maps in order to ascertain which brigades fought in that particular area during the three periods considered in the book. Several of the maps are, however, designed to show trenches and strong points at particular times of the campaigns. These do, of course, also provide information as to the relative position of the villages and their connecting roads.

The larger present-day roads are shown and given their designated number. Drivers new to France should be aware that road numbers frequently change without notice when they cross *département* boundaries. With the exception of completely new roads, and the disruption to the established routes their construction caused, the old roads generally closely follow the same path as they did before 1914. Dotted lines on the maps represent what were largely originally sunken lanes but which have since become access tracks for the fields and recognised walking routes.

Some of them are navigable by saloon cars but many of them are not. They should be treated with extreme caution, especially in wet weather. Many of them peter out some distance on; the only route back then is to turn around, often with difficulty, and retrace your steps. If biking, these former lanes provide ideal cross-country routes with almost the only traffic encountered being the occasional tractor.

Map 1	The Northern Devastated Zone (Frontispiece)
Map 2	Le Transloy–Villers-au-Flos–Reincourt-les-Bapaume
Map 3	Beaumetz–Louverval
Map 4	Beugny–Vélu
Map 5	Boursies–Havrincourt
Map 6	Havrincourt–Trescault
Map 7	Beaucamp–Gouzeaucourt
Map 8	Gouzeaucourt
Map 9	Metz-en-Couture – Fins
Map 10	Équancourt – Léchelle
Map 11	Lagnicourt-Marcel
Map 12	Vaulx-Vraucourt – Frémicourt
Map 13	Vaulx-Vraucourt
Map 14	Écoust-St-Mein – Noreuil
Map 15	Croisilles
Map 16	Croisilles–St.Léger
Map 17	St.Léger–Mory
Map 18	Ervillers–Béhagnies
Map 10	Béhagnies–Bihucourt
Map 20	Hamelincourt–Courcelles-le-Comte
Map 21	Bucquoy–Puisieux
Tour Maps :	1. Le Transloy
	2. Bapaume
	3. Favreuil
	4. Ervillers

Illustrations

The photographs representing the landscape today are sequenced to coincide with recommended tour routes: Tour 1 – numbers 1-6; Tour 2 – numbers 7-11; Tour 3 – numbers 12-21; Tour 4 – numbers 22-30.

1

Advance to the Hindenburg Line: March-April 1917

The decision by the German High Command to withdraw their forces to the newly-constructed *Siegfried Stellung* in early 1917 was a consequence of the attrition caused by the Battles of the Somme and Verdun. Allied losses had been huge, but the Germans had also suffered heavily. For the Germans, the withdrawal could be viewed as a strategic, an operational, and a tactical necessity. By geographically shortening their line the Germans could save on manpower and compel the Allies to hurl themselves against what the enemy considered to be an impregnable defensive system. When the strategic necessity of the plan was acknowledged by the Kaiser the preliminaries of the highly detailed and timetabled scheme were put into operation on 24 February.

The first British division to realise that the anticipated withdrawal had commenced was 18th Division in II Corps. Shortly afterwards patrols from I ANZAC and V Corps also began to submit reports stating that they were in occupation of German trenches from which the original occupants had disappeared. Serre was taken and, gradually and cautiously, the line was advanced towards Miraumont and the Beauregard Dovecote.[1] Puisieux village was cleared on 26 February and the following day the Australians drove the Germans from Thilloy. It was not a straightforward and easy advance as German rearguards fought hard at certain points and in several key tactical positions, A successful set-piece attack by 2nd and 18th Divisions on Grevillers Trench and the village of Irles on 10 March did, however, cause a further withdrawal whereby the Germans evacuated a stretch of the so-called R.1 Line between Bapaume and Achiet-le-Petit. By 13 March I ANZAC and II Corps were facing the R.2 Line to the south-west, west, and north-west of Bapaume.

The enemy's withdrawal caused a dilemma for the British forces following closely behind. The extent of the Hindenburg Line had been established from intelligence gathered from aerial photography and agents' reports. It was realised that the further south the British forces were, the greater distance they would have to traverse before they approached the new line. Those corps which lay closest to Arras had the shortest distance to cover. General Gough, GOC Fifth Army, knew that his corps would have to be closed up to the new line by the proposed date in early April for the start of the Arras offensive. Fifth Army was tasked to cooperate in

1 Beauregard Dovecote was the name of a German strong point on the now D107 north-west of Miraumont. It stretched across and around a fork in the road about 600 yards north of the village.

the Bullecourt area with the main thrust by Third Army to the east of Arras. This meant that although his and the southern corps of Third Army had comparatively shorter distances to cover, Gough was forced to make as rapid an advance as the logistics, communications, and tenacity of the enemy rearguards allowed. He could not, of course, throw caution to the winds but if he was to have his army in position by early April he had to take rather more operational risk than, for example, Rawlinson's Fourth Army to the south.

Furthermore, as it advanced on a generally north-eastwards axis the faster Gough's army could progress, the greater was the chance of trapping German forces withdrawing from south of Arras in front of Byng's Third Army. This need for quick progress resulted in mistakes and unnecessary losses. On 27 February, 16/West Yorks of 31st Division made a premature attack on Rossignol Wood; it went very badly wrong and led to a court of inquiry. Two companies of the battalion lost two officers and 68 ORs killed or died of wounds with a similar number of wounded. The court wanted to establish what had happened to a further 61 unaccounted for ORs. It was concluded that at least one NCO and roughly 16 men had gone across to the German trenches unarmed and shouting *Kamerad*. Two weeks later, and in the same corps as 31st Division, an attack on Bucquoy was forced on 7th and 46th (North Midland) Divisions. Despite protests from its commanders that insufficient artillery was available, and the troops would not have enough time to assemble and reconnoitre the ground, Lieutenant General Fanshawe insisted the attack should go ahead. The result, on 14 March, was a disaster with both divisions losing heavily for no gain. In 137 Brigade, 5/South and 5/North Stafford were tasked for the operation. The march up to the jumping off tapes was done in intense darkness and pouring rain, the heavy artillery shoot lasted for only 30 minutes and, because the infantry's zero was delayed for 75 minutes, fell nearly three hours before the assault. The field artillery barrage was weak and the German wire strong. A few Staffords did get into the enemy trenches but were forced to withdraw after severe fighting culminating in a Germans counter-attack. The brigade war diary noted: "Nothing was seen of the attack of the 7th Division on the right." For its part, 7th Division, which had detailed 22/Manchester and 2/Queen's to undertake the attack, suffered equally as severely as the North Midland. After its failure, Brigadier Cumming, GOC 91 Brigade, wrote a stinging critique of the operation. His earlier protests about its very rushed nature, the state of the ground, the intensity of the wire, and the fact that the Germans had been alerted by the increased patrolling and the heavy artillery barrage in the hours before the attack had been largely ignored. The entry in the divisional war diary diluted Cumming's comments but still blamed the thickness of the wire and for having been "forced to carry out the attack by night despite vigorous protests."

Approximately two miles to the south of Bucquoy, on 14 March the enemy had withdrawn from Loupart Wood. On the body of a dead German officer inside the wood troops of 2nd Division discovered papers specifying the timetable of the *Alberich* operation. These papers suggested that the main withdrawal of the enemy forces was to have begun either on 13th or two days later on 15 March. It was assumed by Fifth Army that it was thus likely to be now the night of 15-16 March when the bulk of the German forces would begin their retreat. It issued a memorandum to all corps: "It seems probable that the enemy may evacuate Bapaume-Rocquigny Line on 15th or 16th March. If that happens they are to be followed by advanced guards of all arms who will act vigorously against any small parties of Germans to cut them off by attacking their flanks." Further orders instructed V Corps to advance in the general direction of Béhagnies; II Corps towards Favreuil; I ANZAC towards Frémicourt.

Gough was informed that the Lucknow Cavalry Brigade would be at his disposal from 18 March. The brigade, along with the corps cavalry regiments, would form part of divisional all-arms advanced guards which were to keep in close touch with the withdrawing forces. In the meantime, patrols were sent regularly to examine the still occupied sections of the R.1 and R.2 Line defences but were invariably met with machine-gun fire. Small bombing engagements involving rifle-grenades, and sometimes hand-to-hand fighting, occurred. During the night of 15-16 March, patrols from Major General Maxse's 18th Division found their way through Bihucourt Trench and on into Bihucourt village. Lacking immediate support they withdrew to their own lines; by next morning the trench was again manned by the enemy. When 12/Middlesex and 7/Bedford of 18th Division, with 2/South Stafford of 2nd Division on their right, tried to advance from a position about 300 yards from the Bihucourt Line they were immediately held up by fire from the high ground between Achiet-le-Grand and the trench to their front. Furthermore, divisional HQ (DHQ) believed the Germans had actually moved their artillery *closer,* rather than *away* from the front. What did arouse particular interest in senior commanders were reports which mentioned a number of fires and explosions occurring in Bapaume and some of the villages further behind the lines. Patrols ordered forward to investigate were heavily fired on and had to keep their distance. There were also a few changes made to army and corps boundaries along the front. One of these altered the direction of II Corps advance which was now to pass to the north of Favreuil and *en route* pass through Achiet-le-Grand, Ervillers, St-Léger, and Croisilles. Meanwhile, British artillery continued to pound Bucquoy; to the rear the generals and their subordinates decided on which railways and roads should be given priority in order that advancing troops could be kept supplied.

The fires and explosions were the precursor to the enemy's withdrawal during the night 16-17 March. Early on 17 March, 5th (Aust) Division, the right-hand formation of I ANZAC, discovered the R.1 Line to be empty. On further progress it found the R.2 Line, which almost joined the R.1 close to Bapaume, also to have been evacuated. The Australians of 8 Brigade quickly entered the town and engaged in some small-scale and quickly completed street fighting. To their left patrols of 6 (Aust) Brigade entered Avesnes and Biefvillers; further south, patrols of the right brigade of 5th (Aust) Division found Le Transloy and Beaulencourt empty. These were quickly occupied, and patrols pushed on into Rancourt, Reincourt, and Villers-au-Flos. All this was achieved at the cost of a reported two dead and one officer and 28 other ranks (ORs) wounded.

In V Corps, 62nd Division advanced through Achiet-le-Petit and most of Logeast Wood. In the early afternoon one officer reported that although he could "see for miles" he could spot in total only three Germans. He also counted a precise number of 15 fires burning in Gomiécourt. The battalions of 186 Brigade had held positions between the two Achiets and in front of the Bihucourt Line. Three German machine guns had fired at them for most of the day but disappeared as night fell. During the darkness one company of 2/5th Duke of Wellington's was ordered to push forward "with vigour," particularly towards Gomiécourt. Corps HQ was coming to the conclusion that the Germans were probably falling back along the entire corps front. Fanshawe had already ordered divisional staff officers to go and see for themselves what was happening and, in particular, to ascertain whether Bucquoy had fallen to 7th Division. If it had, Fanshawe wanted to know how far further to the east patrols were exploring. The cavalry components of the divisions' advanced guards were to reconnoitre ahead to keep touch with units on divisional flanks and with the withdrawing enemy. The yeomanry attached to

6 Brigade, 1/1st Yorkshire Dragoons, were to keep in touch with the left of I ANZAC; 29/Lancers were to push on into Ervillers and Mory and make contact with the mounted component of V Corps at Courcelles.

By the afternoon 7th Division reported it was through Bucquoy and into the burning Ablainzevelle. Its infantry was ordered to follow the cavalry and make contact with patrols of 62nd Division on the main Amiens – Arras railway 1,500 yards south-east of Courcelles. Once it had taken Courcelles it was to move onto the high ground north-east of the village.[2] The left division of V Corps, 46th (North Midland), reported that it had occupied Dierville Farm[3] and Essarts, patrols were passing to the north of Ablainzevelle, and its cavalry was advancing in the direction of Achiet-le-Grand. Its orders for the following day were to occupy Ayette and Douchy and to get in touch with 7th Division on the Courcelles – Ayette road. Between I ANZAC and V Corps, II Corps, with 2nd Division on its right and 18th Division on the left, crossed Bihucourt Trench, with 17/Middlesex taking the empty village beyond. Patrols were in contact with the Australians near Biefvillers and pressed on to Sapignes on the main Bapaume – Arras road. While the advanced guards pushed roughly north-eastwards with the stipulated "vigour," and the cavalry reconnoitred towards Moyenneville and Hamelincourt, all other available troops were employed on mending the cratered roads. The night sky was lit by fires to a depth of three to four miles behind the advancing lines. Abandoned dugouts were ablaze, dumps were being blown up, and enemy shells rained down on the ruined trenches and villages that their troops had so recently occupied.[4]

Early in the morning of 18 March, 4th and 5/Lincoln of 46th Division occupied Douchy and Ayette respectively; 62nd Division cleared the remaining pocket of resistance from Logeast Wood and continued its advance in the direction of Gomiécourt. An enemy machine gun positioned in the cemetery on the north-western outskirts of Achiet-le-Grand held up the advanced company of 2/5th Dukes but withdrew when it was about to be out-flanked. An RFC aircraft had reported Gomiécourt to be still burning but empty. By about 0900 the vanguard of 7th Division had occupied the evacuated Courcelles and moved on towards the railway and its intended contact with the West Riding Division.

The Lucknow Brigade, which had been reunited with 29/Lancers, passed through Achiet-le-Grand and headed north north-east towards Moyenneville.[5] According to a report from the RFC the brigade passed through the village and was in Ervillers and Hamelincourt by about midday. An estimated half battalion of German troops, complete with field kitchens and in full marching order, was observed marching eastwards from Hamelincourt. It remained unmolested because there was no immediate artillery support. The cavalry was told it was to be relieved in Ervillers by the infantry of 62nd Division, who would then hand over the village to II Corps. In Moyeneville and Hamelincourt the cavalry were to be relieved by troops of 7th Division. The Lucknow Brigade would then be released to reconnoitre towards St-Léger, where German cavalry had been seen, and try to block the retreat of any Germans withdrawing from Third

2 When an airfield was later built on this high ground it became known as Aerodrome Spur.
3 Dierville Farm is the present la Brayelle. It lies on a minor road about 1,000 yards east-south-east of Essarts.
4 In preparation for the coming Arras offensive, orders were received that 17th, 31st, and 63rd (RN) Divisions were shortly to be transferred to Third Army.
5 One source notes it passed through Achiet-le-Petit.

Army's front. When the infantry again caught up with the cavalry posts were established by II Corps to the east and north of Mory. The cavalry next continued its advance towards St-Léger and Ecoust. The former village was occupied by 54 Brigade of 18th Division by late morning but the section of advanced guard on the right was held up by machine-gun fire from Ecoust. As part of the thinning out of Fifth Army, V Corps was told that in addition to its own sector it would be taking over that of II Corps by 21 March. In preparation for this move 2nd Division was to be relieved by 54 Brigade; that brigade would then take over the entire front of II Corps until being relieved by units of 7th Division.

Further south, in the morning of 18 March 2nd (Aust) Division had entered Favreuil and Beugnâtre. Vaulx was occupied during the afternoon. The division continued its march on a north-easterly axis. Outposts were established near the German cemetery a little to the north of Vraucourt and north-west of Vaulx-Vraucourt on the Croisilles road. That morning the advanced guard of 5th (Aust) Division consisting of two battalions, one battery of field artillery, sections of sappers and medical orderlies, a machine-gun company, and a squadron of Light Horse had begun to operate. The infantry made its way into Frémicourt while the Light Horse patrols continued east and bumped into a strong point at Delsaux Farm 1,500 yards south of Beugny. The position was taken and inside it on the body of a dead officer was found another set of plans for the retirement. A small garrison was chased from Beugny while the right flank of the van advanced towards Lebucquière without immediate opposition. The following day 2nd (Aust) Division's outposts were pushed forward and, against some opposition, Maricourt Wood, Vaulx Wood, and Vraucourt Copse were all taken. The Light Horse squadron attached to 5th (Aust) Division on the right flank came under quite intense fire from Vélu and Lebucquière and waited for 60/Battalion to come up. By the afternoon 18 pdrs were in position to provide a barrage while the infantry attacked and took the two villages.

While to the south of the main Bapaume – Cambrai road the advance was reasonably straightforward, on 20 March the Australians to its north experienced a setback. The combination of what had been a slightly ambiguous message from Fifth Army and its interpretation in an unintended manner, caused Brigadier General Gellibrand, GOC 6 (Aust) Brigade, 2nd (Aust) Division to launch a pre-dawn attack against Noreuil. Gellibrand used two battalions, 21st and 23rd. Their companies fought their way into the south-west corner of the village and then came under severe machine-gun and artillery fire. The flanking forces close to Lagnicourt and Longatte also suffered with the result that both battalions withdrew with an initial estimation of about 150 killed and wounded. As 7th Division had discovered earlier, the Australians to their cost learned that the outpost villages were evidently strongly held. To the south of the main road, 5th (Aust) Division continued its advance, with the Light Horse taking Bertincourt and 59/Battalion, Morchies. Heading east from Lebucquière, 60/Battalion approached Beaumetz in the evening. When the companies came under fire from the garrison, rather than attempt a frontal assault battalion HQ decided to pass troops to its north and south and let the artillery bombard the village. This appears to have driven out some of the garrison and the village was partly occupied. A strong counter-attack later developed from Hermies, however, and together with some of the original garrison who had remained within the ruins, the Australians were compelled to withdraw to the west. As an interim measure they contented themselves in establishing posts but during the night the Germans evacuated the village. It was occupied by 60/Battalion soon after dawn.

To the south of the Australians the divisions of XIV and XV Corps of Rawlinson's Fourth Army faced substantial opposition in the area to the north of Péronne. A particularly bloody encounter was fought by 8th Division at Bouchavesnes on 4 March. The enemy began to withdraw towards the Canal du Nord eight days later in front of 8th Division but did not follow suite in front of the adjoining 20th Division until 17 March. The following day elements of XV Corps crossed the canal east of Moislains but were held up by strong opposition on the Nurlu – Péronne road. The trenches close to the road constituted part of the R.3 Line. On 19 March, 20th Division was ordered to advance to a line Barastre – Rocquigny with the aim of making it the main line of resistance. The corps cavalry were shelled out of Bertincourt but held a line roughly Bus – Léchelle – Four Winds Farm. By 23 March the infantry had placed standing patrols in Etricourt and Léchelle; on 27 March, 61 Brigade occupied Ytres and 59 Brigade had taken the northern end of Equancourt. Neuville-Bourjonval was cleared by 12/King's against little opposition but an attack on Ruyaulcourt by 7/DCLI failed in the face of uncut wire and machine-gun fire. On its right, against strong opposition 59 Brigade could not get onto the high ground north of Fins but 61 Brigade occupied the evacuated Ruyaulcourt the following day. On the right of 20th Division, 8th Division entered Fins and then worked through Dessart Wood towards the Fins – Gouzaucourt road. On 4 April, and supported by 8th Division, two battalions each of the Rifle Brigade and the King's Royal Rifles constituting 59 Brigade successfully executed what the official historian later described as a "very fine attack" on Metz-en-Couture. The Germans appeared to have been caught by surprise, officers in one dugout having swiftly to abandon a meal of hot coffee and English potted meats. The attack was done during a blizzard, under a very hastily organised and not particularly efficient barrage, and without the supposed support on the right of 2/R.Berks of 8th Division. A later report admitted that the degree of opposition from the garrison and also from machine guns on the edge of Havrincourt Wood was stronger than anticipated. It praised the men, about half of whom had been in the line continuously for eight days and involved in the advance which had gained 2,500 yards since 30 March. Furthermore, 25 percent of the troops were recently arrived drafts; their inexperience and lack of training had, apparently, showed. Nonetheless, the report emphasised that grit and sound sub-unit leadership had seen them through.

The barrage had been fired by guns some of which had only just been brought into position and had not had the time to register on the principal targets. The poor visibility caused by the snowstorms meant that a conventional barrage could be fired but, without the ability to report back on the fall of shot, its effectiveness was open to question. The limited opportunity for the guns accurately to cut the wire caused problems particularly for the two companies of 2/R.Berks on the right of 59 Brigade. They were tasked to secure the high ground to the south-east of Metz and gain entry to the southern face of Gouzeaucourt Wood. Two machine guns fired an overhead protective barrage, but the Berks companies quickly ran into difficulties. The enemy wire remained intact, there was confusion and misunderstanding over the meaning of flares seen above Gouzeaucourt Wood, and the inevitable delays in getting messages back to the artillery. The Berks did eventually get into the wood but by the time they did the operation by 59 Brigade was all but completed.

Simultaneously with the advance by the Berks, another of 25 Brigade's battalions, 2/RB had been ordered to advance up the Fins – Gouzeaucourt road and secure a strong point on the site of a ruined mill about 300 yards to the south-west of Gouzeaucourt. The companies were hit from the left by fire from inside Gouzeaucourt Wood as well as from the garrison in the strong point. The attack was thwarted, as was another in the late evening. A third attempt, this time with the help of a Stokes mortar drove the Germans from the mill but the pursuit was halted by fire from the village. The RB took refuge in the former enemy trenches. There was then a pause of a few days before 8th Division made an attempt on Gouzeaucourt itself.

Larger than most settlements in the area, Gouzeaucourt has the main Péronne – Cambrai road running through its centre. The next coordinated attack was to come from the south and the west on 12 April. Again, the weather was foul, but it did help the attackers because the snow was blowing into the faces of the defenders. On the far right, 2/West Yorks was to advance and take a position known as Meunier House on the Villers-Guislain road; on its left, 2/Scottish Rifles was to pass up the railway from the south, clear Gauche Wood, a strong point called Quentin Mill, and the eastern side of the village; in the centre, and with its left on the main road, 2/East Lancs was to get into the centre of the village from the south-east; on the far left, 1/Notts & Derby was to approach from the west and clear westwards as far as the main road. The attack proved to be relatively simple. The Germans possibly did not realise how large and organised the assault was or had standing orders to put up a fairly token resistance before withdrawing.

In the expectation that resistance would be stronger than it turned out to be, 8th Division had thoroughly prepared itself for the attack. There was plenty of time for officers to reconnoitre the ground and memorise natural features such as hollows, cuttings, and ditches. Compass bearings were taken from points of departure to objectives and the artillery was to fire desultory shots on certain points to assist direction-keeping. Advances were to be made in short bounds so that in the darkness better control could be exercised over platoons and sections. These factors all helped the operation to go smoothly and to cost only 15 OR fatalities. Being about two miles in front of the Hindenburg Line the village itself had no particular strategic or tactical importance but, as the line was pushed further forward, its still comparatively intact buildings could be used by units resting or waiting to return to the front. Before, however, 8th Division, 20th Division, and the recently arrived 40th Division could settle down at least temporarily within close reach of the Hindenburg Line, five outpost villages needed to be taken and secured.

Third Army held the city of Arras as a salient. Where the opposing lines curled around the south-east, south, and south-west environs of the city, the enemy defences were strong. Because it was known new stretches of formidable defences had been built to their rear the British assumed that if there were to be any evacuation of the current defences it would be of limited distance and only as far as the new lines. This did prove to be the case. Meanwhile, the usual trench routine of raids and shelling continued into mid-March. On 19 March, in VI Corps sector which included the Arras – Cambrai road and Tilloy, only on 3rd Division's extreme right, and thus on its boundary with VII Corps, was there any abandonment of the enemy's line. The trenches had been filled in and the dugouts deliberately collapsed. To harass the new occupants the Germans attacked their former positions twice on 20 March and then contented themselves with shelling them heavily.

On the southern side of the VII Corps boundary, 30th Division discovered the enemy had withdrawn north-east of Wailly at dawn of 18 March. The division began to "feel its way forward" and came across some resistance in Beaurains. This was soon cleared and under orders that the advance was to be carried out "cautiously" and to "avoid becoming involved in a serious engagement" it progressed "practically unopposed." Corps orders for the next day again stressed the need for a slow, deliberate advance in coordination with XVIII Corps on its right.

Commanders were instructed to tell their officers that "any inclination of leading troops to press forward to insecure positions in close proximity to the main defensive line must be checked." The division's principal objectives for 19 March were to reach the Arras – Bapaume road, which it did near Mercatel, and to ascertain whether Hénin was still occupied. Because no equivalent of the R.3 Line existed north of Achiet-le-Grand, once the withdrawal started in this sector it was executed rapidly. With the British and Dominion corps to the south through the R.1 and R.2 Lines it was thought unlikely that those German divisions to the north of Achiet-le-Grand would offer any substantial resistance. If they did, they ran the risk of being cut off by the Allied north-easterly advance.

On the right of 30th Division, troops of 58th (2/1st London) Division began their advance during the night of 17-18 March. This 2nd Line Territorial Force (TF) had spent its trench acclimatisation period attached to 46th (North Midland). It had taken over the Ransart sector earlier in the month and, by the evening of 19 March when it was transferred to VII Corps, the novice 58th had been the only division remaining in XVIII Corps. It moved forward with 46th, of V Corps on its right and 30th Division on its left. The 2nd London Division made good progress through the R.1 Line towards Adinfer Wood against slight opposition. Monchy-au-Bois, Ficheux, and Blairville were occupied and then, with the cavalry leading, its advanced guard went through Boiry-Ste-Rictrude and Boisleux-au-Mont. By the evening of 19 March, it was in Boiry-Becquerelle and Boyelles. Its DHQ later recorded that for some undisclosed reason it had rather trailed behind the divisions on its flanks. Nonetheless, it did gain touch with 18th Division at the mill on high ground to the north of St-Léger in the evening of 19 March. On the following day, 46th Division was squeezed out and a little later, 2/1st London Division was relieved by 30th Division. The divisions of VII, II, and V Corps now lay close to the Hindenburg Line as it tracked south-eastwards from about Tilloy. Two outpost villages remained to be taken before the corps could confront the line itself. These were the twin villages of Hénin-sur-Cojeul and St Martin-sur-Cojeul, and the more formidable Neuville-Vitasse.[6]

Accompanied by cavalry and cyclists, 6/Northants of 54 Brigade had occupied St-Léger on 19 March. By the evening the battalion had pushed outposts to the north and north-east of the village. It was joined shortly by elements of 2nd Division's advanced guard on its right on the St-Léger – Mory road and also by units of 22 Brigade, 7th Division at the nearby Judas Farm. Orders were received that 18th Division was to take over 2nd Division's front that day; on the following day 7th Division would relieve 18th Division. Those moves would then allow the withdrawal of II Corps and its replacement in the line by V Corps.

As preparations for the assault on the outpost villages, and also for the intended set-piece Battle of Arras continued, 2nd and 18th Divisions were to be allowed a period of rest. They were not to be used again until the final days of April and early May respectively. A few days after being withdrawn from the line, GOC 2nd Division wrote a reflective piece on what had been learned over the previous few weeks. He decided that tactics for trench to trench attacks had not altered but had, in fact, been reiterated. He acknowledged, however, that in the conditions of semi-open warfare which had existed once the R.1 and R.2 lines had been breached

6 The village of Neuville-Vitasse was bisected by a deep trench which formed a forward defence of the Hindenburg Line itself. The village was not attacked until 9 April in the operation which constituted the opening day of the First Battle of the Scarpe. As such, and because it was not a discrete outpost village, it will not be considered here.

alternative tactics had of necessity been developed. The paper discussed possible means by which an enemy holding a string of villages sited within rifle range of each other might be turned or taken. Important as this discussion on tactics was, the paper concentrated more on the means by which the cavalry might operate, the work of the engineers, and on how the advancing forces could be supplied and supported. The damage wrought by the enemy on the roads – the craters, deliberately felled trees, destroyed bridges, etc, – had severely disrupted the supply of ammunition, water, and rations as well as the forward movement of the artillery. For example, there were reports of dung and arsenic having been poured into village wells and of two howitzers of D/310 brigade being stuck in a ditch near Achiet-le-Petit. These guns blocked the road and prevented the passage of B/310 for several hours until the immobilised guns were excavated. Major-General Malcolm, MGGS Fifth Army, admitted that the logistics difficulties had been "enormous" and that "we got beyond our communications." This had "restricted artillery action to the minimum." By 28 March the broad gauge railway had been repaired as far as Achiet le-Grand but two days later Malcolm noted that although the field artillery was now "well forward", the supply of ammunition for the heavy guns and the movement of the guns themselves was still severely hampered.

In general, the advance so far had been fairly straightforward. It had not always, however, gone quite according to plan. For example, GOC V Corps had become very frustrated at what he considered to be the poor reporting regime of the Lucknow Brigade, and by the troublesome ability of a single well-positioned machine gun to bring an entire battalion's progress to an, albeit temporary, halt. On a more positive note, casualties had been relatively light. In the week ending 22 March, V Corps casualties had amounted to three officers and 44 ORs killed; 13 and 239 wounded; 29 ORs missing. In the following week, which included a failed attack on Croisilles on 28 March, 7th Division recorded only four officers and 63 ORs killed; 12 and 84 wounded; 28 ORs missing. While the German rearguards fought delaying actions other enemy units continued to burn and destroy the villages through which they withdrew. Amidst the destruction Sapignies church was blown up, that of Wancourt's was recorded simply as having "disappeared." Whilst the British troops concentrated on road repairs and consolidation of captured areas, a summary of the week 23 -30 March by VII Corps concluded that the lines had been "practically unchanged."

German raids and local counter-attacks were a nuisance but the principal problem was the weather. March had been mainly wet, with only the odd day of a drying sun. As the month turned to April, snow returned. The roads along which the heavy guns and ammunition had to be hauled in preparation for the coming attacks deteriorated further; some stretches became almost impassable for wheeled traffic. With the devastation of the landscape and villages the troops lacked protection from the elements. Cellars had been blown in, huts burned, and roofs destroyed. Across the new no man's land the garrisons of the outpost villages were comfortable and considerably warmer in their dugouts and shelters. Furthermore, they knew that behind them lay the strength of the Hindenburg Line to which they were destined to withdraw. In order to make the final stage of the Allied advance as costly as possible, until the instruction to withdraw was issued the enemy troops were to offer organized, coordinated, and thoroughly determined resistance.

2

Battles for the Outpost Villages: II, V, VIII Corps

As dusk fell on 19 March, troops of 54 Brigade in several of the newly-established posts on the eastern outskirts of St-Léger could see across the open ground the darkening shapes of three ruined villages. To the north-east lay Croisilles, one of the larger villages in the area with a network of sunken lanes radiating from it in all directions. About a mile to its south-east and due east of St-Léger were the twin villages of Ecoust-Saint-Mein and Longatte. Then, as now, these two small settlements line the main Croisilles–Lagnicourt road. It is difficult to know quite when the clusters of housing of Ecoust become those of the adjoining Longatte. As elements of the outpost system of the Hindenburg Line, all three of the villages were to be defended tenaciously by small garrisons who had been ordered to hold them until resistance was no longer feasible.

Encouragingly for the British, when an aircraft of 15 Squadron RFC flew over Croisilles during daylight on 19 March it reported that the village was in the process of being evacuated. The observer had obviously taken what he thought to be about 300 of the enemy "retreating" from the site in a north-easterly direction as a full-scale withdrawal. When the machine proceeded south-eastwards to fly over Ecoust its observer noted that there was at least one machine gun and probably 50 riflemen in the village. Presumably without knowledge of the RFC's report, later in the day Lieutenant Colonel Norris, CO of 1/King's, 2nd Division's vanguard unit, had doubts as to whether the village was occupied at all. He was quickly proven wrong when one of his patrols advanced to within about 200 yards of the cottages on its south-western outskirts. It was fired on by not only machine guns and rifles but also by two light field guns, and an anti-aircraft weapon. The following day a squadron of King's Dragoons and a RHA battery received the same treatment when they approached too closely. The aerial observer's earlier suggestion that Croisilles was unoccupied was initially given further testimony two days later when another machine flew over the village unmolested and unperturbed. When it tried a return flight, however, it was fired on from the buildings as was a patrol of the Lucknow Brigade on the ridge to its south-west.

As his 54 Brigade was in the process of relieving 2nd Division, Major General Maxe, GOC 18th Division, knew that his own troops were to be relieved by 7th Division the following day. Maxe was told by II Corps, however, that if he thought it was feasible he was to attack Croisilles the next morning. GOC II Corps did also specify that if Maxe believed the affair would of necessity be too rushed, and if there was in his perception insufficient available artillery, he could opt to leave the task for the incoming 7th Division and V Corps. Maxe decided 54 Brigade should make the attempt on the morning of 20 March.

The division's advanced guard consisted of 6/Northants supported by B/82 Battery, a battery of RHA, a section of 54 Machine Gun Company, and some sappers. A machine-gun barrage was fired over the heads as the Northants advanced; their flanks were protected by "strong" cavalry patrols. With all four of its companies deployed the Northants' war diary chose to call the operation a "battalion reconnaissance in force." Intense enemy fire from some of the estimated 14-15 machine-guns operating from within the village and a chalk pit north-east of the cemetery prevented one company from debouching from a wood to the north-east of St-Léger; another company took an enemy post in the shallow Sensée valley before being halted; the other two were stopped after gaining about 500 yards. The cavalry on the battalion's flanks had similarly failed to make any significant advance. As it was obvious the village was still strongly held the order to withdraw was given. Because D Company was in dead ground from the Germans and would come under heavy fire once the men showed themselves, it was decided to postpone the escape until nightfall. During the afternoon, however, Germans assembled for a counter-attack against the company's position. Leaving several of their wounded and whilst the Germans were still organizing themselves most of the company escaped in small groups,[1]

Having relieved 18th Division, and with the knowledge that 54 Brigade's assault had failed, initial orders were drawn up by V Corps for 7th Division to attack once sufficient artillery and ammunition were in place. With additional heavy artillery ordered to assemble Major General George Barrow, GOC 7th Division and his staff drew up plans for a simultaneous attack on Croisilles and Ecoust.[2] Outpost lines were gradually pushed closer towards Croisilles, but patrols sent to investigate the village defences and the higher ground to the north, were inevitably swept with fire. They did, however, ascertain that there was at least one belt of wire 20-30 yards deep. It was a similar picture to the south. All of 20 Brigade's patrols sent towards Ecoust and Longatte reported the villages to be strongly held. Posts were advanced by 8/Devons, but 2/ Gordon Highlanders tried for three successive days and on at least four occasions to clear strong points close to the roads running into Ecoust from Mory and Vraucourt. All the attempts were repulsed. It was clear that only the developing fully planned and organized attack would have any chance of taking the three villages. The decision was made on 27 March that the major assault should take place the following day. But, because the approaches to Ecoust and Longatte were proving so difficult to secure the proposed simultaneous two brigade attack was replaced by a single brigade assault only on Croisilles.

Another forced alteration to the original scheme came when Major General's Barrow's request for cooperation from 58th Division of VII Corps on 7th Division's left was declined. The reason behind the refusal was simply because the London Division was about to be relieved by 30th Division. Barrow was possibly relieved by the London Division's response because he very probably wanted to postpone the attack until 21st Division was in a position to assist and

1 The wounded were apparently collected by 8/Devon who relieved the Northants that night. The battalion later reported it had sustained about 60 casualties.

2 One of the more unusual elements of the subsequent orders was that any single trees were to be cut down lest they be used by the enemy artillery as range marks. Barrow was clearly uneasy about expecting his troops to advance across such a wide area of open ground. This order about the trees and the slow progress made in pushing posts forward may have been designed by Barrow as delaying tactics.

the situation in front of Ecoust and Longatte had improved. But such was Gough's impatience that Barrow felt compelled to act and decided 91 Brigade should attempt it alone.

Two battalions, each with two companies up and one following in support, were to be used: 1/South Stafford on the left was to be supported by a company of 2/Queen's and four Vickers; 22/Manchester was to be on the right. The Stafford was expected to advance and take a line of about 1,500 yards in length as well as form a defensive flank of about 1,200 yards facing north. To the Staffords' right, and south of the Fontaine-les-Croisilles – St-Léger road, 22/Manchester was to advance to the *sucrerie* on the Bullecourt road and work northwards to join with the Stafford at the north-east of Croisilles on the road to Fontaine. Despite the accepted need for significant support from the artillery, what was in reality a fairly thin field gun barrage was to creep forward at 50 yards every two minutes. While the troops advanced the heavy artillery was to concentrate on the village itself and its nearby sunken lanes.

The assault opened at 0545. The two companies of 22/Manchester were quickly held up by uncut wire. Captain Duguid and about 12 men managed to force a passage through one section and then became trapped for 36 hours before they finally managed to withdraw. The remaining platoons dug themselves in just in front of the wire. The GOC brigade ordered the attack be renewed at 0800 by sending the reserve company of the Manchester on an arc to the right in order to try to outflank the village. This was across open ground and the company was hit hard from the right flank by machine-gun fire and halted. On the left, 1/South Stafford's right company made some progress but, together with elements of the support company became held up. It successfully drove off a counter-attack but remained in an exposed position. The troops withdrew to a nearby sunken lane and stayed there under fire for the rest of the day. On their left the other company of South Stafford virtually disappeared after being held up and then probably counter-attacked whilst fixed in an exposed position. Only a handful of men returned. An attempt to reinforce the right company with the reserve company and two Vickers at 0800 also failed as they tried to cross open ground. The two battalions, each less one company, were relieved by 2/Queen's and 21/Manchester. These battalions had been ordered to renew the attack next day. Fortunately, at 2100 those troops heard that their attack was to be postponed in favour of a larger one to be conducted at a future date.

In his report GOC 91 Brigade went probably as far as he dared to suggest that, given the exposed ground over which the advance took place, the strength of the enemy defences, and the defenders' resolution, the attack had been misconceived and was unlikely ever to have succeeded. He perhaps had no need to have minced his words. Barrow's delay in launching the attack, together with what Gough considered to have been Barrow's poor and hesitant command during the earlier assaults on Bucquoy, had greatly annoyed and frustrated the much pressured army commander. Gough sacked Barrow.[3] Brigadier General Shoubridge, GOC 54 Brigade, whose own brigade had already tried and failed to take Croisilles, was promoted to command 7th Division. Gough made it clear to Shoubridge that he expected the new divisional commander to organise a rapid and successful attack on Croisilles, Ecoust, and Longatte.

On 29 March, and on the left of V Corps, 21st Division completed the relief of 58th Division; aerial torpedoes fired from the sunken Hénin road north-west of the village were reported to

3 J. Walker, *The Blood Tub: General Gough and the Battle of Bullecourt, 1917* (Barnsley: Pen & Sword, 2000), pp.60-1 discusses Barrow's removal.

have been used for the first time against 7th Division; patrols again failed to get into Croisilles. The enemy also bombarded Ecoust for about half an hour during the evening. A patrol sent to investigate whether it had been evacuated drew fire and the assumption was made that the German artillery had accidently fallen short. The following day, and at its second attempt, 2/Border managed to capture the posts which had earlier so frustrated the Gordons' efforts. The British occupation of the posts was to be short-lived. The Border battalion was relieved by 2/1st Honourable Artillery Company (HAC) and, on 31 March after a crushing bombardment which had reduced the garrison of one platoon to just eight men, a daylight attack by the enemy recaptured them. An attempt by the HAC to re-take them on 1 April failed with heavy casualties. By the time this tactical action had occurred orders had arrived for a set- piece attack on the three villages on 2 April. The villages were to be pinched out by 21st Division from the north and 7th Division from the south. All of V Corps' heavy artillery was to be available together with the divisional brigades and an army brigade of the RFA. After the attack, 62nd Division was to relieve 7th Division and the captured villages handed over to 21st Division.

On 27 March, VIII Corps HQ had issued orders that its 30th and 21st Divisions were to advance their lines closer towards the outpost villages during the night of 30-31 March. This was part of the preparation for the larger attack which had been initially scheduled for 1 April. On 29 March, Brigadier General Goodman, GOC 21 Brigade, received a note from his counterpart of 62 Brigade, Brigadier General Rawling, on the other side the divisional boundary. Rawling's note explained that he was going to advance his left battalion that night and asked if 21 Brigade would cooperate. As the message had only arrived at 21 Brigade HQ at 1959 little could be organised to help 62 Brigade that night. Brigadier General Goodman informed the CO of 2/Yorks of the request; he replied with the suggestion that his battalion should attempt to establish a lodgement in Hénin on 30-31 March. This was to be attempted simultaneously with the general advance of posts towards the village. Brigadier General Goodman agreed to the proposal. Three companies of 2/Yorks subsequently pushed into the south-west part of the village. After a series of confused encounters with German posts and fearing encirclement, the Green Howards were eventually forced to withdraw. Nonetheless, a new series of posts were established, as ordered, to the west of the village. On their right, 21st Division had not managed to achieve a similar yardage towards Croisilles. This limited success caused the next stage of the advance against Hénin and Croisilles to be postponed for 24 hours.

Hopes that the main attack might not be necessary had been temporarily raised on 30 March. On receipt of a report and in the belief that Croisilles had been evacuated patrols were despatched by 1/Royal Welsh Fusiliers (RWF) in the afternoon of 30 March. Two of them made no more than 300 yards before they were fired on from the village. Further difficulties struck the fusiliers when the battalion was informed it was to hand over some of its posts on the left to the incoming 13/Northumberland Fusiliers (NF) of 62 Brigade. The *Official History* later noted that the forthcoming attack was unusual because two armies cooperated on the scheme. Predictably, the cooperation was not without some minor but frustrating difficulties. For example, there was an ongoing dispute between Third and Fifth Armies about boundaries. Although reliefs had been agreed between the COs of 13/NF and the RWF, the former subsequently decided to change his mind about which of the posts he would actually garrison. Blaming the fickleness of the Northumberlands, the adjutant of the RWF recorded his annoyance at the "unnecessary" delay in the eventual relief which still left one of his companies having to conduct a daylight withdrawal in full view of the Croisilles' garrison.

When the attack on Hénin was launched on 2 April, 21 Brigade employed 2/Yorks, with two attached companies of 19/Manchester as mopper ups. The Green Howards' companies encountered some very determined resistance whilst trying to establish posts at tactical points inside the village. Its south-eastern part fell fairly easily but a flanking party on the left, which had captured several Germans, came under severe fire. Most of the party and its captives were killed. Another centre of resistance came from the houses on the south-western side of the village and from the nearby *Mairie*. The street fighting lasted for nine hours until, having destroyed the *Mairie* and its garrison with Stokes mortars, most of the surviving enemy in posts further east withdrew to the adjoining village of St Martin. As this was not an objective for 21 Brigade, 2/Yorks, the two companies of Manchesters, and a squad of the brigade pioneer section set about consolidation. Touch was made with 62 Brigade of 21st Division on the right during the afternoon. Brigadier General Goodman praised the support of 21st Division but put the success of the operation down to the "sheer grit and pluck" of the men, the initiative of small unit commanders, effective coordination between the infantry, machine guns, and Stokes teams, and the prompt and accurate work of the artillery. Ninety-two dead Germans were counted in the village.

With Shoubridge's 7th Division having still only two brigades available (22 Brigade was only just about to re-join the division having spent days working in the rear areas), it fell again to the unfortunate 91 Brigade to attack Croisilles. To its south 20 Brigade was to go for Ecoust while 62 Brigade was to attack the Croisilles -Hénin road and establish a line of posts on the slopes of the ridge to its north-east. Three battalions of 91 Brigade were to be used with the first objective being the railway line running between the village and Ecoust. The assaulting troops were then to link up with 62 Brigade at a point on the Fontaine road in the north-eastern outskirts of Croisilles. Lewis gun posts established in that area would catch any Germans withdrawing from the village as the support battalion, 22/Manchester, cleared the ruined buildings. The battalions were to advance under a creeping barrage, especially intense on their flanks, while the heavy artillery was to concentrate on the village itself and remain pounding it until 22/Manchester had begun advancing through it. The heavies would then lift and shell the furthermost outskirts. Stokes mortars and Vickers were to assist from earlier selected positions. There was a slight hitch during the assembly when the bright moonlight revealed one company of the Queen's advancing down the exposed spur towards the railway. In response the Germans sent up some "golden rain" rockets and barraged the valley on the Queen's right. This caused a temporary difficulty, but all battalions were in place for zero at 0515.

The objectives of the South Stafford on the right were gained quite easily but 21/Manchester had an uncomfortable time when one of the division's own batteries fired short. There were further problems when the battalion tried to cross the railway embankment particularly where it ran about 50 yards south of and parallel to the Bullecourt road. The embankment was in places 40 feet high and covered in brambles which concealed wire as well as a machine-gun post and snipers. Another machine gun was hidden in a culvert. Hit from the front and enfiladed by a machine gun in Croisilles, the Manchesters finally managed to get over the obstacle and continued the advance. On the left 2/Queen's had also suffered from their own RFA barrage but progressed towards the strong point known as The Tooth. Its garrison offered determined resistance so when the Queen's had exhausted their supply of rifle grenades and being enfiladed by a machine gun from their left, they withdrew to allow the artillery to hammer the site. This worked and about 100 Germans were seen to be escaping from the position. These joined with other parties who were evacuating the village by several routes. A Lewis gun post prevented them using the Fontaine-les-Croisilles road but, as GOC 91 Brigade later ruefully reported, if 62 Brigade had advanced to the prescribed contact point with his own brigade or "even had a post" on the sunken lane to Héninel a large number of Germans would not have escaped. For its part, 13/NF of 62 Brigade had advanced well but was counter-attacked from a series of dugouts in two sunken lanes running down from Hénin to the west of Croisilles. The Northumberlands' positions were "with difficulty maintained" before they managed to drive the enemy back into his dugouts. Six attempts were made to clear the Germans from the intended contact point with the Queen's in the northern end of Croisilles and several small groups of Germans were seen to slip away from these dugouts; some were caught in the open by the Lewis guns of the Lincolns. The Northumberlands were relieved in the evening by 10/East Yorks. This battalion sent patrols into Croisilles and discovered the troublesome dugouts in the two sunken lanes to have been evacuated. It linked with 91 Brigade at the sunken crossroads on the north-western outskirts of the village at about 0230.

Several hours before the link was made with 10/East Yorks and under pressure from Shoubridge, Brigadier General Cumming had sent two companies of 22/Manchester into the village. Many of the garrison remained and stood their ground until surrounded or enfiladed. A third company of the Manchester was sent up and gradually the three, although badly mixed and often losing direction worked their way through the ruins. Two further platoons were shortly also deployed. They knocked out two strong points, met up with some Queen's, and then attacked another strong point at some crossroads from the rear. Having softened up the garrison with bursts from three Lewis guns Lieutenant Robinson and his platoon charged the post and captured 22 Germans. The brigade commander later praised the men's behaviour when forming up for the assault and the assistance of the RE. The artillery he noted, apart from the "unfortunate accident" at the start when the troops were hit by their own guns, was reported on "favourably by all."

The CO of 21/Manchester thought the men had done well but criticised his officers for failing to indicate the time at which their messages were despatched and to give accurate map coordinates. This oversight had caused "misunderstandings" at battalion HQ. The CO of 1/South Stafford was also pleased with his men's work. They had inflicted heavy casualties as the Germans retreated across the open to the Hindenburg Line, had advanced 1,700 yards, and captured 20 of the enemy. This was achieved for a total, he thought, of one officer and 26 ORs wounded. The CO of 22/Manchester contented himself with a purely factual account of the operation but, like his counterpart in 21/Manchester, did mention that incorrect coordinates submitted by one officer had caused confusion at battalion HQ.

To the south of 91 Brigade, 20 Brigade's assault on Ecoust and Longatte was also to be made with three battalions. On the right, next to the Australian attack on Noreuil, 2/Gordon was to take the southern part of Longatte and establish posts on and beyond the Longatte – Noreuil road; 8/Devon was to take the central and northern sector of Longatte; on the left, 9/Devon was to assault Ecoust. As a preliminary, two platoons of Gordons were to seize the post on the Ecoust – Vraucourt road which on 31 March the Germans had re-taken from the HAC. In the event once the barrage began the Germans evacuated the post. These two platoons of Gordons were later able to fill the gap which developed between the rest of their battalion, which had strayed to the right, and 8/Devon in Longatte. There was some house clearing to be done in Longatte, but two platoons of Gordons surged beyond their boundary and reputedly came close to capturing some German field guns near to the Noreuil – Bullecourt road. A little to their left, 8/Devon, which had been held up by uncut wire until a gap was found close to the church, also became engaged in some hard street fighting. One enemy post on the Croisilles road with two machine guns and a garrison of two officers and 22 other ranks had held up the battalion's left company and the right of 9/Devon. Surrounded and pummelled, it eventually surrendered. Some of the posts established by the Devons, especially one at Ecoust Station, came under such intense fire and the occasional counter-attack that they were later withdrawn. The left company secured the railway embankment and gained touch with 9/Devon. Battalion HQ received no reports about the right company's progress because all of its officers became casualties. The battalion later reported three officers and 25 ORs killed in what had been at times hand-to-fighting. At the northern end of Ecoust, 9/Devon was halted by the fire from its right and from a strong point housing three machine guns at the cemetery just to the north of the village. One company pressed on east from the railway embankment but was held up by its own barrage as well as by enemy machine guns. Posts were established but, like those of its sister battalion, some were forced later to be withdrawn. The brigade subsequently reported a total of 17 officer and 304 OR casualties, including about 70 dead.

The British corps of Third and Fifth Armies had succeeded in fighting their way through to their intended objectives by the date set by Haig. The devastated area had been crossed and the divisions now confronted the untouched and supposedly impregnable Hindenburg Line. The German resistance had frequently been determined and the British casualties, consequently heavy. The preliminary bombardment for the forthcoming Battle of Arras began on 4 April; on 5 April the date for the infantry assault to commence was pushed back a day from the 8th to the 9th. Daily reports from the RFC mentioned the arrival and departure of enemy trains at the sidings in Buissy, Quéant, and Vaulx, and also the evidence of work continuing on the trenches and wire of the Hindenburg Line. Any British soldier who looked at the opposing defences through a trench periscope had a limited view of the obstacles to be overcome. He would see some outpost positions, but the real defences lay out of sight on reverse slopes. Patrols continued to try to ascertain how strongly the forward defences were held, and there were several tentative preliminary attacks. For example, 1/London of 56th Division twice tried to take an advanced German strong point on the site of Neuville Mill. It lay in a forward position on the Mercatel – Neuville-Vitasse road and unless neutralised would be able to enfilade the main attack. The failures to achieve its capture resulted in 56th Division requesting that a tank be allotted specifically for this task for when the operation began.

The build-up of equipment, shells, and guns for the Arras offensive continued as 9 April approached. The German defences had observation over much of the area where the concentrations were taking place. The few sunken lanes could provide cover for some guns, but many field artillery brigades were compelled to deploy their batteries in almost full sight of the enemy. Under Gough's relentless driving his divisions had traversed the Wastelands and reached their objectives on schedule. They had also pushed their lines forward usually to within about 400 yards of the enemy's outposts. But the hardest work was still yet to come. On 10 April, to assist the major offensive by Third Army two divisions of Gough's now reduced command, 62nd (West Riding) and 4th (Aust) Divisions, were to attack towards Bullecourt. The first attack was to be aborted, and the subsequent one, a disaster. The southernmost divisions of Byng's army were also to attack from positions gained from the advance across the devastated area. The Germans knew an attack was imminent and were confident that with the withdrawal to the Hindenburg Line and their revised defensive doctrine they would be able to hold and then destroy the assault. As he read through the corps' instructions concerning the role his division was to play in the offensive and the objectives to be seized, a staff officer in 30th Division could have been writing for many when he commented: "The task set us may … be assized as a long advance over an exposed tract of land on a wide front against a trench system which might or might not be stoutly defended, but which was certainly strongly wired and which we were unable properly to reconnoitre."[4]

4 TNA WO 95/2311: General Staff WD, 30th Division, Operations April 1917.

3

Battles for the Outpost Villages: I ANZAC

During a conference with his corps commanders on 20 March, General Gough decided that rather than wait for both V and I ANZAC to come abreast and for the two to act in unison, they should conduct their individual operations when they considered the time was right. Cooperation would still be important but as the Australians believed their outpost objectives were less strongly wired and defended than those confronting V Corps, Lieutenant General Birdwood wanted to maintain both tempo and momentum by continuing his attacks.

As the advance continued increasing numbers of artillery pieces were brought forward and dumps of ammunition, engineering stores, and rations established. Patrols reconnoitred the German positions but if spotted were invariably met by fire. On 21 March a German Albatross crash landed in front of Australian posts between Vaulx and Lagnicourt. When the pilot scrambled from his aircraft and began running towards the German lines the Australians opened fire and brought him down. He was collected and taken to an aid post where it was discovered he was Prince Frederick Karl of Prussia. Son of the almost legendary Prince Frederick Leopold, Frederick Karl was himself a cousin of Kaiser Wilhelm II and married to the younger sister of the Kaiser's wife. Two days later a German aircraft flew over the lines and dropped a canister requesting information on the prince's condition and location. He had, in fact, died from his wounds.

On 23 and 24 March the Germans made determined attempts to re-take Beaumetz. After a heavy bombardment and then infantry assault the Australian garrison was driven out. An immediate counter-attack was organized, and the Germans forced from the village leaving about 60 dead in the streets. On 24 March, the enemy attacked from the north-east with about 350 troops and, when that attacked was repulsed, from the south-east. The Australian infantry held their ground and with the help of the artillery dispersed and broke up the attacks. On this occasion about 80 dead were strewn across the approaches. As part of the preparation for the main assault on Lagnicourt and the outpost villages further east, Australian guns regularly shelled the areas east of Noreuil, Lagnicourt and its approaches, and Hermies. Posts were pushed forward from the south of Beaumetz and east of Vélu Wood. The small enemy garrisons fled from their positions in the open as troops of 5th (Aust) Division advanced; others were caught by shrapnel as they retreated up the sunken lane running south from Beaumetz towards the railway crossing. Over the course of almost three days a farm on the north side of the Bapaume – Cambrai road at the junction with the sunken lane to Beaumetz was taken, lost, and retaken by the Australians. In the early hours of 24 March, a body of an estimated 300 Germans was spotted in column marching down the lane towards the village. Machine guns were turned on them from short range and 18 pdrs fired a creeping shrapnel barrage over the area where the enemy had scattered to seek refuge. Later, 72 dead Germans were counted along the lane and its adjoining area.

The principal operation, an attack on Lagnicourt, took place on 26 March. There was, as Gough had insisted, cooperation from V Corps. Its artillery and machine guns fired barrages on Noreuil, Longatte, and Ecoust to complement a severe and well-coordinated bombardment by the heavy and field artillery on Lagnicourt and its immediate surrounds. Companies of 26th and 27/Battalions of 7 (Aust) Brigade virtually encircled the village while others worked through the housing. One strong point within the village proved particularly troublesome. Troops under the command of Captain Cherry destroyed it with Stokes and then fought hand-to-hand with garrisons in its supporting posts. German counter-attacks approaching from south of Noreuil and south-west of Quéant pushed back the posts to within 200 yards of the village but were eventually beaten off over a two-hour period and the ground re-gained. By the afternoon posts were established 800 yards to the east and north-east of the village; to the south they continued across the open ground to join with those in and around the contested farm on the Cambrai – Bapaume road. To the north, the line of posts overlooked the Hirondelle valley east of Noreuil and swung back to pass south of the village, which remained in German hands. It then turned north to meet up with those of V Corps in front of Longatte. The German infantry had fought hard and well, leaving about 100 dead from the counter-attacks but had been ill-served by their artillery which was described as "feeble" in its response. Various pieces of booty were captured including an electric searchlight and about 70 prisoners. Some of these apparently told their captors that their orders had been to resist strongly and hold the Australian advance because sections of the Hindenburg Line were still incomplete. One also stated, with probably a degree of exaggeration, that almost his entire battalion had been annihilated during its counter-attack.[1]

There followed something of an operational pause while preparations were made for the next stage of the advance. Patrol work continued and there were regular amounts of shelling by both sides. General Gough decided that the set-piece attack on the outpost villages by V Corps and I ANZAC should be coordinated affair to take place on 2 April. While V Corps went for Croisilles, Ecoust, and Longatte, the Australians were to take Noreuil, Doignies and Louverval. On the left of the ANZAC front, 4th Australian had relieved 2nd (Aust) Division. The plan was for 13 (Aust) Brigade to attack Noreuil with two battalions and others in support. The thrust by 50/Battalion was to come from the south-east from the recently captured Lagnicourt, take the south and eastern parts of the village and then wheel right to consolidate on the Lagnicourt – Bullecourt lane. Meanwhile, 51/Battalion was to advance from the south-west go through the northern part of the village and meet with 50/Battalion on the same lane. The battalions had been in the forward area long enough to have reconnoitred the land and knew it fairly well. The right company of 51/Battalion entered the village without much difficulty but to its left, the other company had to overcome some resistance from the garrison of a trench lining the Noreuil – Longatte road. Once the company was through, a machine-gun was positioned on the road to control the low valley which ran away to the north-east. To the south-east, 50/Battalion

1 The Australians initially reported about 57 dead and just over 200 wounded. Captain Cherry was killed on 27 March. He was posthumously awarded the Victoria Cross for his conduct during the Lagnicourt battle. He is buried in Quéant Road Cemetery

had to overcome several barricades and strong points with Stokes, rifle grenades, bombs and enveloping movements before most of the enemy was silenced. Private Jorgen Jenson won the Victoria Cross here for his work. The right company then swung to the right but was hit hard by machine-gun fire from the right where 52/Battalion, which had pushed up to the Lagnicourt – Bullecourt lane about 900 yards north of Lagnicourt, had been trying to make contact with 50/Battalion's right. This caused some confusion and heavy casualties in 50/Battalion. These numbers were increased when Germans who had not been mopped up and driving some of their own captives in front of them were deluged by shrapnel as they headed east along the valley road towards Quéant. The enemy tried on several occasions to exploit the gap between 50th and 52/Battalions before it was closed. Another attempt was broken up by the artillery when the German were seen to be massing. During the approach of night, the gap was closed and the companies consolidated along the intended objective.

To the south, 5th (Aust) Division, which had been in the line for a long tour, was to attack the hamlet of Louverval and the village of Doignies. Louverval was a small collection of farm buildings and a chateau about 300 yards north of the main Bapaume – Cambrai road; Doignies lies approximately 700 yards to its south. The bulk of the available artillery was to be used to support the attack against Noreuil which meant that only three heavy batteries and a brigade of field artillery with two attached batteries could be used against Louverval and Doignies. The original plan was scrapped when patrols discovered previously reconnoitred gaps in the enemy's wire had been closed. It was decided that 56/Battalion, with its right on the main road at about the contested farm would take the *sucrerie* at the Louverval – Doignies crossroads and then swing left to take the higher ground to the north and encircle the hamlet. Once the *sucrerie* had been taken, 55/Battalion would follow behind 56th and pass to the north of Doignies before turning south and encircling it from the east. The attack began over an hour before that of the one further north, and with no preliminary bombardment. The *sucrerie* was taken and 56/Battalion followed through, but things quickly went badly wrong. Instead of passing to the north of Louverval Wood companies of 56/Battalion went through it. They came under severe fire and had difficulty in overcoming the obstacles of deliberately felled trees. To the south, 55/ Battalion also turned too soon and attacked Doignies from the north rather than the east. The enemy blew four mines as the Australians entered the village and fought well until making their escape unimpeded towards Demicourt, a mile to the east. Consolidation began and when aircraft spotted the enemy massing for counter-attacks called down fire upon them from the heavy and field batteries. Five major assaults were launched by the Germans during the day from the north-east towards Louverval and east from Demicourt. They were all either shattered by the artillery or beaten off by the infantry. As the infantry consolidated the heavy artillery began the deliberate and systematic bombardment of Hermies, Demicourt, and Boursies.

These Australian assaults had been successful but had been costly. Initial casualty reports suggested a total of 45 officers and 957 other ranks, with six and 178 respectively thought to be dead and a total of over 200 missing. The Germans had continued to resist strongly in these outposts but on the positive side all-arms cooperation had appeared to work well. Communications between the artillery and RFC had proved to be efficient, as had those between the guns and the infantry. Brigade and battalion command and control also seems to have been effective. When it devolved to junior ranks, they were reported to have shown initiative and courage. With the capture of Croisilles and Ecoust by V Corps, and Noreuil by the left of I ANZAC, the two corps were in position to launch the flank attack in support of Third

Army's offensive at Arras. Before that attack was launched, or as part of it, however, I ANZAC was expected to take the three remaining outpost settlements in its area.

Today, Hermes is large enough to be called a small town. It sits on top of a ridge and dominates the surrounding, undulating land. In April 1917 it had strong wire and trench systems to its west, north and south. To its north north-east, and about 2,000 yards away, lies the small village of Demicourt, It had some wire and trenches but was not a particularly strong position. About 1,000 yards to its north-west is Boursies. This village straggles along the main Cambrai – Bapaume road and was well defended, with posts established on the higher ground to its north-west. Hermes was identified by the planners as being the most significant and the most difficult target for the attack. It was decided to employ deception and try to fool the Germans into thinking that Boursies was the main target. As the attacks on Louverval and Doignies had intended to circle around both objectives to the north and take them from the rear the planners thought that if a similar tactic were used towards Boursies the enemy would be lulled into thinking that it was another typical attack on just one village and not expect a simultaneous attack on Hermes. This led to an operation on the night of 7-8 April whereby the enemy posts to the north-west of Boursies would be taken in what they hoped the Germans would assume was the precursor to a major attack on the village. After some hard fighting, 3 (Aust) Brigade took the objectives which meant the Australians were in the western end of the village and on the high ground overlooking its remainder. To the south, 1 (Aust) Brigade was to advance from Doignies in a south-easterly direction on Hermies. On the right, 2/Battalion, with its right on the Doignies – Hermies road, was to attack the town from the north-west with the right company heading for the station and railway on its western edge. Once these had been reached, 3/Battalion would attack eastwards between the railway and the canal. It would have to overcome what were assumed to be the strongest of the town's defences. Zero was at 0415 on 9 April. The advance of 2/Battalion was checked temporarily at a couple of strong points, particularly by one on the lane which ran east north-east away from Hermies but by 0600 a series of hand-to-hand engagements, in one of which Private Thomas Kenny earned a Victoria Cross, had taken the town. South of the railway 3/Battalion came under fire as it approached its jumping off points. It continued and pressed through the defences and, as 2/Battalion pushed the Germans from the town, pressure on 3/Battalion eased. It took the cemetery and met with 2/Battalion scouts to the east of the town on the Hermies – Havrincourt road.

North of the main road 12/Battalion of 3 (Aust) Brigade was to attack Boursies from the recently won high ground to its north-west. A German counter-attack had disrupted the forming up stage, but 12/Battalion advanced on time and fought its way into the housing. It took some bitter fighting until the remaining Germans withdrew and by 1400 the village was secured. A few hundred yards to the rear and south, and when 2/Battalion began its attack, 1/Battalion moved into Doignies. Some premature reports that Boursies had fallen caused 1/Battalion to advance eastwards towards Demicourt. Enemy artillery and machine-gun fire hit the companies with the result that Australian artillery was again instructed to shell the village. Gradually, and with the capture of the *sucrerie* about half way along the Hermies – Demicourt road, 1/Battalion entered the village. By 1100 posts were established east of the village with 1/Battalion in touch with 2/Battalion on its right and with only a small and soon to be closed gap between it and 12/Battalion in Boursies on its left. Casualties had been heavy on both sides. The Australians put German casualties at 8-900, with 90 dead counted on the front of 2/Battalion alone. They put their own at 497.

The Australians pushed forward posts as far as they could especially towards the railway embankment south of Bullecourt. On 11 April in conjunction with 62nd Division on its left, 4th (Aust) Division launched its attack on Bullecourt. That village, together with the other objective of Riencourt and Hendecourt, were technically either part of, or to the rear of the Hindenburg Line. As such they are beyond the scope of this narrative. Despite the disaster of 11 April General Gough was determined to attack again when further preparations had been completed. On the other side of no man's land, Lieutenant General Otto von Moser, GOC *XIV Reserve Corps*, was also convinced the British and Australians would try again. Following the Allied attack Moser's corps had been strengthened by an additional two divisions. He decided to use infantry from four of his divisions in a pre-emptive strike on Lagnicourt with the intent of disrupting Allied preparations for the anticipated renewal of the offensive. The principal objective of his troops was to destroy as much of the British artillery as possible. As a bonus the attack might also force British divisions to be moved down from the Arras front.

The line between the Canal du Nord to a little north of Lagnicourt was held by two brigades of 1st (Aust) Division. The length of the division's fan-shaped line was excessive by any standards. Each of the two brigades had two battalions in the forward defences which consisted largely of picquets, and posts widely separated along their average front of about 3,100 yards. The defences were stretched further during the night of 13-14 April when the four front battalions advanced their lines by up to 1,200 yards north and south of the Cambrai – Bapaume road. In places the Australians had to overcome some stiff resistance but by morning a series of strong points had been established. Just before mid-day two of them south-east of Pronville were rushed and occupied by the Germans. A counter-attack which re-took the posts was organized immediately. The enemy withdrew talking with them nine captured Australians. With the front so under-manned the battalions tended to try to camouflage their posts by covering any turned earth with grass and leaving many of them with no protective wire. The more unobtrusive they could be the better, but it did leave them at greater risk of being surprised and surrounded.

To the left of 3 (Aust) Brigade, 2nd (Aust) Division held the front from north of Lagnicourt to the southern end of Longatte. The division had relieved the battered 4th (Aust) Division and was now itself preparing for the next assault on Bullecourt. Much of its field artillery was massed in the shallow valleys behind Lagnicout and Noreuil within a mile of the outpost positions. The gunners were concentrating more on the help they were to provide to the infantry rather than worrying too much about the security of their own gun pits and ammunition dumps. Consequently, battery commanders had failed, or neglected, to issue their gun crews with rifles when they moved to the forward positions.

At 0330 on 15 April a short, very violent bombardment fell on Hermies. About 40 minutes later hordes of Germans began advancing towards 1 (Aust) Brigade's front east of Hermies from the canal Spoil Heap to the north of the Hermies – Havrincourt road. Lewis gun and rifle fire from the scattered picquets halted two such rushes which, according on one report, left 150 enemy dead on one company of 3/Battalion's front alone. To their left in and around Demicourt and Boursies the posts of 4/Battalion were attacked by *flammerwerfer*. In the face of these weapons and against what appeared to be insurmountable numbers the Australians fell back. With the arrival of reinforcements, however, the two villages were held and again secured. North of the main road the Germans penetrated between several posts of 11th and 12/Battalions and worked behind those still holding their ground. Although often completely surrounded, many posts, including that commanded by Lieutenant Charles Pope, continued to resist. The company of 12/Battalion on the extreme left of the unit's front, and thus the closest to the divisional boundary, held a line of 1,000 yards with only three platoons. The fourth platoon moved up to a position 400 yards east of the Lagnicourt – Bullecourt lane, north-east of Lagnicourt but was also virtually destroyed. That company lost an estimated 70 percent of its strength. Its troops, and the other companies of 11th and 12/Battalions, did delay the advance long enough for reserves to come up and form a new line of resistance. But, with penetrations of 17th and 18/Battalions' fronts of (5Aust) Brigade north of the Hirondelle valley, huge numbers of Germans were now inside several of the field artillery's gun lines. A machine gun had been moved to a position south-west of Lagnicout in the sunken lane running south from the Lagnicourt – Vaulx road. It took a heavy toll of Germans as they advanced over the crest further up the lane and almost to the gun pits. Despite this effective supporting fire many of the weaponless gunners withdrew in some disorder. The enemy took four batteries to the west of Lagnicourt and were closing in on another nine in the Hirondelle valley behind Noreuil. Further Australian reserves were moving up from Vaulx and Morchies but in the meantime, Captain James Newland was to be awarded the Victoria Cross for his leadership, and Sergeant John Whittle for his courage in rushing a German machine-gun crew. This gun was about to enfilade their platoon of 12/Battalion as it fought in the sunken Lagnicourt – Beaumetz lane, about a mile south of Lagnicourt village.[2]

To the north of Lagnicourt, 19/Battalion in reserve formed a flank on the ridge between Lagnicourt and Noreuil to protect the latter village; at the same time 20/Battalion moved forward towards the high ground close to Vaulx Wood. On the north side of the Hirondelle valley 300 yards east of Noreuil, elements of 17/Battalion had been pushed back to the sunken Lagnicourt – Bullecourt lane. Here, Captain Shephard and Lieutenant Dakin with a mixed platoon attempted to hold the enemy but small groups of Germans moved up the valley and enfiladed them from the south. The platoon withdrew to a trench nearer Noreuil where it was reinforced by the appearance of two Lewis guns crews. Despite continuing losses, the small garrison managed to hold the enemy on the eastern edge of the village. Earlier, and as the Bullecourt – Lagnicourt lane drops into the northern sector of Lagnicourt village, four Vickers of 21 Machine Gun Company had also temporarily halted the enemy advance. When they were fired on from the right rear the crews successfully disengaged and withdrew through the batteries in the valley running west of Lagnicourt. Once the Vickers teams had left, German machine-gun crews moved 200 yards north of those positions and from the northern side of the lane's crest were able to fire along the valley into Noreuil and towards the close packed ranks of field artillery further west.

The enemy thrust had taken the Australians by surprise and had shaken them severely. Gradually, however, as the reserves were ordered to move and the situation on the ground became clearer, it was realised that the enemy had boxed himself into a salient west of Lagnicourt. Some of their troops were too busy looting the battery positions to worry about continuing their advance. The Australian artillery, some now firing over open sights, received coordinates as to where their own infantry was now deployed and brought down a barrage which effectively

2 There is some uncertainty as to whether the action was fought in the Lagnicourt – Beaumetz lane or in the Lagnicourt – Doignies road. Both men had distinguished themselves during the attack on Boursies on 2 April. The award of the VC took into consideration the work they had done on the earlier occasion as well as their actions on 15 April.

trapped the Germans in the salient. The counter-attack by 19th, 20/Battalion and elements of 9/Battalion closed in on the salient from its three sides. Realising their predicament scores of Germans surrendered; others who tried to escape through Lagnicourt were caught by the stationary barrage. Those further to the east were pounded by the heavy artillery which ranged on the gaps in the enemy wire. As the Australian infantry regained their lost posts and positions the breach blocks removed from the abandoned guns were replaced and brought back into action. There was a slight delay in clearing the northern part of Lagnicourt because, as the Australians later claimed, it took time to discover and then inform the guns of 62nd Division that they were inadvertently ranging their fire over the divisional boundary.

If the objectives of the enemy were to cause troops to be brought down from the Arras front and to wreak such destruction on the Australian batteries as to prevent the expected next attack of the Allies, the attack failed on both counts. The reserve infantry brigades of both the involved Australian divisions were not engaged and the intended destruction of the Australian artillery brigades was not achieved. The Germans claimed they had destroyed 22 Allied guns; the actual total was five. Nonetheless, although the operation had failed it had cost the Australians dearly and had certainly caused a degree of panic amongst the unarmed gunners. The Germans reported their casualties to have been the very precise 2,313. Initial Australians reports put the casualties from their two divisions at about 26 officers and just under 1,100 ORs. They also claimed to have counted about 800 enemy dead on the front of 1st (Aust) Division and roughly 1,000 on that of 2nd (Aust) Division.

Lieutenant General Birdwood's I ANZAC remained fighting in the Bullecourt sector until relieved on 26 May. The corps had been in almost constant action since the previous autumn and more than required an extended period of rest and recuperation. Brigades of 20th Division quickly assumed command of Noreuil and Lagnicourt, followed in June by 62nd Division; 48th Division moved into the Hermies sector. Shelling and raiding continued throughout the summer months as the British brigades developed the trench system in front of the Hindenburg Line. There were to be no major engagements in the area until the Battle of Cambrai in November.

4

Battles for the Outpost Villages: XV Corps

To the south of the Canal du Nord and largely north of the Péronne–Cambrai road, XV Corps was also to be involved in some stubborn fighting as its divisions worked further towards the Hindenburg Line. With the capture of Gouzeaucourt on 12 April, five outpost villages remained to be taken. With the Australians on the left, 20th Division was to go for Trescault and 40th Division, Villers-Plouich and Beaucamp. South of the main Cambrai road, 8th Division was to capture Villers-Guislain and Gonnelieu. These last two villages were taken by 23 and 25 Brigades respectively on 17 and 25 April. These were fairly simple operations, as was the advance by 20th Division into Trescault. The precise sequence of events of what happened in Trescault is, however, a little unclear

The report in DHQ war diary notes that posts had gradually been pushed closer to the village but before any assault on it could be made the Germans began shelling it on the morning of 21 April. A small patrol led by Second Lieutenant Thornton-Smith, Intelligence Officer of 12/KRRC, entered the village and, save for the occasion shell and machine-gun burst coming from the Germans on the other side of the shallow valley, wandered about quite happily for several hours. Troops of 12/KRRC filtered into the west side of the village during the rest of the day. What Thornton-Smith and his scouts did certainly discover was that the enemy was digging trenches in the area known as Bilhem. This was a former farm with a courtyard wall and several ruined buildings. The report in 12/KRRC diary suggests that Thornton-Smith's patrol entered the still-occupied village at 1030 but received no enemy fire from within the cottages and farms. He established posts at the southern end of the village; these were increased and strengthened during the night. At 0930 on 22 April, Lieutenant Sampson established more posts in the village which, it was assumed, had been evacuated by the enemy at or before dawn. On the right, 40th Division opposite Beaucamp was supposed to have advanced its left to link up with the KRRC but failed to do so. What followed was almost a textbook little attack on Bilhem.

On 24 April, as part of another attack by 40th Division on Beaucamp, 12/KRRC was ordered to take Bilhem. As a preliminary measure during the day a patrol of 6/Ox&Bucks cleared the civilian cemetery north of the Ribécourt road; 12/RB fired Lewis guns on Bilhem only infrequently to try to convince the garrison an attack was not imminent. Second Lieutenant Benson of the Ox&Bucks set off to reconnoitre towards the farm but failed to return. By 2100, KRRC battalion HQ of had been established in a ravine on the side of the Metz–Trescault road and its companies were in position for the assault. On the left, D Company was in touch with the Ox&Bucks in the cemetery and A Company lined up just below the crest of the Gouzeaucourt road south-west of Trescault. Behind this company, C was in support and B in reserve. At 2300 a barrage fired by field and heavy artillery opened on the enemy trench in front of Bilhem and then crept back 100 yards every two minutes. To supplement the barrage 60 TMB dropped 120 rounds on the farm area in the space of five minutes. At 2302 A Company advanced and took the trench but, instead of consolidating the gain, pressed on. Seeing this error and fearing a counter-attack, OC C Company took his platoons forward to occupy the ground where A Company should have dug in. On the left, D Company moved towards Bilhem from the cemetery and occupied it from the north. The assault and capture had taken 25 minutes. The Germans did shell the newly-won positions which compelled a short retirement, but the land was quickly reoccupied when the shelling died down. The German infantry had not put up much of a defence and most had escaped to the rear. Consequently only 10 prisoners were taken for a cost of about 30 KRRCs killed and wounded. It had been a simple but very effective manoeuvre, the results of which were later to provide valuable protection for 40th Division's next attack on Beaucamp.

The front of 40th Division stretched from the Péronne–Cambrai road in the south, climbed slightly west by north to embrace the western sections of Beaucamp ridge, and Trescault spur. The division was a hybrid. One of its original brigades, 119, had been composed of bantam units – men below what had been the official height regulation. The other eight battalions had also contained large numbers of bantams. Many of these men had subsequently been weeded out as unfit for active service and by the time the division sailed in 1916 the remaining fit men in the eight battalions of 120 and 121 Brigades had been amalgamated into two battalions for each brigade. Another four new battalions were then transferred from 39th Division to bring 40th to establishment. It had fought on the Somme and joined XV Corps in March 1917.

Before it could assault the outpost villages of Beacamp and Villers-Plouich the division had first to establish suitable jumping off positions. Preparatory work began on 15 April when the divisional artillery, some of whose guns were described as "worn out," began wire cutting to the west and south of the two villages. The first objective for two battalions of 119 Brigade was a depression known as Fifteen Ravine and its various associated strong points on the north-eastern outskirts of Gouzeaucourt. In conjunction with 8th Division's attack on Gonnelieu south of the main Cambrai road, 12/South Wales Borderers (SWB) and 19/RWF attacked at 0420 on 21 April. The barrage was not particularly good but once the attacking companies were through the wire many of the Germans fled in the direction of Villers-Plouich. The garrisons of several strong points did offer resistance and had to be mopped up before consolidation could begin. On the left, 13/East Surrey and 11/King's Own of 120 Brigade had found the work rather easier. Unwittingly the Surreys had advanced beyond their objective of the sunken lane leading to Beaucamp from the western exit of Villers-Plouich; the King's Own had made their way onto the Trescault spur with little real difficulty. Casualties had been remarkably light – those in 119 Brigade amounting to about 157. The brigades were now in positions close enough to attack the two villages.

The next operation, again as part of a larger effort by XV Corps, was scheduled for 24 April. Two brigades, each with two battalions leading, were to be used: on the left, 18th and 17/Welch of 119 Brigade were to establish strong points on the lane which ran across the main Cambrai road from Gonnelieu to Villers-Plouich; in the centre and left, 13/East Surrey and 12/Argyll & Sutherland Highlanders were to take Villers-Plouich and Beaucamp respectively. Supported by artillery and machine-gun barrages, and with 8th Division protecting their right flank, the two Welch battalions were thought to have the somewhat easier task. Similarly, taking Villers-Plouich which lay in a hollow of ground was not thought to pose too many difficulties. But, if Bilhem remained in enemy hands observers and machine-guns there would be able to bring enfilade fire on the Argylls as they crossed the exposed ground towards Beaucamp. The assumptions proved correct. Parties of 18/Welch left their trenches well before zero and had established advanced posts by the time the barrage opened. They had been followed by the other companies who had formed up in no man's land. When the enemy guns responded to the British barrage most of the Germans shells thus fell behind the advancing waves. Companies of 17/Welch had the task of working round to the higher ground south-east of Villers-Plouich from about Farm Ravine while the East Surrey's attacked it a little south of west. The division had been unsure of the depth of the enemy wire, and it proved to be stronger and deeper than anticipated. It did cause some problems, but the Welch reached the lower slopes of Welsh ridge and mopped up the few Germans who had remained within their dugouts.

The East Surrey formed up on the Gouzaucourt–Trescault road about 1,500 yards from Villers-Plouich. At zero the companies advanced to the enemy wire and trench about 250 yards in front of them, fought their way through both, and moved on towards to the village. Several strong points in between had to be silenced with bombs and Lewis gun fire. Once the outskirts of the village were reached the battalion split into three groups. The right group was to link up with 17/Welch around a ravine and the Monument on the lower slope of Welsh ridge east of the village. Fierce opposition confronted them and the company commander, Captain Crocker, was killed. To regain momentum Corporals Reed and Foster used their Lewis guns to knock out several of the enemy positions and made contact with 17/Welch. Foster was later awarded the Victoria Cross and Reed the DCM. In the centre the company went through the village and along the Ribécourt road to establish posts on Highland ridge about 500 yards north of the village. The left party cleared the western part of the village and stormed a strong point in the sunken lane running between Villers-Plouich and Beaucamp. Here it was realised that Beaucamp had not been taken and that trying to advance any further would merely draw fire from that hamlet. The company dug in about 300 yards west of Villers-Plouich and sent the 100 prisoners taken to the rear. The village and its immediate surrounds were then subjected to intense enemy artillery fire.

The East Surrey battalion had effectively achieved its objectives. The centre company was now north-east of Beaucamp. Were it not for the fact that many of the farm buildings in the hamlet were not entirely ruined and able thus to provide cover for German troops in trenches and the buildings themselves, the company could in theory bring fire to bear on the rear of the defenders. Yet even if the cottages and barns had not obscured the lines of sight and fire, it would have been of little consolation to 12/A&SH. The highlanders had advanced their jumping off points to within about 100 yards of the enemy's front trench. When the barrage began the two lead companies found the wire uncut. The men carried wire cutters, but heavy losses were taken as they cut their way through. Fire hit them from the front and from the exposed left flank. Once through the wire they cleared the enemy trench and continued towards the hamlet still 200 yards away. There was little opposition in the buildings but as they emerged from the eastern and northern sides, again fire ripped into them. Most of it was coming from posts on the banking of the sunken lane going down the valley to Ribécourt and also from a series of posts south of Bilhem. The support company was unable to get forward, but a message did get through to the artillery and fire was brought down on the posts on the valley lane. Numbers of enemy troops were killed by Lewis fire as they left their positions to escape the shelling but once it had stopped they were seen to be returning to the posts in small, ordered squads with good distance between them. Once there, they resumed their fire. Against such odds, and with few officers remaining, the survivors of the two leading Argyll companies made their way back almost to their jumping off points. There, in a new trench of connected shell holes they joined with the support company.

One company of 11/King's Own had come under the orders of the Argylls during the attack; the rest of the battalion came up to relieve the Scots and resume the attack after dark. At 0420 on 25 April the King's Own advanced through Beaucamp meeting little opposition. They began to dig posts across the valley road from where the Argylls had been so heavily hit the day before and, although under fire for most of the day, consolidated the ground won. From their new positions they looked down on the outpost line of the Hindenburg Line. That they were able to do so was the result of the action during the previous night by which 12/KRRC of 20th Division had cleared Bilhem and thus secured the King's Own left flank.

5

Hindenburg Line Reached: Conclusion

A few miles to the north, Byng's Third Army continued to hammer away at the German defences east of Arras. Patrol activity and shelling continued along the Bullecourt sector in preparation for another attack against the village. The operational pause allowed time for training and advancing some of the outposts closer to the enemy's main defences. It also allowed a little time for reflection on what I ANZAC had achieved since it had come within range of the outpost villages of the Hindenburg Line. In the same away as GOC 2nd Division had done when it was withdrawn from the line in March a staff officer at I ANZAC HQ wrote a critique of the actions of the preceding weeks. There was nothing especially novel in what he wrote – there were some comments on the use of mounted troops and the necessity of better coordination of all arms in semi-open warfare – with the bulk the report concentrating on the communications, the need for more rifle practice, and the utility of close infantry support weapons. These points echoed those in post-battle reports written during the later phases of the Somme and were to be reiterated endless times in those written by commanders from the Arras offensive until the end of the war.

Although there remained much to be done in the ways and means of improving training and in the provision of sufficient and effective equipment, the advance across the evacuated zone had been done reasonably efficiently. There was the need for a cautious advance because the Germans could pick the time and place where the advanced guards would meet resistance by rearguards. Third, Fourth and Fifth Armies knew they were expected to be close to the Hindenburg Line by 8 April at the latest. The pressure to be in position for when the Arras offensive began was greatest on Gough. His army had the shortest distance to cover and also faced the least formidable of the geographical and physical obstacles. If, however, his corps were not in position on schedule the start of the Arras attack, and thus the associated Nivelle Offensive, could have been thrown into jeopardy. Gough was prepared to push his commanders and his men hard, as the sacking of Major General Barrow demonstrated. The advancing troops and their commanders had learned some of the skills required for semi-open warfare while the job was in hand. Tactical and operational mistakes had been made and the enemy was always in control. By direct and indirect methods, the enemy did much to determine the tempo of the Allied advance. The principal problems for the British and Australians had been to keep their troops supplied and capable of communicating with each other as progress was made across the devastated area. The Hindenburg Line had been reached and, indeed breached east of Arras, but along most of its length it was to remain intact for more than another year. With the exception of the Battle of Cambrai, British attention moved north to Flanders. Those corps and divisions garrisoning the evacuated zone resumed the attrition and hardships of trench warfare. The villages which had been destroyed during the withdrawal offered the new occupants little or no shelter from shells or weather. Camps, horse standings, training areas, artillery positions, and a network of trenches had to be constructed, roads and railways needed to be restored and repaired. Life in the zone was hard, dangerous and demanding with shelling, working parties and patrolling filling the days and nights. The cemeteries made during the advance and those begun once the lines settled down became testaments to how deadly conditions in front of the outpost villages could be.

6

Losing the Wastelands: Introduction

There was a general assumption and expectation amongst the Western Allies in the early months of 1918 that the enemy would launch a major offensive on the Western Front. The objective was assumed to be the separation and destruction of the Allied armies before the arrival of Americans forces swung the balance in favour of the Allies.[1] Intelligence suggesting that the Germans were transferring divisions from the Eastern Front to the West confirmed the belief that the offensive would start sometime in March. The precise date, and the actual area or areas to be assaulted were speculative but the expectation was that the attack would be on a massive scale. In order to meet the anticipated assault, the winter months had seen the British take over more sectors of line from the French. British divisions and any available corps and army ancillary units concentrated on preparing and developing their defensive ways and means in order to counter the threat. Opportunities for training during the winter months had, however, been infrequent. The reorganisation of divisions' infantry brigades into only three battalions each had also disrupted divisional and brigade coherence. General Gough, whose Fifth Army had recently taken over the extended British line from the French, was unsure of how adequate his defensive arrangements, coupled with the possible lack of tactical understanding amongst his troops of what those arrangements demanded, would prove to be when the attack came. GOC Third Army, General Byng, whose corps held the northern Wastelands, was more confident than Gough. He believed his troops would be able to hold the assault in the Battle Zone of his divisions' defensive systems.

British defensive doctrine had emerged in the post-Somme period but had only been codified with any real coherence in late 1917. The enemy's development of defence in depth supported by strong and swiftly organized counter-attacks had frustrated many of the British assaults during Third Ypres and later at Cambrai. The resultant evolution of the British doctrine was a combination of lessons learned from bitter and costly experience, captured German doctrinal documents, and the consequence of assessments of the state of British force preparedness and defences in late 1917 and early 1918. A GHQ memo of December 1917 explained the principles on which an accepted but only temporary period of British defensive posture should be

1 This was certainly a strategic objective, but Ludendorff's operational objectives were less clearly defined. To paraphrase his oft-quoted comment, Ludendorff said that he would, "Punch a hole in the Allied defences and see what happens." It was probably three days into the offensive before he decided the rail hub at Amiens should be a prime objective.

grounded. The document emphasized the need for such components as economy of force, the timely employment of reserves, the organization of successive defensive zones, and the extensive construction of protective shelters and posts. It advised on the role of the artillery and machine guns and reiterated the need for constant aggressive patrolling and raiding. Frequent rehearsals of counter-attacks over ground likely to be contested, and the "maintenance of confidence and fitness of the troops" were also to be prioritized.[2]

Along the front of Byng's VI (Haldane), IV (Harper), and V (E.A.Fanshawe) Corps the divisions had had a reasonable time to prepare their defences. The Forward and Battle Zones had been well constructed, and there were stretches of the Rear Zones which had some obstacles and trenches in place. Possibly the weakest point in Byng's defences was the section of line near Flesquières taken up in December 1917 following the German counter-attack towards the end of the Cambrai battle. The so-called Flesquières Salient required three divisions of V Corps to hold the front line, with another in reserve. As a salient it offered an open invitation for any offensive to pinch it out and trap its divisions by attacking its northern and southern shoulders.[3] The Battles of Bullecourt and Cambrai had allowed the British and Australians to push some of the lines captured in the advance of March and April 1917 a little further forward into what had been the Hindenburg System itself. These defences, for example those at Havrincourt and Bullecourt, had been incorporated into the British zones. The infantry garrisoning what had been the former enemy outpost villages, and the stretches of open land in between them, manned the defences with two brigades up and had devised various schemes for counter-attacks over what were the anticipated German lines of approach. The artillery had concentrated on disruptive shoots and counter-battery work and had registered on their SOS and protective barrages lines. Field company personnel and pioneers knew their roles and positions to be adopted when the onslaught broke. Many of the main communication cables and networks had been buried up to a depth of six or eight feet.

The new doctrine provided essential guidelines, theories and practices for a BEF forced to confront the unexpected realities of fighting defensive battles in the near future. Unfortunately, its tardy appearance had allowed little time for its strategic, operational, and tactical elements to be fully understood by those who were to operate under its aegis. Elements of *Field Service Regulations(2)* and the numerous centrally-published instructional pamphlets were essential reading for commanders about to face the forthcoming test. Their over-riding concern was, however, the lack of time their men had had to become accustomed and trained for a system of defence that was both largely unfamiliar and widely disliked.[4]

2 *Military Operations* Appendix VI, 14 Dec.1917
3 When the attack began on 21 March, Fanshawe had five divisions in his corps. At 1255, 19th Division was transferred to IV Corps.
4 See *Military Operations*, Appendices: IV, 24 Nov.1917; XIII, 24 Jan.1918; XI, 1 Feb.1918 for concerns over manpower, etc.

7

Losing the Wastelands: VI Corps, March 1918

The three forward divisions in Lieutenant General Aylmer Haldane's VI Corps were 59th on the right, 34th in the centre, and 3rd on the left. The latter, whose southern flank lay to the east of Hénin, was little affected on 21 March. The few assaults which were made against its right brigade were fairly easily repulsed. The main German thrust against the corps was aimed against 59th (2nd North Midland) Division, the formation which held the shortest front of the corps' three divisions. The enemy's aim was to drive a wedge down the Hirondelle valley and take Vaulx-Vraucourt. The valley and the twin villages lay just within 6th Division's sector of IV Corps. Another assault was to come through Ecoust and Longatte directly against the front of the North Midland. The thrust would then swing north-west to trap the forward troops of 59th Division and penetrate the right rear flank of 34th. The Battle of Bullecourt in April and May 1917 had captured the village and the new British front line had been established to its east. The Forward Zone of 59th Division's 1918 defences incorporated the village and the land lying between it and, roughly, the easternmost outskirts of Noreuil, Longatte and Ecoust. Those villages contained the front system of the Battle Zone. This zone stretched back across the open land south-westwards as far as Banks Trench and Banks Support. These were the front of the Third System and ran in a north-west – south-east direction between St-Léger and Vraucourt.

The 2nd North Midland Division's four battalions in the Forward Zone were two Sherwood Foresters' units of 178 Brigade on the right in front of Noreuil and Longatte, and two Stafford battalions of 176 Brigades on the left inside and to the east and north-east of Ecoust. The third battalion of each brigade were in the front of the Battle Zone. Those in the Forward Zone were accurately targeted by the enemy barrage and then assaulted by overwhelming numbers of German infantry. Against the two Sherwood Forester battalions, and with the assistance of the heavy mist, the enemy poured through the forward defences of Horseshoe Redoubt, Joyride Trench, over the railway embankment and then through Pontefract and Dewsbury Trenches to Iggaree Corner. Because communications to the rear had been broken by the bombardment, Lieutenant Colonel Gadd whose 2/5th Sherwood was in support and manning the front of the Second System could ascertain little of what was going on.

Several days before the offensive opened Gadd had expressed disquiet about how strongly the Forward Zone of 178 Brigade was held. He argued that it should be thinned out, and greater weight put instead into the Battle Zone. Standing orders preventing any counter-attacks from the Battle into the Forward Zone meant he could do little to assist the two front battalions unless, or until troops of 177 Brigade, the reserve formation, had been ordered to move to the Battle Zone to replace his. All he could do was to call forward his own reserve company and try to discover what was going on to his front. Events remained unclear until huge numbers of Germans appeared on either side of his battalion HQ. He regained contact with 2/7th Sherwood Foresters and, until about 1400 according to one later report, the two COs believed the advance had been stopped. Having regrouped, the Germans attacked again and destroyed Gadd's command, the advance down the Hirondelle valley having exposed the Foresters' right flank. The Germans then swung north-westwards up the Noreuil-Longatte road and were thus able to take the front sections of the Battle Zone from the south and rear.

To Gadd's left, 2/6th South and 5/North Stafford had also been virtually swept away. As the enemy advanced through Bullecourt and on into Ecoust, Stanhope and Station Redoubts had fallen fairly quickly. The dire position confronting the brigade and the entire division in the morning and afternoon of 21 March required unit and sub-unit commanders sometimes to take instant decisions about where to deploy their dwindling number of men. Brigadier General Cope, GOC 176 Brigade, asked DHQ to send up two companies of 177 Brigade to replace two companies of 2/6th North Stafford, the support battalion in the Battle Zone. Despite the standing orders Cope wanted to send the two companies of 2/6th North Stafford across the boundary of the Battle and Forward Zones. Telephone communications were down so a runner was sent to DHQ but, probably unknown to Cope, two companies of 177 Brigade had already been ordered forward to occupy the second line of the Battle Zone west of Ecoust. Before any answer arrived at 176 Brigade HQ, however, the enemy was through the Forward Zone in considerable force and had attacked the two North Stafford companies just as they were about to counter-attack eastwards. With his CO already dead, Major Keating of the North Stafford had now to turn intended attack into hasty and desperate defence. Keating and his men, confronted with constant explosions and dense phosphorous smoke from a nearby burning ammunition dump, were compelled to wear gas respirators for two hours. There was no communication with any other company or battalion and no possibility of obtaining any SAA and Lewis drums. He held a post on the railway embankment in front of Ecoust and was frequently over-flown by enemy aircraft that dropped flares over his position. He sent out runners in pairs to contact other companies and seek reinforcements, but none returned. As sparse information came in and with the enemy hitting him from all directions Keating did what he could to shuffle his diminishing sections around. His aim was to fight his way to the higher ground near the civilian cemetery but, with wheeled enemy machine guns being run up towards him and ammunition almost exhausted, he and his 12 surrounded survivors surrendered.

At least one of Keating's runners seems to have reached brigade HQ because DHQ placed 1/East Lancs of 34th Division at the disposal of GOC 176 Brigade. The plan, rapidly extemporized rather than one taken from the prepared defence scheme, was for a coordinated counter-attack using one battalion of 177 Brigade, the division's reserve brigade, and 1/East Lancs to retake sections of the Battle Zone. The attack was cancelled because the East Lancs proved too slow in assembling its companies and 2/4th Leicester, which was four miles behind the Battle Zone, was unable to reach its supposed jumping off point beyond the Third Line. With hindsight, if two advanced companies from two of the three battalions of 177 Brigade had been despatched as soon as it had become clear Noreuil was under severe threat, they may well have arrived in time to have offered substantial help to 2/5th Sherwood Foresters and 2/6th North

Stafford in the Battle Zone.[1] Major General Romer did eventually order 177 Brigade forward to man the rear defences of the Battle Zone and, once there, companies from two of its battalions attempted counter-attacks towards Ecoust and Noreuil. Both ran into heavy German resistance and lost the equivalent of about two companies. In the afternoon enemy forces continued to pour along the spurs and the Hirondelle valley. In a desperate attempt to halt the flood, transport details, cooks, and batmen were rushed up hurriedly from the rear to join the eight surviving machine-gun crews of 59 Bn MGC.

Little is known of what happened to the three forward companies of 59 Bn MGC. Their deployment, thought at the time by DHQ to have been unsatisfactory, meant they were probably hit very hard in the opening bombardment. It was believed that some crews fought on with borrowed Lewis guns and even revolvers, but those in the Battle Zone did certainly inflict massive casualties on Germans emerging from Ecoust and Longatte. B Battery claimed to have shot down about 1,500 on the Hog's Back, and C Battery "virtually demolished" a further two battalions. Eventually, shrapnel fire and a threatened turning movement by the enemy from the south forced the crews to withdraw. The survivors were joined near Mort Homme by about 100 partially trained machine-gunners and some gunners of the artillery despatched forward as platoons of infantry. The 18 pdrs of A/296 Brigade RFA firing HE with 106 Fuzes from positions overlooking Maida Vale, south-west of Ecoust, were considered to have had "a tremendous effect" when they targeted Germans debouching from Noreuil. Other of the surviving batteries to the east of Mory fired over open sights as hordes of Germans approached their positions along the Hog's Back.[2] The OC D/295, whose 4.5 inch howitzers were sited about 200 yards north of Vaulx-Vraucourt, had fired on Iggaree Corner, which was "packed with Huns," and on other concentrations as they appeared on the ridge carrying the Noreuil–Longatte road. The "decisive factor" which in the end compelled him to disable his guns and withdraw his shrinking number of men was the appearance of Germans emerging over the crest to the north-west of Vraucourt Copse. What was left of the artillery was eventually ordered to the rear some hours later. It managed to salvage 20 of its 18 pdrs and 4.5 inch howitzers.

In the early afternoon the division's pioneer battalion, 6/7th RSF, moved up to Vraucourt Trench, about 400 yards west of the position from where D/295 had destroyed its guns. Within 20 minutes of arriving the pioneers were firing into waves of advancing Germans. For the next 18 hours the battalion was at times out of touch with both flanks and under fire from British heavy and field artillery. It kept its snipers active in preventing enemy patrols emerging from Vraucourt Copse and even managed to bring up an additional three Lewis guns from their anti-aircraft positions in the rear. The battalion maintained a steady fire into apparently never ending masses of Germans heading for Mory. It remained in the line under 40th Division when most of what remained of 59th Division was later relieved.

1 This assertion is, however, open to some debate. The times of the orders and movements for the counter-attack given in 177 Bde's Report on Operations (TNA WO 95/3022) are at significant variance with those in Edmonds, *Military Operations*, p.233 and also the WDs of 2/4th Leicestershire (TNA WO 95/3022) and 2/5th Lincolnshire (TNA WO 95/3023) Those in VI Corps WD more closely reflect those of 177 Bde. It may be that Romer acted rather more swiftly than some sources indicate.

2 An 18 pdr firing over 'open sights' usually meant firing at targets at a range of between 1,000-1,500 yards. This was well within the effective range of the German MG08/15 light machine gun employed by German *Sturmtruppen*. The effective range of the 18 pdr was about 6,000 yards.

On the division's left flank, touch had just about been kept with 34th Division; on the right, a "serious gap" had developed between 59th and 6th Divisions. A meeting at about 1930 between an unnamed brigade major of 59th Division, Brigadier General Dobbin, GOC 75 Brigade, and two newly arrived battalion COs of 40th Division, discussed the situation. The gap of about 500 yards lay in a stretch of the Third System roughly where Vraucourt Trench became Vaulx Trench, a little to the north-east of Vaulx-Vraucourt. Despite the discussion the gap remained empty but, fortunately, fighting eased off during the night. At 0055 on 22 March, Major General Marden, GOC 6th Division, telephoned Major General Romer and asked if 59th Division could attempt to work southwards and get in touch with 6th Division's left. With what little remained of 177 Brigade constituting virtually the whole of his command, Romer declined the request on the grounds that his remnants were in the process of being relieved by 40th Division.

The 2nd North Midland Division was probably the hardest hit on 21 March of any under Byng's command. The divisional command believed it was the left of 6th Division that had allowed the enemy to penetrate the Hirondelle valley and then roll up the North Midland's right. Casualties had been enormous and although a huge casualty list does not necessarily mean the men "fought to the last," 59th Division suffered the highest losses of any formation involved that day. Lieutenant Colonel Gadd's earlier concern that the Forward Zone was too strongly held at the expense of the Battle Zone proved to have been justified. As the Germans swept into and around the positions of 2/6th and 7/Sherwood they were left with the option of surrendering or dying at their posts. Initial returns late on 21 March gave the combined number of survivors of those two battalions as 59 ORs. Gadd's battalion, 2/5th Sherwood, had just three ORs at the first roll call. The Foresters' Brigade casualties were recorded as 88 officers and 1,899 ORs. Casualties in the three Stafford battalions of 176 Brigade were noted as 70 officers and 1,683 ORs.[3] By 2200, 177 Brigade's fighting strength was probably little more than the equivalent of one battalion and one machine-gun company.

The centre division of Haldane's VI Corps had also suffered heavily, partly as a consequence of the ferocity of the assault on 59th Division. The former outpost village of Croisilles lay in 34th Division's Battle Zone. The Forward Zone's left front sector was held by 101 Brigade, with 11/Suffolk on the left and 15/R.Scots on the right. The right sector was held by 102 Brigade, with 22/NF adjoining the Staffords of 176 Brigade, and 23/NF next to 15/R.Scots. The brigades' two support battalions were 16/R.Scots and 25/NF respectively. The division's reserve formation, 103 Brigade, had 1/East Lancs in close support in St-Léger. The other two battalions, 10/Lincoln and 9/NF, were held further back. The enemy bombardment fell most heavily on 102 Brigade but there appears to have been no infantry attack until enemy troops appeared behind the front line posts. These had penetrated the Staffordshire Brigade and then turned north to attack the two Tyneside Scottish battalions from the rear. A well-practised defensive flank facing south was executed by 22/NF and extended to beyond Bunhill Row by one company of 25/NF. The fusiliers were forced back along the communication trench known as Queen's Lane that ran down the gentle slope towards the eastern edge of Croisilles.

3 According to *Soldiers Died* the two battalions of 178 Brigade and the two of 176 Brigade in the Forward Zone suffered a combined loss of 452 OR fatalities.

Fighting continued during the afternoon in and around the area of the sunken lane which ran from the sugar factory down to the north-western edge of Bullecourt. Many of the fusiliers' sections and platoons were cut off or overwhelmed north of where the railway crossed the main Croisilles–Ecoust road. The situation took another turn for the worse when the thrust that had swept through Longatte and Noreuil turned north and crossed the Battle Zone of 59th Division. Three companies of 25/NF not in the defensive flank counter-attacked across the spur to the south-east of St-Léger and were not heard of again. Rearguards of 102 Brigade held the enemy for a time in the area west and south of the railway where it ran from Croisilles towards St-Léger, and also from a trench just south of the railway crossing on the main road to Ecoust. They were assisted by two batteries of 160 Brigade RFA which fired on the massed enemy ranks from a distance of about 800 yards. Just to the north of the railway the mortars of 102 TMB "found most favourable targets" from a range of 500 yards. This combined resistance, which entailed much hand-to-hand fighting, was sufficient to hold the enemy until 9/NF had taken position in the defences on the ridge to the west of Croisilles. There, with remnants of 102 Brigade and with the help of a counter-attack by two companies of 1/East Lancs supported by D Battery of 34 MGC, the Germans were held until nightfall. The four guns of D Battery were reported to have fired off about 30,000 rounds from their positions a little south-east of St-Léger Wood. The enemy had not penetrated Croisilles itself and the switch which ran north-south on the west side of the village remained garrisoned. This allowed corps HQ to approve the proposal of 34th Division GOC, Major General Nicholson, to withdraw his remaining troops from the village.

The two forward battalions of 101 Brigade had not been assaulted quite so ferociously as those in the division's southern sector. Nonetheless, 11/Suffolk, and particularly 15/R.Scots, had been forced from the Forward Zone into the Battle Zone. By dark the brigade was manning Croisilles Switch North with a mixture of units and details. The Germans attacked at 0800 on 22 March just to the north of the village against elements of the pioneer battalion and some details. A counter-attack by remnants of 23/NF drove them back but having regrouped the enemy attacked again. They over-ran several machine-gun posts and sections of the scattered 15/R.Scots to hit the Suffolks' right flank from the south. The Suffolk battalion was gradually forced back towards Hill Switch, a very shallow trench on the slopes to the north-west of Croisilles and manned by details of 25/NF and 16/R.Scots. An enemy aircraft directed artillery onto the trench and, according to one report, the garrison was "literally blown" out of it. The bombardment was followed by an infantry assault which forced 16/R.Scots to withdraw, either "slowly" or "pell-mell," to the Third System to the east of Boyelles.[4] They passed over the trenches which 2 Guards Brigade had recently arrived to garrison. Meanwhile on their left, and although attacked from its right rear as well as its front, 11/Suffolk had managed to contain three assaults on Hénin Hill. The battalion was finally forced to withdraw north-westwards to a bank on the lower northern slope of Hénin Hill 800 yards south of Héninel.

During the night of 21/22 March units of 40th Division arrived to relieve 59th Division and to act as reinforcement to 34th Division. Two battalions of 103 Brigade, 10/Lincoln and 9/NF, were manning Croisilles Switch South. This trench curled round the west of Croisilles and then to its south and south-east. At 1030 on 22 March in front of St-Léger Wood, 9/NF repulsed

4 The manner of the withdrawal depends on which source is taken. *Military Operations* Vol.I, p316 described it as "pell-mell"; the divisional war diarist recorded it as "slowly."

an enemy attack with the crucial assistance of machine-guns which fired over the heads of the fusiliers to break up the massing enemy forces. At about 1430 Germans who had crossed the Hog's Back and the boundary between 34th and 59th Divisions assaulted a line to the south-east of St-Léger Wood. This had only just been filled by 13/Yorks of 40th Division. The Green Howards began to yield ground which, in turn forced 9/NF on their left, and 10/Lincoln on the left of the fusiliers, to fall back.[5] Garrisons withdrew through St-Léger towards Judas Farm Switch and the Sensée valley. A counter-attack from Judas Farm by 13/East Surrey of 40th Division supported by two tanks with the objective of regaining St-Léger village was proposed, but the idea was abandoned when the tanks were commandeered to assist 18/Welch in Sensée Switch to halt a separate enemy attack. Although very much spread out along the trench, the Welch, the two tanks, and an 18 pdr whose crew had "the time of their lives " knocking over Germans in "scores," managed to convince the Germans that the line was held in great strength. By the afternoon it was known that 2 Guards Brigade was in the Third System in front of Boyelles and that it was to come temporarily under the orders of 34th Division. DHQ was told, however, that the Guards were not to be used as a counter-attack force. Further encouraging news came in the later afternoon. Two brigades of 31st Division were to debus about Boyelles and relieve the much weakened and "wavering" 34th Division that night.

Very soon after they had deployed in what had been 59th Division's sector, two battalions of 120 Brigade of 40th Division were attacked between Ecoust and Vaulx-Vraucourt. It was believed for a time that 6th Division on their right had given way, but the CO of 14/A&SH decided to hold on in case a counter-attack was being organised to his rear. D/181 was in support and managed to destroy several enemy machine-gun teams as they attempted to establish their positions. Contact was made with 6th Division and a defensive flank was formed by 10/11th HLI and 14/HLI along the Vaulx-Vraucourt–Beaugnâtre road. The left of the brigade should have been in touch with either 6/7th RSF (P), elements of 177 Brigade, or 20/Middlesex of its own division but appears not to have been. The lack of clarity and certainty about where all of the division's units actually were on the morning of 23 March is apparent in the war diary.

It is clear that the battalions of 120 Brigade had relieved the three units of 177 Brigade by about 0230 on 22 March. The Leicester and Lincoln battalions had withdrawn to the Third System, which in this sector was known as Banks Trench. This trench roughly followed the line of the St-Léger–Vraucourt road. During the course of several attacks throughout the day, especially those which drove in the left front of 6th Division, the brigade withdrew to the Army Line which ran a little to the east of Mory. In the evening further attacks developed simultaneously on both flanks and several posts were over-run. Having been ordered again to withdraw the brigade took up positions in Mory village. The crossroads close to the church was defended by 2/4th Leicester. The Leicester had 4/Lincoln on its immediate right and the five officers and 80 ORs who constituted 2/5th Lincoln on the far right. On the left of the Leicester were elements of 12/Suffolk and 20/Middlesex. The Suffolk, which according to a later report had already lost three companies at Le Mort Homme in the late afternoon, was thought to be holding Mory Copse. At about 2315 an attack drove in the remaining company which caused 2/4th Leicester to throw back a defensive flank on the left along the Mory – Ervillers road.

5 Second Lieutenant Ernest Beal of 13/Yorks was awarded the VC for bravery and leadership during this fighting. He was to be killed the following day and is commemorated on the Arras M.M.

At 2320 the brigade received orders to counter-attack and regain the Army Line. Brigade HQ was informed by battalion COs that this was impossible and would be a waste of men because the enemy had already taken Mory L'Abbaye, just east of the defended crossroads. During the next four or five hours 2/4th Leicester in particular was heavily pressured by enemy attacks trying to envelop its left flank. These assaults were accompanied by the sound of bugles and assisted by light trench mortars and a field gun at close range. Eventually the pressure told. With 119 Brigade HQ having received a report at 0404 on 23 March that 20/Middlesex, which was somewhere between the village and west of Mory Copse, "was breaking," the two Lincoln and the Leicester battalions were ordered to withdraw to the higher ground to the east of the Ervillers–Behagnies road.

By dawn on 23 March, 4/Lincoln was on the right about 1,500 yards south-east of Ervillers; in the centre, 2/5th Lincoln held a short front between the Ervillers–Behagnies road and the Ervilllers-Mory road; on the left, 2/4th Leicester held an even shorter line as far as the Ervillers – Mory road about 600 yards in front of Ervillers. By that time, and to the north, the three battalions of 119 Brigade had withdrawn from St-Léger and were digging in to the north-east of Ervillers. Its southern battalion, 13/East Surrey was in touch with 2/4th Leicester on the Ervillers – Mory road.

The northernmost of 119 Brigade's units, 21/Middlesex, assembled in a quarry in the Sensée valley north of the Ervillers – St-Léger road at about the same time as 177 Brigade began digging in on its new positions a little closer to Ervillers. Two companies of the Middlesex were to attack south-eastwards while one company of 13/East Surrey on its right was to advance east-south-east. The objectives were Mory and part of the Army Line to its north. The advance began at 0920 but the Middlesex was held up by machine guns firing from around Mory Copse, their own artillery firing short, and by an enemy aircraft which strafed the advancing troops. When they reached the section of the Army Line it was found to be 18 inches deep and very wide. It offered no protection from machine guns firing from the higher ground. The East Surrey was halted within 20 yards of advanced enemy posts a little south and on the lower slopes to the west of Mory. These posts had good fields of fire along the valley between Ervillers and Mory. The East Surrey was ordered to make another attempt in the afternoon with all four companies. Two companies were to go straight for the village, while another on the left was to take the high ground near Mory Copse. The fourth was to give supporting fire from the spur to the south and then move into the village and mop up. Fierce fighting took place in the village but most of it was eventually taken. With all officers having become casualties the three companies involved regrouped under a company sergeant major. To the north of the village, 21/Middlesex reoccupied the area close to Mory Copse. During the night 23/24 March, however, the enemy counter-attacked and forced the East Surrey down into the valley between Ervillers and Mory. Very confused fighting took place which eventually forced the East Surrey back towards Ervillers. By dawn of 24 March the position was precarious. The Germans were massing to the west of Mory and, despite being savaged by machine guns and artillery, advanced towards the much weakened 119 Brigade. If the Sensée Switch to the north fell the brigade, as well as 4 Guards Brigade of 31st Division on its left, could be taken from the rear. When the switch was captured by the enemy at about 1600 the order to withdraw from the Mory valley was given. What was left of 13/East Surrey was temporarily combined with the remnants of 21/Middlesex and 18/Welch. To the brigade's right, 120 Brigade had withdrawn from its defensive positions on the Beugnâtre road towards the village of Favreuil.

Further north, the Guards Division held the line roughly from Bank Copse to Hénin. Any enemy attack towards the village would have to cross open ground; those that were attempted were repulsed. The line between the Guards Division and the now severely-tried 40th Division was filled by the newly-arrived 31st Division. This division had relieved the remnants of 34th Division on the night 22-23 March. Its reserve brigade, 92 Brigade, had taken a position about 300 yards to the north of Ervillers in order to offer support to both 40th Division in its defence of Mory, and its own 4 Guards Brigade. Despite 31st Division being a New Army formation, 4 Guards Brigade was the right brigade of 31st Division. The three Guards battalions were positioned along the Ervillers – St-Léger road and would be overlooked if the Germans took the high ground around Mory Copse. Attacks against 4 Guards and 93 Brigades either side of St-Léger on 23 March were all broken up by 31st Division's artillery and infantry. German cavalry appearing to the north of St-Léger suffered the same fate. The Guards extended their right further towards Ervillers from the Sensée valley and were thought to be in touch with units of either 40th Division or 177 Brigade.

On 24 March, the CO of 2/4th Leicester reported that the Germans had again pushed along on the north side of the Mory–Ervillers road and were now able to enfilade his posts. He had formed a defensive flank along the south side of the road and was trying to hold under "great difficulties." Attempts by 11/East Yorks of 92 Brigade to organise groups of stragglers from units of both 40th and even 34th Divisions coming into Ervillers met with indifferent success because the men were exhausted and could offer little in the way of support. It was also realised that enemy patrols were mixed up with the withdrawing troops. At 0130 on 25 March, one company of 18/Welch was frustrated by bright moonlight in its attempt to reinforce the harassed 2/4th Leicester and, when 119 Brigade HQ ordered 13/East Surrey which was still on the left of 2/4th Leicester, and the Leicester to counter-attack along the road, it was told succinctly that there were no men available to launch such an assault. Relief was, however, on its way.

Major General Solly-Flood's 42nd Division had been swiftly bussed down to Adinfer from close to Lillers. The convoy of London buses had been driven at reckless speed and arrived late on 24 March with the men onboard having been tossed about in the freezing cold. They then marched off to the south-east. Solly-Flood requested that Haldane allow his division a day's rest before relieving 40th Division. He cited the uncomfortable journey followed by a long approach march and the obvious tactical difficulties any battalions would face when relieving other units on such a fluid front. Haldane demurred and informed Solly-Flood the relief was to take place that same night. At about midnight two battalions of 126 Brigade took up a preparatory position to the east of Logeast Wood while 125 and 127 Brigades moved further forward to the south-west of Ervillers and due west of Sapignies. Shortly after having taken their positions in the rear, 126 Brigade was instructed to move quickly on Ervillers. On arrival, two companies of 10/Manchester were hastily pushed through to the east of Ervillers and were in touch with 4 Guards Brigade on their left. Some two hours later the two companies were withdrawn through Ervillers and rejoined the rest of the battalion. They, together with 5/East Lancs, were ordered to become part of the garrison of Ervillers Trench from north of Bee Wood to about the Ervillers–Courcelles road.

The two forward battalions of 126 Brigade were told they would be bolstering a garrison of 18/Welch of 119 Brigade in the stretch of trench that covered the southern and south-western outskirts of Ervillers. When 5/East Lancs arrived to take over its allocated section it found it filled with men from a mixture of battalions. In contrast, 10/Manchester discovered its allotted sector of the trench to be empty. The Welch had apparently "disappeared." During the remainder of the night 24-25 March some but not all of the divisional relief took place.[6] Before it could all be completed, however, the Germans rushed the left of 2/4th Leicester in large numbers and took all of its posts. A few men did struggle back to the centre of Ervillers but the right of 13/East Surrey and the left of 2/5th Lincoln were now in the air. Later in the morning, and although by that time Ervillers was now technically outside VI Corps' sector, 10/East Yorks of 31st Division counter-attacked the northern arm of the enemy attack on the village and succeeded in temporarily driving him from it.

After another massed attack at 1015 the enemy took Sapignies and advanced on Bihucourt. This caused DHQ of 42nd Division to order any remaining troops of 40th Division and 177 Brigade to fall back to the line running 200 yards west of the Ervillers – Behagnies road. With the East Lancashire Division now having taken over command of 40th Division's front, Haldane asked IV Corps to assume command of Solly-Flood's division. As the principle but not the precise timing of the transfer had been previously agreed by both Third Army and Lieutenant General Harper, the order was issued. Thus, at 1030, on 25 March, 42nd Division was moved from Haldane's VI Corps to Harper's IV Corps.

To the north-east of Ervillers another heavy enemy attack was met by the rifles and Lewis guns of 93 Brigade. They ensured the enemy's assaulting waves "withered away." Later, 4 Guards Brigade complained that the artillery was so effective that the guardsmen were not "given a fair chance of using their rifles." The artillery's good shooting was in contrast to the criticism it had attracted the day before. Heavy batteries in particular, which were later thought not to have belonged to VI Corps, together with some RFA brigades had repeatedly shelled 4 Guards and 93 Brigades. The former complained that shells were regularly falling a good 1,000 yards behind their own front positions. To make matters worse RFC aircraft strafed and bombed the division's trenches. The divisional war diary decided, "It was evident that some units of the RAF (sic) from other districts had not quite made themselves acquainted with the new area." Given the constantly moving front this was hardly surprising.

At about 2130 on 25 March, and after more heavy fighting, 92 Brigade of 31st Division evacuated its positions on the northern outskirts of Ervillers. The battalions withdrew to what had become identified as the Yellow Line which was essentially the embankment of the Albert-Amiens railway. The manoeuvre was achieved while their own corps heavy artillery shelled the open land over which the troops had to pass. Because DHQ was unsure of what was happening over the corps boundary Major General Bridgford ordered a defensive flank to be established facing south. This was hurriedly created by the 31st Division's three field companies and pioneer battalion, as well as a mixture of men from the Welch, Middlesex, Suffolk, and East Surrey Regiments of 40th Division.[7] These troops were organised under the command of 11/East Lancs of 92 Brigade. On their left, 4 Guards Brigade had also withdrawn from its posts north of Ervillers and then passed through 93 Brigade and into reserve. On their way the Guards

6 The only unit of 59th Division actually to be relieved during that night was 6/7th RSF (P).

7 Those troops of 40th Division who were still with their units were withdrawn on 26 March and, by stages, moved to Bienvillers to recuperate and rest. The sorely tried survivors of 177 Brigade were withdrawn to Sailly-au-Bois. Both 40th and 59th Division were rebuilt and then almost destroyed again during the Battle of the Lys. In early May their battalions were reduced to training cadres. The divisions were reconstituted in June-July as Garrison Divisions and resumed active operations.

marched through an evacuated but mercifully temporarily no longer shelled Gomiécourt. The village remained unoccupied for some hours while both sides again decided to shell it heavily. The Germans advanced into its ruins on 26 March.

Having occupied and made hasty and improvised improvements to the Yellow Line, 92 Brigade was told at 0100 on 26 March that it was to conduct another withdrawal. This time it was to be to a line Ablainzevelle – Moyenneville. The new line was to run from 500 yards north of Ablainzevelle in a north-easterly direction to about 1,000 yards north of Courcelles. From there 93 Brigade would continue the line to join with the Guards Division north-east of Moyenneville. To the south of 92 Brigade, 42nd Division was to hold a line Bucquoy – Ablainzevelle and gain contact with the right of 31st Division. This next withdrawal by 31st Division meant that Courcelles would have to be evacuated. There was thought to be no need for an organised rearguard in the village, but the last troops did leave the village under small arms fire.

In Haldane's northern sector the Germans had made only limited attempts against 3rd Division. The division had voluntarily withdrawn from some of its Forward Zone in order to conform to a similar withdrawal by 15th Division on its left. It was ordered now to remain in its Battle Zone whilst on its right, the Guards Division was to pivot on the inter-divisional junction on the main Arras–Bapaume road north of Boiry-Bequerelle. The Guards Division was then to throw back its line to the north-west of Hamelincourt. The enemy followed on the heels of the withdrawal, but a counter-preparation show of force by the heavy artillery dissuaded the Germans from anything more than patrol activity. During the early hours of 26 March, the right of the Guards Division made firm contact with the left of 4 Guards Brigade north-east of Moyenneville. This latter brigade was digging in on a line Courcelles – Moyenneville but before dawn, it received orders to withdraw to Ayette as the reserve brigade of 31st Division. The Guards apparently marched back in column of fours but did not occupy the village itself. Its three battalions dug trenches and machine-gun positions to its north, south, and west. The divisional front was to be held on the left by 93 Brigade, in contact with the Guards Division, and 92 Brigade on the right which was to gain touch with the East Lancashire Division. Haldane was concerned about whether 92 Brigade would be able to extricate itself because he had intelligence that the enemy was advancing on Courcelles from Gomiécourt. If 92 Brigade was to reach its allotted position on the new line it would have to move north and thus probably create a gap between itself and the left of 42nd Division. Further bad news arrived at about noon on 26 March. Reports suggested that marauding Germans armoured cars had reached as far as Hébuterne, well to the south-west. This caused something of a panic in the rear area, but the report was later to be proven false.[8] By that time and as a precaution, one battalion of Guards had been despatched to Quesnoy Farm on the Bucquoy – Monchy-au-Bois road. What was certain, however, was that the enemy was known to be pressing hard on Moyenneville.

During the morning of 26 March, GOC 31st Division, Major General Bridgford, called at the Guards Division HQ. There, Major General Fielding told Bridgford that two battalions of 93 Brigade had recently been seen "quietly" marching back towards the Purple Line. Fielding asked Bridgford if he would like the Guards to extend their right to cover what was now something of an inviting gap between their two divisions. On investigation Bridgford discovered

8 Later reports suggested that the 'armoured cars' were, in fact, farm vehicles being towed by tractors.

that two battalions of 93 Brigade were indeed about a mile west by north of Moyenneville but that 15/17th West Yorks was still in the village or very close to it. A story emerged that a shell-shocked or possibly concussed brigade major had ordered the brigade to withdraw. It seems that 13/York&Lancs and 18/DLI did so but that the West Yorks did not receive the order. The West Yorks battalion was on the lower slopes of a ridge south-west of the village and in some trenches to its west. When it was realised there was no friendly unit on its left, the battalion began to extend northwards in order to get in touch with the right of the Guards Division. Meanwhile, however, the Germans had entered the unoccupied village and established several defensive posts; other sections had taken positions on the ridge to the south-west of the village. Their machine guns were then able to enfilade some of the West Yorks positions west of the village. The same guns were also able to break up an attempt by the York&Lancs and DLI to re-join the West Yorks. When the error of their withdrawal had been discovered the two battalions had been ordered to return to the village. The newly-positioned enemy machine guns ensured they managed to get only within about 400 yards of it. The CO of the isolated West Yorks decided to conduct a counter-attack with two companies to eliminate the machine guns and secure the ridge. Simultaneously a platoon was to sweep through the village and trap any of the enemy fleeing from the frontal assault. The attack succeeded but gradually during the day enemy pressure forced the West Yorks back to a sunken lane running from the south-west of the village and to trenches on its western side. The men were too exhausted to attempt another counter-attack and it was decided to try to withdraw during the evening. Caught in enfilade by the enemy from both flanks, eventually only four officers and 40 ORs made it to what was only comparative safety. The battalion had held a front of 2,000 yards for about 36 hours and had been all but wiped out in the process. Sergeant Albert Mountain was awarded the Victoria Cross for commanding a section of five men that managed to hold up an estimated 600 Germans for 30 minutes. This action allowed the rest of his company to withdraw.

Lieutenant General Haldane was aware of the punishment taken by 31st Division and grew increasingly concerned about its durability. On 27 March he acknowledged that the division's overall condition "is not good." Major General Fielding, GOC Guards Division, also expressed his doubts about whether the division on his right would hold. In order to bolster his neighbour, Fielding despatched 2/Irish Guards to help 93 Brigade in its position around Moyenneville. When he visited Major General Bridgford's HQ later on 27 March, Haldane was unpleasantly surprised to hear that the division had withdrawn from Ayette. Bridgford blamed this withdrawal on the fact that his heavy artillery had fallen short of ammunition. He insisted it was not the result of any incompetence on the part of his own CRA but because the expected ammunition train had not only been unintentionally side-tracked at Doullens but had then been diverted from its original destination. Haldane pointed out that Bridgford's CRA had been informed of the changed destination and had even sent a telegram acknowledging receipt of the information. The eventual cause appears to have been that the CRA had failed to send any wagons to collect the shells because "his horses were tired." Later that night a disconcerting report from air reconnaissance caused Haldane to comment, "I hope that the 31st will pluck up courage and gain some ground tonight." He presumably remained disappointed because the following day Major General Fielding described 31st Division's performance as "shaky."

Until the late morning of 27 March, the artillery was able to break up any enemy advances towards the lines of 92 and 93 Brigades. The right brigade whose two front battalions held a line north-east – south-west about 1,300 yards behind Courcelles, was fired on from Ablainzevelle which had for some reason not been occupied by 42nd Division. The brigade suffered repeated and almost continuous frontal attacks between 1130 and 1630 originating from between Ablainzevelle and Courcelles. Four times the enemy took the outpost line but was driven out every time by the bayonet. After much hand-to-hand fighting by the late afternoon, however, the Germans had established themselves on both flanks. The brigade had lost touch with 42nd Division north-east of Ablainzevelle (a gap which the Germans tried to exploit) and then suffered a major attack against its centre. The brigade's three battalions shared a common HQ at the nearby aerodrome. This HQ was supposed to be in telephone contact with the brigade HQ in Adinfer.

In the event of broken communications between brigade and DHQ the senior CO of 92 Brigade, Colonel Hickman, had been instructed to use his initiative. As the man on the spot he was given authority to make tactical decisions. Under increasing enemy pressure, Hickman informed 15/17th West Yorks of 93 Brigade on his left that he was ordering a withdrawal. The much denuded 15/17th West Yorks and 18/DLI held 93 Brigade's line and had inadvertently echeloned themselves behind the left of 92 Brigade. This allowed the Germans to enfilade the left of 11/East Yorks. GOC 93 Brigade had been forced to use 13/York&Lancs in a counter-attack role when the Germans penetrated the left forward post. Despite having regained some ground, the brigade's right remained to the left rear of 92 Brigade. This, and the fact that the divisional artillery was shelling 92 Brigade's positions, caused the two senior officers to agree that the two brigades should fall back through the trenches of 4 Guards Brigade about 2,000 yards to the rear. Once this had been achieved, 92 Brigade manned the Purple Line between Adinfer and Essarts; by 0600 on 28 March contact had been made with 10/Manchester 300 yards west of Ablainzevelle. In cooperation and support, the Guards Division on the left extended its divisional sector southwards. This resulted in 31st Division's front being reduced from 9,500 to a more manageable 6,000 yards.

During daylight on 28 March the enemy attacked the Guards Division from the bed of the Cojeul north of Ayette. A combination of artillery and small arms fire, the latter largely by 2/Grenadier Guards, was sufficient to deny the Germans any progress. There was heavy shelling on 31st Division as well as some infantry engagements which caused another counter-attack to be conducted by 13/York&Lancs. What seems to have been the day's most noteworthy event according to DHQ, however, was what was recorded as a "curious incident." An estimated three enemy battalions began massing south-west of Courcelles with the supposed intent of attacking towards Ayette. The SOS was put up by 4 Guards Brigade and the artillery crashed down. The diary noted that the enemy battalions "simply seemed to dissolve in the barrage, and nothing materialised against our lines." Shelling and patrol activity continued but apart from 3rd Division, which was heavily engaged in halting *Operation Mars* on 28 March, VI Corps had a few peaceful days. To reinforce the Guards Division, Haldane allotted 97 Brigade of 32nd Division which had arrived at Hendecourt early on 28 March. Following the day's engagements fought by 31st Division, 97 Brigade was, however, later placed under the command of Major General Bridgford.

On 30 March, and after an exceptionally intense bombardment which obliterated many of the Guards' front trenches, the Germans attacked the left and centre of the the Guards Division with two battalions of what were described as "storm troops." Another three battalions were in support. The attack came up the sunken road from Boyelles towards Boiry St Marc; simultaneously, another assault debouched from the north of Hamelincourt. The objective was assumed to be the high ground between Boisleux-au-Mont and Boyelles. With the support of over a dozen bombing and strafing aircraft the attackers penetrated the Guards' line at one point but were driven out by an immediate counter-attack. The division was to remain in the line for another two weeks until relieved by 2nd Division. Like those of 32nd Division which had by 1 April relieved 31st Division, the Guards battalions were to suffer frequent and regular shelling and gassing but with only limited infantry activity. The most significant action was that taken by 15/HLI of 32nd Division on 3 April to recapture Ayette. Supported by two platoons of 5/6th Royal Scots on their flank, three companies of HLI, each of only about 35 men, went through the village in the face of opposition from a weak battalion of the enemy supported by a machine-gun company. The artificial defences, ruined buildings, shell craters, and fallen trees presented major difficulties to the HLI. Furthermore, intelligence had suggested there would be only a one company garrison. Nonetheless, with the advantage of complete initial surprise the HLI overcame the very stubborn resistance of the defenders who, "flushed with success of his recent operations" enjoyed "good" morale. The HLI men and officers were later praised for the initiative and improvisation they displayed during an operation which had cost almost 40 percent casualties. The corps' overall priority for the weeks to come was, however, to prepare defence schemes and consolidate the lines and posts for defence in depth.

The distance as the crow flies from Joyride Trench, east of Bullecourt and VI Corps' easternmost position on 21 March, to near Ayette where the line settled in the west on 3 April, is about 10 miles. Of all the Third and Fifth Army corps involved in the withdrawals from the 21 March positions, VI Corps had the shortest distance to cover. It was also probably the most fortunate in the lie and condition of the land over which it withdrew as well as in the proximity to its resupply routes and rail heads. The distance may not have been great, but the fighting had been severe and the casualties suffered by both sides very heavy. Haldane had managed to keep a fairly tight control over the battle but there had been several unsettling occasions. The "panic" in the rear areas on 26 March certainly caused him concern and as a precaution he was ordered by Byng to move his HQ further back. He had had to despatch some of his Q staff to resolve the traffic chaos and restore calm and confidence amongst the supporting arms. The move of his HQ certainly did create temporary communication problems with his divisional commanders.

By the second day of the battle Haldane was reasonably confident that his northern flank was not in any real and immediate danger; the attacks on 3rd Division were comparatively light and there was no firm indication until 26 March that the Germans might attempt a major offensive against Arras. When *Operation Mars* was launched two days later it was defeated in one day. It was on his southern flank where the real danger lay. The assault against his own 59th Division certainly caused him anxiety, and this was exacerbated by the rapid advance of the enemy against 6th and 51st Divisions of the adjoining IV Corps. His somewhat tetchy relationship with Lieutenant General Harper probably did not help his confidence. He had been able to get 40th and 31st Divisions into the battle quickly in order to lessen some of the pressure on his own right sector but he did still run the substantial risk of being rolled up from the south. Much as he was wary of how well 31st Division might continue to perform, he was even more concerned about the reliability of 41st Division which was brought into the line by IV Corps on his right. Neither did 42nd (East Lancashire) Division before the battle have a particularly sound reputation. The stubbornness shown by 10/Manchester and 126 Brigade at Ervillers should have done much to assuage that opinion. The knowledge that he was to receive 32nd and 2nd Canadian Divisions convinced him that his line could ultimately be held.

Haldane's divisions had certainly been aided by the quality and depth of the prepared field defences. The two Forward Zones, especially that of 59th Division were, as events turned out, probably held too strongly. Yet, despite the unprecedented violence and intensity of the opening bombardment the initial assaults were generally met, where the mist allowed, with determination. Machine-gun positions had been sensibly sited, the field artillery had registered on the SOS lines, and counter-attacks had been rehearsed over the most likely avenues of approach. Field companies and the pioneers knew their battle positions and their casualty rolls suggest they fought hard. There were plenty of lessons to be learned but apart from the need for better ways and means of communications, the biggest criticism was directed against the heavy artillery. Major Generals Fielding and Romer, who after the battle on 28 March were also supported by Major General Deverell of 3rd Division, thought the heavies had been badly handled. Haldane defended his corps CRA and the criticism of the divisional GOsC was later toned down. However, now that the battle's intensity had subsided and trench warfare resumed, little was to change in VI Corps' sector until August when Haldane's divisions began their offensive to retake the Wastelands.

8

Losing the Wastelands: IV Corps, March 1918

The two forward divisions of Lieutenant General Sir George Harper's IV Corps formed a front of about 10,000 yards. This extended from Lagnicourt to a little north of Hermies. Both divisions had all three brigades in the line; 25th Division was in corps reserve in Achiet-le-Petit.

In the corps' right sector, 51st (Highland) Division's front was about 5,500 yards as the crow flies. It stretched from a point in the front line south-east of Demicourt and ran north-westwards across the main Bapaume–Cambrai road 200 yards east of Boursies, to the north-east of Louverval chateau and wood, until meeting with 6th Division's right at Lark Post. This point was roughly halfway between the trunk road and Lagnicourt. The Highland's Division front crossed three spurs and two valleys and was dug largely on forward slopes which ran north-east from the main Lebucquière–Hermies ridge. The division had been in the area since December and had done a considerable amount of work to improve the trenches and posts. The disadvantage was that with the Forward Zone lying on forward slopes, much of the system was under direct enemy observation. It was considered a quiet sector, with the enemy front being in places 1,500 yards distant.

The Forward Zone of 6th Division suffered from the same disadvantage; furthermore, its defences were not as well constructed or numerous as those of the Highland Division. The Forward and Battle Zones lacked sufficient dugouts and defended posts, and several sectors of the front system of trenches were not as robust as the garrisons and their commanders might have preferred. Nonetheless, Major-Generals Carter-Campbell, who had only just taken command of 51st, and Marden, GOC 6th Division, were reasonably confident that their troops and the defences would be able to disrupt any enemy attack in the Forward and then defeat it in the Battle Zone. Their respective Defence Schemes had been signed off by the previous corps commander, Lieutenant General Sir Charles Woollcombe. That of 51st Division had been drawn up by the former GOC of the division, the now GOC Corps, Lieutenant General Harper.

Within its front, 6th Division had two valleys running into its system. The northernmost, the Hirondelle, lay just inside the division's boundary; 59th Division's right flank lay on the northern slope of the valley about 200 yards from its floor. In peacetime this valley carried the Quéant – Noreuil road and also a standard gauge railway. The other, Cornhill valley, carried the Quéant – Lagnicourt road. The front system, Leeds Trench, with Leeds Reserve as its support, crossed both valleys about halfway along their respective roads. There were several communication and switch trenches, mostly with Yorkshire place names, in the area of Lagnicourt. A long support trench known as Lagnicourt Trench ran on the east side of the Noreuil – Lagnicourt road. Another, Travel Trench, followed the east side of the Lagnicourt–Louverval road. This crossed the boundary with 51st Division about 1,500 yards north of the Bapaume–Cambrai road. On the morning of 21 March, 16 Brigade was on the left, covering the Hirondelle valley with its right boundary on Cornhill valley. In the centre, 71 Brigade covered Lagnicourt village down to a shallow valley on the Louverval road about 500 yards to its south. This sector had several pre-war tracks running north-eastwards towards enemy-held Pronville. On the right, 18 Brigade faced a large expanse of open terrain but one riven with trenches and some dead ground before joining with 51st Division at Lark Post.

As was the case along most of the British front, 6th Division's nocturnal patrols on 20-21 March noted very little enemy movement in no man's land. When it began, the opening bombardment was especially intense on 6th Division's defences. By 0700, 75 and 74 Brigades of 25th Division, together with two divisional machine-gun companies had been ordered to Favreuil to come under orders of Major Generals Marden and Carter-Campbell respectively. Field companies were instructed to take their reserve positions and two additional brigades of field artillery had moved into positions close to the Vaulx-Vraucourt– Beugnâtre road. The reserve division later bemoaned its fate of being divided between the two front brigades of another division. Its war diary described it as having fought continuously under "strange commanders and a strange staff. To a Division full of Esprit de Division, no more cruel a fate could have been reserved than the manner in which it was unavoidably used throughout the battle."

The moves of the two reserve brigades coincided with a report from the Forward Zone that the enemy was massing in both the Hirondelle and Cornhill valleys. By mid-morning it was clear that the main enemy weight seemed to be concentrated against the centre and left of 6th Division. Two battalions of 75 Brigade were ordered to a position behind Maricourt Wood. One, 8/Border, was to hold the Morchies-Vaulx Line between Vaulx Wood and the railway running along the Hirondelle valley between Vaulx-Vraucourt and Noreuil. If required it was also to act as a counter-attack battalion along the valley. The other battalion, 2/South Lancs, was to hold the continuation of the same line between Vaulx and Maricourt Woods.

By noon the two forward battalions of 16 Brigade, 2/York&Lancs and 1/KSLI, had lost Leeds Reserve and were falling back, some over the open and some along Macaulay Avenue to Lagnicourt Trench. By 1125 the Germans were in Noreuil and Lagnicourt. A section of 6 Bn MGC positioned on the crest of Lagnicourt Trench caught large numbers of Germans as they approached the sunken lane to the section's east. It then moved back to Dunelm Avenue to cover the withdrawal of the York&Lancs towards Vaulx Wood. The remnants of the battalion escaped but four platoons of 1/KSLI were known to have been trapped in Lagnicourt Trench. Another section of the MGC battalion fired along Cornhill valley and, with the help of a company of 1/Buffs, held up the enemy for a time. The CO of 1/KSLI was last seen firing a rifle towards Lagnicourt from the junction of the Noreuil road, Lagnicourt Trench, and Dunelm Avenue. GOC brigade, Brigadier General Walker, proposed a counter-attack by 8/Border, the designated battalion of 75 Brigade, but as its companies had not reached their positions in the Morchies–Vaulx Line the counter-attack was delayed. Meanwhile, the OC of a company of 1/Buffs positioned to the south-east of the Vaulx-Vraucourt–Lagnicourt road saw that a stretch of the Morchies–Vaulx Line close to Vaulx Wood was unoccupied and ordered his men to advance. According to the OC, "This took the form of a race" between the company and the advancing Germans and resulted in "an easy victory" for the Buffs because the enemy were held up by wire in front of the trench. At the same time, three companies of 8/Border were by then in position to launch their intended counter-attack. In the same way as the Buffs, the Borderers drove back the enemy and the section of the Corps Line was reoccupied. One company of the Border was sent to the *râperie* at Vraucourt to form a defensive flank to the left. For their reconnaissance work during these operations Lieutenant Bell was awarded a bar to his MC and Sergeant Bowman the DCM. The third member of their, Private James Steward, was killed.

By mid-afternoon the remnants of the front two battalions of 16 Brigade had fallen back as far as the Morchies-Vaulx Line. Two companies of the Buffs manning Vraucourt Switch running along the southern side of the Hirondelle valley had also withdrawn to the line. As the survivors of the York&Lancs and KSLI approached the trench, the OC C Company of the Buffs who had won the "race" against the Germans, organised them into bays. Once he had moved on down the trench, however, many men drifted away to the west. Officers struggled to stop the withdrawal but did manage to rally sufficient of them to repulse a limited attack on the line. That was only a temporary reprieve because by 1620 the Germans had forced a way into the line a little in front of Vaulx Wood. The pioneers of 11/Leicester and two companies of 8/Border drove them out three times but with the right of 59th Division having lost Noreuil and falling back towards Vraucourt, 11/Cheshire, the final battalion of 75 Brigade, was ordered to fill the gap between the North Midland Division and 16 Brigade until 40th Division came up. The brigade ammunition dump in Vaulx was blown up by a shell in the late afternoon and in 59th Division's sector to the left, the enemy was in the Morchies-Vaulx Line. Some posts behind Maricourt Wood were lost by 1/Buffs and by about 1900 the remnants of the York&Lancs and KSLI were withdrawn to the sunken road running from the south-east corner of Vaulx-Vraucourt to Beugny.

In the centre of the divisional front, 71 Brigade deployed 9/Norfolk on the right and 2/Sherwood on the left. A working party of about 200 from the reserve battalion, 1/Leicester, had been digging near Lagnicourt during the night. Because the transport failed to arrive at the end of the shift the party had had to march back to Favreuil; when the bombardment began the men had to march back up to their assembly area 800 yards south-west of Vaulx Wood. Unsurprisingly, the battalion arrived "somewhat weary."

Little is known of what happened in this sector immediately after the initial enemy infantry attack. There was certainly strong resistance in Bradford Reserve, which ran across the Cornhill valley road about 500 yards east of Lagnicourt, and in Skipton Reserve and Skipton Post. Both of these lay on the north side of the Lagnicourt–Louverval road 2-300 yards east of the village. The reserve company of 9/Norfolk counter-attacked across the road in support and two companies of 1/Leicester were sent up to replace the Norfolk company to the south of the village. They were supported by four machine guns which helped to stop the enemy from debouching south of Lagnicourt. A later account even describes how at the height of the attacks on Skipton Reserve two hares dashed between the Norfolk and the advancing Germans. Allegedly, the Norfolks halted their fire on the enemy masses and switched it to the two hares until they were bowled over. As pressure on the Sherwood and the Norfolk grew they were warned that if the enemy could not be held they were to withdraw to the section of the Morchies-Vaulx Line running parallel to the southern arm of a track which joined the Lagnicourt–Morchies road north of the latter village. In view of the worsening situation, soon after noon the third battalion of 75 Brigade, 11/Cheshire, moved forward towards the Morchies–Vaulx Line to be in a position to support 71 Brigade.

Prior to 1300, reports reached DHQ that the enemy was through 71 Brigade and about to break out to the west of Lagnicourt; to the north, it was known the enemy had penetrated Lagnicourt Trench, crossed the Noreuil road, and were pressing on to the Lagnicourt–Vaulx – Vraucourt road. With the enemy now behind its left rear, 71 Brigade was in danger of being cut off. German field guns had been brought into the brigade's former front system and had helped to finish off the resistance in Skipton Reserve and the southern part of Lagnicourt. Waves of Germans were next reported to be advancing up the shallow valley near the boundary with the right brigade. The remaining Norfolk and Sherwood withdrew fighting into the Morchies-Vaulx Line immediately south of Lagnicourt, from which two companies of 2/South Lancs launched two counter-attacks. These temporarily recaptured a couple of strong points close to the south-west of the village; another company of the South Lancs was ordered to prepare to attempt a counter-attack into Vaulx Wood. Some personnel of 459 Field Company and at least one company of pioneers were also in the Morchies–Vaulx Line close to Maricourt Wood. In the evening, Major Roy Wingate, a much-decorated RE officer who had served overseas since August 1914, was killed by a shell a little north of Maricourt Wood.[1] By 2100 the survivors of the Norfolk and Sherwood, with a combined strength of about 250 all ranks, joined with approximately 340 all ranks of 1/Leicester to occupy the line. Garrisoning the continuation of the line on their right were battalions of 18 Brigade.

The reserve battalion of 18 Brigade, 11/Essex had, as had those of the other two brigades, been digging. The Essex had been working near Maricourt Wood in the evening and into the night of 20 March. With the non-arrival of the train scheduled to take them back to the rear, the 300 men marched back and collapsed with exhaustion. When the alarm was raised they were issued with tea and rum and sent back up to Maricourt Wood. They passed through clouds of gas and, having marched 10 miles during the night, were in their assembly area by 0630. About 2,500 yards in front of them the brigade's other two battalions manned the Forward Zone with 1/West Yorks on the right and 2/DLI on the left. Two runners from the DLI managed to reach brigade HQ at 0730 but for the next three hours nothing was heard from the two battalions. It was known that by about 1000 the enemy had reached Lynx Support, about 300 yards behind the front line in the centre of the brigade's front. A post-war report noted that battalion HQ of 2/DLI had fallen by 1030. The HQ dugout was at the junction of Leech Avenue and Travel Trench; this latter trench ran parallel to and 40 yards east of the Lagnicourt –Louverval road. As an element of its defence scheme the brigade had the "Galloping Gun", an 18 pdr which travelled up and down the road behind the trench firing a few rounds before moving to another position. Further defensive measures included mortar bombs laid in front of the wire in the forward area as anti-tank mines, and a 15 pdr or 18 pdr situated nearby in an anti-tank role. The field gun had been knocked out by the bombardment and the first thing HQ knew that the infantry attack had begun was when grenades came bouncing down the dugout steps. The occupants evacuated through another entrance and reorganised in a trench on the other side of the road. Second Lieutenant McBain and two other men embarked upon a bombing counter-attack which killed about 30 Germans and captured four machine guns. McBain was finally forced back but in the words of another officer his effort, "completely cowed the nearest attackers and saved the battalion front till evening."

1 The monument erected post-war by his family is very close to where he fell.

At about the same time as MacBain's action, two companies of 11/Essex were despatched to protect 1/West Yorks' pressured right flank. The other two companies joined the sappers of 12 Field Company and a company of pioneers in the Morchies–Vaulx Line. At 1230 one of the Essex companies was sent up to assist the DLI. Attempts to get forward some SAA were frustrated by the continued shelling and, at 1430, brigade HQ reported to DHQ that the situation was "critical." Brigade HQ believed 1/West Yorks, 2/DLI, three companies of 11/Essex, and one of 9/Norfolk to have been "practically surrounded." DHQ urged the brigade to hold on until dusk in case a counter-attack could break through to them. If this did not happen any survivors were ordered to withdraw to the Morchies–Vaulx Line at dusk. The position grew even more precarious when enemy trench mortars were established in former field gun pits close to the boundary with 51st Division. The supporting enemy infantry worked their way round behind the HQ of 1/West Yorks and at 1600 the battalion's CO, Lieutenant Colonel Boyall, despatched a message stating the position to be "hopeless." With the enemy on both flanks and about to cut off the HQ, those survivors who could escaped to the Morchies–Vaulx Line. From the brigade's three battalions only about 12 officers and 370 ORs reached the line. For the West Yorks, for example, that meant something like 17 officers 530 ORs were killed, wounded, or missing. For 2/DLI the figure were 28 and 571 respectively.

Of the two other brigades of 25th Division, 74 Brigade had been sent forward to assist 51st Division; 7 Brigade was kept in reserve at Frémicourt. Its three battalions occupied the Army Line from about the main Cambrai road west of Frémicourt to a position 1,000 yards north of Beugnâtre. These battalions were essentially in the rear of 6th and 40th Divisions and manning what were reasonable trenches. The two forward battalions, 10/Cheshire on the right and 1/Wiltshire on the left, spent much of the night improving them as best as their available tools allowed.

The diarist of 25th Division described the position of 6th Division and his own left and reserve brigades on the night of 21-22 March as being "very favourable." This was a somewhat optimistic assessment because, in reality, 21 March had been a bad day for 6th Division. Its losses had been severe, and its setbacks had had consequences for other formations. This was especially the case for 59th Division because the enemy's penetration along the Hirondelle and Cornhill valleys had exposed the right of the North Midland with, as we have seen, the knock on effect for 34th Division. Nonetheless, one officer of 2/DLI wrote of the "great sport" they had had "sniping at the Bosche." Another, with some justification, wrote: "2/DLI was the only battalion in the front line of the division, and probably in the IV Corps that held its battle positions for the whole of 21 March, and only retired when ordered to do so."

During the night 21-22 March battalion and brigade officers tried desperately to re-establish some order in the badly inter-mixed groups of men manning the Morchies–Vaulx Line. Trains bringing up 41st Division began to arrive at The Monument near Favreuil and, by 0800, 11/Cheshire had moved up to the rear of 18 Brigade's sector south-east of Morchies. A Corps Reinforcement Battalion had also been organised, two companies of which extended the Maricourt Wood Switch westwards towards Vaulx-Vraucourt. There were conflicting reports as to who held Vaulx Wood, but it was later learned that 1/KSLI, which had been reinforced by a draft of 200 men originally intended for 51st Division, had made three counter-attacks against the enemy occupying the wood. The attempts had, however, faltered on the open ground to the wood's front. A report did reach DHQ that 2/York&Lancs was involved in heavy fighting in the northern-eastern parts of Vaulx and that Lewis guns and a detachment of 6 Bn MGC had held up for a time the enemy advance along the Vaulx-Vraucourt–Lagnicourt road. In the late afternoon the enemy certainly did force his way into Vaulx-Vraucourt. A counter-attack led by the Corps Reinforcement Battalion drove him out but, again, weight of numbers told. The few survivors of 16 Brigade evacuated the twin villages but remained sufficiently strong to prevent the Germans from debouching down the Beugnâtre road.

With sections of the Morchies-Vaulx Line also having fallen, remnants of 9/Norfolk and 2/Sherwood held a trench following the lane running along the southern face of Maricourt Wood between the south-east of Vaulx-Vraucourt and Morchies. They were supported by sections drawn from the division's three field companies. To their right, a brigade of 19th Division was digging in 500 yards south of the lane facing north in preparation for any enemy advance coming south-west from Morchies. Another of 19th Division's brigades had arrived to form a line along the Vaulx-Vraucourt–Beugny road. Despite these reinforcing moves, the situation in mid-afternoon remained grim. It was decided to throw in three companies of tanks with some infantry and artillery support in a counter-attack between Morchies and Vaulx-Vraucourt. The artillery was provided by 51st Division's 256 Brigade RFA. In the morning its four batteries had been occupied in breaking up several formations of massing troops; in the afternoon the guns were taken from their pits and fired over open sights at enemy infantry and unlimbering artillery. For the counter-attack, one battery fired smoke to mask the advance of the tanks whilst the other three concentrated on the infantry.[2] The tanks of 2nd Tank Battalion forced the enemy from both Maricourt and Vaulx Woods, but it proved to be only a temporary respite.[3] Later, an enemy thrust came down the valley north of Morchies and drove the force of about 30 men of 2/DLI and 1/West Yorks through the village ruins. They attached themselves to 74 Brigade south of the cottages. About 60 survivors of 11/Essex first formed a defensive flank before being moved south of Chaufours Wood, with their right on the Morchies–Beaumetz lane.

The units of 6th Division and the attached 75 Brigade of 25th Division heard during the day that they were to be relieved by 41st Division that night. The relief was completed, and the depleted three brigades of Marden's division withdrew to the Achiet-le-Grand area. On 20 March the trench strength of 71 Brigade had been 76 officers and 1,730 ORs. By the early hours of 23 March of that number 11 and 252 respectively reached Berkeley Camp. Two battalions of 75 Brigade, 8/Border and 2/South Lancs, withdrew eventually to Savoy Camp east of Bihucourt. There were a few reinforcements waiting to join the units but the numbers available for digging on the spur east of Sapignies the following day remained small. The brigade's third battalion, 11/Cheshire, seems not to have received any orders to withdraw. The unit had been in reserve during the two days but had moved about considerably in order to be in a position to despatch companies to the three brigades of 6th Division when necessary. It is known to have occupied a position about mid-way between Maricourt Wood and Beugny before at least one company went to Chaufours Wood; another went to an area south-west of the wood, north of the Cambrai road. With the enemy seemingly to have penetrated behind the supposed front, such was the confusion that it was later confirmed the order to withdraw had not been received

2 During 21-22 March the 18 surviving guns of 256 Bde RFA fired 36,700 shells. The Highland Division's RFA brigades had lost heavily on the first morning and during the night of 22-23 March, three new brigades of field artillery were brought up to reinforce the division.

3 Of the 25 tanks that went into action, 16 failed to return. Casualties amongst the crews were about 70 percent of ORs and 80 percent of officers. The Germans were credited with having shown "considerable enterprise" when attacking the tanks.

by all the Cheshire companies. Two had simply disappeared. Over the next two days a total of about 90 men of the battalion eventually arrived in Savoy Camp.

The formation of 25th Division attached to 51st Division, Brigadier General Armytage's 74 Brigade, had also had a difficult time in its task of supporting Campbell-Carter's division. From right to left on 21 March, the Highland Division had 154 Brigade (Demicourt Sector: 4/Gordon and 7/A&SH) with V Corps and the Flesquières Salient on its right; 152 Brigade in the centre (Boursies Sector: 6/Gordon and 5/Seaforth); 153 Brigade (Louverval Sector: 7th and 6/Black Watch), adjoining 18 Brigade of 6th Division at Lark Post. In brigade reserve, respectively, 4th and 6/Seaforth were in Lebucquière, and 7/Gordon in Beugny. All of the front battalions seem to have had two companies up and two in depth behind. The three battalions of 74 Brigade moved forward with orders to deploy around the crossroads where the Morchies–Beaumetz lane met the main Bapaume – Cambrai road. This position, with 9/LNL north of the road, 11/LF to its south, and 3/Worcester in support 1,000 yards behind, was 1,000 yards to the rear of the Corps Line.

The enemy assault on 153 Brigade north of the main Cambrai – Bapaume road was overwhelming. As they did against 6th Division, the Germans advanced in huge numbers and swept away the front posts and the trenches of the Intermediate Line in Louverval Wood. The chateau and its grounds fell within about two hours and immediately bristled with enemy machine guns. These, and others established in a large former RE dump close to the divisional boundary, almost annihilated three companies of 7/Black Watch. Something of a stand was made on the Lagnicourt–Louverval road, largely by details of the two Black Watch battalions, but one report suggests that many men who tried to withdraw became lost and then captured by inadvertently choosing trenches which ended as *cul de sacs*. What few remaining men there were who did succeed in escaping the advancing Germans, the shelling, and strafing by an enemy aircraft, joined 7/Gordon in the Beaumtez–Morchies Line north of Beaumtez village by about 1500. The left of the Gordon was in contact with 11/Essex and its right with 6/Seaforth.

In the centre, 152 Brigade fought well in front of Boursies and along Sturgeon Avenue and Support a little to its south. The brigade later recorded that its own front was not broken, and the attacking forces do seem to have approached from the flanks. The great difficulty was that as there were few British trenches sited for flanking fire parties of 6/Gordon and 5/Seaforth were likely to be cut off. Once in possession of Sturgeon Support, and thus behind the Intermediate Line, the Germans approached Doignies from the north. A resolute defence was still being made, however, in Sturgeon Avenue. The diarist of 152 Brigade believed that it "is beyond doubt that the stand here saved the flank of 154 Brigade, and the 17th Division beyond them." That claim is perhaps open to some dispute, but the stand did certainly delay the attack on Doignies. By late morning the village had fallen; this compelled the remnants of 5/Seaforth and 6/Gordon to fall back to Hermies Switch. This trench ran in a north-west – south-east direction some 1,500 yards west of Doignies. The withdrawal was covered by one pair of machine guns commanded by Second Lieutenant Bentley of 25 Bn MGC at Bruno Mill, south-west of Doignies, and another pair under Lieutenant Potter of 51 Bn MGC in the sunken road between Doignies and Beaumetz. These guns fired throughout the day and the next taking a heavy toll of the enemy masses.

A few hundred yards to the north, along the Bapaume – Cambrai road, an evening counter-attack was proposed by brigade HQ. The intent was to drive the enemy back along the north side of the road at least as far as the *sucrerie* on the junction of the Lagnicourt – Doignies road.

The idea was abandoned when it was realised no artillery support was available. Instead, the battalions of 74 Brigade were instructed to move closer to the Corps Line, the garrison of which had already been ordered to "hold at any cost." If it looked as if the line was in immediate danger of being overwhelmed, 9/LNL and 11/LF would reinforce or retake it 1,000 yards either side of the main road. For the time being the two battalions remained in support to the mixed elements of 152 Brigade which continued to hold the line. The several breaches of it near Vaulx Wood caused two companies of 3/Worcester to move closer to Morchies. There, together with 130 Field Company and a company of 6/SWB (P), rather than attempt to dig a continuous line 3/Worcester dug trenches of between 30-40 yards, in echelon.

In the evening of 21 March, two battalions of 57 Brigade were brought into action in support of the Highlanders. The brigade belonged to 19th Division which until 1500 had been in Army Reserve. It had spent most of March training around the Haplincourt area and was earlier supposed to have relieved 17th Division of V Corps. Because the relief was postponed several times, the division assumed it was being kept as a counter-attack formation for when the expected offensive began. In the morning of 21 March its three brigades were ordered by V Corps to move to positions that would ensure the safety of the Hermies – Lebucquière ridge. The brigades subsequently moved to Gaika Copse, Vélu, and Bertincourt. In the afternoon of 21 March, the division was allocated to IV Corps. Within 15 minutes of the transfer, IV Corps phoned to order a brigade, supported by tanks, machine guns, and trench mortars, to counter-attack and re-take Doignies. GOC 57 Brigade and the OC 8 Tank Battalion were instructed to attend DHQ where a plan was hatched. There was some delay until artillery support could be organised but at 1840, and supported by 10 tanks, 10/Worcester on the left and 8/Gloucester on the right advanced from Vélu. By the time they reached Beaumetz it was dark and difficulty with direction keeping immediately became apparent. The Gloucester managed to get as far as Doignies church but on coming under enfilade fire both battalions withdrew. Two companies of the Worcester remained in the Beaumetz – Morchies line just to the east of Beaumetz while the other two companies and the Gloucester reorganised in the sunken lane running about parallel to and behind Hermies Switch to the south-east of the village. As one post-operation report noted, troops of 57 Brigade were for a time inextricably mixed with elements of 51st Division.

The counter-attack was well-intended but was later, understandably, criticised. The original plan was altered "at the last moment" and allowed no time for the new objectives to be adequately explained to the men. The artillery barrage did not materialize and in the dark and heavy mist the tanks lost direction and the men lost the tanks. There was no support on the flanks which meant the attackers were caught from both sides as well as frontally. The lack of a supporting move against the high ground on the left meant the brigade's approach up the valley towards Doignies was bound to be dangerously exposed. As another report noted, rather than being squandered in attempting to retake a pile of ruins which held no tactical value the two battalions would have been of far greater use had they been added to the garrison of Hermies Switch and other positions close to Beaumetz.

On 51st Division's southern flank, 154 Brigade suffered to a degree from the morning bombardment but there was no infantry attack until the afternoon. On the left, 7/A&SH knew of the loss of Louverval and Boursies but it was not until 1445, following a *flammenwerfer* attack on the right of 6/Gordon, that the left front of 7/A&SH withdrew to conform. One company of 4/Gordon was detached and holding a portion of the Beaumetz – Morchies Line with 4/Seaforth which had moved up from reserve. A half company of 4/Seaforth and a section of 154

TMB were sent to form a defensive flank facing Doignies on the Hermies – Doignies road 500 yards south of the village; another company was in Hermies Switch. These companies could hear if not see the counter-attack by the tanks and two battalions of 57 Brigade on Doignies. At least one company of 7/A&SH formed a flank facing north-west south of the Demicourt – Doignies road but a message from the CO at 1640 announced that the bulk of his battalion to the east of Demicourt was in danger of being surrounded. On his right, the front of 4/Gordon remained secure. The fighting died down after dark but as V Corps on the right had been ordered to withdraw from their forward positions, 154 Brigade had to adjust its line to conform. By morning, the new front line was effectively the old Intermediate Line. This ran from the divisional southern boundary 500 yards north of Hermies on the Demicourt road, north-west to about 200 yards south of the Demicourt – Doignies road, and then westwards along part of Hermies Switch, south of Doignies, until it joined the Beaumetz–Morchies Line.

Overnight as the readjustments were made, 10/Worcester, 10/R.Warwick and 8/Gloucester were placed under 154 Brigade. The Warwick had not yet been in action, but the Gloucester and Worcester close to Beaumetz had lost quite heavily during their counter-attack. Nonetheless, the additional troops were a welcome addition to 154 Brigade. Before 1100 on 22 March, 7/A&SH and 4/Gordon reported the enemy were through the Intermediate Line and were attacking the Beaumtez–Morchies Line. Around mid-day the enemy had penetrated Hermies Switch but during the remainder of the afternoon things quietened down. Two attacks were made in early evening but with the success of the enemy north of the Cambrai road it was decided that Beaumetz village and the Beaumetz–Morchies Line should be evacuated. To conform with 152 Brigade's moves to the north and to the immediate south of the main road a defensive flank of two parallel lines was to be established between the west of Beaumetz and Lebucquière, and from the south of Beaumetz to Vélu. The moves were made during the night by the "very exhausted" troops.

Corps HQ recorded a fairly upbeat assessment at the end of the two days' fighting. It praised the achievement of 51st Division and 74 Brigade in halting the evening attacks on the Beaumetz- Morchies Line and the attempted advance down the Cambrai road. It accepted that the left of the corps had been pushed back a "considerable distance" but that the right was still well forward and flanking the enemy advance. The Highland Division had certainly lost ground but its decision to fall back some 2,000 yards was in part made to conform to Byng's decision to withdraw V Corps from the Flesquières Salient. The corps' right flank was still held by the weakened 51st Division and a brigade each of 25th and 19th Divisions. The rest of 19th Division was holding a line north-east of Beugny and the Army Line south of the Cambrai road. On the left, the much depleted 6th Division and its attached 75 Brigade were about to be relieved by the fresh 41st Division. The almost equally fresh 7 Brigade of 25th Division had also been attached to the arriving 41st Division.

Fighting erupted on the morning of 23 March at about 0530. North of the main Cambrai road there was a considerable confusion of battalions and brigades. Huge numbers of enemy troops emerged from the dead ground of the valley north-east of Chaufours Wood. Three assaults were held and repulsed by 11/LF of 74 Brigade, but the battalion was eventually forced to withdraw on 4/KSLI of 56 Brigade, the support brigade of 19th Division. With its right on the *sucrerie* at the crossroads of the main Cambrai road and the Morchies road coming in from the north, 6/Wiltshire, the right battalion of 58 Brigade, lined the sunken Morchies road facing east. On the Wiltshire's left, 9/RWF continued the line of the road before throwing back its left on the higher ground to the south-west of Morchies. On its left during the night 22-23 March, two battalions of 123 Brigade, 41st Division had deployed. The brigade's third battalion, 9/Welch was in Beugny, about 1,600 yards to the rear astride the main road. With the withdrawal of 11/LF and the continuing heavy shell and machine-gun fire, 58 Brigade was ordered to fall back on the Green Line at 0930. The plan was for 9/RWF to withdraw first and hold the Green Line while the other two battalions passed through. The confusion was such that at 1300, the CO of 6/Wiltshire ordered his battalion and 9/RWF to withdraw to the outskirts of Beugny because, he believed, 4/KSLI on the right of the Wiltshire had "disappeared." Fortunately, two companies of 10/Cheshire of 7 Brigade had been discovered and they were put into a line running south-west from the *sucrerie*. To the north-east of Frémicourt, 1/Wiltshire, also of 7 Brigade, was heavily attacked during the day. Captain Reginald Hayward, although already badly wounded, showed exceptional leadership and courage that was to earn him the Victoria Cross.

In the early afternoon, an enemy thrust against 9/Welch from troops that had turned north-west from Lebucquière, attacked Beugny from the south-east. The orders for the Wiltshire and RWF to fall back were not delivered until 1400 and because the withdrawal would have involved moving across open ground to the village it was decided it should be postponed until darkness. The fighting continued and by 1600 the enemy had worked around from Morchies and the *sucrerie* and was about to encircle the Wiltshire and RWF. All codes and maps in the battalion HQ were burned as "escape seemed most improbable". About 60 men of the two battalions managed to withdraw through 9/Welch and reached the Green Line. The Welch hung on and fought hard for Beugny so as to allow any other groups of Wiltshire or RWF to make good their escape. Their "fine defence" of the village was acknowledged as having been crucial to the withdrawal of the brigade. The battalion joined the other two in the late evening and worked on consolidating the Green Line. The line was filling with troops from a variety of brigades and divisions, but an order of sorts was achieved.

To the south of that road, at 0700 the Germans attacked 152 Brigade from the valley in front of Beaumetz. The two Black Watch battalions, sections of two of the division's field companies, and 10/Worcester held them for a time but when at 0930 another attack developed against 154 Brigade on the right, the pressure became too great. The dense masses of the attackers were described as "an inspiring sight …[and] a magnificent sight, yet terrible to behold." The Germans fell "in their hundreds" but pressed on over their dead and wounded comrades until a wedge was driven between the two brigades. This threatened to cut off 8/Gloucester and 10/Worcester. Elements of these two battalions managed to withdraw and formed a defensive flank along the railway facing the northern edge of Vélu Wood. To their north, the Lancashire Fusiliers and Shropshire had fallen back to the Green Line and other enemy thrusts had reached the western edge of Lebucquière. These were now in the rear of 152 Brigade. Consequently, at 1015, corps HQ ordered Major General Carter-Campbell to instruct 152 Brigade to withdraw through the Green Line by passing to the west of Lebucquière and then to reassemble at Bancourt. By the evening the sector of the newly-designated Red Line from the Cambrai road due north of Bancourt to Villers-au-Flos to its south was manned by the remnants of 152 and 153 Brigades' battalions, 8/R.Scots (P), about 40 men of 252 Tunnelling Company, and 100 sappers from the divisional field companies. Unfortunately, 70 of the latter were quickly withdrawn from the line when it was discovered they had "no knowledge of the rifle."

By about 1300, the Germans were in occupation of Vélu Wood. The defensive flank to its north contained them inside the wood but the flank itself became exposed by the appearance of

Germans on the higher ground south of Beaumetz. The resistance continued, with both Captain Manley James of 8/Gloucester and Captain Julian Gribble of 10/R.Wawick showing leadership and bravery which earned them both the Victoria Cross. Another group of about 100 men from the Gloucester and Worcester under the command of RSM Hopcroft of 8/Gloucester dug slit trenches in front of 104 Brigade RFA of 2nd Division. They held the enemy at bay until the guns had been galloped away. Nonetheless, by 1400, and despite the machine guns of 51st and 19th Divisions shooting down scores of the enemy as they tried to debouch from Vélu Wood, the enemy's numbers were overwhelming. The two battalions had not received any orders to retire until a message arrived ordering survivors to retire to the Green Line. Just to the left of the Warwick, 4/Seaforth and 7/A&SH managed to hold on until 1530. They had come under fierce enfilade fire when 17th Division on their right had evacuated Hermies at 1300. One company of 7/A&SH fought hard, with both flanks turned in the sunken lane running south-east from Beaumetz until about 1130. It then withdrew to the sunken crossroads due south of the village. There, as the company came under enfilade fire of machine guns it withdrew 300 yards to the railway on the east side of Vélu Wood. Using the embankment as cover it formed a defensive flank to protect the rear of the troops still fighting in the Corps Line between Beaumetz and Doignies. Although by this time the enemy was well to the rear of the position which stretched for some 800 yards, resistance by some Seaforths, who later recorded that the Worcester "on our left ran away," and the Argylls, remained strong.

For *its* part, 19th Division later claimed that its battalions had become exposed because troops on their flanks had withdrawn without notice. Whatever the precise truth might be, Major Harcourt, the OC of one company of 51 Bn MGC, galloped a limber up to his guns to bring forward more ammunition. Two companies of the Argylls were cut off when their comrades were eventually forced to withdraw but fighting continued until enemy field guns and machine guns caught the Highlanders at close range from several directions. Under the cover of smoke from burning grass German infantry launched another assault. Having exhausted their grenade supply the survivors fell back towards the railway, passed Vélu Wood, which technically lay in V Corps area, to the section of the Green Line covering Bertincourt. Major Harcourt positioned two of his guns on the railway embankment alongside the lone company of Argylls to cover the withdrawal. In the early hours of 24 March, the scattered elements of 51st Division assembled in and around Villers-au-Flos. Close by, the survivors of the attached three battalions of 57 Brigade were re-organised and once again came under the command of 19th Division.

At 1330, the Green Line between Delsaux Farm and Hill 120, 1,200 yards north of the Cambrai road and north-west of Beugny, had come under command of 19th Division. This meant that the day was not yet quite over for the division's troops. The decision had been made to improvise a so-called Red Line. This was to run roughly north-south, east of Bancourt, to Monument Wood near Favreuil, and then back to the north-east of Achiet-le-Grand. The line was to be held by 51st Division on the right and 19th Division on the left. As the support brigade of 19th Division moved back to its intended position on the proposed Red Line close to the brickworks on the Cambrai road immediately east of Bapaume, three weak battalions of 58 Brigade accompanied by two companies of 5/SWB (P) were moving in the opposite direction to the Green Line. The brigade was to hold this line from the Cambrai road west of Beugny north to Hill 120; 56 Brigade's sector ran from just south of Delsaux Farm to the main road where it joined with 58 Brigade. Once these moves had been completed the troops could get some much-needed rest. As the troops slept reports from the RFC informed IV Corps that on the far side of V Corps' boundary the enemy had taken Nurlu, Etricourt, Equancourt, Fins, and Metz, and was closing in on Ytres and Neuville-Bourjonval.

During the night enemy attempts at massing troops between Beugny and Lebucquière were thwarted by the artillery; heavy fighting around Mory forced 75 Brigade of 25th Division again to strengthen its left flank. Dawn of 24 March was heralded by a bombardment fired by the British artillery for over two hours with the intent of dissuading any further early German attacks. Possibly the over-riding concern for Lieutenant General Harper on the morning of 24 March was how he was somehow to create a reserve. As we have seen, 9/RWF and 6/ Wiltshire of 123 Brigade had lost considerable numbers of men on 23 March; to bolster its strength 18/KRR and 19/Middlesex (P) were placed under 123 Brigade's command. Harper wanted to get all three battalions of 7 Brigade to the rear so that it could re-organise with the rest of 25th Division. This procedure was helped by 18/KRRC covering part of its withdrawal. Nevertheless, 41st Division was itself weak and badly stretched; 19th Division on its right was not a great deal better off.

At 1000 the first of the day's enemy attacks on the central and southern sectors of the corps began. At Delsaux Farm, 9/Cheshire was confronted by attacks of "sheer recklessness" when hundreds of Germans advanced in close order. The enemy gained a footing, but a counter-attack led by Captains Milner and Palmer at about 1100 restored the line. The Cheshires intended to occupy the recaptured trench but found so many dead and wounded Germans lying in it that there was no room. Pressure continued to grow along the line, but the principal concern was what was happening in V Corps area. The withdrawal of the corps and the widening of a gap with it and Fifth Army on its southern flank both threatened and influenced the actions of IV Corps. Harper issued several orders during the day instructing Major Generals Jeffreys and Lawford (19th and 41st Divisions respectively) as to where they could either concentrate or withdraw their brigades should the situation on the right grow ever more threatening. At 1115, for example, 8/North Stafford reported that 2nd Division on its right was moving back but that, for the time being, the Staffords were confident of holding their sector of the Green Line.

Although the Staffords were confident of maintaining their position, by 1400 troops of 2nd Division had indeed fallen back to their sector of the Red Line. At 1530, DHQ 19th Division ordered 56 and 58 Brigades to withdraw fighting to a line roughly Bancourt– Frémicourt 400 yards north of the main road. Although a combination of a motor machine-gun section and the guns of 19 Bn MGC did manage to break up some of the German masses forming north of Frémicourt, the brigades found it difficult to disengage. With the help of the artillery and several local stands and counter-attacks the battalions did manage to pass through 57 Brigade holding the Red Line. The latter brigade was north of the main road in the vicinity of the Old Sugar Factory and the Brickyard and came under orders of 153 Brigade who held the line to its south. In the evening a withdrawal by 51st Division south of the main road and west of Bancourt exposed the right of 10/R.Warwick. It was obvious the current line had become untenable. A defensive flank was thrown out along the main road and the brigade withdrew to the south-eastern outskirts of Bapaume. Meanwhile 58 and 56 Brigades had formed a line east of Bapaume through which 57 Brigade was to pass. Once those two brigades had retired, and covered in turn by 51st Division, the battalions of 57 Brigade were to march through Bapaume to their new positions stretching from Le Barque to the Bapaume –Achiet-le-Grand railway at Avesnes. Until the remnants of the battalions arrived all bandsmen, cooks and other details were to man the line. When the tired survivors of 58 Brigade, for example, did appear during the night the initial total was 270 rifles. Rather than maintaining their momentum and occupying Bapaume in hot pursuit, the Germans were content to shell the town. The infantry strength of 19th Division was thought to be around 2,200. Its artillery and machine guns were quickly tasked to close the western and south-western exits from Bapaume. On its right, although not in contact, was 2nd Division; on the left was 41st Division. Once 19th Division had withdrawn the covering Highland Division was to retire and take up a line Warlencourt–Loupart Wood in corps reserve.

Before this most recently proposed withdrawal had begun, the Highland Division was facing south-east on a line Beaulencourt–Riencourt–Bancourt. The men had been able to put out some wire but had been handicapped by a shortage of stakes. A collection of huts south of the Cambrai road and also those of Middlesex Camp had been fired on the orders of 153 Brigade and, to his annoyance, the CO of 7/Black Watch discovered that two posts near Bancourt supposedly manned by personnel of 252 Tunnelling Company had been abandoned. In the late afternoon troops of 19th Division began to pass through the Highlanders' lines followed closely by the enemy. The diarist of 152 Brigade later questioned the resolution of the men, noting, "There is no doubt that, had the men held on and used their rifles and Lewis Guns, they could have checked the enemy's advance." He felt the men did not "feel secure in the open" and "did not appreciate the great strength of the shell hole positions they were in." The alleged lack of fighting power may also have something to do with the fact that as the guns had been ordered to withdraw there was no artillery support. The officer also bemoaned the action of an OC tanks with about 20 machines under his command. The tanks had parked below a bank south of Bancourt before moving off in the afternoon. On terrain which was according to the diarist ideally suited to tank action, it was "Beyond doubt that they would have exercised an enormous influence on the result of the action."

As they withdrew across the Bapaume–Peronne road the Scottish battalions encountered intense traffic congestion, but 152 and 154 Brigades were at Loupart Wood by 2200. They were joined there at 0100 of 25 March by 153 Brigade and sections of two attached field companies and pioneers. An outpost line had already been organised by about 1,000 reinforcements, hot food from the field cookers was available, and SAA issued. The food and other rations will have helped lift morale but had any of the tired troops known with certainty what was going on to their right, morale would probably have again been shaken, At 1600, Third Army wired its various DHQ to report that the enemy was in Combles, Morval, and Lesboeufs. In an attempt to block further progress, IV and V Corps were to hold a line Bazentin-Martinpuich–Le Sars-Grevillers–Sapignies. The army boundary was to run through the Butte de Warlencourt. In simple terms, the enemy was already well behind the right rear of IV Corps.

It had been a difficult day for 41st Division and 7 Brigade of 25th Division in the northern sector of the corps line. The fighting around Mory largely concerned VI Corps but a reconnaissance by IV Corps cyclists reported at 1030 that two battalions of 122 Brigade and some supporting machine guns had formed a defensive flank to the south of the village. Of equal concern was the large concentration of enemy infantry gathering in the valley between Vaulx-Vraucourt and Beugny. The divisions' field artillery had been divided into two groups, each with a heavy artillery brigade attached. Four additional brigades of heavy artillery remained under corps command. In response to the massing Germans, the northern group of 16 field and three heavy batteries fired a preventive barrage. Many of the shells fell short and caused casualties amongst the battalions of 7 and 123 Brigades. To add to the brigades' difficulties unmolested enemy aircraft directed German fire onto their positions. The build-up of enemy forces was assumed to be a precursor to yet another major assault towards Favreuil. In anticipation of this a defensive flank running north-east-south-west across the Sapignies– Bapaume road was formed by 12/East Surrey. Between Vaulx-Vraucourt and Frémicourt, 123 Brigade had 19/Middlesex (P) holding a line south-west of Beugnâtre, with 23/Middlesex reorganising just to its rear. Further back the badly mauled 11/Queen's and 10/R.West Kent were also trying to reorganise.[4] Having managed little rest, 23/Middlesex was ordered at 1255 to occupy a line across the Beugnâtre – Bapaume and Favreuil – Bapaume roads and to gain touch with 57 Brigade of 19th Division. At 1600, 18/KRR fell back to conform to a move of 58 Brigade, and 19/Middlesex (P) raised the alarm that its left was in the air. Brigade HQ told the pioneers that Beugnâtre was still held by 124 Brigade and to maintain their position. Further attacks during the afternoon in the direction of Beugnâtre drove back what little was left of 123 Brigade and the attached 7 Brigade. To assist with their withdrawal Brigadier General Towsey, GOC 122 Brigade, sent up from Sapignies six tanks of 10 Tank Battalion which he had at his disposal. They acted "vigorously" around Favreuil to offer some protection to the retiring brigades.

At dusk, and according to orders issued at about 1800, 19/Middlesex (P) withdrew across the Bapaume – Arras road. There it was joined by 23/Middlesex which had withdrawn when it received enfilade fire from the north and its right rear. Both battalions began digging trenches north and south of the Biefvillers – Favreuil road close to the sunken lane connecting Avesnes with Sapignies. They were in touch with 18/KRR and with 4/South Stafford of 7 Brigade. This latter battalion had held a line astride the main road to cover the withdrawal of 10/Cheshire and 1/Wiltshire. Despite the stand by the Staffords both battalions were hit hard as they crossed open ground. The left of 23/Middlesex was thought to be protected by 124 Brigade which was still believed to be holding Favreuil. This information was incorrect because 124 Brigade had withdrawn to a line west of Favreuil at 1900. Brigade HQ moved to Sapignies and, during the night of 24-25 March, ordered its battalions to fall back and continue the line being dug and manned by the two Middlesex battalions. Understandably the turmoil of events and consequent disjointed communications caused some remnants to miss their allotted positions. Elements of all brigades began digging in what were technically the wrong places. Sapignies, for example, was supposed to have been held by 124 Brigade until relieved by 40th Division. The brigade was then meant to withdraw to a line being dug by three field companies east of Achiet-le-Grand and north of Bihucourt. Most of its men established themselves instead in scrapes 1,000 yards in front of the intended line. Battalions and brigades became inter-mixed which in the general confusion and the darkness allowed a gap of about a mile to be created between the right of 41st and the left of 19th Divisions. This was discovered by the enemy who then dribbled men through. When the danger was realised, Major General Lawford ordered the three field companies then digging north of Bihucourt to move and dig a trench across the Achiet-le-Grand – Bapaume railway south-east of Biefvillers. By dawn the gap had been closed but the daylight revealed that 74 Brigade of 25th Division was actually dug in on the Biefvillers ridge some 600 yards behind the new trench. It was also discovered that 4/South Stafford, with about 60 attached stragglers of 10/Cheshire, was manning a trench close by.

4 On 23 March 11/Queen's had reported 15 officers missing, including the CO, 14 ORs killed, 31 wounded, 15 wounded and missing, and 391 missing. Whilst reorganising, the remainder of the battalion, about 120 all ranks held a line west of Bihucourt.

As part of Lieutenant General Harper's scheme to create a reserve the other two battalions of 7 Brigade, 10/Cheshire and 1/Wiltshire, had been withdrawn overnight to Bihucourt. Only three officers and 54 ORs of the Wiltshire arrived at the camp. Possibly in the belief that they were covering the withdrawal, the South Stafford had dug in east of Biefvillers. The following morning the battalion, with its CO Lieutenant Colonel Blackall having been killed during the nocturnal shelling, withdrew to rejoin the division near Logeast Wood. It was there joined by 74 and 75 Brigades and again came under the command of its own DHQ. In their new trench the field companies of 41st Division were in touch with their own 20/DLI of 124 Brigade. This battalion, which had 23/Middlesex on its left, had been fortunate. It recorded a very low casualty rate for the day of only two killed, 33 wounded and 15 missing. In comparison, 23/Middlesex reported 19 killed, 57 wounded and 22 missing. That figure was fairly typical of battalions in the division. Although the division had established a line west of the Bapaume – Arras road, its occupiers were tired and very inter-mixed. Some of the positions they held were not those intended by either IV Corps or their own DHQ. It was, however, at least a line of sorts.

At 0230 on 25 March, Major General Lawford ordered 123 and 124 Brigades to move to their originally assigned positions. The remaining brigade, 122, went into reserve near Bihucourt. To the rear, the artillery of several divisions was on the move, the last batteries not having left the Bapaume–Sapignies line until after midnight. This move caused a serious blockage at Achiet-le-Grand and an even bigger one at Achiet-le-Petit. For a couple of hours most of IV Corps' artillery was stationary in and around the village. The diarist of 12/East Surrey, 122 Brigade, believed the rearguard fought by one of its companies (which was virtually annihilated during the action) saved 60 guns blocked in Achiet-le-Grand. "But for this stand", he wrote, "the guns would have been captured."

The action also gave 15/Hampshire of the same brigade time to dig a trench to the rear. Only one officer and one NCO of the East Surrey company initially escaped from the scene. If the company had not delayed the Germans it seems likely that the enemy would have then gone through the left of 41st Division and thus also the right of VI Corps. Strangely, however, once the company of East Surrey had been effectively wiped out, the enemy did not press on. An attack on Sapignies was halted by the rifles and Lewis guns of 14/A&SH and, except on the left between Ervillers and Béhagnies where 120 Brigade and the about two-company strength 177 Brigade were forced back a short distance, the line held. The failure to break the Sapignies–Béhagnies–Ervillers line was assisted by the arrival of the first of 42nd Division's battalions. As far as IV Corps was concerned their appearance was one of the day's two encouraging events.

The inclusion of the fresh 42nd (East Lancashire) Division to IV Corps' strength and its relief of 40th Division were important even though, as we saw, there was some initial confusion as to when and where it should deploy its first brigade. The second encouraging piece of news was that 62nd (2nd West Riding) Division was also on its way to bolster the corps. Its three brigades had left Arras in the early hours of 25 March; after enduring much frustrating traffic congestion, two brigades eventually reached Bucquoy in the early afternoon. From there they marched to Achiet-le-Petit. The remaining brigade, 187, reached Bucquoy in the late afternoon and sent one battalion into a trench to the east of the village newly dug by 9/DLI (P). Although grateful for its allocation, corps HQ was disappointed by the tardy arrival of the division. It had been hoped that its brigades would cooperate with 19th and 51st Divisions in eliminating the salient around Warlencourt–Eaucourt created by the German penetration of IV and V Corps' boundary.

While troops of 62nd Division struggled to reach their allotted positions, the battle continued. Several early attempts by the enemy, including cavalry, to cross the Albert-Bapaume road were thwarted by 4/KSLI of 19th Division but when ammunition stocks began to dwindle, and with pressure from the direction of Warlencourt, the battalion was forced to withdraw towards Serre. Meanwhile, of the other battalions of 56 Brigade, 9/Cheshire was west of Loupart Wood and 8/North Stafford north of Irles. From about 0900, 56 and 58 Brigades began to withdraw towards the Pys – Bihucourt line; cover was to be provided by 57 Brigade. This brigade was ordered to make a stand at the crossroads mid-way between Grevillers and Irles and to gain touch with 51st Division at those crossroads. Repeated counter-attacks by 10/R.Warwick and 10/Worcester frustrated enemy attempts to debouch from Grevillers and Loupart Wood until about 1620. When the Germans instead advanced around the southern end of the wood, 57 Brigade withdrew to the ridge north of the Grevillers – Irles road. As they did so they came under fire from British machine guns. Under pressure from enemy forces close to Irles the brigade crossed the railway south of Achiet-le-Petit. The division's other two brigades had by dusk taken up a line running north-east – south-west from the outskirts of Achiet-le-Petit, across the valley, and to a point south-east of Puisieux. On the left, but probably not in touch, a brigade of 62nd Division held a line just east of Achiet-le-Petit. Much of the new line was garrisoned by stragglers collected by the staff of 19th Division from around Puisieux. The officers had stationed themselves to the north of the railway as it swings south of Achiet-le-Petit to halt and re-organise all men passing through without officers. Once leadership and command were reasserted the men were apparently prepared to dig in and fight where and when they were ordered. Another approximately 4,000 men were collected from roads leading west from Puisieux towards Colincamps and Beaumont Hamel.

The fighting troops had been handicapped during the day by a growing shortage of SAA mainly because traffic congestion was hampering attempts by transport sections to refill dumps. This had been especially felt by 57 Brigade. There were also rumours circulating that Puisieux had fallen, and that traffic was blocking all roads heading west. Staff officers of 19th Division were sent to discover what the situation actually was in Puisieux. The village was found still to be in British hands, but it was evident the enemy was not far away. The division was to re-organise between the village and Hébuterne while the southern exits from Puisieux were to be guarded by elements of 41st and 25th Divisions. By dusk a scheme of sorts was put in place whereby the gap between IV and V Corps was to be protected, if not closed, and that by 0900 on 26 March, 57 Brigade would have by stages reached Foncquevillers in order to rejoin 56 and 58 Brigades. With their locations largely unknown at dusk collecting the various battalions of the division had been difficult. When, for example, 56 Brigade struggled into Hébuterne, "Practically the whole of the 9/Cheshire were unaccounted for." The brigades were re-organised as battalions, with each of the battalions forming one company of between one and three platoons.

Once 19th Division had passed through the Highland Division's positions, 51st Division again became the front line. On its right, 154 Brigade's flank lay on the Albert-Bapaume road about opposite the Butte de Warlencourt; 152 Brigade in the centre stretched to the edge of Loupart Wood; 153 Brigade's front passed around the wood's eastern edge to its north-eastern corner. The line was really one of occupied shell holes rather than a continuous trench, but the ground was held in as much depth as the available manpower allowed. When the day began the division was not in touch with other forces on either the right or left. The enemy's penetration of 2nd Division on the right was witnessed clearly by 154 Brigade and although the enemy seems to have been held by the brigade, by noon it was forced to make constant withdrawals in order to avoid envelopment. The Germans headed in a north-westerly direction towards Pys with, at times, the fighting becoming hand-to-hand. Several stands are known to have been made. One, for example, by 6/Seaforth under the command of its CO, Lieutenant Colonel McDonald, apparently held to the last man. Counter-attacks made with the bayonet by the company resulted in only one prisoner being taken. The defensive flank thrown out by 154 Brigade to the north-west of Pys came under continual pressure and, as the other two brigades withdrew towards the high ground east of Irles, 154 became separated from them by the Pys valley. As on so many occasions during the previous days the masses of advancing Germans presented remarkable targets for the guns and the infantry. However, this was the fifth day the division had been in almost constant action and exhaustion took its toll. Units were inter-mixed, "control by officers had practically disappeared and we were again without artillery support."

The divisional artillery was in fact stalled at Miraumont. Until sufficient staff had been ordered to sort out the chaos a block lasting nine hours existed at a point where five streams of traffic converged. There remained a limited amount of artillery support for the forward troops but because the infantry's positions were constantly altering there was a great danger of shells falling in the wrong places. One diarist recorded that the enemy continued to be met on the division's front with Lewis gun and rifle fire, but with the men running short of ammunition and in their exhausted state, "A protracted resistance was out of the question." As a growing number of stragglers was also heading towards the rear brigade staffs were despatched to halt the drift, re-organise the men, and send them back towards the front. GOC 153 Brigade tried to get officers from various divisions to grip the withdrawing men but found that with a few exceptions the officers were either incapable or unwilling to exert command. If a group of stragglers was organised and ordered forward once the officer's back was turned the group quickly disappeared again to the rear. There was no panic, just apathy amongst the stragglers. On the right, 2nd Division was, "Utterly exhausted…and as soon as the enemy appeared…[the division] was seen retiring down the slopes to Miraumont." The pressure on the right was extreme and at about 1800 the remnants of 51st Division fell back towards the southern end of Achiet-le-Petit, then to Puisieux, and eventually Colincamps. At the latter village a degree of re-organisation was achieved. After dark, the groups moved to Sailly-au-Bois. The cookers had arrived before them, and hot meals issued before the men collapsed to sleep. The division had reached at least temporary safety, but it was not in the place where its former GOC, Lieutenant General Harper, had intended it to be. Harper was recorded as having personally been "much shaken" at the parlous state of his old division.

At dawn on 25 March, Harper was unsure of how widely 41st Division's troops were scattered across the northern sector of his front. There were a few formed bodies of men manning a line of sorts which stretched about from the railway south-east of Biefvillers, then north passing perhaps 1,000 yards in front of the village and past the western outskirts of Sapignies. There it met troops of 40th Division awaiting relief by the East Lancashire Division. The northern end of the line was held ostensibly by 122 Brigade, but such was the inter-mixing over the last two days that it was estimated perhaps 300 of the men were from battalions other than those of the brigade itself.

An early attack by Germans debouching from Bapaume hit the three field companies manning their newly dug trench across the railway south-east of Biefvillers. Having sustained "heavy" casualties the sappers managed to drive it off. A report from the corps cyclists received at 1030 noted that 41st Division's line actually ran almost to the Albert-Bapaume road, south-east of Grevillers. This report was quickly forgotten because another, timed at 1025, announced that troops were withdrawing from Biefvillers. A few minutes later another, from air reconnaissance timed at 0730, reported something like 7,000 German troops massing on the eastern edge of Bapaume. Orders were quickly issued instructing the subsequent withdrawal to go due west and form a line running from an old German trench south-west of Bihucourt, round the eastern outskirts of that village to about 2,000 yards due west of Béhagnies. Over the preceding days the general direction of the corps' withdrawals had been north-westerly; on its right, V Corps was tending to retire more or less due west. A westerly withdrawal by IV Corps would thus help to prevent the gap between the two corps widening further. It was, of course, one thing to issue orders and completely another thing for them to be delivered. It seems unlikely any of the battalions did receive them and even if they did, the line could not be held. Air reports believed that by about 1400 the corps line ran along the Irles ridge to a point west of the Bihucourt–Gomiécourt lane, east of Achiet-le-Grand. There it was believed to be in touch with 127 Brigade of 42nd Division.

It will be remembered that on the morning of 25 March 42nd Division was officially transferred from VI to IV Corps. It thus became Harper's corps left division. At 1015, after yet another massed attack, the Germans took Sapignies. The village was recaptured at 1130 by two companies of 8/Lancashire Fusiliers attacking from Béhagnies and the line was re-established south of the village. The respite was to be short-lived, however, because by 1330 it was known that 125 Brigade and 6/SWB (P) of 25th Division had been forced from both Sapignies and Béhagnies. The enemy tried to press his advantage and at 1430, the CO of 5/East Lancs ordered three companies to attack infantry massing astride the lane linking Sapignies and Gomiécourt and close to Bee Wood. The counter-attack was successful, and the East Lancs battalion maintained its positions on the lower slopes of the Gomiécourt ridge to the south-east of Gomiécourt village. The machine guns of a detached company of 31 Bn MGC were also crucial to the defence of this southern flank. They fired over open sights for three hours at masses of Germans sometimes only 300 yards away.

To the right rear of 5/East Lancs, and on receipt of information that Germans were approaching the village from that direction, 8/Manchester was brought forward from the railway cutting to form a line facing south-west of Gomiécourt. Shortly afterwards a message was received by DHQ from 126 Brigade HQ optimistically requesting assistance of mounted officers to rally stragglers who were passing through its line around Ervillers. The brigade was informed none were available. When reports arrived from various sources outlining the growing pressure on Gomiécourt, the five brigade HQ occupying the village chateau decided it was time for them and their approximately 400 attached ORs to leave. At 1600 the ORs were directed to make their way towards Courcelles; the five brigade staffs agreed to move together to dugouts in the railway cutting. At the time scheduled for the coordinated evacuation it was discovered staff of two of the brigade HQ had already disappeared without informing the other three.

Shortly afterwards news was received that the enemy was massing east and south-east of Bihucourt; one company of 6/Manchester of 127 Brigade was sent to investigate. The company arrived simultaneously as the enemy attacked 15/Hampshire's position. The Manchester attacked the superior German forces and, in spite of two counter-attacks, was gradually forced from the village. To prevent the enemy debouching from Bihucourt and thus threatening the rear of 127 Brigade, at 1600 the recently converted 7/Northumberland Fusiliers (P) was put at the disposal of 6/Manchester.[5] With the assistance of the pioneers the CO was ordered to retire on Achiet-le-Grand and to defend it "at all costs." In the centre of the division's front 125 Brigade was withdrawn to the Gomiécourt ridge in touch with the Manchester Brigade to the south and 126 Brigade between Gomiécourt and Ervillers to the north. There had been little artillery support for the three brigades during the day because many of the divisional batteries were still on the move. Furthermore, because they had had no opportunity to register their guns those batteries which were available often fired short causing casualties amongst the division's own troops. With the very heavy expenditure of SAA by the infantry there was during the afternoon a shortage among battalions of 127 Brigade. To rectify the position fresh and sufficient supplies were brought up by the brigade's TMB personnel on their hand carts.

Re-supply was disrupted by the enemy's shelling of the support areas and by a shortage of limbers. There are stories of machine gunners stealing Lewis pans, of Lewis gunners stealing machine-gun belts, and of men looting the pouches of the dead. Some batteries of the corps heavy artillery and several of the RFA brigades did have to be careful about their rates of fire and certainly suffered from unreliable communications with the forward infantry. At times the arm was brutally efficient; at others it either failed to target observed massing Germans or deliberately declined infantry requests lest it run short of shells.

In spite of the stands made by various companies and battalions against the oncoming hordes, and the wonderful targets those massed ranks had presented to the defenders, the Germans, equally bravely, just kept on coming. The attackers' gallantry and tactics were praised by many of the defenders. There were occasional periods of relative quiet which allowed ammunition and rations to be brought forward and patrols sent out to ensure contact on the flanks. On one such occasion the mud-splattered, dishevelled and unshaven Second Lieutenant Henry Lawson of 10/Manchester crossed some open ground with the intent of conferring with an officer of a Guards battalion on his left. Having fought for over 36 hours and looking every bit the resolute warrior, Lawson launched into a monologue about the precariousness of their position to an immaculately dressed subaltern of the Coldstream Guards. Wearing a look of abject horror on his face the young officer listened politely as Lawson regaled him with tales of his own troops' heroism. After a few minutes the Coldstreamer brought Lawson's flow to an abrupt halt with a short valediction of, "Good afternoon. Thank you for coming over. We don't need anything, thank you. Goodbye." Lawson returned to his own platoon somewhat deflated.

The sheer weight of numbers inevitably told on the defenders. By the evening of 25 March, the defence of Ervillers had run its course. Lieutenant General Haldane had been receiving reports that several villages in IV Corps area had been lost. Although concerned, he believed: "All reports from the IV Corps have been of a very alarming nature, and the report about the situation on their left proves to be exaggerated." However, by mid-day Haldane knew the enemy was through Sapignies and by mid-afternoon that he was now west of Bihucourt. Apparently, "10,000 Germans were on the line Bapaume – Ervillers." Knowing that 42nd Division on his immediate right was under considerable pressure, Haldane anticipated that his VI Corps would be obliged to conform to a withdrawal by Harper's IV Corps.

5 Much to its chagrin, during February 7/NF had been converted from a battalion of line infantry in its 50th (Northumbrian) Division to a pioneer battalion in 42nd (East Lancashire) Division.

Lieutenant General Harper did indeed order his divisions to withdraw to the west. For the time being, however, 126 Brigade of 42nd Division fought on whilst the division's other two brigades were taking up positions further to the south and west. Major General Solly-Flood's division was eventually to cover a front of nearly 10,000 yards. Its own transport had still not arrived, but it had managed to borrow a few horses from other formations. Nonetheless, the staff still had acute difficulties in getting orders delivered in good time to the disparate battalions along the very congested roads. At about 2130, 10/Manchester, which by that hour had repelled no fewer than eight determined attacks on Ervillers, evacuated its positions on the western edge of the village and withdrew about 1,000 yards. At the height of the day's engagements, Lieutenant Colonel Peel had despatched a defiant message to brigade HQ of, "Got the blighters. Can hold as long as you want." With his battalion now pretty much isolated Peel accepted the need to withdraw. To its south, and after they had halted yet another enemy attack, the Lancashire Fusiliers of 125 Brigade withdrew from their positions between the south of Ervillers and the open land west of Béhagnies. Both brigades prepared to fall back to the railway east of Courcelles. As if to help them on their way, at about 1900 IV Corps heavy artillery began shelling Gomiécourt. At that time 8/Manchester, the reserve battalion of 126 Brigade, was perilously close to the southern part of the village; 10/Manchester and 5/East Lancs to its east were about to receive orders to withdraw through it.

In recounting their daily actions, the various unit war diaries make little mention of battalions other than those of their own brigade or division having any role in the fighting. In those of 41st Division, which was to the immediate south of 127 Brigade, there is no mention of the Manchesters' involvement in the fighting around Bihucourt. They record the enemy as attacking in force at 1500 and driving many of the defenders of 122 Brigade back from roughly where a branch line left the main Achiet-le-Grand – Bapaume railway. A detailed report of the situation was apparently despatched by 122 Brigade to DHQ but never arrived. Neither were any of the orders sent from DHQ to GOC brigade delivered. Further down the chain of command GOC 123 Brigade stated that he had been out of touch with all units of his brigade since 1100. There were widespread rumours that 62nd Division was on its way up to relieve the division. Rather than wait, however, for the West Riding Division to arrive, many men simply headed straight for Achiet-le-Grand, refusing to be halted by any officers *en route*. Hearing of the retirement and loss of control, staff of 41st Division HQ were sent to stem the flow and organise the men on a line along the railway south of Achiet-le-Grand. In the mid-afternoon it was discovered that 124 Brigade had also been forced back to the line of the railway as it curled to the south-east and south of Achiet-le-Petit. The enemy did not follow up the action and fighting in the sector tended to die away for the remainder of the day.

With 62nd Division now in place on the high ground east of Bucquoy, at 1700 41st Division received the welcome news that it was to withdraw through the West Riding Division and fall back to the area east of Gommecourt. There it was to go into corps reserve. On the division's left flank, the left company of 15/Hampshire only disengaged with difficulty and there was a slight gap created to the north through which the enemy filtered. According to the brigade war diary only the "most adroit handling" by the OC company, Captain Oxborrow, assisted in a counter-attack by some of the few 12/East Surrey then in support, allowed the withdrawal to be affected. Oxborrow's company certainly did fight a rearguard action, but they were also assisted by one company of 6/SWB (P), 10 tanks, and three companies of 6/Manchester who attacked the advancing enemy forces on their right flank. The company of pioneers occupied several positions before its OC, Major Deane, was asked by "a colonel of 42nd Division" to help in clearing the enemy from Bihucourt. Deane considered, "This was the proper course" of action and agreed to the request. He succeeded in getting his men in position to assault the wood on the north-west side of the village but just before the attack was launched he received word that tanks were on their way to do it. Deane decided that as his men had been fighting for four days and nights, and because many had since become detached or disappeared, his company had done its bit. He withdrew his survivors through Achiet-le-Grand where he lost more men to enemy shelling. The tanks cleared the wood but only two of them survived the encounter. The counter-attack had halted the enemy's progress long enough for 122 Brigade to get away through 185 Brigade of 62nd Division which had been sent forward to assist. The battalions of 41st Division had struggled back to their new positions by dawn of 26 March. Unit strengths were low: 200 ORs of 11/Queen's arrived under the command of Second Lieutenant Baker, the senior of the battalion's only two officers.

By the time the hugely depleted battalions of 41st Division had reached Gommecourt, the planned withdrawal of the entire corps line had been achieved. Following its remarkable stand at Ervillers, 10/Manchester fell back to the south-east of Courcelles, west of the railway. Its division's front then ran from that point south-west towards Logeast Wood where it joined with the left of 62nd Division. That division's right flank was about Achiet-le-Petit. Behind it at Puisieux the very battered units of 19th and 25th Divisions formed a defensive flank facing south. Lieutenant General Harper had managed to shorten his line, but the day had been costly. As the *Official History* later observed, "A battering ram" of six enemy divisions had been hurled against IV Corps that day. The general direction of the relentless German thrusts had again been north-westwards. At the commencement of the day's fighting the corps had faced east, with a small gap between itself and V Corps; by the end of the day, it faced south-east with a three mile gap between its southern flank and V Corps. If the enemy was cooperative, the corps' five very tired and depleted divisions were now to re-organise behind a screen formed by two still comparatively fresh TF divisions. The enemy losses had been tremendous, and he was equally as tired as his opponents. The unanswered question during the night of 25-26 March was whether he had sufficient fresh troops to maintain his momentum and tempo the following morning.

When the first two of 62nd Division's brigades had arrived in the area during the afternoon of 25 March they had taken up positions covering Achiet-le-Petit. Major General Braithwaite met with other senior officers of the several divisions and the corps commander to obtain as full a picture as possible of what was happening on his front. At 1900 he assumed command on his sector and established his DHQ initially in Bucquoy and then shortly afterwards in Gommecourt. With 51st Division on the right having withdrawn, his own 186 Brigade's right was exposed. He quickly withdrew the brigade to the railway south of Achiet-le-Petit and sent 9/DLI (P) to the right of 186 Brigade to fill the gap between it and 51st Division. From about the position of the current German cemetery, 185 Brigade continued the line northwards. At 2300, Harper phoned Braithwaite to inform him that as VI Corps on the left had withdrawn, IV Corps would have to conform. Presumably neither of them was aware that Major General Solly-Flood had opted to delay the withdrawal of his 42nd Division until 0200 on 26 March. Braithwaite despatched orders to his three brigades that they should begin the withdrawal to the new corps line of Puisieux–Bucqouy–Ablainzevelle as quickly as possible. The orders were not received until 0200-0300 but the withdrawal began soon afterwards. This caused problems for 42nd Division because as it was forward of 62nd Division when the West Riding Division began to withdraw, its own right flank became further exposed. Because Solly-Flood had been unable to inform all of his brigades promptly he had pushed back their departure until 0730. Consequently, by about 0800 on 26 March, 185 Brigade on the 42nd Division's right was in position on the high ground east of Bucquoy a good mile behind Solly-Flood's division. On the right of 185 Brigade, 186 Brigade continued the line southwards to about 500 yards north-east of Puisieux. The pioneers were in close support, and 187 Brigade in reserve near Biez Wood.

The enemy had closely followed the withdrawal, harassing it with machine-gun fire and then at 0800 by an organised attack against the left of 186 Brigade. This was checked but another by troops heading north from Miraumont advanced through the gap between V and IV Corps' sectors to the high ground south of Puisieux and thus threatened the village itself. The brigade's right threw out a defensive flank facing south along the ridge north-west of Puisieux. With the help of a section of 62 Bn MGC, 5/Duke of Wellington's halted the advance. The situation was not helped by the panic resulting from the supposed appearance of German armoured cars in Hébuterne. This caused, according to 62nd Division, the issue of "totally unauthorised orders…by persons unknown" for all transport to be evacuated to the west. The result was traffic chaos which took the staff several hours to resolve. Meanwhile, the enemy was clearly attempting to maintain his tempo of attack and was concentrating on pushing along the valley from Puisieux towards Hébuterne and Gommecourt. These villages were held by the resting troops of 19th and 41st Division. The three-mile gap between 62nd Division's right and the left of 12th Division of V Corps was to be closed by the arrival of the New Zealand Division and 4 (Aust) Brigade. Before the closure of the gap was achieved, the Germans continued to press attacks on Bucquoy and between Bucquoy and Puisieux. Several assaults on Bucquoy and from across the Logeast Wood–Ablainzevelle road were broken up the artillery and machine-gun fire of 42nd Division as well as by those of the West Riding Division's units. During one such attack, an exchange of shelling by close range enemy field guns and mortars, killed the CO of 8/West Yorks, Lieutenant Colonel A.H. James.

Other enemy forces were also advancing west from Serre towards Hébuterne. To cover the exits from Puisieux, 5/Dukes and 9/DLI (P) were moved towards Rossignol Wood with orders to face south; one company of 2/4th Dukes was moved from support to face Fork Wood.[6] A battalion of 187 Brigade was sent up to the right of the Dukes and by 1900, 4 (Aust) Brigade had assumed command of the Hébuterne defences. Enemy pressure on the front between Rossignol Wood and Bucquoy continued well into the evening and finally a break was made in the Dukes' line. A counter-attack supported by 11 tanks leaguered close to Rossignol Wood restored the position. The defence of 62nd Division's sector had been bolstered by the arrival of 100 specialist machine gunners under the command of Lieutenant Colonel Edmund Ironside. He arrived at DHQ and casually asked if he could be of any assistance. Major General Braithwaite did not hesitate long before answering. Further good news arrived at 2200 when it was known that the leading brigade of the New Zealand Division had moved into the southern section of the three-mile gap around Colincamps. After some confusion and misdirected orders, at about 0630 on 27 March, 4 (Aust) Brigade wired that it was in touch with the New Zealanders south of Hébuterne.

6 Fork Wood lay on the west side of the main Bucquoy–Puisieux road about half-way between the two villages. On IGN maps today it is known as *le Bois des Chapelains*.

The gap between the two corps had been all but closed and as if to emphasise this success, Third Army issued a wire stating that there were to be no further withdrawals. This was somewhat qualified by the addition of a stipulation that if one did become necessary its direction had to be east-west rather than north-west. During the night there had been some additional difficulties as the corps boundaries were changed several times. This caused yet more predictable confusion over wagon lines and the location of various HQ. During the following morning of 27 March several enemy attempts against the New Zealanders and Australians were made but a lack of coordination between the two German armies involved assisted in their repulse. Other attempts at massing troops were broken up by the artillery and machine guns of 42nd Division. One concentration near Ablainzevelle cemetery and another in the village wood were smashed. This latter one was pounded by the enemy's own artillery. An attack emerged from Logeast Wood in mid-afternoon and was quickly broken up but, at 1715, a wire from 59th Division's CRA warned that because the enemy was through into the Ayette valley he was withdrawing his guns from Douchy.[7] Solly-Flood warned his reserve 125 Brigade to be prepared to form a defensive flank facing north but the CRA's action turned out to have been a somewhat hasty decision. He had made it in response to the attack against 92 Brigade of 31st Division on the Ablainzevelle–Moyeneville spur. It was a heavy attack but patrols from 8/Lancashire Fusiliers discovered that 4 Guards Brigade of 31st Division had held its lines and had remained in touch with 126 Brigade on the left of 42nd Division. The Lancashire Fusiliers Brigade remained in support and was not required to offer any assistance when the East Lancashire Brigade was assaulted from Ablainzevelle in the evening.

While the troops of 42nd Division had a comparatively quiet day on 27 March, those of 62nd Division on their right had been heavily engaged. Early attacks on Bucqouy were beaten off but at mid-day the Germans again attacked 5/Dukes positioned east of Rossignol Wood. Assaults across the open ground were repulsed easily but a shortage of bombs hampered the efforts to disrupt those working up the old trench systems. During the afternoon, 2/4th KOYLI was forced from the higher ground east of Hébuterne and 2/4th York&Lancs evacuated Rossignol Wood. The result was a potentially very dangerous gap between 4 (Aust) Brigade and the right of 186 Brigade. A counter-attack was ordered immediately but communication difficulties between 187 Brigade HQ and its battalions delayed the attempt. The Australians launched their part of the counter-attack against trenches to the south-east of Gommecourt and met with some success; 5/KOYLI attacked at 2200 with the help of four tanks. The enemy fled from most of the wood and the higher ground to its south-west.

An early two hour bombardment on 28 March was followed by an attack on the southern end of Bucquoy. This was broken up by artillery and Lewis guns, but other great masses of Germans began advancing towards Fork Wood and the ridge to its south-west. The assault was destroyed by rifles and Lewis guns of 186 Brigade, with over 200 dead Germans reportedly lying in front of one company alone. More attacks were made against positions between Hébuterne and Rossignol Wood and sometime in the early afternoon 5/KOYLI was driven from the wood and the ridge east of Hébuterne. The detail of this tactical set-back is unclear, but it resulted in the removal of the temporary GOC brigade and his replacement by the CO of 2/7th West Yorks of

7 The divisional artillery had stayed in the line when the Staffordshire and Sherwood Foresters Brigades of 59th (North Midland) Division were relieved late on 21 March.

185 Brigade. One report suggests that until the early hours of 28 March the KOYLI had not attempted fully to garrison the section of the wood it had recaptured the night before. In the meantime, the Germans had re-occupied it and converted two of the tanks which had broken down and abandoned in the previous attack into strong points. While the precise chronology of what actually happened inside the wood is vague, three companies of 5/KOYLI and one of 2/4th KOYLI were surrounded. The CO of 5/KOYLI, Lieutenant Colonel Oliver Watson, was killed as he led the other company into the wood in an attempt to rescue any of the other platoons which may still have been inside.[8] During the morning, Lieutenant General Harper had instructed 41st Division to send two brigades forward to the Purple Line. This ran north-south to the east of Gommecourt. The brigades reached the line by mid-afternoon but when Harper heard that Rossignol Wood had again fallen he ordered a battalion of 122 Brigade in the Purple Line to re-take the wood. The attack was misdirected, became engaged with garrisons of posts well away from the wood, and never reached it.[9]

In view of the wood's tactical importance, 8/West Yorks was the next battalion ordered to retake it. The Australians were to cooperate by simultaneously driving the Germans from trenches to the south-east of Gommecourt. So crucial was the attack that the Australian brigadier was told that if necessary he should use all his reserves. Again, delays in issuing orders and a failure to coordinate meant that the Australians launched their assault well before the West Yorks. The Australians pushed the enemy back about 500 yards but in the dark and over unreconnoitred ground, the West Yorks was held up in the northern edge of the wood. The war diary of the battalion simply states that it inflicted "severe casualties" and captured two prisoners. Neither of the assaults gained their full objectives but a potentially dangerous gap in the line had been filled by the Australians. The wood had cost 187 Brigade dearly and it was for the time being pretty much a spent force. The Duke of Wellington's Brigade was holding on but 185 Brigade was relieved when 42nd Division extended it right during the night 28-29 March. It still had, however, to hold itself ready to strengthen the positions held by 187 Brigade.

In the early morning of 28 March, and following a three-hour barrage, 42nd Division came under a heavy attack from Ablainzevelle. This was stopped but later another emerged from Logeast Wood. So dense were the enemy masses that troops of 126 and 127 Brigades were reported to have climbed out of their shell holes and scrapes in order to get better aim. The Germans were mown down by the score. Some did manage to enter the division's line but were ejected by counter-attacks from 6th and 8/Manchester. Another attack from Ablainzevelle in the afternoon was also halted by intense SAA fire and a brief counter-attack by 6/Manchester. As the division's war diary later noted, in 48 hours the enemy had launched eight major attacks on the division's front. Having extended its line during the following night it had a front of

8 Lieutenant Colonel Watson DSO of the Middlesex Hussars was posthumously awarded the Victoria Cross for his leadership and bravery in the wood. The battalion recorded 268 missing at the end of the month, most of whom will have been those captured or killed during the attack in the wood.

9 There is a good deal of confusion about this operation. The information above comes from 62nd Division's narrative. The war diary of 122 Brigade, 41st Division, which had been instructed by DHQ to select two companies to undertake the job, makes no mention of it actually being conducted. The diary of 15/Hampshire indicates that it ordered a "fighting patrol" to reconnoitre Nameless Farm. According to that account over a period of a few hours orders for the operation were cancelled and re-instigated a total of five times. The final cancellation was received as the patrol actually began its advance. The order was "immediately complied with, to the satisfaction of all."

3,800 yards held by two brigades and the pioneer battalion. One brigade remained in support and one field company was attached to each of the two brigades in the line as additional infantry. The division had also formed a Composite Battalion from the battle surpluses of individual battalions.

The next few days were quiet in comparison, but fighting did still continue. Gas attacks, bombardments, and bombing fights were conducted regularly but both TF divisions had some time out of the line. The fresh 37th Division appeared at the end of March and relieved both 42nd and 62nd Divisions on 1-2 April. In early April the final phase of the intense fighting was to culminate in the capture by the enemy of the bulk of Bucquoy's ruins. The action on 5 April coincided with an attempt by 63 Brigade of 37th Division on Rossignol Wood. This operation went disastrously wrong – the tanks failed to arrive, the weather and trenches were appallingly wet, troops lost the barrage and direction, the supply of bombs was quickly exhausted, and the enemy resisted strongly. In contrast, the German effort on Bucquoy achieved most of its objective. After a heavy hurricane bombardment, the enemy fell on the positions of 8/LF on the high ground to the east of the village. The companies were forced quickly to fall back but what happened next is unclear. The Lancashire Fusiliers blamed 13/RF of 112 Brigade on their right for withdrawing prematurely; 13/RF blamed 8/LF. One account from 13/RF claims that when the writer saw 8/LF withdrawing, his own CO, Lieutenant Colonel Smith, went to the fusiliers' HQ and, "From thence onwards practically took over the re-organisation of the line by turning back the men of that battalion." How much of this is correct is contested but 8/LF did make a counter-attack before noon. Heavy fire prevented it getting any further than the main crossroads in the middle of the village. In the northern sector of the built up area, 7/LF threw back a defensive flank on its right, but 13/RF seems to have withdrawn. By 1400 the Royal Fusiliers certainly occupied a lane to the west of the village and also the orchards to its north-west. One company of 6/Bedford was sent up in support of 13/RF and two companies of 5/LF, together with the few remaining troops of 8/LF, were tasked to counter-attack at 1630. The Royal Fusiliers joined in the attempt, but the effort was again halted at the main road by machine-gun fire and snipers. When the attack failed, "practically the whole" of 8/LF had been wiped out and the Germans pushed machine guns and TMs into woods on the western side of the village. More Germans were seen massing on the slopes to the east, but these were broken up by the artillery.

By 2000 both sides in the village were consolidating and the fighting died down. Between them, 112 Brigade and 125 Brigade had lost most of the ruins and COs of two of the Lancashire Fusiliers battalions had been killed: Lieutenant Colonel Percy Clive, of the Grenadier Guards, MP, CO of 5/LF; Lieutenant Colonel Oswyn Davies of the Manchester Regiment, CO of 7/LF. The lines were to stay pretty much static in the area from then until the beginning of the offensive on 21 August. The summer campaign was to involve the same divisions which had been active there in April.

The lines held by IV Corps in early April were thus very close to those occupied at the close of the Somme Offensive. The Wastelands had been lost and the line stabilised within the space of about 10 days. For the Germans, Operation *Michael* had failed to achieve its principal objective of splitting the French and British armies; Operation *Mars* towards Arras had been foiled in one day; Operation *Valkyri* had been cancelled; Operation *Georgette*, a scaled down version of that originally intended, was about to open on the Lys Front. The northern and central corps of Third Army had bought time at the expense of ground and although suffering very heavily themselves had inflicted massive casualties on the Germans. It is useful to remember that Byng's army was not always master of its own destiny. As IV Corps HQ wrote on 25 March when V Corps on its right had fallen back west of the Ancre and when the Germans were thought to be in Pozières, "The situation south of the Bapaume – Albert road was still the deciding factor in the line that could be held by IV Corps." What Lieutenant General Harper might also have added was that Third Army's fortunes depended greatly on what was happening to Fifth Army situated on the right of V Corps.

9

Losing the Wastelands: V Corps, March 1918

The front of Lieutenant General Sir Edward Fanshawe's V Corps extended for approximately 15,000 yards. His command deployed three divisions forward and kept one in reserve. Another division in the sector, 19th, was in Third Army Reserve. The divisions held the Flesquières Salient, a position which many senior officers judged to be untenable. There was a fairly widespread belief that if a major enemy offensive did occur the salient should be immediately evacuated to the defensive positions across its base.

On the morning of 21 March, from north to south, the line was held by 17th Division, 63rd RND, and 47th (2nd London) Division. The London Division had relieved 2nd Division that night and officially took command of its sector at 0540. Intensive gas attacks on five successive nights before the offensive began had hit the corps badly: 63rd RND recorded it had suffered 102 officers and 2,748 serious, and many more or less severe gas casualties since 13 March. In 2nd Division the battalion with the highest fighting strength of the three units of 99 Brigade was 1/KRRC with 20 officers and 404 ORs. There had been something like 800 gas casualties when the brigade held the forward sector. As the division's infantry withdrew towards Barastre and Equancourt to rest, it came under yet more shelling and gas discharges.

Almost an hour after the enemy bombardment began Major General Jeffreys' 19th Division was ordered to stand by; within four hours the pioneer battalions of 2nd and 47th Divisions, 10/DCLI and 4/RWF respectively, were ordered to man Dessert Switch and the Metz inner defences. The reserve battalions of 63rd RND were in the Battle Zone by mid-morning and, an hour later, 19th Division was ordered to its assembly positions and told to push strong patrols onto the ridge Hermies–Beaumetz. Within another hour the division was told it was now under orders of V Corps, that it was to hold the Hermies–Lebucquière ridge, and that a battalion of tanks currently leaguered in the tankdrome in Vélu Wood was at its disposal. There were several local attacks on all three of the forward divisions, but few penetrations were achieved. Those troops that did enter the British positions, such as in Hughes Trench in 17th Division's sector and Ostrich Trench in 47th Division's, were either ejected or contained. The former, for example, was retaken by 10/West Yorks but a proposed counter-attack by 10/Lancashire Fusiliers on the right of the West Yorks was denied on the grounds that as the Forward Zone was considered to be only an outpost line no significant counter-attack should be attempted. For a similar reason Hawke Battalion's offer to recover the loss of the Prémy Salient was also rejected.

Gradually news came into corps HQ about what was going on to its north and south. The danger was that if 9th Division of VII Corps and 51st of IV Corps continued to be pushed back towards their Battle Zones, it would become even more difficult for V Corps to escape from its salient. Gas and shells continued to hit the three divisions and enemy tanks, which were later believed to have been infantry in artillery formation, were reported to be approaching Boursies and Louverval Wood along the main Cambrai road. The discharged gas was phosgene and, as this clears more quickly than mustard, an imminent attack seemed likely. What was described as the "disquieting news" from 51st Division caused 10/Sherwood Foresters and a company of the pioneers to be sent up to Jargon Trench to support 7/Lincoln in the Hermies defences. A little before 1700, corps HQ issued a warning that the corps might withdraw to Highland ridge and the Intermediate Line during the night. The latter was the old German Hindenburg System. Its still substantial trenches and dugouts with good fields of fire was generally a better line to defend than the divisions' own Battle Zones. It also became apparent as the day wore on that the enemy attacks were not really meant to create major gaps in the corps' lines. It was later acknowledged that they were intended as raids designed to fix the corps in the salient. By working around its flanks, the enemy would then pinch it off and trap the divisions within.

By the evening of 21 March, the corps' artillery was instructed to fire off as much of its ammunition as possible in order to facilitate any possible withdrawal. An initial warning order from corps was issued at 1730, with a firm order following at 2000. The withdrawal to the Highland Ridge–Chapel Wood Switch was to commence at 0130 and be completed by 0430. The distance back to the new lines was on average about 4,000 yards. In addition, 2nd Division was ordered to move to the corps' northern sector and to be prepared to man the Green Line from Haplincourt to Bertincourt. In 19th Division, 58 Brigade was to hold the switch running almost east-west about mid-way between Doignies and Hermies; 56 Brigade was to move two battalions to the east side of Vélu Wood; and sections of the divisional MGC battalion were to cover Hermies Switch. For most of the brigades the withdrawal was done easily, there being some difficulties for 47th Division when guides could not locate the positions of some aid and collecting posts. A certain amount of destruction was done although as there was thought to be the possibility of a return to the area fairly quickly, the extent was deliberately limited. In 17th Division's area trench stores were carried back, Lock 7 on the canal was blown up and a bridge "dismantled." Battalion HQ of 12/Manchester was burnt with the assistance of a liberal application of rum. Some forward ammunition and RE dumps were blown up and dugout entrances blown in. By 0730 all infantry brigades had reported they were in their allotted positions. The artillery was also on the move but not all divisional batteries were in their new sites until just before noon.

Dawn of 22 March was misty and cool. In 17th Division's sector the withdrawal meant that 52 Brigade was still east of the canal in the Havrincourt Defences; 50 Brigade was west of it in Lurgan Switch which ran north-west across the eastern edge of Hermies from the brigade boundary north of the railway and east of the canal to join with the Hermies Defences; 51 Brigade was in the Hermies Defences themselves. The three field companies were in and around Hebburn Spoil Heap. It appears to have taken some time for the Germans to realise the division had pulled back overnight and the first attacks against the outpost trenches of Jermyn Street and then Gong Trench were more for reconnaissance purposes than large scale assaults. These were easily repelled. A lack of coordination, however, meant that because 7/East Yorks withdrew from the outpost line west of the canal without informing the outposts east of it in the Jermyn Street zone, the latter became enfiladed from the Spoil Heap. This was the well-known feature on the west side of the canal 600 yards north of the railway. The outposts were forced to withdraw. With 51st Division on the left having fallen back, at 1115 a major attack developed from Doignies on 7/Lincoln in the Hermies Defences. The attack was beaten off by a combination of steady field gun and machine-gun fire with, reportedly, "several hundred" of the enemy dead in front of the wire. Several other attacks from the same direction throughout the day, including one with a *Flammenwerfer,* were dealt with in the same manner. To support the Lincoln and 10/Sherwood in Jargon Switch, 7/Border was divided between the two forward battalions. At 1400, 5 Brigade, 2nd Division was put at the disposal of 17th Division and held in reserve to the west and south of Hebburn Spoil Heap. East of the canal 52 Brigade comfortably repelled four attacks, one of them involving the capture by the CO of 12/Manchester of a "yelling German" caught in the wire by "the seat of his pants." Other attacks during the day on the Havrincourt Defences were also easily repulsed but it was what was going on elsewhere which forced the issue.

The division realised that these were merely fixing attacks and aroused no major concern. The factor that did worry DHQ was that liaison and communication with 51st Division had been virtually non-existent all day. The rapid initial withdrawal of the Highland Division had exposed 17th's left; the problems facing 9th Scottish Division of VII Corps on the right of the corps were also causing concern. At 1205, V Corps issued a warning order that the corps would withdraw further that night and, at 1535, 47th Division reported that VII Corps was falling back and that the London Division was forming a defensive flank. At 1726 corps warned that the withdrawal might have to go as far as the Metz Switch and issued instructions that if that were to be the case, its divisions were to leave fighting patrols in the Second System. Their purpose was to convince the enemy to deploy for an attack on a false front. The withdrawal was to be covered by the heavy artillery.

In the centre of V Corps sector, 22 March had been a quiet day for 63rd Division. The attacks on 17th Division on its left had had little impact on the RND. There was some shelling but the positions the three brigades now held were good ones. There was, therefore, some surprise when the orders came for a further withdrawal that night. Liaison officers were sent to the divisions either side and arrangements agreed. The only real excitement came when Commander Beak of Drake Battalion discovered a group of RE trying "with the utmost zeal to blow up his battalion." Drake had not received any orders to withdraw but when enemy patrols were heard on both flanks, Beak ordered a retirement. He covered it himself with a Lewis gun fixed on a limber. When the battalion reached the line held by 189 Brigade at 0700 on the morning of 23 March it learned immediately that there was to be another withdrawal.

The action on the front of 47th Division on 22 March was rather more intense than that experienced by the RND. The two forward brigades were on the Highland Ridge Line and managed to keep the Germans east of the railway running through the Couillet valley. The third brigade, 142 Brigade, was in position in the Second System; the pioneers of 4/RWF were on Dessart ridge. The pioneers were supposed to be in touch with the rear troops of 9th Division on their right. Similarly, GOC 140 Brigade was told to concentrate his reserves, such as they were, on his right to be able to counter-attack should a gap develop between his brigade and 9th Division. The danger posed by this potential rift was all consuming and when 9th Division announced that it was going to make another withdrawal, probably back as far as the Green Line, 47th Division was told it would have to conform. Furthermore, it was informed that in addition to occupying the Metz Switch it would also have to garrison New Switch. This trench ran across the open ground north of Gouzeaucourt Wood to north-west of Gouzeaucourt village, thus connecting Metz Switch with the Second System. Arrangements were made for the subsequent disposition of its battalions.

During the day the two front brigades on Highland ridge fought off several attacks. The London Irish in particular were active in repulsing the assaults but it was becoming increasingly obvious that there would have to be a further withdrawal to at least the rear of the Second System. At 1920 a warning order was issued whereby 140 and 141 Brigades were to fall back through 142. This latter brigade would then withdrawal to the Metz Switch. The pioneers on Dessart ridge would be joined by 140 Brigade with the intent of securing contact with 9th Division about 1,000 yards north of Fins. To assist with this task, No.11 Motor Machine Gun Battery was detailed to occupy positions where it could bring fire to bear on the enemy who, it was believed, had occupied Fins. Only 20 minutes after receipt of the warning order the corps instruction arrived ordering the move to be executed that night. The withdrawal was hardly hampered by the enemy. By the early hours of 23 March, 140 Brigade garrisoned Metz Switch from the village cemetery on its eastern edge, north to a position a few hundred yards inside Havrincourt Wood. There it joined with the RND. To its south, 142 Brigade was also in Metz Switch; 141 Brigade and three field companies were in open ground 1,000 yards south-east of Neuville–Bourjonval. The detached 99 Brigade of 2nd Division was in support around Equancourt. At 2230 it was placed under 47th Division's command with the intent that it should serve as a reserve link between 47th and 9th Divisions. Unfortunately for the tired troops it was swiftly realised by senior command that these new positions would quickly become untenable.

One of the great problems facing corps and divisional commanders was how to receive and despatch reliable intelligence. All over ground lines had been destroyed but there were still some buried networks functioning. For example, at 0600 on 23 March, V Corps wired 47th Division HQ that 99 Brigade was definitely holding Dessart Switch as far north as where Fins civilian cemetery is now located. In fact, 99 Brigade's troops were still around Equancourt, a good 2,000 yards to the west. Nonetheless, Major General Gorringe was told to link with 99 Brigade and hold Dessart ridge "strongly." No.11 Motor Machine Gun Battery was despatched to the position 99 Brigade was reported to be holding and came under severe machine-gun fire itself from that very position. At the same time as V Corps sent the wire concerning the position of 99 Brigade, 141 Brigade was instructed by DHQ to go to the Third System in order to cover the withdrawal to the Green Line of 140 and 142 Brigades. The brigade was to hold the line from Fins civilian cemetery north-westwards to about where Neuville–Bourjonval British Cemetery is today. The CO of 18/London was ordered to "fight to get in touch" with 99 Brigade and to use the three attached field companies to extend his right to ensure he did.

Fighting along the London Division's positions in the Dessart and Metz Switches and the rear of the Third System was heavy for most of 23 March. The London Irish reported at 1002 that the enemy was behind its line and closing in on Equancourt. Attacks and counter-attacks failed to gain touch with 99 Brigade or to clear the enemy from north of Fins. Closer to Metz, as 15/London was being heavily attacked the two companies of 4/RWF (P) at Metz Cemetery were ordered to join the third already to the right rear of 15/London. Before the reserve company of 21/London could move to replace the pioneers, the Germans penetrated the vacated area. One company of 15/London, whose stand in combination with the divisional sappers was described by the divisional history as having saved "the right of Third Army from disastrous results" never managed to extricate itself. It was either wiped out or captured. In 142 Brigade's sector 23/London had been attacked from the direction of Scrub Valley. At least large assaults were repelled by the battalion aided by the artillery but one fairly close to the cemetery was successful. A counter-attack did drive the Germans back a little way but a gap of about 3-400 yards opened between 21/London, which had been forced back to the Fins-Metz road about one mile north of Fins, and 23/London.

Because the situation had become impossible to hold against successive waves of attacks, at 1300 the order to withdraw from the Metz Switch was executed. With their right flank exposed both 140 and 142 Brigades suffered severely from enfilade fire as they withdrew through 141 Brigade in the Green Line. Once the other brigades were through, 141 pulled back to the area of the Rocquigny–Equancourt road roughly to the south of Léchelle. The cookers of 23/London were waiting for the withdrawing troops but as the last platoon reached them a shell landed killing about half of the 30 men and destroying several of the cookers. The cookers of 19/London had also been lost but for a more mundane reason: there were no horses to pull them. Furthermore, the CO and adjutant had been adrift for some hours because they could not locate their battalion. They did rejoin late in the evening but by that time 9th Division had already gone to the Green Line and 99 Brigade was unable to plug the gap between the Third and Fifth Armies. By about 1600, 142 Brigade had formed a defensive flank facing south-east with its right close to the southern portal of the canal tunnel and Vallulart Wood. It was in vague touch with the RND on the left and with 140 Brigade and a few troops of 99 Brigade on the right. There was little to no coherence, and it could hardly be considered a coordinated defensive position. The pressure remained incessant and 142 Brigade was forced again to pull back.

On its right, 140 Brigade's battalions were similarly dispersed and inter-mixed. The GOC, Brigadier General Kennedy, realised the enemy were now behind most of his brigade. This stark realisation came when he was fired on from the near-by slag tip as he crossed the canal south of the tunnel. Those elements of his brigade which he was able to contact withdrew to the areas of Four Winds Farm, the aerodrome on the south side of the Rocquigny– Equancourt road, and Léchelle village. There were already a few score men of mixed units when they arrived to form a line facing south-east. There were elements of several battalions' details, the best part of two companies of 22/London that had become detached when their battalion withdrew from close to Winchester Valley, and a small party of 23/London. This handful of 23/London men later attempted a dramatic but failed attempt to escape from a farmhouse in Léchelle village. There were also some 200 of 99 Brigade's 1/R.Berks and 1/KRRC.

Since its detachment from its own 2nd Division on 22 March, 23/RF, 1/R.Berks, and 1/KRRC of 99 Brigade, whose average battalion fighting strengths were by now reported to be 20 officers and 360 ORs had, in theory, been ordered to reconnoitre the Green Line around the boundary with Fifth Army. This was meant to be in preparation for bridging the gap between 47th and 9th Divisions. Understandably, because there was so much uncertainty about who was where, Brigadier General Barnett-Barker had acted with some misgivings. Late on 22 March the brigade formed a defensive flank to protect Equancourt and stood by as steams of traffic and labour units poured west from the forward areas. When the brigade did receive a message from 47th Division despatched almost eight hours earlier it learned there was a gap of about 2,000 yards between its left and the right of the London Division. That was the gap 140 Brigade had been sent to fill. Barnett-Barker despatched six machine guns to Mouettes Trench west of Equancourt and also a section to the higher ground on the aerodrome west of the main crossroads north of Manancourt. It seems probably that guns of No.11 Motor Machine Gun Battery were also in and around the aerodrome. All these enjoyed good fields of fire along the Rocquigny-Equancourt road. But, during 23 March, the enemy had gradually pushed 1/R.Berks out of the *sucrerie* at the main crossroads and then back to Léchelle Wood. The CO was killed, and the survivors attached themselves to details and elements of 140 Brigade close to Four Winds Farm.

North of the main road and under intense shelling and machine-gun fire, the 1/KRRC withdrew from its position on the Equancourt–Neuville–Bourjonval road across open ground to pass through Vallulart Wood. Hearing that there were some GOC brigades of 47th Division apparently meeting close to the CCS at the railway halt near Vallulart Wood, the CO, Lieutenant Colonel Stafford, went to investigate. Following consultations, his battalion was put first under 140 Brigade but when a little later this brigade "suddenly vanished" Stafford attached his unit to 142 Brigade. The KRRCs dug in south-east of Léchelle facing Little Wood and thus extended the approximate line which ran north-east from the aerodrome. The Germans approached the assorted units from the *sucrerie* at the crossroads and from the Rocquigny–Equancourt Road British Cemetery. The first assault was halted but as more of the enemy arrived and the barrage intensified, first 140 withdrew to Léchelle Wood and then 142 Brigade fell back towards Ytres. There, an outpost line was established. Some of 140 Brigade gained touch with 141 Brigade on the right. This brigade had been tasked to occupy some old trenches to the south-east and east of Mesnil-en-Arrouaise. At about 0730 on 24 March, and after a circuitous route, 142 Brigade arrived at Rocquigny. Once it had left Vallulart Wood it had marched north-westwards, reaching Ytres about midnight. As there were reports of the enemy already in Bus, a conference of battalion commanders decided to circle to the north of Bus and march via Bertincourt and Barastre to Rocquigny.

When 1/KRRC, still holding its line to the south-east of Léchelle, discovered that 142 Brigade had disappeared it realised that both of its flanks had immediately become exposed. Harassed by low flying aircraft, running short of ammunition and knowing that as soon as the enemy reached the aircraft hangers his battalion would be enfiladed from the higher ground, Stafford decided to take his remnant back towards Bus. The third battalion of 99 Brigade, 23/RF, had started the day on the left of the brigade in the Green Line a little east of the sunken Equancourt-Metz lane. When 24/London on its left withdrew at about 1500, the battalion pulled back through Hayettes Wood and then, via Ytres, Bus, and Rocquigny to Le Transloy. It reached that village soon after dark.

The RND to the north of 47th Division had an equally difficult time. The brigades had hardly arrived in the Second System on the night of 22-23 March when they were told that another withdrawal was shortly to be made. By 0700, 190 Brigade held the right sector of the divisional front of the Metz Switch while 188 Brigade held the left. The remaining brigade, 189, went into reserve in the Third System east of Neuville-Bourjonval. Within 30 minutes of the arrival orders were received that the Metz Switch was to be thinned out immediately and that rearguards were to be clear of it by 1300. Strong posts established by 189 Brigade in the Third System would cover the withdrawals, which were to be completed by 1500. As much as what could be swiftly physically destroyed was ordered to be either burned or blown up. The Germans did not interfere strongly during the operation and the withdrawal to the Green Line was completed by 1700. For practical technicalities as well as possible fire support each brigade was to have one company of pioneers and a field company attached. On the right, 190 Brigade was in touch with 47th Division; on the left, 188 Brigade had contact with Major General Pereira's 2nd Division. Pereira's division had just relieved 17th Division. In the centre of the RND, 189 Brigade was joined on both flanks.

During the afternoon of 23 March, 190 Brigade submitted reports indicating that 47th Division on its right seemed to have disappeared "for some reason unknown to us." The brigade formed a defensive flank and DHQ informed V Corps of its action. About midday a report from the left brigade informed DHQ that the enemy was in occupation of both Bus and Léchelle. The brigade was ordered to send Hawke, its reserve battalion, to retrieve the situation. It was about this time that Lieutenant Colonel Stafford of 1/KRRC arrived west of Bus. There he found elements of his own division's 5 Brigade and having had no contact since the morning with his own brigade HQ, went on to Barastre to report to GOC 5 Brigade. Brigadier General Bullen-Smith's brigade faced north and when Stafford explained what had happened around Equancourt and Léchelle, Bullen-Smith expressed complete ignorance of the seriousness of the situation. When the news was transmitted to V Corps it apparently "flatly refused to believe that the enemy were in Léchelle." Stafford rejoined his remnant west of Bus where the CO of Hawke Battalion suggested that Hawke, the KRRC, and 24/RF should conduct a counter-attack to retake Bus. Stafford and the CO of 24/RF were reluctant and when shortly afterwards the Bus ammunition dump exploded they demurred on the grounds that their men would be short of rations, water, and ammunition.

Under orders from his own division the CO of Hawke decided to make the attempt and sent a company with the objective of clearing the village. The company was held up at once. The CO later reported that he had possession of the north-wester end of Bus and the enemy, the south-eastern. It was now well into the night. A wire from V Corps instructed all battalions to hold their ground in the Green Line because in the morning 17th Division was to make a counter-attack to recapture Bus. GOC 190 Brigade, Brigadier General Hutchison, was non-plussed by that response. He reported that the position on his right was "becoming serious" because 47th Division had gone and because the right of his two front battalions, with whom he had no communication, were now exposed. He said he would withdraw his troops to Rocquigny unless something was done about the enemy in Bus and Léchelle. Again, he was told to hang on until the morning.

The RND was in a difficult position. Although it was weak in strength on 21 March owing to the gas casualties it had not lost particularly heavily during the withdrawal; its three brigades were also reasonably well concentrated. But the worry about what was happening on its right caused the Drake, Artists, and Bedford to withdraw from the Green Line and form a flank facing south along the Ytres-Bus road. The division's remaining battalions were to stay in the Green Line. Their positions were not secure and 188 Brigade wired DHQ to explain the "critical state of the Brigade." The next German attack came from the south-east and drove 190 Brigade north-westwards. The ammunition dump at Ytres exploded which caused some hesitation on the part of the enemy but the attack brought results. The RND was running short of ammunition, the artillery was also running low because the DAC had lost it wagons, and the broken communications meant any kind of central control by DHQ was almost impossible. The only bright spot on the horizon seemed to be that the ration dump at Ytres was largely undamaged. At least there were cold rations available. A message from corps did get through during the night stating that it was still intended that 17th Division would counter-attack in the morning. In reality, there was little hope that even if the attack did take place it would achieve anything.

On the morning of 23 March, Major General Robertson's 17th Division was still a reasonably fortunate formation. Its three brigades had coped with the fairly limited encounters on 21-22 March and had then, according to orders, withdrawn from its front system. At 0400 on 23 March its sappers demolished the railway bridge over the canal and DHQ learned there was to be a further withdrawal to the Green Line. The division was to pass through 2nd Division in the Green Line and then man the Red Line as corps' reserve. Major General Pereira's 2nd Division had been ordered to occupy the corps' northern-most sector of the Green Line. All three brigades were to garrison a stretch, each with a battery of 18-pdrs and a MG section in support. The Red Line was a mixture of old and largely ruined British and German trenches then in the process of being swiftly renovated. Robertson's division was to man a section from the eastern edge of Villers-au-Flos, eastwards to pass west of Barastre, and south towards Rocquigny.

The withdrawal began at 1000 on 23 March: 51 Brigade evacuated Hermies; 50 Brigade from the area west of the canal between the canal and Hermies; 52 Brigade from the bend in the canal at Yorkshire Bank to the northern part of the Metz Switch in Havrincourt Wood. The attached 5 Brigade of 2nd Division guarded the flank between Hermies and Bertincourt, south-east of Vélu Wood. Once the withdrawal had been completed 5 Brigade was to rejoin its own division in the Green Line. Just before the retirement began, 6/Dorset suffered a *Flammernwerfer* attack and then, once the withdrawal had begun, narrowly avoided being enveloped. The enemy followed the rearguards but without launching any massed attacks. The Germans quickly occupied Hebburn Spoil Heap and from this position of advantage were able to cause "fairly heavy" casualties amongst 10/Sherwood. Two companies of 7/Lincoln were also cut off a little west of Hermies. One battery of 79 Brigade RFA and some sections of 17 Bn MGC effectively engaged strong enemy forces debouching from Vélu Wood but by 1700 the brigades had passed through the Green Line and were taking positions in the Red. To the delight of 12/Manchester the battalion took over a camp recently vacated by a heavy artillery brigade. The gunners left behind stocks of new clothing, boots, fresh meat, and other assorted rations. The pioneers and field companies were temporarily camped near the two British cemeteries west of Beaulencourt. Most of the pioneers and sappers were shortly to move forward to join the brigades in the Red Line..

At 2100 on 23 March, DHQ 17th Division received a wire from 2nd Division stating that a battalion commander (presumably Lieutenant Colonel Stafford) had reported that the enemy were in Bus and Léchelle. This was confirmed by another wire at 2240. DHQ ordered 52 Brigade to push out patrols to cover approach roads and for 50 Brigade to send patrols towards Bus. The realisation was that if the Germans were now in Bus, the enemy was in front of the Red Line and to the rear of the RND in the Green. Despite what the RND and 99 Brigade had been told during the night it was not until 0600 on 24 March that a message arrived at DHQ 17th Division from V Corps ordering a counter-attack to be made on Bus. GOC 50 Brigade was told to organise the operation and that 78 Brigade RFA was at his disposal. Before the counter-attack could be launched, corps changed its mind and cancelled it. Because corps HQ intelligence officers had failed to find 47th Division, 51 Brigade was now tasked with filling the gap between Rocquigny and Sailly-Saillisel. There, it was supposed to gain touch with 9th Division.

As did commanders at all levels, Major General Robertson suffered greatly all day from the lack of reliable and recent intelligence from V Corps. Vulnerable despatch riders and mounted messengers were used during the withdrawal to carry messages between DHQ and brigades; air reconnaissance reports from corps HQ had been "very scanty" and "always arrived too late to be of any value." It would have been much better, DHQ argued, had a contact aircraft been provided for every division. Unsure of what was going on to their front the infantry, sappers, and pioneers set to work to improve the trenches of the Red Line and lay wire. Their senior officers, however, knew from a V Corps wire received at noon that a further withdrawal was likely to be ordered the following day.

In front of 17th Division, 2nd Division, less 99 Brigade which to all intents and purposes had temporarily ceased to exist, was in the Green Line in what had become known as the Bertincourt Salient. In the afternoon of 22 March, 6 Brigade had been sent to man the Green Line from about Delsaux Farm southwards. With the enemy's breakthrough at Morchies, 5 and 6 Brigades were to be reunited and to hold the Green Line from the farm (the corps' northern boundary) to where the line crossed the railway 600 yards north-east of Bertincourt. The norther sector was to be held by 6 Brigade, with 5 Brigade on its right. The line was continued south by the RND. The pioneers of 10/DCLI and the divisional field companies worked with the infantry, who had only their entrenching tools, to improve what in many parts was only a spit-locked trench. By lunch time of 23 March suitable machine-gun positions had been prepared and all of the infantry had reasonable cover in what was a good defensive position. Stragglers from 17th and 19th Divisions were recruited to swell the garrisons.

In the afternoon Germans appearing over the ridge west of Lebucquière offered "excellent" targets for the infantry and 36 Brigade RFA. After darkness had fallen another attack emerged from Ytres. The Germans had clearly looted the village's abandoned canteen and came down the slope towards Bertincourt singing and shouting. Ammunition dumps along the light railway were ignited which gave the Lewis gunners and infantry of 24/RF well-illuminated targets. The divisional machine guns kept up a steady fire in the direction of Bus and Ytres for most of the night and no more attacks were forthcoming. Effective as this night action was, however, it was obvious that the Bertincourt Salient could not be held. During the night pioneers were put to digging a trench between Bertincourt and Barastre. This would effectively become a cord for the salient.

A heavy enemy barrage greeted the dawn of 24 March and at 0900, 5 Brigade and the RND began the withdrawal from the salient. The shelling continued, especially on the Haplincourt valley, as the retirement proceeded over open ground. At 0935 massed attacks came from Lebucquière and Vélu Wood but over the exposed ground they were hit hard by four Vickers of the divisional machine-gun battalion. On the left, 9/Cheshire of 19th Division withdrew about 200 yards but a counter-attack by 2/South Stafford of 6 Brigade pushed the enemy back to the high ground west of Lebucquière. A company of about 100 10/Worcester of 19th Division was placed under the command of 2/HLI and apparently told to plug a gap between 5 and 6 Brigades which had developed during the withdrawal. According to 5 Brigade the Worcesters withdrew "completely and independently." A "misunderstanding" between 1/King's and 9/Cheshire caused another gap and two platoons of 17/RF were sent forward to seal it. But it was to no avail as the enemy continued to surge forward. Two companies of 2/South Stafford were cut off and 1/King's was down to about 60 men. There was clearly now no alternative other than to make a general withdrawal towards the Red Line. The most direct route was to the section running roughly between the east of Villers-au-Flos and ground to the west of Haplincourt. This operation was assisted by the arrival soon after noon of eight tanks of 8 Tank Battalion. Besides bringing forward supplies of SAA the monsters cruised about between Barastre and Haplincourt Wood to help disorganise the enemy attacks and pursuit. Once the infantry was in the Red Line the tanks departed and rallied at Courcelette.

The divisional account gives numerous tales of how individuals and gun teams delayed the enemy's advance towards the line; of how rearguards of a few men, such as that commanded by Lieutenant Armstrong of 1/King's, opted to stay where they were and pour as much fire as possible into the advancing hordes; of the courage shown by Second Lieutenant Sheridan and two platoons of 2/HLI who stayed to protect the flank of 6 Brigade as it retired; of Sergeant Callender of 17 Bn MGC who was credited personally with having knocked out seven enemy machine guns. The leadership demonstrated by sub-unit commanders during the action, as well as that shown by men with no stripes on their sleeves, helped to slow but not stop the advance.

The Red Line actually offered very little protection and the withdrawing troops barely paused in it. Within minutes the men of both brigades were again heading west. They came across elements of 51st Division as well as their own pioneer battalion, 10/DCLI, in front of Beaulencourt on the Bapaume – Péronne road and dug in alongside them. Both flanks, however, seemed to be in the air. To add to the woes, the position was also being shelled by both British and German artillery, and all about them troops were withdrawing. Recognising the futility of their situation and with the Germans pressing up from Le Transloy and Lesboeufs, at 1800 the personnel of 2nd Division and the remnants of the Highland Division joined the flow heading west by north towards the Albert- Bapaume road. After the action near Léchelle, the 200 men of 23/RF and 60 of 1/R.Berks of the detached 99 Brigade withdrew with elements of 47th and 63rd Division via Rocquigny and Le Transloy to Gueudecourt. The other battalion, I/KRRC, claimed never to have received the DHQ orders to evacuate the Bertincourt Salient. It finally received word from Hawke Battalion to retire and rendezvous to the north of Villers-au-Flos. British artillery was shelling a line Rocquigny–Barastre so, after "trying in vain to get the FOO to stop this", Lieutenant Colonel Stafford borrowed a horse and galloped round every battery he could locate. Having achieved that objective he looked for any elements of 2nd Division that might be able to inform him of where the rest of the division was located. He failed to find any and with chaos everywhere decided to take his men, who "could now hardly stand," towards Gueudecourt.

When Brigadier General Barnett-Barker was killed on 24 March,[1] Lieutenant Colonel Winter, 23/RF, had assumed command of 99 Brigade. He, too, decided his two battalions should head west from Gueudecourt. Somewhat east of Eaucourt L'Abbaye he received orders from his own DHQ that his brigade was now once again under command of the division and that he should stay where he was. The division's other two brigades were said to be on their way and would establish a line south of and parallel to the Albert-Bapaume road covering Ligny-Thilloy. Winter's brigade was to get in contact with 17th Division on his right and go into reserve. The two divisions were to be part of a line then in the process of forming by several brigades running from Ligny-Thilloy to High Wood. When they arrived the strength of 5 and 6 Brigades was each about 150 all ranks. They were disposed in small posts along a line nearly 5,000 yards in length. Clearly, it was unlikely such a force would be able to hold for long.

This proved to be the case. In the early hours of 25 March, the three brigades of 2nd Division were ordered to withdraw to a line Pys-Courcelette. This line was, according to V Corps, to be "held at all costs." Fighting did take place, especially by 17/RF and 1/King's, but a further withdrawal followed. By the end of the day the division had crossed the Ancre south of Beaumont Hamel. It stayed in and around the same area until it was finally relieved on 3 April. It was then sent to Halloy for rest and rebuilding.

1 Captain E.Bell (Middlesex Regiment), Barnett-Barker's staff captain, was also killed by the same shell. Both bodies were apparently carried back by a brigade party and later buried in Albert Communal Cemetery.

About four hours before the brigades of 2nd Division began their move towards the Albert-Bapaume road, Brigadier General Elles of the Tank Corps had witnessed the scenes on the old Roman road. He telephoned GOC 2 Tank Brigade and instructed him to gather as many serviceable tanks, crews, and support personnel as possible to mobilise the tanks and also to establish Lewis gun positions further down the road towards Albert. Elles explained: "Our own infantry [are] demoralised and [are] retiring without apparently fighting." That may, of course, have been true in regard to many men but was probably not the case for most of those who fought their way back from the front lines of the Flesquières Salient to the Bapaume–Péronne road. Amongst some of those trudging westwards were elements of 17th Division.

Major General Robertson's 17th Division had had a busy day on 24 March. The activity had begun in the early hours when V Corps instructed the division to hold the Red Line from a little north of Mesnil to about Barastre. It was told 47th Division was holding Mesnil. At 0500, corps told DHQ to send 51 Brigade, which was then at Villers-au-Flos, to the south of Sailly-Saillisel. There it was to come under the command of the London Division and be prepared to support either the right of V Corps or the left of VII Corps. DHQ next received the message warning that 50 Brigade was to undertake the proposed counter-attack against Bus. As we know this order was quickly rescinded. This cancellation came at the same time as another which changed the orders for 51 Brigade. Because corps HQ had no idea where 47th Division actually was, 51 Brigade was now to fill a gap between Rocquigny and Sailly and get in touch with 9th Division. Brigadier General Bond's units moved forward and took up a line from 600 yards due south of Rocquigny south-westwards to the Bapaume-Peronne road some 800 yards from the northern end of Sailly-Saillisel. It was in touch with 52 Brigade in Rocquigny where there were also some troops of 47th Division. On the right it pushed south-eastwards from the main road and made contact with some troops of 9th Division. The contact was, however, brief because 9th Division continued its withdrawal westwards. The right of 51 Brigade was then pulled back to the Bapaume-Péronne road about halfway between Le Transloy and Sailly-Saillisel.

Having been relieved of making the counter-attack against Bus, 50 Brigade was next told to hold a stretch of a line north-south from 1,000 yards due east of Rocquigny to 1,200 yards north-east of Barastre. This was a length of almost 4,000 yards. The objective was to cover the withdrawal of 2nd Division and the RND to the Red Line. Within an hour of spreading out its battalions as best it could the enemy attacked the line. On this occasion it was repulsed but another attack against the right of 51 Brigade and against Loon Copse had turned the flank. In the view of DHQ this latest attack confirmed the belief that "47th Division had ceased to exist" and that 51 Brigade was now the right of Third Army. Late on 23 March, and at the entreaty of 9th Division, GHQ had instructed Third Army that *it* had the responsibility of maintaining contact with 9th Division. The latter was already technically in what was V Corps' area and wanted to reduce its front in order to close the gaps between its own brigades. General Byng was told that at 0400 on 24 March, 26 Brigade, whether it had been relieved or not by V Corps, would leave its position close to Government Farm and move south. Byng instructed V Corps to fill the space and to hold from Government Farm to the Green Line "with the greatest determination." It was to be the task of the London Division to fill that space. When 26 Brigade made its move, what constituted the right of the dispersed 47th Division was still some two miles to the north-east of Government Farm.

At dawn of 24 March, 51 Brigade had no idea where 9th Division was, and knew only that some units of 47th Division were in Rocquigny and had attached themselves to 52 Brigade.

Neither did V Corps have any firm information about where other elements of 47th Division might be. It despatched a hopeful message soon after midday ordering the division to move any troops it may have collected to a line Sailly-Saillisel -Combles and to cover all roads running through that line. By that time, the enemy was already through Combles, had occupied Morval, and was moving towards Lesboeufs. To the north, at 1400, 50 Brigade reported that 2nd Division and the RND had passed through the Red Line and that the brigade itself was retiring. At 1430, and with the enemy beyond Bapaume, V Corps instructed 17th Division to extricate itself from what had become virtually a salient and make for a line Montauban-Bazentin-le-Grand. Given how far the enemy was now behind its brigades, DHQ decided this was impossible. When this was pointed out to corps HQ, Lieutenant General Fanshawe told DHQ to work out itself what was practicable. Orders were issued at 1530 whereby 50 Brigade, which had already reached Beaulencourt, was to pass through Gueudecourt and take up a position on the Ginchy road facing south-east; 51 Brigade was to act as rearguard around Le Transloy whilst 52 Brigade passed through en route for Flers; 51 Brigade would then follow and assemble at Gueudecourt. The pioneers and field companies were also to concentrate close to Gueudecourt. All three brigades were then to move to a line Bazentin-le-Grand – Martinpuich.

As evening fell confusion reigned as the brigades tried to make their way back. In Brigadier General Yatman's 50 Brigade the withdrawal of 6/Dorset and 7/East Yorks from Rocquigny was assisted by tanks. Both battalions reached Gueudecourt and then Le Sars. The third battalion, 10/West Yorks, had split into two groups. Two companies with Lieutenant Colonel Simner were attacked by "hordes" of Germans near Eaucourt L'Abbaye. Simner was presumably captured and the 60 survivors of the 150 men were then divided between the Dorset or the East Yorks. At Le Sars, Brigadier General Eden had learned of the new corps line and placed his 52 Brigade between 2nd Division and the RND. The battalions of 51 Brigade withdrew through Le Sars and then, after 7/Border had been scattered by a British barrage, took position on what was probably the ridge between Longueval and Bazentin. In 52 Brigade, 10/LF was also split into two groups. One of the parties, of about six officers and 200 ORs, reached Flers by the evening and then went into a line east of Martinpuich. When 12/Manchester was ordered to retire and rendezvous at Flers the men had to cross a road barraged by four field and several machine guns. CSM Lamb was awarded the DCM for having rescued the wounded Lieutenant Addison from the road. Lamb carried Addision away first in a discovered barrow, then on a bicycle, and finally on his back until he found an aid post. As the diarist wrote, however, the German guns "should have wiped out the battalion." Some dozens did make it across and reached Flers. It was apparent at Flers that the battalion would soon be surrounded so it moved on to Martinpuich. At 0400 on 25 March, it was in contact with brigade HQ and rejoined the other two battalions at the crossroads south of Courcelette on the Albert-Bapaume road. The transport section had dumped the day's rations there in anticipation, but another unit had requisitioned them. It was now that the bonus of the rations left by the departing heavy gunners at the Rocquigny camp came into their own. Together with 9/Dukes, which had experienced "overwhelming difficulties" on its way back, the Manchester went into the line near Pozières. The 17th Division remained active in the area around Albert and the Ancre until it was finally relieved on 3 April. By 7 April it was in the rear areas of Halloy and Canaples for rest and recuperation.

When Brigadier General Hutchison, GOC 190 Brigade of the RND had reported to his DHQ in the early morning of 24 March that the situation on his right was "becoming serious," he was told to hold his position. Hutchison informed corps HQ during the night of his concern about the absence of 47th Division and politely suggested that the London Division "should be asked to restore touch" with 190 Brigade. Major General Gorringe's division was in no state to do that. The situation about the Bertincourt Salient had become impossible and a withdrawal from the Green to Red Line had become inevitable. The Germans attacked at dawn along the front which lay east of a line Rocquigney–Barastre – Villers-au-Flos just as the brigades were about to retire. Hutchison's two forward battalions east of Rocquigny, 4/Bedford and the Artists Rifles, were almost surrounded and had great difficulty disengaging. They did so only after some severe hand-to-hand fighting and joined the third unit, 7/RF, at Beaulencourt. The battalions of 189 Brigade close to Bertincourt also had to fight their way free of the enemy. The best part of two companies of 2/RMLI were cut off or captured but the remainder, with 1/RMLI and Anson Battalion which had been in support behind the village, regrouped at Le Transloy *sucrerie*. Although attacked, the three units of 189 Brigade were not so heavily engaged. Hood Battalion was in the line just to the rear of the railway cutting in Ytres and Hawke still to the north-west of Bus. The two foremost battalions may not have received the order to retire but had an easier task; they passed north of Barastre and through 52 Brigade occupying the Red Line. They assembled with the other two brigades between Beaulencourt and Le Transloy, east of the Bapaume -Péronne road. All three brigades had, however, suffered severe losses. Of the 26 officers and 400 ORs of two days earlier, Hood's fighting strength was recorded as 11 and 140 respectively.

There was little time to rest because corps orders arrived instructing the division to retire to the Bazentin-le-Grand Line. As masses of Germans were reported to be through Morval and close to Lesboeufs, Major General Lawrie decided to withdraw to a line Martinpuich – Bazentin-le-Petit. Huts, water points and anything else which might have provided shelter or succour to the enemy were destroyed. At 1530, the three brigade columns moved off. A reserve of 12 machine guns kept in Lesboeufs was activated and for four hours kept the pursuing Germans at bay as the infantry columns, each supported by artillery, pioneers and sappers, moved westwards. The old Somme battlefields proved difficult for the field artillery to traverse, and several guns had to be ditched. Corps orders arrived in the late afternoon instructing the division to man a line High Wood–Eaucourt-L'Abbaye. The London Division was to be on its right and, as we saw, 52 Brigade appeared on its left. There was some "panic" amongst several parties of gunners and infantry when a strong German patrol in High Wood fired on them as they "rushed" through Drake Battalion's lines. Despite this incident the night was fairly quiet.

The morning of 25 March brought yet more attacks and withdrawals across the wilderness of collapsing trenches, shell holes, and wire of the old Somme battlefield. Drake Battalion even made a counter-attack in an effort to distance the enemy and captured two machine guns in the process. But the pressure remained intense and by stages, covered by rearguards provided by the machine gun battalion, the division, often with its flanks in the air, withdrew across the Ancre. Coincidentally this same area had been the scene of the division's first actions on the Western Front in late 1916. On 26 March, the west bank between the southern end of Aveluy Wood and the bridge at Hamel became the division's sector. The division was gradually relieved by the recently arrived 12th Division. Even so 188 Brigade had still to make a successful counter-attack to retake Mesnil and clear a section of Aveluy Wood in the early hours of 27 March. Later in the morning, 190 Brigade also had to restore the line near to the railway north of Albert. By the evening of 28 March, the RND had been relieved and was on its way at least temporarily to the rear.

During the course of the retreat the RND criticised the London Division for what it considered was poor liaison and for making decisions about withdrawals without consulting with, or informing, the RND. For its part, 47th Division criticised the RND for precisely the same reasons. If blame is to be apportioned both divisions were probably equally culpable. In the same way as did all divisions and brigades during the first five or six days of the withdrawal, both formations had lost a significant degree of cohesion. It was difficult enough for GOsC to remain in contact with their own brigades, and brigades with their battalions; trying to maintain contact with those of other formations on the flanks was even more problematic. The difficulties really began once the divisions retired from the Metz Switch; they were exacerbated by the withdrawal from the Bertincourt Salient and when 26 Brigade of 9th Division drew back from Government Farm. At this stage the battle evolved into one of open warfare which made communications between formations and units even more complicated. It took something like four hours for Brigadier General Bailey, GOC 142 Brigade, to learn that his battalions had withdrawn from Bertincourt and well on their way to Rocquigny.

When Bailey subsequently heard that his 142 Brigade had reached Rocquigny he ordered it to form a line facing south-east across the Bapaume–Péronne road about midway between Le Transloy and Sailly-Sallisel. By the time 142 Brigade had formed the line, 141 Brigade reported enemy forces were in Mesnil and were advancing westwards to its north and south. If Brigadier General Mildren's brigade was forced to withdraw it was instructed to take a position on the Lesboeufs–Le Transloy road west of the latter village. At 0900 on 24 March, 141 Brigade was at least in touch with 51 Brigade holding a section of line between Rocquigny and Sailly. In case the line did not hold, V Corps issued instructions at 1030 that the route for the division's withdrawal should be via Lesboeufs and Longueval to Albert. If that route proved to be impossible, which to all intents and purposes it already was, it was to go via Gueudecourt. As events were to prove few of the units were to receive the orders until after the withdrawal had begun.

In the early morning of 24 March two battalions of 140 Brigade held a trench of about 200 yards in length south-east of Rocquigny on the road to Equancourt. The third battalion of 140 Brigade was a little to the west where it was in touch with 20/London of 141 Brigade. The support company of 1/R.Berks of 99 Brigade was also in the immediate vicinity south of the village. The enemy was seen massing to the north and north-east of Mesnil; once they came within range of the rifles and Lewis guns of 140 and 141 Brigades the first attack faltered. Later attacks on the right around midday forced back 10/Sherwood of 51 Brigade, which had come up during the morning, and fought their way into the south-west corner of Rocquigny. This allowed the Germans to enfilade 18th and 19/London from the right. Under intense fire these battalions were compelled to withdraw to the edge of the village but appear to have regained touch with the Sherwood. The brigade's left battalion, 20/London, was in touch with 12/Manchester of 52 Brigade. The two COs agreed to support each other and to endeavour to defend the positions held. Three tanks arrived from behind the Manchester and whilst they cruised about the Germans fled. Once they departed, however, the attacks resumed.

In the afternoon, 140 Brigade could hold no longer. Field guns and machine guns poured fire into the village from the open ground to its east. When, according to a later report the RND on its left began to retire, the brigade decided to conform. The Blackheath and Woolwich Battalion fought a rearguard while the London Irish and St Pancras Battalions disengaged. Eventually the remnants of the brigade fell back, harassed all the way by shell fire and low flying enemy aircraft through Le Transloy and Gueudecourt. They rendezvoused in the evening at High

Wood. When it also withdrew from Rocquigny, 141 Brigade involuntarily split into two groups. The larger of the two held on until 1400 but then pulled back towards Le Transloy. There, the troops became intermingled with those of 17th Division. The smaller force fought on until 1530 before also withdrawing. When the party approached Le Transloy it saw German patrols within the village so skirted around it to the north. The third brigade, 142, had spent most of the day in its position across the main road mid-way between Le Transloy and Sailly-Saillisel.

Orders to withdraw did not reach all units and companies but Brigadier General Bailey met with at least one GOC brigade of the RND and agreed to withdraw in unison. They headed north-westwards with the intention of moving towards High Wood. When orders did finally catch up with the brigade it was already marching very much in the stipulated direction. On the way, Brigadier General Bailey and his brigade staff were captured close to Delville Wood. On the right of the brigade, 24/London became separated from the other two battalions and also split into two parties. Finally, earlier in the day the pioneers of 4/SWB, 34 Brigade RFA, sappers from the field companies, and a section of No.11 Motor Machine Gun Battalion had been sent to guard the Lesboeufs–Ginchy road. The road was full of transport trying to escape before the route was cut. The mixed group held its ground and stopped several attacks until the final wagons had passed over the Ginchy crossroads. They also then withdrew towards High Wood and took position to its south along the Longueval–Bazentin road. By midnight of 24 March, two of the brigades were in Bazentin-le-Petit; 142 Brigade and the pioneers with their group were at High Wood. There were some troops of the RND on the left, but these were not in touch with their own division. As one of the two parties of 24/London passed High Wood the men saw the divisional memorial constructed in September 1916 in memory of its ferocious battle inside the wood. The battalion diarist noted the exhaustion of the men and the fact that some of them had marched 14 miles that day. The *Official History* makes the point that when they had crossed the devastated area the troops had been led to believe there were fresh troops waiting to relieve them. As they tried to get some sleep and warmth the men realised their assumption was mistaken. Their ordeal was clearly not yet over.

The war diary of V Corps for 25 March contains scattered peremptory orders and messages to its formations insisting, for example, that they must hold and "must dispute ground," and that "under no circumstances" should 47th Division retire to La Boiselle ridge. It also has texts saying that if they are forced back across the Ancre, 47th and 63rd Divisions "must" secure certain river crossing points. The fresh 1st Cavalry and 12th Divisions were arriving in the area, but it is clear from the diaries that the situation, especially at the junction of Third and Fifth Armies, was still extremely precarious and that uncertainty about what might happen next was widespread.

The early morning brought some shuffling of remnants and attempts to make contact on either flank with recognised brigades rather than merely dispersed units. The division concentrated on the Contalmaison ridge which it considered to be a "very strong position." Further work was done on it in the expectation that it was to be held for at least the day. One attack was broken up and "severe" casualties inflicted on Germans attempting to debouch from Bazentin Wood on the right. A flurry of messages to and from V Corps during the afternoon caused some consternation and protests on the grounds that what was being asked was simply impossible to achieve with the number of troops available. As far as the London Division was concerned, it was again the RND which caused it to withdraw from its "strong" position. At about 1800, RND units on the left began to withdraw. In view of what he believed to be a critical situation, Major General

Gorringe assumed command of the recently arrived 12th Division's 37 Brigade and ordered it to counter-attack and retake Pozières. Before the attack could take place, V Corps learned that the RND had begun crossing to the west bank of the Ancre. The counter-attack was cancelled and 37 Brigade deployed to try to link the London and Royal Naval Divisions. The momentum of withdrawal was, however, still gathering pace and just before midnight V Corps HQ conceded the inevitable and ordered a general retirement across the river. The London Division crossed near Aveluy covered by 37 Brigade. That night, 12th Division took command of that sector of front and 47th Division withdrew. After six days of almost constant fighting and marching the troops were to have a couple of days of respite. It was not yet over, and the still much weakened division was soon to return to the line in Aveluy. But for at least a few precious hours there was the opportunity to eat, sleep and wash.

The area to the north-east of Mesnil-en-Arrouaise where the much dispersed troops of 141 Brigade and elements of 51 and 52 Brigades fought desperate delaying actions on 24 March 1918.

Taken from Four Winds Farm looking north-east over Five Points Cemetery (centre right), to Vallulart Wood and the site of the former Hayettes Wood beyond. The buildings comprising what is today known as Gare, close to the canal's southern portal, are on the right.

From Vallulart Wood above the southern portal of the canal east-south-east towards the area cut by Mouettes Trench. This was originally part of a German trench system and was used in turn by both sides. By September 1918 it was part of the system known to the British as the Ytres-Equancourt Line.

The present day remains of Dessart Wood from the D55 north of Fins are centre left. Dessart Ridge Switch ran right to left in front of the camera and then joined with Metz Switch a little further to the north. The March 1918 southern boundary of V Corps with VII Corps ran roughly parallel to the switch a few hundred yards further to its east.

Looking north-west on the D55 Equancourt – Neuville Bourjonval road from about where Neuville Switch joined the Green Line in March 1918. Ytres church is centre. The line of trees in the foreground marks where the northern end of Hayettes Wood once reached.

From the northern end of Dessart Switch to the east of Metz showing part of Winchester valley and Gouzeaucourt Wood. The D7 (which becomes the D29B east of the wood) is just visible in the centre. Metz Switch ran through the camera position, which is close to the communal and British cemeteries. In March 1918, 47th Division fought hard here in the switch to stem the enemy advance; in September the New Zealanders advanced across the area with 38th Division on their right.

The pre-war railway forked about 800 yards east-north-east of Delsaux Farm. The southern fork crossed the road here 1,200 yards west of Lebucquière and ran on down to beyond Ytres. The western edge of Vélu Wood can be seen in the centre. German troops debouching from the wood in March 1918 were cut down in swathes by machine guns on this slight ridge and by artillery in the Green Line to their rear.

The old railway embankment to the east of Vélu Wood. The original trestle bridge over the track was probably destroyed by the Germans during their withdrawal to the Hindenburg Line. Its stone replacement was constructed post-war. It was from the embankment that two companies of 7/A&SH fought their dogged rearguard in March and close to where both Captains James and Gribble won their Victoria Crosses.

The site of Bruno Mill, with Doignies church centre. On 21 March 1918 hundreds of Germans were killed as they advanced towards Hermies Switch by crews of a pair of machine guns of 25 Bn MGC positioned on the mill's ruins.

Spoil Heap on the west bank of the canal east of Hermies was a major German strong point both once the advance to the Hindenburg Line was halted and again in September 1918. Its garrisons caused significant Allied casualties during the offensives and the more routine life of trench warfare.

Yorkshire Bank was another of the canal's spoil heaps. Today is it cut by the A26 *péage.* From 1917 it was riddled with British dug outs and command posts. There are a few lumps of concrete on its surface but these appear to come from a date later than the Great War.

The north-west corner of Maricourt Wood in the valley running south-west from Lagnicourt- Marcel. The Wingate Memorial is behind the camera, with the position of the important Vaulx Trench, part of the March 1918 Battle Zone, running in front of the wood and across the valley to the site of the former Vaulx Wood. In this sector, Vaulx Wood Switch ran along the valley to link Lagnicourt village defences with Vaulx Trench. This trench crossed Vaulx Wood's northern face. Vaulx-Vraucourt lies in the lower ground beyond the ridge in the far distance.

Looking from about the position of Lark Post south-east to Boursies. The post marked the boundary between 6th and 51st Divisions on 21 March 1918. The Hindenburg Line south of Pronville lay about 1,800 yards to the north of the post.

Part of the complex of sunken lanes on the north side of the Hirondelle valley a few hundred yards east of Noreuil. On 2 September 1918, 2/Royal Scots and 1/RSF suffered heavily as they tried to clear enemy garrisons from the dugouts and posts lining the lanes. The track climbing the hill on the opposite side of the valley leads into Lagnicourt.

This partly sunken track runs south past Noreuil Australian Cemetery to join the D36 west of Lagnicourt. The area just north of the junction was known to the British as Dunelm. It was something of a strong point protecting the western exits from Lagnicourt and had a communication trench linking it with the important Lagnicourt Trench to the east.

The valley of the Hirondelle between Noreuil and Vaulx-Vraucourt. Vraucourt Copse is in the right distance. The pre-war broad gauge railway ran along the flat land just beneath the bank. In March 1918 the valley marked the boundary between 59th and 6th Divisions, and thus also the boundary between VI and IV Corps.

The Hirondelle west of Noreuil. Today this path offers a pleasant, shaded walk between Vaulx-Vraucourt and Noreuil. On 21 March 1918 it was the scene of confused and desperate fighting between the advancing Germans and troops of 6th Division.

The Hog's Back, with the shrouded church tower of Ecoust-St-Mein in the centre distance. On 21 March, hundreds of Germans were cut down on this plateau by machine guns and artillery of 59th Division. The ill-fated counter-attack by two battalions of 177 Brigade also crossed the area as they advanced over their division's Battle Zone towards Ecoust and Noreuil.

Frequently used as a brigade HQ and an assembly area, Judas Farm lies to the north side of the Sensée valley and west of St-Léger. Today's farm complex is significantly larger than the original but the route of the old railway and its embankment can still be seen to its north and east.

St-Léger Wood from the south. The TGV and the *péage* are off camera to the right. The lane goes under the two and connects with the track climbing from Croisilles British Cemetery.

With Favreuil church central, this shows the ground crossed in August 1918 by troops of 111 Brigade in the somewhat confusing attack on the trench west of the village. The tree on the extreme left lines the lane linking Sapignies to Favreuil down which 2/4th Dukes may also have advanced.

The land north-east of Ervillers as it begins to climb towards St-Léger. It was in this lower ground that troops of 34th and 40th Divisions tried to reorganise on 23-24 March, and from where 13/East Surrey assembled for its attack on Mory. Guardsmen of 4 Guards Brigade held the ground on the slope to the right.

The copse in the centre lies immediately north of the D36 linking Mory with Ervillers. The southern end of the latter village on the D917 is seen beyond the trees. The copse did not exist before the war and grows on what was then very heavily contested land during the March Offensive. Exhausted remnants of 31st and 40th Divisions garrisoned hastily dug slit trenches and shell holes on the slope immediately east of Ervillers.

Ervillers from the south. The lane was crossed by Bee Wood Trench and Bee Wood Support as they reached down towards Béhagnies. In March 1918 this area was defended by remnants of 40th and 41st Divisions and later by 125 and 126 Brigades of 42nd Division.

By German standards Sapignies cemetery is small. This sometimes untidy site contains the graves of 1,550 soldiers. Most of those troops interred in the mass grave died in March and April 1918.

The spire of Biefvillers church is left of centre. The photo looks across from the quarry close to the junction of the track running down from Sapignies to the D10E3. In March 1918 the fields here were cut by quickly dug trenches manned by units largely of 41st and 25th Divisions. In late August that year, troops of, 2nd, 37th and 62nd Division assembled in and around the village for their attacks on Sapignies and Favreuil.

The higher ground to the east of Bucquoy, with the dark mass of Logeast Wood in the left distance. This was the area held for a short time by 62nd Division on 25 March. Its defence allowed remnants of 41st Division to pass to the rear. The enemy poured out of Logeast Wood in hot pursuit.

The Cojuel valley from between Douchy and Ayette. On 28 March 2/Grenadier Guards of 4 Guards Brigade, 31st Division, halted an attack on Douchy by Germans advancing down the valley towards the camera.

From west of Courcelles looking north-east from the British position known as the Milk Work on the D12. Ridge Work was to the left on the ploughed field, with Coffee Redoubt further over and to the right. Moyenneville lies on the other side of the high ground on which the RFC established an airfield in 1917.

Railway Cutting Cemetery, west-south-west of Gomiécourt. The cemetery holds the graves of men of 2nd and 3rd Divisions killed in August 1918. The cutting was an important rallying point and command centre in March and August 1918. Its banks were mined for dugouts by both German and British forces.

Taken from the lower slope of the Gomiécourt ridge looking north by east towards Ervillers. The village church is central. This is the ground defended by battalions of 42nd Division in March 1918 and the scene of offensive actions by tanks and troops of 2nd and 3rd Division in August. Bee Wood was about in the centre of the photograph nestled on the bank which is marked by the broken line of trees running across the ground left to right.

Lt Gen A. Haldane, VI Corps.

Lt Gen C. Shute, V Corps April-November 1918.

Lt Gen C. Jacob, II Corps.

Lt Gen G. Harper, IV Corps.

Lt Gen E.A. Fanshawe, V Corps August 1916-April 1918

Lt Gen I. Maxse, XVIII Corps.

Lt Gen Sir W. Birdwood, I ANZAC Corps.

Maj Gen C.E. Lawrie, 63rd Royal Naval Division.

Maj Gen C. Romer, 59th Division.

Maj Gen G. Gorringe, 47th Division.

Maj Gen G.P. Fielding, Guards Division.

Maj Gen G. Jeffries, 19th Division.

Maj Gen C. Deverell, 3rd Division.

Maj Gen G. Barrow, 7th Division.

Maj Gen G. Bainbridge, 25th Division.

Maj Gen Sir J. Ponsonby, 40th Division.

Maj Gen T. Cubitt, 38th Division.

Maj Gen W. Braithwaite, 62nd Division.

10

Losing the Wastelands: Conclusion

Brigadier General Kennedy, GOC 140 Brigade, concluded his account of the six-day withdrawal with the observation: "During the whole of this fighting the brigade always held its own and in every case where withdrawals were made they had to be done in order to conform to our flanks that had been pushed in." These, or words very similar were echoed by almost all units and formations in post-battle reports. Rarely was it acknowledged that a withdrawal was entirely or solely because the writer's own unit or formation had failed to halt an enemy assault. Conforming to the movement of others was the default position in almost all accounts.

It is completely understandable that no battalion, brigade or divisional scribe would want to paint his unit or formation in a lesser light. The period was one of great drama, crisis, and trauma. Although Third Army had lost the Wastelands and suffered huge casualties, it did eventually stem the German tempest. Thousands of its men had been captured, some of whom were perhaps not unhappy to be out of danger *pro tem,* while others had endured and continued to fight despite overwhelming fatigue and the loss of comrades. Some divisions had spent longer in battle than others but all those that were engaged during the initial week of the enemy offensive, and particularly after the first day, faced similar difficulties and problems. Many units drew attention to these in reports composed both whilst the battle continued or in its aftermath. The extent of the reflection depended very much on the GOC or CO and, of course, on their own interpretation of what did happen. Many of those in command arrived during the operation to replace casualties and would thus perhaps have a less rounded picture of how the crisis evolved; others managed to remain in command for its duration and were able to assess it from a wider perspective. Most, however, recognised that certain aspects of the battle were common to all.

As it had been since before Third Ypres the primary concern for commanders was the lack of a consistently reliable means of communication. The inability to stay in touch and report what was happening from all parts of a division's and corps' front to senior commanders was, naturally enough, greatly accentuated during the period of open and mobile warfare. Because they were awkward to extricate and transport, power buzzers and amplifiers were of little use once the withdrawal began; wireless was generally good until shelling destroyed wireless stations and aerials; pigeons were unreliable; visual signalling useless in the morning mist and when shelling threw up clouds of dust and smoke. Signal company officers had long complained that the infantry had become too reliant on the telephone. Lines were continually being cut and the casualties amongst personnel attempting to repair them heavy. An additional difficulty was that when the offensive began several divisional signal companies were only at about 40 percent of establishment. Despatch riders (DRs) were used especially between corps and divisional headquarters but their limited number, the clogged and damaged roads, and the lack of spare parts for the motorcycles meant that they could not cope with the sheer number of orders issued and were often too slow in delivering them. Several divisions formed a mounted detachment of one officer and up to 15 ORs. The Highland Division put great store in its detachment and suggested all units and formations should create a similar section. It believed the value of the horse for reconnaissance and communications had "decayed" in trench warfare, with one senior officer recording his astonishment in not seeing one mounted officer during the withdrawal through Bapaume. He concluded that was the reason why officers looked as exhausted as their men. Most headquarters at different levels still relied on the vulnerable runner as their principal means of communication. One officer of 51st Division wrote that commanders should never underestimate the value of well trained runners. He believed they were "the one absolutely reliable means of communication between brigades and battalions."

Inconsistent and unreliable communications, of course, impacted heavily on how well commanders could influence the battle. It made sense during the withdrawal that those infantry brigade HQ that could, sholuld operate from the same dugout. Many were thought to be located too far forward because when the front fell back, HQ had to conform. Valuable and perhaps crucial time was subsequently lost when runners and DRs were unable to locate the new HQ. When they were not under enemy observation, HQ were instructed to show flags and lamps so that they could be found more easily. They, and the more local report centres, were also urged to fall back along existing and selected telephone lines; the fewer separated HQ there were, the fewer lines needed to be kept under repair. For practical reasons it was also thought sensible for infantry brigade HQ to house the OC of their attached artillery group and their own section of "Q" Branch. There were also instances of two DHQ sharing a command dugout: 19th and 51st Divisions used a common facility for two days behind Bapaume. Joint occupation allowed actions to be more easily coordinated, especially those on divisional boundaries. This proximity of staffs was thought to be particularly invaluable when attempting to establish which roads should be used by which division's transport, guns, and troops. Such liaison was ideal when it could be organised but that was not always possible. During the chaos of 23-24 March there are several tales of GOC brigades and their brigade majors riding around the congested rear areas hoping to bump into other GOsC of their own divisions or separated parties of men of their own brigade's battalions. If chance did allow them to locate one or more of their fellow GOsC, and if they actually knew where some of their units were, a degree of concerted action could be attempted.

Commanders were sometimes criticised for being too sensitive about losing contact with units on their flanks. It was always a major concern in trench warfare and, understandably, during the withdrawal the anxiety deepened. The RND was out of touch with both flanks for 24 hrs from 25-26 March. Its diarist noted rather innocently, "The reason for this is not known." It was believed the result of such ignorance was that good positions, even if well defended, could be turned more easily. DHQ suggested that each division should place on each flank echeloned posts to the rear in an outward direction. Such a practice would consequently make it easier to maintain contact with adjoining units because it would make it harder for the enemy to out-flank the division. If contact was lost, the number of stragglers increased, and troops' confidence and morale dropped. Other suggestions about how contact could be maintained were for the corps reconnaissance squadron permanently to patrol the flanks and for troops on the flanks to use a system of indicator lights. This was a method used by the Germans and one much admired by British officers. The Highland Division suggested that each brigade's signal section should have ready access to a cable wagon. Some but not all divisions had extemporised such a vehicle and considered them useful. When available, contact aircraft did prove useful but, for example, although troops of 6th Division had flares to attract the attention of pilots and observers no aircraft were seen above the division on 21 March. Overall, the RFC is little mentioned in the war diaries. One aircraft was acknowledged to have done valuable work in protecting disorganised troops near Serre, but most mentions noted the absence rather than the assistance of the British air component. The diarist of 51st Division believed that pilots should be trained in close support tactics so that they could eliminate forward enemy field guns.

The lack of information certainly had a negative effect on many of the defenders and on their morale. On 22 March the diarist of 1/R.Berks noted "many disquieting rumours were rife [and that] rumours of disaster were generally prevalent." The following day he recorded, "We have absolutely no official enlightenment as to the true situation." On 24 March, HQ of 1/KRR admitted, "We had almost given up any hope of receiving orders" [about a withdrawal from the Bertincourt Salient]. The only reliable answer to the ongoing problem of a lack of lateral and depth communications was the availability of buried cable. Where it existed, it largely survived the shelling but there was simply not enough of it in the right places. One officer in 6th Division gloomily suggested that rather than having had men digging reserve positions for the artillery, time and effort in the pre-offensive period would have been better expended in burying cables.

Opinion was somewhat divided on how the artillery had performed. Generally, it was thought to have done well in covering the withdrawal, often with 18 pdrs firing over open sights and only limbering up or destroying their guns when the enemy infantry was almost upon them. The two HA batteries attached to each division were also thought generally to have done well. It was those batteries held under corps command, or rather how they were used, which attracted the most criticism. They were accused of having withdrawn too quickly and of failing to inform the infantry that they were going. They were regularly thought to have fired short and to have consistently ignored pleas to increase their range. They were not, however, the only batteries thought to have done that. Furthermore, when the enemy opened his barrage on 21 March, the RFA brigades of 6th Division fired on their SOS lines which were largely on no man's land. There was no infantry assault for about three hours and when the enemy did eventually advance the division's protective and SOS barrages had reduced in intensity. On several sectors of the front the SOS barrages were considered to be so thin that many infantry officers reported they had no idea whether it was being fired or not.

DHQ 31st Division advocated the need for significantly more observation posts and, in order to avoid the danger of firing short, that RFA batteries should not target within 700 yards of their front until the fall of shot had been observed and reported back. Heavies, it was argued, should leave 1,500 yards when firing blind. This might have worked in periods of static trench warfare but maintaining barrage accuracy and safety during a war of movement posed difficulties for gunners and infantry. The brigades of 51st Division were accused of not landing one shell on Germans massing in Louverval Wood, despite repeated requests, throughout the whole of 21 March. Nor did they shell the enemy traffic on the Cambrai road. There was also widely thought to have been a "noticeable absence" of artillery support between 23-25 March, while the London Division wrote of their artillery support as being "uneven." In contrast, another division recorded that the artillery assistance afforded the infantry "cannot be over-estimated." There were so many targets that the divisional artillery simply could not cope with them all and there were times when fire was reduced in case re-supply was not possible. On 24 March the RND warned that unless lorries could get up overnight to replenish stocks their artillery might have to cease fire. There were shell stocks at Pozières and Courcelette and loads were lorried up in time to keep the guns firing. Throughout the period most batteries reported they had sufficient shells for immediate use but did admit to having husbanded stocks from time to time. There were significant losses of guns in the divisions on 21 March so even if there were sufficient available shells the intensity of the barrages were frequently diminished.

There was considerable thought given in the post-battle reports to the tactics used by the enemy to break into the forward and successive defensive zones. There was widespread admiration at the way the first, thin, wave of troops armed with light and heavy machine guns swept through the destroyed wire and obliterated trenches. If resistance was shown they moved round its flanks and pressed on. There were rarely more than two men to a machine gun and empty belt boxes were quickly rushed to the rear, re-filled and brought forward. The attackers made good use of shell holes and were swift to bring up light trench mortars and *flammenwerfer*. Snipers and heavy machine guns then gave covering fire for the advance of the second waves. Field artillery was brought forward with the third wave and used to good effect often from the former no man's land against strong points and defended posts. In the dense early morning fog of 21 March many British troops, however, would not have realised they were being first assailed by storm troops and then by more conventional infantry. What did surprise the British as the days wore on was the profligacy with which the German High Command was prepared to expend its troops. Often the infantry advanced in what were almost Napoleonic columns. British artillery and machine-gun fire ripped them apart causing huge casualties. There are stories of great piles of enemy dead in front of the British wire, with their comrades stepping Agincourt-like over the growing heaps of corpses. The concentrated masses tended to advance along the high ground with skirmishers moving in the valleys. This was not always the case, however, as 6th Division found to its cost when hordes of the enemy came along Cornhill valley. It was quickly realised by the British that instead of leading their platoons, German officers tended to be in the rear driving their men forward. It was assumed this tactic was used because officers would better see where there had been breaks and were then able then to push or dribble their men through.

While there was general admiration of the ways and means by which the offensive was begun, there was a sense that the British had themselves facilitated the German success. This self-examination usually concentrated on the lack of training of the British troops and on the defensive system adopted by the BEF. Although Third Army had occupied its stretch of front longer than Fifth, some divisions' fronts were still inherently linear. Brigadier General Hugh Bethell of 74 Brigade, 25th Division, although something of a maverick, considered, "Continuous lines of trenches should be henceforth as extinct as the Dodo." Strong points and redoubts had been added but there were still too many machine-gun positions not housed in champagne emplacements or deep dugouts. The Forward Zones were not as strongly held as some of those in Fifth Army, but the paralyzing power and intensity of the bombardment and the speed of the enemy advance was sufficient to kill or capture large numbers. With the inadequate number of buried cables linking forward observation posts and battalion HQ with batteries, the enemy was quickly into the rear of the Forward Zone. Overwhelming numbers told but so did the layout of the trenches.

The shortage of labour in the winter and early spring had meant that efforts were concentrated on the strong points and emplacements in the Forward and front of the Battle Zones rather than on the Support Line of the Battle Zone. What had been needed, and it was obvious once the enemy was through, was for all communication trenches to have been fire-stepped on both sides, wired, and thus easily converted into switches. They should also have been dug at obtuse angles rather than as more or less direct but zigzagged lines between the front and rear trenches. This would have allowed fire to be brought against attacks which did not come from the expected due east direction. The front trenches also tended to have too much spoil on their parados and parapet; fire could thus really only be directed to the front rather than in enfilade along the zones in front or rear of the trenches. Major General Carter-Campbell argued that defence schemes should be devised by corps rather than by division. His division's trench lines matched with those of 6th Division but not with 17th Division of V Corps to its south. The Beaumetz-Morchies Line should, he stressed, have been continued into V Corps sector. Rather more coherently, in his assessment Brigadier General Burn, GOC 152 Brigade, believed the fault lay in there being no *Army* system for trench layout. He wrote that there was no "policy or plan" for the positioning or construction of trenches, or even for a standardised trench design. Furthermore, work done by one division was often undone by another. The consequences of the lack of a system and poorly constructed trenches were, he thought, "Our enormous casualties… misery…inefficiency…and sickness." There were not enough deep platoon-sized dugouts – 6th Division, for example, claimed 24 of its platoons had no cover – and there should have been more double line systems like the Beaumetz – Morchies Line along the entire front of Third and Fifth Armies. If there had been, he riled, "The Germans would not now be nearing Amiens." Strangely, perhaps, one of the GOC's own battalion commanders disagreed with Burn's views on deep dugouts. The CO of 6/Seaforth Highlanders believed "too many deep dugouts seem to be death traps." Brigadier General Walker, GOC 16 Brigade, wanted more deep dugouts and believed that if there were too few for a trench garrison when a bombardment started the men should be ordered out of the trench and secure what cover they could to its front and rear. Trenches should not be regarded as an actual line of resistance, he wrote, but as a means of "providing living accommodation in the immediate vicinity" of the battle area. Rather than deep dugouts being so, he considered *trenches* to be "death traps."

The wiring policy was also criticised. Belts in front of the Vaulx – Morchies Line were thought to have been too thick because the troops had difficulty firing through them. Apron wire was considered not to be nearly as effective as thick belts and was too often badly placed. It was not thought to have been a "serious obstacle" to the Germans squads sent out under cover of darkness and the bombardment to cut it. The ideal to some would have been a series of belts none of which would run parallel to the trenches and so designed as to channel attackers towards the machine guns. In the rear areas the belts were recommended to be at least 100 yards in depth.

The excellence of the enemy's training in open warfare was contrasted with that of their own men. Troops were, "unavoidably under-trained and overworked" with long trench tours having "eradicated all mobile warfare teaching, particularly with regard to the use of ground." Furthermore, troops "had no idea of fighting a delaying action." The tactical inability of troops and their officers to affect what the more senior officers considered to be a well organised withdrawal was a source of significant exasperation. Troops too often simply went back from one trench to another and once they had gone, those who had covered that withdrawal then fell back as well. That meant that on occasions no troops were actually in action because they were all on the move or masking defenders' fire. It was extremely rare for snipers or strong patrols to be left behind to hinder the enemy's advance; heads were shaken in disbelief when withdrawals were made in daylight. It was all very well for these pre-war Sandhurst-trained regular officers to bemoan the drop in standards of junior officers, but they did at least acknowledge it to be a "great unavoidable weakness." Despite their perceived shortcomings, however, the troops needed to see and hear their officers because without them, as many reports confirmed, the men were "lost." Many NCOs and privates did, of course, respond magnificently when a crisis arose and the men themselves were praised for their courage and endurance. There is at least one official mention of British troops, in this case 1/Buffs, firing on Germans trying to surrender but given the fact that there were widespread rumours that hordes of Germans were wearing British uniforms there may well have been other, unrecorded instances. Bethell described the "staying power" of the army as being "most remarkable, considering its physique."

Many senior officers, as they had done since the arrival of the New Armies in France, despaired of the standard of shooting. Since the Somme the men had been accused of relying too much on the Mills bomb rather than their rifle. Attempts to rectify the practice were thought to have failed. There was a general lack of fire control which led to an enormous wastage of ammunition with "every Lewis gunner and rifleman shooting every man in sight." On witnessing one of the reputedly few instances of a section's correct and efficient fire control, an officer realised how effective such fire could be. There was a widespread demand amongst senior officers for more ranges in the rear areas where men's confidence in the weapon could be developed. At the moment, that confidence "did not exist."

The Lewis gun had again proved its worth and had taken a heavy toll of the attackers. Nonetheless, in the hands of so many half-trained men one officer thought that it might be better to have a slightly inferior weapon but one which was rather more dirt and fool-proof than the existing "excellent" gun. In the same way as for musketry, in order to address the issue of training and the excessive use of ammunition there were demands for more ranges in the rear. It was a fact that until they first used it in anger, few Lewis gunners had fired their weapon on anything more than a 30 yard range. The heavy machine gun had also played a major role in the withdrawal process. Divisional machine-gun battalions had only recently been formed and their performance was thought to have been "an excellent start" to the new system. Brigadier General Bethell agreed and wrote that the new battalions must be formed of picked officers and ORs and be highly trained. Despite their successful first actions he believed their lack of training meant that their full potential had yet to be realised. There were differences of opinion in how the MGC battalions should be managed, the real bone of contention being who should actually control them. DHQ 17th Division blamed what was described as the "heavy wastage" of guns on their "faulty handling" by infantry COs who had assumed command of their allocated sections. GOC 34th Division thought that sections on Hénin Hill had done "yeoman service" but because they had not all been given infantry protection they were vulnerable and could be easily turned. One gun, he noted, was taken from behind without having fired a shot.

There were arguments about how best the guns should be grouped. Divisional opinions differed as to whether they should be deployed in batteries of eight, four, or pairs, but with a consensus that single guns were normally "unsatisfactory." When sited for defence they were usually echeloned in depth and positioned for direct fire. They needed to be mutually supporting and capable if necessary of also providing barrage or indirect fire. Some divisions, however, had them sited for indirect fire and then, when called upon to support or cover the infantry, lost heavily when they moved to new positions. With sections so dispersed it was difficult for the MGC battalion CO to control the batteries. It was generally thought best to attach a section to each battalion, with the infantry CO deciding what area he wanted the machine guns to cover and for the OC MG section to decide on the actual sites or positions. These tended to be between trench lines rather than amongst or in them. Cooperation and consultation between the infantry CO and the machine guns was vital but there were occasions when the infantry CO demanded that the OC machine-gun section, who was inferior in rank, comply with his orders. This sometimes caused friction and avoidable loss of guns and crews. What little criticism there was of the performance of the machine-gun battalions concerned the excessive range at which they tended to open fire.

Other infantry support weapons played an important but hardly a decisive role in the battle. There are reports of rifles grenades failing to explode and others of them being used with good effect in counter attacks and in silencing machine guns crews. The CO of 6/7th A&SH, however, claimed that his battalion did not use any after 21 March because none were available. The dumps holding the unit's reserves had all been blown in. The diarist of 31st Division recorded that his troops made good use of rifle grenades but, rather strangely, asserted that the Mills bomb was useless in the type of fighting seen during the offensive. Those trench mortars that were not knocked out in the opening bombardment were able to put down local barrages and assisted in at least one counter-attack made by 6th Division. As many were apparently fired from between the knees it was unnecessary to move the bulky and heavy base plates with the guns. It was acknowledged in post-battle reports that dumps of light mortar ammunition had not always been in the sensible positions. They needed to be in places where stands were most likely to be made or counter-attacks launched. Some teams managed to withdraw with their light mortars but, with no transport available the crews of the RND became so exhausted when carrying their 6 inch Newtons back to the Green Line that their OC decided to abandon and bury the weapons.

The problematic issue of re-supply whilst a mobile battle was in progress was addressed by senior commanders when the battle was over. One suggestion from 51st Division was to provide all brigade HQ with a limber capable of carrying a reserve of 10,000 rounds of SAA, 168 Lewis pans, and 100 rifle grenades for each of their battalions. Senior commanders of the RND believed that with "very few exceptions" SAA and rations were well delivered. They did also admit, however, that it had been difficult to get staffs to appreciate it was now a war of movement and that, consequently, stores, ammunition, and rations should no longer be dumped but kept on wheeled transport until delivered directly to units. Transport section themselves had to overcome the problems of traffic chaos when bringing supplies forward from the major dumps in Albert, Aveluy, and Méaulte. Corps defence schemes had laid down routes by which, *in extremis*, individual divisions should send their transport to the rear. Events quickly overtook the prepared plans and until sufficient traffic control points and straggler posts were organised and manned by troops who knew what had to be done, the jams, circuitous diversions, and delays continued.

Also frequently caught up in the traffic jams were the motor and horse-drawn ambulances. One of the essential and most important elements in maintaining soldiers' morale, and thus their will to continue fighting, is to assure them that medical provision will be prompt and efficient. There was a detailed plan within every divisional defence scheme about how the medical provision would be delivered during an enemy offensive.. Like so many other things the German assault made many of those plans immediately obsolete and put the medical services under huge pressure. Because the advance was in places so swift many British wounded could not be collected by their comrades and lay until picked up by the Germans. Nonetheless, thousands of casualties were fed through the system from regimental aid posts, collecting points, field ambulances, and casualty clearing stations to the base hospitals. There were certainly choke points close to the front and there was an acceptance that some wounded would not be evacuated. There were various schemes and later suggestions about how stretcher bearers should be organised and what the proportion should be between battalion and RAMC bearers. There are several instances of ADMS going forward personally to arrange the provision of ambulances from collecting posts and field ambulances. Lorries were requisitioned and light railways employed to carrying back stretcher cases. As the enemy advance continued, casualty clearing stations and field ambulances were forced to pack up and move further back. Such moves added to their operational difficulties. The CO of 1/King's recorded. "Medical arrangements appeared to have broken down very badly." In some areas there was an acute shortage of ambulances which caused many wounded to be abandoned and there are stories of empty ambulances refusing to stop until troops physically stood in front of them. One medical officer claimed that the RAMC bearers deserted his aid post as soon as the enemy attacked. There may well also have been similar instances elsewhere, but most diaries praise the work of the bearers and the orderlies at the field ambulances. It is, perhaps, remarkable that given the disruption and uncertainty of the transport systems so many men were successfully passed down the evacuation channels.

By the end of March, Third Army's line was beginning to stabilise. The Wastelands created by the enemy in the spring of 1917 were again under German occupation. He had made gains, but the land was of little real strategic value and his extended lines of communication were now handicapped by having to cross the devastated country. The German Army had not yet culminated but the tempo of operations against Third Army was beginning to slacken. There were to be fresh offensives in April and May but already his casualties had been enormous. Byng's Third Army remained intact, albeit battered; the command structure had not collapsed but it had been severely jolted and shocked. Byng's role in the battle had been largely to coordinate his corps actions as best as he could and to obtain and deploy what reserves existed. His corps commanders acted in similar fashion. Hampered by unreliable communications they used their reserves in as adroit a manner as possible. At times they knew little of what was actually happening but Haldane, Fanshawe, and their staffs did visit their divisional commanders to try to ascertain information and make informed decisions about where to use their resources. Apart from that they had little real control of the battle. Divisional commanders, too, could really only respond and react to enemy actions.

Until at least the end of the month the Germans held and retained the initiative. Local counter-attacks were rarely successful because the few men available to make them were assaulting the enemy masses where they were strongest. Although not as short of men as Fifth, Third Army was hugely undermanned. German deception aimed at convincing the British that the expected offensive was likely to fall on First or Second Armies had been successful. The prepared defence schemes unravelled quickly because there were insufficient men to implement them; what men were available were sometimes not in the most advantageous deployments. The psychological impact of the opening bombardment, the fog, and broken communications made men and garrisons feel isolated. The sheer weight and fury of the attack was enough to convince many that surrender was acceptable. Battalions, brigades, and divisions disintegrated under the pressure and ceased to be coherent fighting bodies. Many men fought on in small groups or platoons alongside those of other units and, in the end, with the help of arriving formations and extemporised staff work, managed to halt the advance. In their exhausted state, few probably gave much if any consideration to the thought that the Wastelands would once again have to be contested and retaken before the war might end.

Despite the loss of land and the enormous cost in manpower, Major Johnston, acting CO of 6/Seaforth Highlanders, did see some hope for the future. In a balanced and perceptive assessment of what had occurred he observed:

> We have been allowed to forget much of what we learned about semi and open warfare in attack and defence. The Germans have not neglected this. If men had remembered this it is certain that in many cases a finer stand would have been made and the withdrawal would have been carried out with fewer casualties and with greater precision. A great deal of confusion and mixing up of units, resulting in loss of personal control, would have been avoided if lines withdrawing always withdrew through a line formed behind. …It is now proved that with plenty of machine [and light machine] guns, well-handled and backed with courage, determination and good leadership, a well-planned attack can be developed into the enemy after his first resistance has been broken.

Between roughly mid-June and early August there was to be something of an intermittent hiatus on the Western Front. Fighting did not of course cease, but time had been gained for more American divisions to arrive and be trained, and for munitions and ordnance stocks to be replenished. Ludendorff's great gamble for a swift victory had failed. In mid-August Third Army was again to advance across the Wastelands and once more re-take the shattered villages, pitted terrain, and felled woods. At least on this occasion the weather and the ground were to be more conducive to a campaign. The enemy was, however, as he had in March and April 1917, prepared actively to dispute their possession.

11

Regaining the Wastelands: August–September 1918

In late July 1918, the Anglo-French counter-attacks in Champagne and Aisne, followed quickly by the opening of the Battle of Amiens on 8 August 1918, heralded the start of what was later to become known as the Hundred Days. This period witnessed a series of Allied hammer blows against the Germans and forced them again onto the defensive. The entry of the United States and its seemingly limitless resources of manpower and materiél were ultimately to prove decisive but it was the British and French armies which dealt the most significant of the early blows. The Germans did not simply acquiesce and accept defeat as inevitable. The Battle of Amiens emphasised that the war of attrition was definitely going against them but, in general, the German artillery and machine gunners continued to fight hard and well. Allied casualties in the final full three months of the war remained alarmingly high but that the tide had turned was apparent to all save the most intransigent and dedicated of German patriots.

The resources concentrated for the attack at Amiens and the surprise which the battle's planners achieved came as a momentous operational shock to the enemy. But, as the battle's momentum slowed, the Allies struck elsewhere to maintain what was to become a relentless tempo of offensive blows. The period known as the Second Battles of the Somme began on 21 August and lasted officially until 3 September. Within that all-embracing title were other named battles and operations. In the area of the Wastelands between 21 August and 3 September, IV, V, and VI British Corps were engaged in the Battle of Albert and the Second Battle of Bapaume. The former was fought mainly in the area of the 1916 Somme battlefield, with VI Corps on the left engaged in terrain which generally was not as broken as that crossed by IV and V Corps. The land was badly battered but not quite so utterly physically destroyed. There was then a period of preparation before the corps became involved in the operations known officially as the Battles for the Hindenburg Line. The Hindenburg Line had been penetrated in places at the Battles of Arras, Bullecourt, and Cambrai in 1917. Those attacks had not achieved the desired breakout into the open and largely unspoiled terrain which lay beyond its trenches and fortifications. In the British sector the system stretched principally across the fronts of Third and Fourth Armies and was to be assaulted and broken irreparably on 29 September. As those attacks have been well covered by historians and guides it is intended here to look only at the operations which carried the BEF again across the Wastelands and once more to within striking distance of the *Siegfrieg Stellung*. For the same reason the initial August advances which regained the bulk of the old Somme battlefields will not be considered here.

The Allied plan for the British Third and Fourth Armies was for a series of preliminary assaults and shaping operations to secure better jumping off points for what would be the major attack on 23 August. Byng's Third Army of IV, V, and VI Corps was strengthened by the allotment of several more divisions and artillery brigades. The northern-most of his corps, Lieutenant General Haldane's VI Corps, was to operate on ground thought suitable for tanks. It was to open the battle by gaining the line of the Albert-Arras railway close to Courcelles-le-Comte. In the centre, Lieutenant General Harper's IV Corps was to take the remaining sections of the Serre-Miraumont ridge, including the much contested Beauregard Dovecote. Once VI Corps had taken Gomiécourt, Harper's divisions were to advance on Achiet-le-Grand. When the railway had been secured VI and IV Corps would push east from Achiet-le-Grand and Gomiécourt towards Sapignies and Ervillers. Byng's southern corps, Lieutenant General Shute's V Corps was to head south-east across the Ancre, take Thiepval from the south and make for Pys via the Pozières ridge.

Once he knew what resources he had at his disposal Haldane was given a more-or-less free hand to decide how to prepare for the main offensive planned for 23 August. For the initial shaping attack on 21 August, he decided to use 2 Guards Brigade, a brigade of 2nd Divisions, and then two brigades of 3rd Division who would pass through 99 Brigade of 2nd Division to continue the advance. The Guards took Moyenneville village but for some unknown reason – probably a result of the thick fog – its supporting tanks disappeared to the south-east. Some of 2 Guards Brigade crossed the railway into quarries to the south-east of the village but were told not to advance any further without the support of tanks or cavalry. To fill any gap in the low ground east of Ayette that might appear between the Guards and 3rd Division, 99 Brigade was to stay in the line once it had reached its limited objective and consolidated. It would then be at the disposal of the Guards. The heavy fog had caused difficulties for 1/R.Berks and 23/RF of the brigade, but the tanks arrived on time and both battalions reached their objectives between Moyenneville and Courcelles. A significant difficulty had arisen, however, when 23/RF moved out of Ayette. The fusiliers crossed gas soaked low ground which compelled them to wear respirators for four hours. Later, the mustard gas absorbed in their clothing oozed out in the summer's heat and caused over 400 casualties. The battalion was swiftly relieved.

The two brigades of 3rd Division continued the advance with the objectives of securing Courcelles and the railway to its east. On the left, 7/KSLI, of 8 Brigade was to pass to the north of the village with 1/RSF clearing the village itself. With the village gained the battalions would advance down the slope to the railway. On their right, 13/King's and 1/Northumberland Fusiliers were to pass south of the village and also head for the railway. Both brigades had tanks in support. Owing to the particularly dense fog Brigadier General Potter, GOC 9 Brigade, went forward to a position known as the Ridge Work, 800 yards west of Courcelles. Here he hoped he would be in a better position to receive and dispatch communications. In the northern sector 7/KSLI ran into some stiff resistance at Coffee Redoubt, 200 yards to the north-west of Courcelles and 1/RSF met with obstinate opposition inside the village itself. That was eventually overcome but until two tanks arrived to silence the posts the withdrawing Germans maintained a firm rearguard on the slope leading down to the railway embankment and the cutting. Reports were received at Potter's HQ in the Ridge Work which confirmed that 13/King's and 1/NF working on the right of the RSF had reached the railway. The line was under fire, but it was believed that whippets would be able to cross the tracks. The King's, which had lost three OC companies during the attack, had at points pushed east of the railway but the

Northumberlands on their right had not crossed it and were dug in 50-100 yards on its western side. This limited advance allowed enemy machine guns further to the south on the western side to harass the right rear of the King's for much of the next day and a half. On the right of the Northumberlands one company of 2/Suffolk of 76 Brigade was acting as flank guard but, on *its* right, 63rd RND was having difficulties near the railway north-east of Achiet-le-Grand. That division's failure to get forward allowed an anti-tank gun in the rear of 9 Brigade to fire into the approaching line of tanks. To avoid unnecessary losses, instead of unloading their ammunition boxes at identified dumps on the railway, the supply tanks were instructed to shed their ammunition boxes 1,500 yards short of it.

The enemy did counter-attack in some strength the following day and forced several of the posts which had been established east of the railway to be withdrawn. More than 200 prisoners had been taken but casualties had been fairly heavy. The GOC's later report noted that the presence of the fog had probably helped to reduce the number. Largely successful as the attack had been, Major General Deverell believed one more advance was required if the objectives of the main assault on 23 August were to be secured.

To the south of VI Corps, IV Corps had mixed fortunes on 21 August. Under cover of an artillery, machine gun, and trench mortar barrage, and with tanks cooperating, 37th Division took Bucquoy and the high ground to its east against little opposition; the New Zealand Division cleared Puisiuex. On its left, 63rd Division passed through 111 Brigade and was held up by fire coming from the cemetery in Achiet-le-Grand. Like 3rd Division on its left, it did not reach its objectives. On its right, 15 Brigade of 5th Division, which had also leap-frogged 37th Division, took Achiet-le-Petit.[1] With the help of a captured battery of enemy guns it pressed on 1,000 yards beyond the railway. This was better progress than that of 95 Brigade on its right, some of whose troops reached the railway but were eventually forced to withdraw about 400 yards. This was done in order to form a defensive flank to join with the New Zealand Division. That withdrawal and the inability of 189 Brigade of 63rd Division to advance any further meant that when 15 Brigade was strongly counter-attacked it, too, withdrew behind the railway and dug in some 700 yards to its west. Finally, 21 August had been a poor day for V Corps. Attempts to cross the Ancre and its marshes between Hamel and Miraumont had met with very limited success. It was unlikely to make much progress until Fourth Army came up on its right.

On 23 August the main attack, another of the huge operational blows designed to keep the enemy off balance, began along much of the British front. Fourth Army did advance with some success and this, in turn, assisted some limited progress by V Corps. Thiepval Wood was captured and an eastward advance from Tara and Usna Hills was achieved. On its left, IV Corps launched a preliminary operation in the early hours in which 10/Manchester and 8/Lancashire Fusiliers of 42nd Division, and 1 NZ Rifle Brigade, recaptured Beauregard Dovecot and the ridge to its north-east. During the morning of the previous day a patrol from 1/Devon of 5th Division captured about 250 Germans who had taken part in a counter-attack against the New Zealanders. Two of the patrol had apparently come across the body of enemy troops resting after their assault in an old trench. Instead of quietly disappearing the two Devon soldiers ordered the surprised Germans to surrender – an order with which the enemy happily complied. A

1 The 5th Division had returned from Italy in mid-April and had fought in the Battle of the Lys with First Army before attachment to IV Corps, Third Army in August. It was to keep its four battalion brigades until up to October 1918.

patrol from 12/Gloucester similarly managed to round up another 100 Germans. After some resistance which had halted the general advance, 1/R.West Kent had taken Irles, and 14th and 15/R.Warwick were on the high ground north-west of Loupart Wood. By the end of the day, therefore, 5th Division had reached its objective of a line running roughly from the eastern side of the village towards Bihucourt. On its left, 37th Division had crossed the railway and taken Achiet-le-Grand. A trench about 200 yards east of the village was taken by 13/RB, 13/KRR, and 8/SLI assisted by tanks. The third battalion of 111 Brigade, 10/RF, then passed through and took Bihucourt against fairly stiff opposition.

Operating between 111 Brigade and 15 Brigade of 5th Division, 112 Brigade had a more difficult time. Having been reformed with three different battalions in the February 1918 reorganisation of brigades and divisions the official historian later drew attention to its lack of cohesion.[2] The brigade's left battalion, 13/RF, was held up by a garrison in the brickworks to the west of Achiet-le-Grand; 1/Essex on the right was similarly contained by Germans in a trench about 400 yards west of the railway. The third battalion, 1/Hertfordshire, was supposed to pass through the fusiliers but lost direction and eventually found itself mixed up with the Essex. Both battalions did finally cross the railway but only the Essex managed to reach its objective. In the late afternoon an order was received instructing 112 and 63 Brigades to continue the attack by securing what had been the original second objectives and then pressing on in cooperation with 5th Division to take Biefvillers. The planning and orders were rushed and resulted in an entirely inadequate and uncoordinated barrage which failed to silence the numerous machine gun positions in the area to be traversed. The troops of the two brigades were driven back to their start lines.

For his corps' attack on 23 August Lieutenant General Haldane decided to use Deverell's 3rd Division to clear Gomiécourt as a preliminary to the main advance by his corps. He believed the village had to be captured before the German machine-gun nests west of the railway could be silenced. Once these objectives had been taken, 2nd Division would leap-frog 3rd Division and continue the advance towards Ervillers and Behagnies. Two battalions of 76 Brigade were to attack the village: 8/KORL to assault the northern half and 2/Suffolk the southern. Other battalions were to act as flank guards. Machine guns were to fire through gaps in the hedge lining the railway cutting whilst overhead a creeping barrage would cover the troops moving towards the village. Eight Mark IV tanks were also allotted to 76 Brigade, but their crews warned the infantry that as they would not be able to cross the railway their support would be necessarily limited. The barrage and the assault began at 0400 and the village cleared with little difficulty. Until 1/NF, 1/Gordon Highlanders, and 13/King's, with the help of a tank, killed or captured their occupants the flank battalions suffered from some machine-gun fire from those enemy posts still west of the railway. The attacking troops consolidated their gains and waited for 2nd Division to pass through.

After the assault Major General Deverell praised his various divisional components. He applauded the initiative and leadership shown by junior commanders, the quality of the staff work, the cooperation of the tanks, the RFC, the heavy artillery, and the machine-gun battalion. He also stressed how platoons had reaped the rewards of the tactical training which had been possible during periods out of the line. The CO of 2/Suffolk was not quite so fulsome with his

2 J.E. Edmonds, *Military Operations 1918*, Vol. IV, p.231.

praise. He believed that "men who dumped their shovels learned to regret it" and blamed a loss of confidence amongst his men in the utility of tanks on a GSO 2 Tanks who had delivered an "over-optimistic lecture." The officer had apparently suggested that once the tanks appeared all the infantry would have to do was round up prisoners. Lieutenant Colonel Stubbs also thought there needed to be more training done on how to conduct successful liaison with units on the flanks and, that in dusty conditions, every man should carry a shaving brush to help keep his weapon clean. He did concede, however, that supply tanks were "invaluable" and that his Lewis gunners had done particularly well.

With Gomiécourt taken on schedule early in the day, 2nd Division troops began to pass through. In 5 Brigade, 2/HLI was to go for Béhagnies with 24/RF echeloned on its right "to carry on the tide of advance" and seize Sapignies and the ground to its east. On the left, 2/South Stafford and 1/King's of 6 Brigade were to take Ervillers. They were to be supported by 17/RF and also by 1/R.Berks attached from 99 Brigade. The right of 5 Brigade was protected by the other two battalions of 99 Brigade tasked to secure contact with the left of 37th Division in the sunken Bihucourt–Gomiécourt lane a little north of Bihucourt itself. Eleven whippets were allocated to the attacking brigades, but several were knocked out quickly or turned away to avoid fire. Probably only three played any significant part in the battle. Passing Gomiécourt to the north and then turning south-east the two battalions of 5 Brigade passed through the enemy barrage and then came under severe machine-gun fire. Lieutenant Colonel Brodie VC of 2/HLI was killed but, in the words of the diarist of 24/RF, "the advance pushed on in a determined manner, the drill-like precision, steady bearing and unfaltering pace... being wholly admirable."

Nonetheless, the attack was halted on the eastern slopes of Gomiécourt ridge about 900 yards short of the two villages. As the troops of the two lead battalions sought shelter in the area to the south of Bee Wood, the brigade's reserve battalion, 2/Ox&Bucks, closed up to the sunken staggered crossroads south of Gomiécourt. There it was bombed by two aircraft.[3] To the left of 5 Brigade, 2/South Stafford and 1/King's of 6 Brigade fought their way into and then through Ervillers. Large numbers of German infantry, with limbered field gun teams galloping alongside, were seen escaping on the light railway to Mory. A line of posts was consolidated on the village's eastern edge but machine guns on the higher ground to the north-east of Ervillers prevented any attempt to debauch towards Mory. To their cost, 1/KRRC and an attached composite company formed from those of 23/RF who had not been gassed on 21 August, discovered that 3rd Division had not eliminated all of the machine-gun posts immediately east of the railway. Assisted by two of the surviving whippets two companies of 1/KRRC took the nests from the rear, captured a reported 420 prisoners, and made contact with 37th Division in the sunken lane. During the night the battalion sent out patrols one of which reached the shrine just south of Sapignies. Another under the command of Captain Austin captured the OC and his orderly of the German machine gun battalion in the trenches opposite. Brigadier General Ironside, GOC 99 Brigade, later noted that a moonlight attack with a couple of tanks would have taken Sapignies.

3 Ox&Bucks officers heard voices from what turned out to be a regimental HQ in Triangle Copse. Approximately 40 Germans emerged when called upon to surrender. The German regimental CO was one Colonel von Proser. He, "being a wise man" according to the Ox&Bucks war diary, was away on leave. On the debit side, Lieutenant Colonel, Crosse, his adjutant and the battalion MO were wounded at the dugout entrance.

On the left of 2nd Division, the Guards Division had made a substantial advance. The Guards had repelled a counter-attack from the Hamel Work on the south-western approach to Hamelincourt on 22 August and had established a few posts inside the village. On 23 August 3/Grenadier of 2 Guards Brigade had begun its advance at the same time as 3rd Division on its right had moved towards Gomiécourt. The Grenadiers were later followed by 1/Scots who cleared the Hamel Work, passed through Hamelincourt without too much difficulty, and crossed the Arras–Bapaume road. On the brigade's right flank, 1/Grenadier of 3 Guards Brigade had been ordered to support 2 Guards Brigade by taking Mory Switch on the high ground between Ervillers and St-Léger. According to a later brigade report 1/Grenadier advanced 6,000 yards on a 1,000 yard front and took its objective. The battalion was "handled with the greatest skill, and all Company and Platoon Commanders supported one another with perfect precision. Whenever opposition was encountered, an outflanking movement was undertaken which invariably succeeded." By the end of the day the Guards were west of Hally Copse but had taken Judas Copse and Leger Mill. The right battalion reported that it was just about in touch with 2nd Division to the south-west of St-Léger.

The remaining divisions of Haldane's corps, the 1st Line TF formations of 56th (1st London) and 52nd (Lowland) were to pass through the 2nd Line TF and recently reconstituted 59th (2nd North Midland). They were then to head in a north-easterly direction to approach the Hindenburg Line. The initial problem for 52nd Division was ensuring that its 156 Brigade reached the start line in time for zero hour. The three battalions (4th and 7/Royals Scots, and 7/Scottish Rifles) were lorried up but were stuck in traffic jams for a considerable period. They did advance on time and crossed the open ground between Boiry-Becquerelle and Mercatel without undue difficulty. On the division's right, and between it and the Guards Division, 56th Division had a more unfortunate time. The division had been relieved from the line in the Arras sector on 19 August and had since been training in the rear. It was ordered to move forward quickly and at short notice. Orders for the attack on 23 August were late in arriving and by the time 168 Brigade, with 1/London attached from 167 Brigade, had arrived in the forward zone it was deemed "far from fresh." There had been no time to reconnoitre the terrain or the enemy defences opposite and the troops had had to wear respirators for part of the march. The first objectives were Boiry-Becquerelle and Boyelles and, once they were cleared, to continue east and take a line of trenches north of St-Léger. Assisted by 21 tanks the three battalions of 168 Brigade advanced under an unregistered barrage and met with mixed opposition. With the help of a tank the London Scots took Boiry-Becquerelle and 80 prisoners and, having outflanked an enemy strong point containing three heavy and eight light machine guns, 1/4th London took Boyelles.

South of the latter village the Kensingtons initially met with little opposition but were halted by machine-gun fire coming from the second objective. Lieutenant Colonel Shaw was killed whilst trying to ascertain what the situation was. At 0930 corps HQ ordered the attack be continued but broken communications meant that the assault did not begin until the early afternoon. In cooperation with some Guards, two platoons of Kensingtons cleared the railway embankment 500 yards north of Judas Farm and pushed on to Bank Copse. During the late afternoon the brigade was ordered to continue the advance as far as Summit Trench on the southern section of Hénin Hill and north-east of Croisilles. By about dusk touch was again made with the Guards on the right and 52nd Division on the left. The brigade was told it would be relieved by 167 Brigade during the night. The attack had taken just under 700 prisoners and nearly 60 machine guns. Brigadier General Loch praised the artillery, machine guns, and tanks but, above all, thought the success was due to the resolution of the men and the use of the 'blob' formation of attack. This, he concluded, had allowed the exercise of firm and effective junior leadership, swift deployment to outflank enemy positions, and fewer casualties than might have been expected.

On 23 August VI Corps had in places gained up to 3,000 yards along its front. Officially, the Battle of Albert finished that day but local fighting continued unabated. For 24 August in VI Corps, 62nd Division was to enter the action by relieving 3rd Division then in reserve on the railway east of Courcelles. The latter division would move a little to the north and take position behind the Guards. For its part the Guards Division was to advance towards Ecoust while 2nd Division on its right was to head in the direction of Vaulx-Vraucourt. On the left 56th Division was to attempt to take Croisilles; on its left 52nd Division was to conform and move towards the Hindenburg Line..

In the same way as 156 Brigade the day before, 157 Brigade of 52nd Division received its movement orders very late and only just reached its jumping off line in time for zero. With 156 Brigade cooperating on the left the two attacking battalions, 1/5th and 1/6th HLI, passed through Hénin village without undue opposition and extended as they approached Hénin Hill. There was no creeping barrage, the guns having been ordered to fire by direct observation. Lieutenant Colonel Neilson, CO of 1/5th HLI, was severely wounded early on but the advance continued until it was halted by undamaged wire and machine gun and trench mortar fire. The two battalions found themselves trapped under their own heavy artillery barrage which was falling both to their front and rear. The acting CO of 1/5th, and Lieutenant Colonel Anderson of 1/6th, conferred and decided it was probably best to stay where they were. Five wires were sent back to brigade HQ asking the barrage to lift but when it did, the two battalions had been underneath it for a full two hours. Four platoons immediately attacked the wire again but were driven back. Another bombardment was requested, with a known trench mortar position being particularly singled out for treatment. The artillery failed, however, to provide anything remotely effective. The two battalions tried again, with some men managing to penetrate the wire but they were halted in front of the enemy trenches by intense small arms fire and a counter-attack on the left. There was no alternative other than to withdraw and dig in about 500 yards from the enemy front line.

On the right, Croisilles was again proving to be a very difficult obstacle in the path of the British advance. The London Division's 168 Brigade was tasked to take Summit Trench and then work to envelop the village from the north while the Guards attempted to do it from the south. On the brigade's right, and if the opportunity presented itself, 8/Middlesex was instructed to take the village by "peaceful penetration". Twelve tanks were allocated for the operation and Summit Trench fell reasonably easily. Conflicting intelligence then began to arrive about the situation inside Croisilles. The centre and left battalions continued to take ground to the north of the village, which some reports claimed had been evacuated. When, however, 8/Middlesex tried to penetrate beyond its outskirts it was evident that the enemy was still in occupation. The GOC 167 Brigade was informed that a prisoner had told his captors that three new divisions had just arrived in the area and that a strong counter-attack was expected. The withdrawal of 157 Brigade on the left had not helped 168 Brigade's position and the Guards on the right had been held up. Nonetheless, and on receipt of a RAF report which claimed to have seen a tank in the village (it turned out to be a wrecked lorry) the brigade was instructed to attack the village and clear it before any counter-attack might be organised. Only one tank managed to arrive to assist, and the creeping barrage failed to silence sufficient of the machine-gun teams and riflemen for the Middlesex to penetrate to any depth. The attack was abandoned, and Summit Trench consolidated as the main line of resistance.

The difficulties experienced by 167 Brigade impacted on the advance of the Guards Division on its right. The scheme was for 3 Guards Brigade to encircle St-Léger by passing 1/Welsh Guards to its north and 2/Scots Guards and 1/Grenadier to the south. The village was known to be strongly held. With its left flank in the air and with 2/Scots over 1,000 yards away on its right, 1/Welsh advanced only as far as the first objective. The Scots mopped up St-Léger and managed to get on a little further but when 1/Grenadier came over the crest of Mory ridge it was hit by fire from the front and right. The attack ground to a halt. It quickly became clear that further progress would not be made until Mory Copse and village had been taken. The acting CO of 1/Grenadier, Major The Hon.W.R.Bailey, was wounded during the operation. This necessitated the return to the battalion of Lieutenant Colonel Viscount Gort who had been temporarily attached to 1 Guards Brigade.[4]

By August 1918 the approximately 80 x 80 yards patch of ground which had originally been Mory Copse bore little resemblance to anything that might once have been woodland. During the withdrawal of 1917 the Germans had destroyed the copse, and the Third Army dug a section of the Army Line through the near acre of land. The March 1918 battles had levelled much of the trench but by August 1918 the enemy had reconstructed it into a substantial defensive work. After it had cleared Ervillers 1/King's of 6 Brigade made a failed attempt to reach the trench during the night 23-24 August. The repulse prompted 2nd Division DHQ to devise another plan. It had been intended that 99 Brigade would attack Béhagnies and Sapignies on 24 August but DHQ decided that the brigade should be used to take Mory and the site of its former copse. Collecting 1/KRR, 1/R.Berks, and the single company of 23/RF attached to the Rifles, as well as coordinating with a company of tanks, required considerable staff work and a good deal of galloping between unit headquarters. While this was being organised, in the early morning of 24 August the attack by 1/Grenadier was joined by 1/King's on its right which sent one company up the hill towards the copse. Both advances were checked. It was then learned that an organised attack by 99 Brigade would be undertaken that afternoon. At 1530, 1/R.Berks advanced up the hill in a south-easterly direction from the Sensée valley north-east of Ervillers. Two companies of I/King's were moving east along the Ervillers – Mory valley road but were to swing north-easterly up the hill in front of the village. They linked with the Berks and a tank called *Dorothy* which "trundled" towards the copse. *Dorothy*'s "enormous moral effect" and the infantry charging with it drove the garrison from their defences. The Guards made progress on the left but although the copse had been cleared Mory village remained in enemy hands. The garrison halted a hastily organised attack by 17/RF which had intended to force the defenders from what would then have become an untenable position by taking the high ground to its south. During the night 24-25 August, 62nd Division relieved 2nd Division's 6 and 99 Brigades. The third formation, 5 Brigade, remained in the line. It had received orders to take Sapignies and Béhagnies "at all costs" on the morning of 25 August.

4 Later Field Marshal and Victoria Cross recipient.

Further south, V Corps, the right of Third Army, advanced in the Pozières and Grandcourt areas; next to it the right of IV Corps was held up until 42nd Division took Miraumont. By the evening 5th Division had captured Irles and Pys but Warlencourt remained well defended and the advance stalled. On the left of the corps 8/SLI of 37th Division had been heavily engaged during the night in clearing out pockets of resistance near to the railway south-west of Bihucourt.[5] The Somerset was supposed to have been relieved by 13/RF in order to allow it time to regroup before attacking Biefvillers in the early morning. That had proved impossible and once it had disengaged it moved immediately eastwards in conjunction with the New Zealand Division.

The New Zealanders had passed through 5th Division and were tasked to clear Grevillers. If the opportunity arose they were to push forward to Bapaume. On the left of the Somerset, 8/Lincoln was quickly held up but with the support of the New Zealanders, 8/SLI entered the unoccupied Biefvillers and pressed on without any tank support. A heavy barrage then came down upon the battalion and forced it to withdraw to the west of the village. Meanwhile the New Zealand Division had taken Grevillers from the rear and had almost reached Avensnes. It was also forced later to withdraw but as the enemy had not reoccupied Biefvillers the village was retaken. As we have seen, 37th Division was in touch with 2nd Division on its left. It was pushing in the general direction of Favreuil and expected that if 2nd Division failed again to get into Sapignies, it would itself have to take the village *en route* to Favreuil.

Progress, albeit not very substantial in terms of yardage, had been made by IV Corps on 24 August. Perhaps, however, the most significant feature of the day was an event which was to cause the sacking of GOC 63rd RND, Major General Lawrie. A proposed attack by the New Zealand Division on Bapaume was postponed because a brigade of 63rd RND on its right, as well as the allotted tanks, had had insufficient time to reach the jumping off point. Two of the division's brigades, 188 and 189, had been ordered at very short notice to march up to the front and attack in conjunction with the New Zealanders. One of the brigades, 188, had managed to struggle through the traffic jams, enemy shelling and gas bombardment to reach its assault position but 189 Brigade arrived after 188 Brigade and the New Zealanders had begun their attacks. Quickly appraising the situation its GOC, Brigadier General Hugo De Pree, used his initiative as the man on the spot and cancelled the operation. Fortunately, the assaulting brigades were halted before they had gone too far. When De Pree reported what he had done to his DHQ, Major General Lawrie condemned his decision and sacked him.[6]

The change of brigadier did not make a great deal of difference to the troops on the ground. In a thick mist at 0500 on 25 August, 188 and 189 Brigades attacked, passed through the trenches south of Loupart Wood fairly easily, and crossed the Albert – Bapaume road. There they met strong resistance from the enemy. Le Barque was taken but repeated attempts to capture Thilloy were beaten back with heavy losses. Several German efforts to counter-attack were similarly dealt with by the British artillery and machine guns. Casualties on both sides were substantial, including the death of the COs of both the Hood and Hawke Battalions. Later in the day Major General Lawrie declined a corps HQ suggestion that another attempt should be made in

5 The CO of 8/SLI, Lieutenant Colonel John Hardyman, was killed. He was aged 23 years and was later buried in Bienvillers Military Cemetery.

6 Following an enquiry, Major General Lawrie was sacked as GOC 63rd RND on 30 August. De Pree assumed command of 115 Brigade, 38th (Welsh) Division on 5 September 1918.

conjunction with an advance by the New Zealander on Bapaume. In justification Lawrie argued that on the right of the RND, 21st Division of V Corps had not come up.[7] It was agreed that any further attack would not take places until Thilloy had again been subjected to a bombardment by the heavy artillery.

The New Zealanders were making some limited progress on the left of the RND. Avesnes was captured by 1 NZ Brigade, but 2 NZ Brigade met with stout resistance as it moved towards The Monument on the Bapaume – Sapignies road. Covering the New Zealanders' left, 37th Division was moving towards Favreuil from Bihucourt. The first objective was to get to the Sapignies – Bapaume road whilst 2nd Division was to take Béhagnies and Sapignies. On the immediate left of the New Zealand Division, and in thick fog made worse by a smoke barrage laid by the Germans, 4/Middlesex and 8/Lincoln of 63 Brigade got off to a slow start. So, too, did 13/RB and 13/KRRC on their left. Assisted by whippets several German machine-gun nests were eliminated and by 0730 the road had been reached. Both brigades had, however, suffered severe losses. Meanwhile in the bright moonlight of the early hours, 24/RF and 2/HLI of 5 Brigade, 2nd Division, had taken Béhagnies despite having to contend with a gas barrage put down by the Germans on their own as well as the British troops. A little to the south, 2/Ox&Bucks found taking Sapignies was rather more difficult. The late arrival of orders had delayed the battalion's start, but an outflanking movement eventually captured most of the northern part of the village. It needed two assaults assisted by tanks and armoured cars, and the capture of a German officer who was persuaded to call upon his men to surrender, before the bulk of the village was cleared. The southern-most part was taken by 111 Brigade which at1030 received orders that it was to take over the entire divisional front and push on to a line Bancourt – Beugnâtre.[8] On the way to the objective it worked in conjunction with the New Zealand and 62nd Divisions, the latter having relieved 2nd Division, to take Favreuil.

Before the attack on Favreuil commenced a large number of German troops in full marching order were captured by patrols just east of the Sapignies–Bapaume road. Those enemy troops had apparently been rushed up and, in their haste, had lost their way. This was a marked success for the British troops but, on the negative side, during the afternoon 62nd Division was strongly counter-attacked and was subsequently considered unlikely to join in the operation against Favreuil.[9] In lieu of 62nd Division, and in order to cover the left flank, 10/RF was sent forward in close support. As the battalions were moving to their assembly positions an intense barrage fell on and behind them. Enemy aircraft bombed and strafed the troops in what was clearly a

7 V Corps had been set ambitious objectives and, unsurprisingly, had failed to achieve them. It had made some progress in the old Somme battlefields but had reached only as far forward as Martinpuich and Le Sars.

8 The relief of 68 Brigade was hampered by a message which was sent to the wrong battalion. Because the code word 'LOGE' was used instead of 'JOGE' a wire intended for 8/SLI went in error to 8/Lincoln.

9 There is some confusion about the role of 62nd Division. Its war diary claims that one company of 2/4th Dukes played a significant part in the attack on the left of 13/KRRs. The Rifles' diary notes that the Dukes crossed behind them heading south-east in what they described as a "mistake." According to 37th Division, attempts to turn the Dukes to a north-easterly direction, and thus get them to where they should have been, failed. In contrast, 62nd Division claims that the company of Dukes advanced in two waves from the sunken lane between Sapignies and Favreuil and helped to clear the copses in the northern part of the village. The times in the several war diaries are also at variance.

preliminary to an enemy counter-attack. Nonetheless, the assault began across the open ground towards a strongly defended trench to the west of the village, The New Zealanders took the area east of Monument Wood and the extreme south of the village; 13/RB secured the centre against some opposition; at the northern end 13/KRRC was held up. Three companies of 10/RF were ordered to close up on the KRRC; as additional support 1/Essex of 112 Brigade moved forward to the shrine at the southern end of Sapignies. The fusiliers seem somehow to have manoeuvred behind the KRRC and, instead of attacking it from the north-west, managed to turn the troublesome trench from the south. The Germans in the trench withdrew and the riflemen and fusiliers entered the village. Many of the enemy evacuated the village and retreated to the east. Here they were caught in the open by machine guns positioned on the main road. Some of their comrades, however, hung on to The Orchard on the northern outskirts. Orders arrived instructing 111 Brigade to clear up the situation during the night because it was shortly to be relieved by 5th Division. Brigadier General Francis, GOC 111 Brigade, ordered 1/Essex to close up and take The Orchard during darkness but the orders "miscarried" and 1/Essex stayed where it was. Later patrols from 10/RF eliminated the remaining opposition during the night and the division was relieved in the early hours of 26 August. Brigadier General Francis noted that over five days of "difficult operations" his brigade had advanced 14,000 yards, fighting most of the way and with "little rest or chance of sleep." Supplies had kept up well and the roads had been in good condition. Critically, he recorded, once Achiet-le-Grand had been captured and the pumping station in the brickworks on its western edge brought quickly into operation water supply had not been a problem.

As it relieved 2nd Division, 62nd Division HQ knew that its objectives were to be Vaulx-Vraucourt and Vraucourt in the south and the land to the east of Mory in the north. The relief of 2nd Division had taken longer than it should have done largely because communications were sporadic. The West Riding Division was supposed to begin its advance at 0900 in concert with the Guards Division on its left which was to continue heading for Ecoust. At 0500, GOC 187 Brigade wired DHQ to report that his battalions would not be ready by 0900. He was told to decide his own time for zero. He had called a conference for 0500 but the CO of 2/4th York&Lancs did not receive the message until 0830. He rushed off to the conference, telling his second-in-command to go ahead with the advance at 0900. When 2/4th York&Lancs set off, therefore, it did so on its own and without a barrage. By 1030 the battalion was held up by machine-gun fire about 300 yards east of Mory Copse. It must have been in touch with the artillery because fire was brought down to silence some machine-gun nests. Of the brigade's other two battalions, 5/KOYLI was west of Mory and 2/4th KOYLI in the sunken Mory–St-Léger road just north of Mory itself.

At 1700 the enemy commenced a ferocious barrage and at 1815 his infantry attacked. The York&Lancs were driven back towards Mory. Seeing this, Lieutenant Spenser led three companies of 2/4th KOYLI from the sunken road in a bayonet charge, in which the York&Lancs turned around and joined in. Another enemy force tried passing to the north of Mory Copse but were cut down in large numbers by six machine guns of 62 Bn MGC as the Germans came over the ridge near Camouflage Copse. By 2000 the West Riding's outpost line was back where it had been before the German counter-attack. During the night 5/KOYLI moved through Mory and advanced a further 1,200 yards to its east. This meant that by daylight it was 2,000 yards ahead of 186 Brigade on the right and 1,000 yards ahead of the other two battalions of 187 Brigade near Mory Copse.

The diary of 62nd Division notes that the Guards Division had been told that zero for 25 August had been altered to 1030. Guards DHQ almost certainly had not been informed and still believed that the time of the advance was to be 0930. In what seems a bizarre misunderstanding or misinterpretation of what Brigadier General Follett GOC 3 Guards Brigade was alleged to have said, his brigade began to advance at 0430 instead of the scheduled 0930.[10] Seven tanks were tasked to operate with the brigade but according to 1/Scots Guards only one was seen. The mist was dense and direction-keeping difficult. The brigade was heading for Hally Copse, Banks Wood, and Banks Trench. This still fairly substantial trench had been 59th Division's Third System's support trench in March. Eight hundred yards further east was Bank Support; this had been the front trench of the North Midland's Third System. The Guards' progress was slow, the intensity of the enemy fire preventing anything other than limited advances. There was hand-to-hand fighting in the sunken roads leading from the south-east of St-Léger and the afternoon German counter-attack against 62nd Division also involved 1/Grenadier Guards to the north of Mory Copse. On the left, 1/Scots Guards also helped to break up a counter-attack against 56th Division. At the end of the day the gains had been marginal. The three battalions of Follett's brigade were relieved by 1 Guards Brigade during the night.

The London Division had had a reasonably quiet day. The division, together with 52nd Division on its left, had been transferred from VI to XVII Corps at 0800. Lieutenant General Fergusson instructed 56th Division to make another attempt at the Hindenburg Line but Major General Hull protested because no tanks were to be made available. Fergusson agreed and ordered Hull to get his troops into Croisilles by a combination of frontal and enveloping manoeuvre rather than the proposed purely frontal approach. Patrols were active throughout the day but whenever they approached too near the village machine-gun fire drove them back. The enemy machine-gun teams were scattered around in shell holes, usually in front of the riflemen. Consequently, they were often missed by the barrage and were best dislodged with TMs and rifle grenades under cover of smoke. Touch was maintained with the 52nd and Guards Divisions but it was obvious that Croisilles and the Hindenburg Line would again only be taken by a fully planned and coordinated assault. Orders were issued at 1730 for 167 Brigade to attack the following morning at 0300.

The 167 Brigade assault started on time but 26 August proved to be another frustrating day for 56th Division. Galling machine-gun fire from in and around Croisilles hit 7th and 8/Middlesex virtually as soon as the advance began. The assault petered out after a gain of about 600 yards east of Summit Trench. With orders that the attack would be continued in the morning 169 Brigade relieved 167 Brigade during the night. A brighter note was struck by 52nd Division, It was ordered to pivot on St Martin, ensure contact with the Canadians on its left and then, in order to take the Hindenburg Line from the flank, to advance south-east. The German line was successfully penetrated by 155 Brigade south-east of Neuville Vitasse and north of the Cojeul. Touch was made with the Canadians about 600 yards west of Héninel and the advance down the trench system towards Hénin Hill continued. Two battalions of 156 Brigade were pushed along the Cojeul on the left of 155 Brigade; 4th and 5/RSF, and 4/KOSB began to ascend Hénin Hill. Enemy opposition was not particularly strong but once the brigade was over the crest of the hill and consolidating it was hit hard by gas and shelling until after midnight.

10 See Edmonds, *Military Operations* 1918.,Vol. IV p. 277.

This had been a successful operation but with 56th Division stuck just east of Summit Trench, Croisilles remained in enemy hands.

The Guards Division had a quiet day. Corps HQ anticipated that the attacks by 56th and 52nd Divisions and the Canadian Corps would drive the Germans away from the Guards' front. This was not to be entirely the case, but the enemy did evacuate St-Léger Wood. In expectation that it would resume operations the following day, 76 Brigade of 3rd Division was put at the disposal of the Guards. To the right of the Guards, 62nd Division made some slow progress towards Vraucourt and kept in touch with 5th Division of IV Corps. This corps had a difficult day. Its right and centre made no progress because yet another attempt by 63rd RND either to take or contain Thilloy failed in the face of intense machine-gun fire. Its further objective of a line north of Riencourt remained far beyond reach. There was little support from V Corps which was still fighting in the High Wood and Flers areas. Two major assaults on Thilloy were tried during the day but made no impact on the German defences in the village. The higher ground to its north also housed many machine-gun nests and until this was taken by the New Zealanders any further attempt on Thilloy would be equally doomed. Major General Lawrie declined corps HQ invitation to make another attack until the higher ground had been cleared.

The only real success in IV Corps sector was that achieved by 5th Division. The travails of the division on 25-26 August reflected the general uncertainty created by the unreliable communications necessarily employed during the advance. The division was in support to the New Zealand Division. Between 0800 and 2130 on 25 August a series of stop-start messages from corps warned 13 Brigade that it would relieve 111 Brigade during the night. When the final orders instructing 13 Brigade to move forward arrived, it soon became clear that the positions held by 111 Brigade following its attack on 25 August were unclear and uncertain. Furthermore, as we have seen, it had also been ordered to clear the remainder of Favreuil before being relieved. The unfortunate battalion tasked to take over 111 Brigade's final positions was 2/KOSB. To add to the difficulties, orders as to where 13 Brigade's other battalions should place themselves arrived late partly because thunderstorms had flooded the roads and motorcycle despatch riders could not get through. Eventually, and with only five minutes before the scheduled zero, 2/KOSB was in a position which allowed it to keep in touch with the northern arm of the New Zealanders' pincer attempt to surround Bapaume.

The KOSB, with 14/R.Warwick in support, moved on to the west of Beugnâtre but were held up by fire from the village. The New Zealanders wired that they could not get on with their envelopment until 5th Division had taken Beugnâtre. The brigade major of 15 Brigade, Captain Lake, had been sent forward to ascertain what the position was with regard to the possible capture of the village. Lake discovered that following the wounding of the KOSB CO, Captain Kappey was now acting CO. Lake decided to take command of the battalion and issued orders for an attack to be made in conjunction with the New Zealanders at 1800 that evening. At 1745 he learned that one of the OC companies had been wounded and that the company's other officers were unclear as to the objectives of the forthcoming operation. Lake decided to lead the company and the battalion to the objective himself. Under cover of a heavy barrage and indirect and direct fire from two companies of 5 Bn MGC the KOSB attacked. The troops swept through the village against modest opposition and consolidated on the ridge beyond its eastern edge. Germans ran away "in their hundreds." Captain Lake was twice wounded but insisted on remaining until the village and the flanks had been secured. A later enemy counter-attack on the newly-won positions was broken up by the artillery.

Beyond the usual artillery exchanges the situation remained largely unchanged in and around Beugnâtre for the next two days. The New Zealand Division made only limited progress in its effort to envelop Bapaume and continued to appreciate that any frontal attack on the town would be foolish. For the time being the town was to be the target for a slow and continuous bombardment by the heavy artillery of IV and VI Corps. The much thrashed 63rd RND made another failed attempt on Thilloy but did take some ground to its north and south. Two divisions of V Corps, 17th and 38th, gained and then lost Flers and Longueval. To the north-east, and despite some excellent coordinated work between bombers and Lewis gunners, 62nd Division took and lost the *sucrerie* on the north-west approach to Vraucourt, and sections of Banks Trench to its north-east. The Guards managed to get into and hold a part of the northern stretch of Banks Trench which ran away south-east from St-Léger Wood. The Guards had been strongly counter-attacked and had lost so heavily that two platoons of Queen's Westminsters had been sent by 56th Division to hold St-Léger Trench in the Guards' sector.[11] As the *Official History* later noted, "the fighting resembled the autumn days on the Somme."

Rather more progress was made in 56th and 52nd Divisions' sectors. The London Division's 169 Brigade was to make another attempt to cross the area between Fontaine-les-Croisilles and Croisilles and thus, with an advance by the Guards to the south, to envelop Croisilles. A post held by 2/London east of Summit Trench was attacked by a *flammerwerfer* squad during the night but at 1000 the London Rifle Brigade (LRB) and 2/London followed a barrage and made some progress heading roughly due east down the exposed slope. They were held up by enfilade fire from the south and wire after about 1,000 yards. Both battalions lost heavily. Two battalions of 168 Brigade were sent to assist 169 while, on their left, 52nd Division made better progress. It passed through Fontaine-les-Croisilles and worked down the Hindenburg Line from the north on the south-west side of the village. An order from DHQ for a preliminary operation by 155 Brigade apparently went "astray," but the advance down the Hindenburg Line by 157 Brigade helped elements of 169 Brigade get forward. Brigadier General de E Coke, GOC 169 Brigade, ordered 2/London and the LRB to enter the Hindenburg Line close to where 157 Brigade's troops had gathered. Congestion in the trenches, however, created difficulties. Furthermore, CO 2/London could only collect about four officers and 60 men because the continuing enemy fire precluded any movement above ground. Nonetheless, in conjunction with the Guards' artillery brigades the village was again subjected to a heavy bombardment. Coke's brigade managed to force its way to the east of Croisilles and continue in the general direction of Bullecourt. To the south of Croisilles 167 Brigade was ordered to continue to despatch patrols towards the village as well as to pass around its southern outskirts in the general direction of Bullecourt. Orders were issued for a continuation of the moves the following morning but at 0800 on 28 August a contact aircraft reported Croisilles appeared to have been evacuated. This was certainly not the first time such a claim had been reported but on this occasion it was correct. The enemy had gone save for a pocket of resistance near the *sucrerie* which held out for a short time until cleared by 8/Middlesex. The village had again proved to be a difficult pile of ruins to take, and it had cost heavy casualties among the battalions of 56th Division. The very weak

11 St Léger Trench was a long trench which continued northwards from the village and became Summit Trench west of Croisilles. A good deal of the area fought over in the attempts to take Croisilles now lies under the motorway and TGV.

battalions were instructed to press on largely south-eastwards towards Bullecourt; the equally badly mauled Guards Division continued its advance towards Ecoust.

The constant bombardment of Bapaume by the heavy artillery finally paid dividends for the New Zealanders. In the early hours of 29 August, the enemy began to withdraw from the town and from the village of Thilloy. Patrols followed them into both places and continued the advance in the general direction of Ytres and Vélu. The following day the New Zealand Division took Bancourt, went through Frémicourt and consolidated a line about 200 yards to its east. On its right, 126 Brigade of 42nd Division, which had relieved the very tired 63rd RND, was held up at Riencourt. An attack by 5/East Lancs and 8/Manchester failed and was followed that evening by another of two companies of 10/Manchester. After some stiff fighting and some adroit manoeuvre, the Manchester took the village and earned the battalion the sobriquet of The Night Jars. Further down the Bapaume – Péronne road the Germans held onto Beaulencourt and Le Transloy. The forward battalions of V Corps were still some distance to the west on the old Somme battlefields.

To the north of the New Zealand Division, 15/R.Warwick of 5th Division had been tasked with maintaining contact with the New Zealanders and gaining the high ground north of Frémicourt and north of the Cambrai road. On the left of the Warwick, 1/R.West Kent ran into heavy fire coming from the old Third Army Line of March 1918. Further to the left the advance of 186 Brigade of 62nd Division had also received fire from that sector. Little progress had been made when 95 Brigade arrived to relieve 13 Brigade in the evening of 29 August. The four battalions of the latter marched back towards Biefvillers when new orders arrived which, much to the annoyance of brigade HQ, "completely upset" all billeting arrangements. The confusion was eventually sorted out and had not caused any difficulties for 95 Brigade as it prepared to attack the old Army Line at 0500 on 30 August.

It was to be a joint affair involving IV and part of VI Corps. In 5th Division's sector 1/DCLI on the right was to cover the New Zealanders' attack on Frémicourt and gain Hill 120 to the north of the Cambrai road. On the left, 1/Devon was to attack the Army Line and maintain touch with 62nd Division on its left. Four tanks were available for the assault but the ground to be covered was open and could be enfiladed from both flanks. The trenches of the Army Line were thought to be still formidable. Following a creeping barrage the DCLI came under severe fire from the right, but once Frémicourt had been taken by the New Zealanders the Cornwall, supported by 1/East Surrey, pushed on to Hill 120. It was an exposed position and any movement in daylight attracted fire. On the morning of 31 August, the enemy counter-attacked. Three tanks supported by infantry penetrated the inter-divisional boundary north-east of Frémicourt. This was beaten off when counter-attacked on the flanks. Many Germans were seen throwing away their rifles and equipment before running into the British protective barrage. The retained positions, however, still constituted an uncomfortable salient over-looked from three sides. To add to the discomfort enemy aircraft strafed the positions.

The advance had been eased by the action of the artillery which had managed to stay in close support. After firing on the first objective the batteries of 27 Brigade RFA limbered up and galloped forward about 1,000 yards to a position from where they could shell the second objective. Under the command of Captain Mayne, D/15 Battery galloped through the enemy barrage to take up positions only 700 yards from the enemy. In order to guide the batteries through the barrage Second Lieutenant Cormack stood at a road junction for 15 minutes in full view of the enemy indicating to the arriving batteries their new positions.

The enemy fire which continued to hit 95 Brigade and 1/Norfolk came from the north-west and was a consequence of 62nd Division's failure to keep up with 5th Division. The West Riding Division had encountered major difficulties as it slogged away at the villages of Vraucourt and Vaulx-Vraucourt. On 30 August two brigades made another attempt, with 5th and 2/4th Duke's on the right heading for the open land south of Vaulx-Vraucourt and the southern half of the village itself. The second objective was the ridge about 500 yards east of the village. The attacking troops fought their way through the ruins and out to the east but did not mop up sufficiently well. Germans appeared from cellars behind them and fired into the rear; machine guns in the civilian cemetery and the northern part of the village caught them in enfilade. In view of this unsuppressed fire the line which had been reached about 200 yards east of the village was pulled back. The northern half of the village was supposed to have been taken by 2/20th London.[12] It was this battalion's first battle since returning from Palestine and had never before followed a creeping barrage or worked with tanks. Its line of approach to Vraucourt involved taking the *sucrerie* and clearing a confusing collection of crossroads, trenches, and the track of a light railway. Once those were taken one company was to continue east to the high ground while the other worked through the northern half of Vaulx-Vraucourt. On the Londoners' left flank, 8/West Yorks was to clear its way along Vraucourt Trench, the continuation in this sector of Bank's Trench. The *sucrerie* was taken and the series of crossroads cleared fairly quickly but, again, the companies failed to mop up thoroughly as they progressed through Vraucourt. Some accommodation huts between the village and the railway housed several machine guns. These had to be eliminated if progress was to be made but the enemy's resistance proved strong enough to prevent the London battalion from gaining control of the village. A heavy barrage came down on the *sucrerie* and the western half of the village and the attack ground to a halt. While the troops sought shelter and suffered under the bombardment, DHQ received a wire from VI Corps. This informed the division that if the ridge to the east and the two villages were not already captured and consolidated they would have to be attacked again the following day.

On 31 August, 185 and 186 Brigades had to try once more. It was decided not to attempt another west – east attack through Vaulx-Vraucourt; 5/Devon was instead to work in a south – north direction to clear the village. Six tanks were allocated to the operation: two quickly broke down; three entered the village and then disappeared; the sixth crawled forward with the Devon. In the southern portion of the village 2/4th Duke's wheeled right and, with the Devon on its left advanced up the ridge to the east. Again, however, the ruins had not been cleared and intense fire raked through the attackers from the rear. This fire, together with 2/20th London having again failed to make any significant progress along Vraucourt Trench to the north of the German cemetery, caused the Duke's and Devon to withdraw to the west side of the village. It had been another day of frustration, hard fighting and disappointment to the West Riding Division.

The difficulties experienced by 62nd Division in the Vraucourt area had impacted on those faced by 3rd Division. Major General Deverell's command had relieved the Guards Division during the night of 29-30 August. Its orders on relief were to maintain pressure but to undertake no deliberate attack towards Ecoust, Longatte, and Noreuil. Patrols and the artillery were to

12 The 2nd Line West Riding Division had been reorganised in mid-1918. It was joined by three battalions brought to France from overseas: 2/20th London and 1/5th Devon were allocated to 185 Brigade, and 2/4th Hampshire to 186 Brigade.

harass the enemy as much as possible and touch was to be maintained with both flanks. The next planned attack was the one of 30 August. While the right of 56th Division on the left of 3rd Division was to go for Station Redoubt in eastern Ecoust and 62nd Division on the right was to make another attempt on Vraucourt, 76 Brigade assisted by six Mark IV tanks was to go for Ecoust and Longatte. When those two objectives had been taken the brigade was warned that it would then probably be ordered to take Noreuil. It was informed that a section of whippets assembled east of Mory would be available for that task.

The attack was made in a south-easterly direction with 2/Suffolk on the left and 1/Gordon Highlanders on the right. In support was 8/KORL. The tanks arrived late and were immediately sent back to their assembly area by their OC. This decision, which was made without any reference to DHQ, was later criticised by the Deverell. Nonetheless, the Gordons advanced with Bank Reserve on their right and reached the objectives in the open ground south-west of Longatte. On the left, 2/Suffolk reached its objectives but could not gain touch with 56th Division in Bullecourt Avenue, a long former British communication running from the southern end of Longatte north-eastwards towards the railway embankment south of Bullecourt. The absence of the London Division was possibly the result of a fierce and successful German defence of Station Redoubt the day before.

There is conflicting evidence in the diaries as to what really happened on 30 August in and around Ecoust. According to 56th Division's account its 167 Brigade was only to take advantage of any opportunities to push into Bullecourt which might have been offered by the attack of 3rd Division. It makes no suggestion that 167 Brigade was to launch a major attack in support of 3rd Division. The London Division had been counter-attacked itself on 29 August and forced out of some gains made in Bullecourt. Station Redoubt had resisted attempts by the Kensingtons to take it and there is no indication in the London Division's account that the strong point was to be deliberately attacked again on 30 August. The few operations attempted by 167 Brigade that day involved bombing engagements in Bullecourt; these were largely unsuccessful owing to fire coming from Station Redoubt on its left. The confusion may have been caused by a lack of consultation between XVII and VI Corps as to how the next operation should be coordinated. Whatever the reason, however, 2/Suffolk suffered very badly from the enemy counter-attack and from a particularly troublesome trench mortar position immediately south of Longatte. Some limited gains had been made but most of Ecoust had been lost. The division was warned that it was to make another attempt the following day.

On this occasion there does seem to have been sound liaison between XVII and VI Corps. The operations of 31 August began during the night when Station Redoubt, Bullecourt, and Longatte were pounded by heavy artillery. When 168 Brigade, with 7/Middlesex attached from 167 Brigade, launched the assault at 0515 Station Redoubt was taken fairly quickly by the London Scots but it took until late afternoon before all but the eastern extremity of Bullecourt was secured. The Kensingtons were ordered to send up one company to assist 7/Middlesex in taking the *sucrerie* on the north-east side of Bullecourt; the London Scottish pressed on and occupied Bullecourt Avenue. Contact was made there with 13/King's of 9 Brigade, 3rd Division.

The direction of advance of 9 Brigade was again mainly south-east. An enemy bombardment fell just as the four battalions assembled (1/Gordon Highlanders had been attached from 76 Brigade) but once the creeping barrage began at 0515, 13/King's on the left made good progress through Ecoust. In the centre 4/RF, which had suffered significantly from the enemy shelling, was further badly cut up by the fire of a machine gun positioned in a sunken lane running south-west from Ecoust. One of the Mark IV tanks tried to assist but became stuck in the lane when its engine failed. A German officer climbed on the top of the hull and, firing his revolver through the open ventilation hatch, called upon the crew to surrender. The enemy squad manning the machine gun continued to cause problems to the advance for the rest of the day. On the right, 1/Gordon met with little opposition and advanced to Vraucourt Reserve. The battalion made vague contact with 62nd Division about 900 yards north-east of Vraucourt.

At about 0700 the OC whippets operating with the infantry across the open ground between Ecoust and Noreuil Switch reported to 9 Brigade HQ that all objectives had been taken and that the enemy were surrendering by the hundred. As his tanks were, he said, no longer needed they were returning to their assembly positions. Why he assumed or believed they were no longer of use was clearly incorrect because 4/RF was still held up by the machine gun, 13/King's had been ordered to extend its right towards the sunken lane, and one company of 1/NF was in the process of advancing through Ecoust, mopping up snipers *en route,* towards the same sunken lane with orders to eliminate the machine gun. The enemy defence was so solid that without any tank support further attempts at crossing the open ground in daylight would be costly and probably bound to fail. It was agreed that nothing more could be done for the time being other than to straighten the line.

Reports came in slowly during the afternoon, with several of them being hopelessly inaccurate. What was obvious was that Ecoust had not been entirely cleared of enemy snipers and that the machine gun, which had since been joined by others, in the sunken lanes south-west of the village continued to hold up any possible advance. To remedy the situation at about 2000 one company of 1/NF made a further sweep through Ecoust; another company under a creeping barrage assaulted the sunken lanes. The fusiliers were successful and continued to advance down Longatte Trench in the direction of Noreuil. During the night 31 August-1 September, 4/RF, 1/Gordon and 13/King's made more progress and by dawn had achieved the objective of securing Noreuil Switch. On the left divisional front this meant that their troops now overlooked the village of Noreuil and the Hirondelle valley.

Although still under the overall umbrella of The Second Battles of the Somme 1918, the period 31 August – 3 September was later deemed to be The Second Battle of Bapaume. Unspecified of course at the time, in Third Army this later period continued to involve the same three corps as had fought The Battle of Albert between 21 – 23August and also the subsequent engagements between 24 – 30 August. These latter actions acquired no particular title. To the troops fighting the battles there was no differentiation and one day was much the same as the next. For 3rd Division, 1 September was largely quiet. The usual exchange of shelling took place and attempts by patrols to infiltrate forward did gain some ground and intelligence. It was not until the evening that a set-piece attack took place in conjunction with 52nd Division on the left. The Lowland Division had relieved 56th Division during the night. The two divisions continued to press in a south-easterly direction largely to the east of the Longatte – Noreuil road and west of the railway embankment. Under the cover of artillery and machine-gun barrages the areas north of Noreuil close to Iggaree Corner, Pontefract Trench and Sydney Avenue were taken by 13/King's and 4/RF without too much opposition. These small operations were thought to have been conducted with "skill and patience." The experience of 8 Brigade on the following day was a lot less straightforward.

The brigade's objective for 2 September was the area to the south-east of Lagnicourt and north-west of Louverval. To achieve this, the brigade's three battalions would have to clear Noreuil and Lagnicourt and much of the area lying to the west of those two villages. Furthermore, they would also have to take part of 62nd Division's sector east of Vaulx-Vraucourt as well as what had constituted much of 6th Division's Forward Zone of March 1918. It was a formidable task and even though it had a battalion attached from each of the other two brigades in addition to 10 Mark IVs and eight whippets, the enemy's strength was unknown. What the staffs had discovered, however, was that the defenders occupied a maze of wired trenches which covered all intended approaches. On the right, 62nd Division was to advance south-east from Vaulx-Vraucourt and take the high ground east of Morchies; to the left 52nd Division was to begin the envelopment of Quéant from the south and west.

The three battalions of 8 Brigade, from right to left 7/KSLI, 2/R.Scots, and 1/RSF, reached their line of assembly south of Langatte; at 0530 they passed through 76 and 9 Brigades. Companies of 7/KSLI worked their way through Dunelm, crossed the Lagnicourt – Valux-Vraucourt road and moved onto the spur to its south. With all three of its allotted tanks already disabled the Shropshire battalion was held up by machine-gun nests sited in the open ground and in the sunken roads to the south-west of Lagnicourt. Most of the platoons were forced to withdraw to the old Vraucourt Switch running roughly parallel to the lane south of the Hirondelle stream towards the north-eastern exit of Vaulx-Vraucourt. In the centre 2/R.Scots had cleared Noreuil but had then run into strong enemy posts on the rise of the Noreuil – Lagnicourt road as it headed south. The Mark IV tanks could not climb the ascent and machine guns in Lagnicourt Trench and on the crest of the hill prevented further advance. On the left 1/RSF had first to clear a strong point in Dewsbury Trench and then when crossing Noreuil Switch at Iggaree Corner, came under intense fire from the sunken lane running parallel to the railway and the Noreuil – Quéant road in the Hirondelle valley. The allocated tanks had not appeared, and three OC companies and eight subalterns were killed or wounded before the sunken lane was crossed. With few remaining officers direction was lost and machine guns in Macaulay Avenue pinned down the fusiliers and prevented them from ascending the ridge beyond which lay Lagnicourt. Macaulay Avenue could not be bombarded because it was believed, quite rightly, that parts of it close to Lagnicourt Trench were occupied by sections of 1/RSF.

In the effort to resume the advance, one company of the attached 2/Suffolk managed to clear a stretch of Macaulay Avenue. But it was evident that until the enemy could be driven from the crest of the Noreuil – Lagnicourt road, and until machine guns were eliminated from a strong point to the north of the Lagnicourt – Vaulx-Vraucourt road 200 yards east of Vaulx Trench, the positions could not be improved. Two of the allocated eight whippets eventually arrived and were ordered to drive down the sunken lane from Noreuil, cross Dunelm Avenue and turn right onto the Lagnicourt – Vaulx-Vraucourt road. Accompanied by one company of 2/Suffolk they took the strong point from the rear as what was left of 7/KSLI attacked it frontally. On the far left, and only when in doubtful contact with 52nd Division, a company of 1/NF was brought forward and worked its way up Leeds Reserve and Halifax Support as far as Macaulay Avenue. A directed bombardment on the enemy-held stretch of Macaulay Avenue allowed 2/RSF and the Northumberlands to eliminate the garrison from the front and flank respectively. By that time, it was known that the Guards Division was to relieve 3rd Division that night. As the Guards decided they wanted a well-defined jumping off and opening barrage line for their continuation of the attack next morning, no further advance was attempted by 8 Brigade. Firm contact had also been made with 52nd Division. The Lowland Division reported that its 156 Brigade was through the Hindenburg Line and in the outskirts of Quéant. With the capture of

Macaulay Avenue, the resolve of Lagnicourt's defenders had weakened perceptively, and it was assumed that with the expected capture of Quéant the following day the Guards would enter Lagnicourt without too much difficulty. This did indeed prove to be the case.

The difficulties experienced by 8 Brigade were similar to those faced by the left of 62nd Division east of Vaulx-Vraucourt. The West Riding Division had tried again to take the twin villages on 1 September from the same south – north direction as it had tried on 31 August. At 0600, 8/West York of 185 Brigade advanced into the ruins and ran into only sporadic opposition. Once the companies emerged from the eastern exits, however, murderous fire again hit them from the high ground and the advance was halted. In the early afternoon DHQ received a wire from Third Army indicating that a major offensive was to begin to the north on the following day.[13] The division was now not only to make yet another attempt at gaining the high ground but then to advance to the ridge beyond Morchies and, if possible, exploit further towards Beaumetz. The task was given to 187 Brigade supported by 9/DLI (P) with zero fixed for 0530. The four battalions marched up from Sapignies and Behagnies during the night 1-2 September and were in position by about 0430. From south to north the lead companies of 2/4th KOYLI lined up on the sunken road running north-south from the eastern edge of Vaulx-Vraucourt to the west of Hill 120 and then to the main Cambrai road east of Frémicourt; 5/KOYLI was north and south of the village cemetery; 2/4th York&Lancs in a sunken lane running from the north of the village, past the German cemetery and up to Vraucourt Trench about 1,000 yards west of the opening barrage line. On the right, 5th Division was to attack Beugny. That division's zero was, however, timed for 0515. The uncoordinated time meant that as soon as 5th Division launched its assault the attacking battalions of 187 Brigade suffered from an intense enemy counter-barrage fired in anticipation of an attack from their sector.

The advance ran into hostile machine-gun fire but made progress. It stalled for a time whilst some Germans who suddenly appeared in the rear of the inner flanks between the two KOYLI battalions were eliminated, and then reached the Vaulx-Vraucourt – Beugny road. The line was forced to withdraw some hundred yards behind the crest of the ridge as machine guns a little to the south of Maricourt Wood poured fire into the slightly lower ground in front of the line. In the centre, 5/KOYLI took and went beyond Vaulx Wood but as the advanced moved towards Maricourt Wood it came under fire from Vaulx Trench and Germans who had filtered past its open left flank. With the German re-occupation of Vaulx Wood three companies of the KOYLI were effectively cut off. The problem had arisen because 2/4th York&Lancs was forced to throw out a defensive flank on its left to try to maintain contact with the right of 7/KSLI. As we saw above, this had proved difficult and had allowed the enemy in sections of Vaulx Trench to contain the York&Lancs north and north-east of Vaulx-Vraucourt. With all but one company of 5/KOYLI ineffective, and with the enemy likely to regain the sections of Vaulx Trench taken earlier in the day by the York&Lancs, any gains along the divisional boundary were in serious jeopardy. To salvage the precarious situation DHQ ordered the pioneers of 9/DLI to retake Vaulx Wood and Vaulx Trench.

The pioneer battalion had moved forward when the initial advance began. Two companies then dug in along the line of the first objective behind the two KOYLI battalions. When he received the order to attack and make contact with the York&Lancs and the assumed position of

13 This later became known officially as 'Battle of Drocourt–Quéant'.

5/KOYLI, Lieutenant Colonel Crouch, CO of 9/DLI, chose one company for the task. Crouch had been something of a thorn in the side of the division since his battalion had joined 62nd Division in February 1918. It had been transferred from its own 50th (Northumbrian) Division and reluctantly forced to accept the conversion from a battalion of fighting infantry to that of pioneers. Despite the conversion it had continued to regard itself as ordinary infantry unit and preferred in its rare periods out of the line to concentrate on maintaining its infantry skills rather than develop those required for its new pioneering duties. Crouch, for example, demanded DHQ should provide more Lewis guns than the stated establishment allowed. The company recaptured Vaulx Wood and the previously won stretch of Vaulx Trench by mid-afternoon. A battalion of 185 Brigade was sent forward to occupy the trenches vacated by 2/4th York&Lancs which, in turn, sent a party along Vaulx Wood Switch from its junction with Vaulx Trench opposite Vaulx Wood. The section pushed on until it made contact with 7/KSLI in the north-south sunken lane 150 yards south of the Lagnicourt – Vaulx-Vraucourt road.

Orders were received during the early evening that 2nd Division would relieve 62nd and continue the attack next morning. Because the West Riding Division had not reached its second objective of the high ground east of Morchies, the corps cavalry returned to Humbercamps and the six whippets ready to exploit any success beyond Morchies remained in their leaguer. Six of the eight Mark IVs allocated to 187 Brigade had been destroyed and casualties among 187 Brigade had been heavy. The division had had a very difficult few days in and around Vaulx-Vraucourt and, on 2 September, it had again come close to failing. But it had rallied and by nightfall had advanced about 1,500 yards. The final objective had not been reached but the jumping off lines taken over by 2nd Division were reasonably well placed to resume the attack next morning. The subsequent advance by 2nd Division and the Guards was almost without opposition. Both Lagnicourt and Morchies had been evacuated. This allowed the Guards to continue to a line roughly Boursies – Pronville while a troop of Oxford Hussars and whippets working with 2nd Division reached a little short of a line Hermies – Dernicourt. This represented a day's advance of almost six miles.

The assault on 2 September by 5th Division on Beugny had not been an easy operation. The objective for 15 Brigade was the village and the high ground known as Chapel Spur to its east. This stretched from Delsaux Farm in the south, crossed the main Cambrai road immediately east of the village and continued for a few hundred yards to its north-east. As the ground was very exposed there had been little opportunity for daylight reconnaissance. On the right 1/Norfolk was to attack Delsaux Farm and 1/Cheshire the village. Four tanks were to provide assistance. The forming up had been disrupted by German aircraft which dropped a succession of bombs on 16/R.Warwick, the support battalion, causing about 80 casualties. Corps HQ had set zero for its three divisions at 0530 but 42nd Division, IV Corps' right division, decided to advance its zero by eight minutes. Once its troops left their jumping off points an enemy barrage came down along the entire front. The Norfolk and Cheshire had to endure it for seven minutes before setting off themselves. The Norfolk took Delsaux Farm fairly easily, but the Cheshire ran into difficulties in the village. Two of the tanks had broken down very early on, another was knocked out, but the fourth trundled through the village and then returned. The Cheshire became trapped by machine-gun and artillery fire in the sunken lane running north from the western end of the village but were in touch with the KOYLI of 62nd Division. The two supporting battalions were shelled as they waited in their assembly positions and some 18 pdrs were drawn up within 1,000 yards of the enemy in an attempt to quieten the machine guns.

One field piece and its crew were knocked out immediately, but another fired over open sights and got off about 70 rounds.

The Germans launched a counter-attack around noon against the junction of 5th and the New Zealand Division. This was fought off, but DHQ decided that a fresh attempt should be made the following morning. The plan for 3 September was for 1/Bedford to work up Chapel Spur from the south and 16/R.Warwick to approach the village from the north-west. Three brigades of artillery were to bombard the village while another, with two attached batteries of howitzers, would provide a creeping barrage. All the planning and shelling was of little avail because when the Warwick entered the village it was unoccupied. All four battalions of the brigade then turned right and began the pursuit in a south-easterly direction towards Lebucquière. On their right the New Zealand Division headed from Haplincourt towards Bertincourt.

On the right of the New Zealanders, and following 126 Brigade's success at Riencourt, 42nd Division's next objective was Villers-au-Flos. On the division's right, V Corps had fought its way through Morval, Lesboeufs, and Gueudecourt but faced continuing resistance from around the civilian cemetery in Le Transloy. The village was finally mopped up by two companies of 50 Brigade, 17th Division on 2 September. The garrison of the *sucrerie* between Beaulencourt and Le Transloy on the main Bapaume – Péronne road had also put up a resilient defence. The ruins had been taken, lost and retaken several times by 21st Division. With 42nd Division's line of advance being in a south-easterly direction Beaulencourt and the *sucrerie* had to be captured or the East Lancashire's right flank would have been dangerously exposed.

The attack by 42nd Division on Villers-au-Flos was to be in conjunction with its own IV Corps moves on its left as well as fresh attempts to get forward by V Corps on its right. Like those of IV Corps, V Corps' operations on 2 September were coordinated efforts to fix German reserves on its front so that they could not be shifted to where First Army was launching its offensive against the Drocourt–Quéant Line. Major General Solly-Flood gave the taskof attacking Villers-au-Flos to 127 Brigade. A heavy bombardment fired by the divisional artillery, supplemented by crews working captured German 77mm field guns and two *Minenwerfers,* deluged the village during the night.

There is no explanation in the divisional war diary as to why 42nd Division decided to alter its zero hour from 0530. It does state that changing it "at the last moment might have been very awkward." As we have seen it was "very awkward" for 5th Division but instead of the change of seven or eight minutes noted by 5th Division the diary of 127 Brigade claims that its infantry began the attack at 0503. Whatever the precise time might have been, 5/Manchester on the right and 6/Manchester on the left advanced from Riencourt in the prescribed south-easterly direction. On its right, 21st Division was to advance more or less west-east. German machine guns in the sunken lane running in the direction of advance on the south-west side of the village halted 5/Manchester until some trench mortars put the machine guns out of action. On the left another trench mortar crew accompanied 6/Manchester and also knocked out several nests. When all their ammunition had been fired the crews picked up rifles and bayonets and joined the infantry. As additional forward support one 18 pdr was released from its barrage duties to follow the infantry and operate against identified German positions. One report also suggests that an aircraft played an active role in knocking out one troublesome enemy post. Two of the intended four tanks appeared but the brigade report gives no mention of how useful they were. What it does mention, however, is the work of a supply tank. This was thought to have been of great value in that it brought forward what was estimated as between 2-300 man loads of SAA and water in one journey.

The advance had been so swift that the two battalions, with one company of 7/Manchester attached, had to throw back defensive flanks to north and south until the New Zealanders and 21st Division came up. Some Germans in huts to the north of the divisional boundary continued to cause difficulties to 6/Manchester until what was described as a "raiding party" of New Zealanders dealt with them.

Once Beaulencourt and the *sucrerie* had been cleared by 21st Division, 64 Brigade moved towards the area where the machine-gun that had caused early trouble to the Manchesters had been eliminated. Two companies of 1/East Yorks took Lubda Copse on the southern extremity of Villers-au-Flos. This enabled 127 Brigade to withdraw its south facing defensive flank. Further south, 17th Division was conducting an operation to envelop Le Transloy. Two battalions of 52 Brigade, 9/Duke's and 12/Manchester, were to work around from the south while 7/East Yorks circled from the north. By the time the two pincers closed to the east of the village the enemy had withdrawn. This left 6/Dorset to move through it unopposed. By the end of 2 September, 50 Brigade had pushed on and taken Rocquigny. The German garrison of Mesnil repulsed an attack by 115 Brigade of 38th Division that evening but when it attempted another in partnership with 113 Brigade the following morning there was little opposition, and the village was secured.

Important as these gains were in themselves, the assaults had also served their intended objective of fixing German divisions. Elsewhere First Army had successfully broken the Drocourt–Quéant Line. This, together with the Australian successes at Péronne and Mont St Quentin compelled the German High Command to order a general withdrawal to the as yet unassailed sections of the Hindenburg Line. Air reconnaissance during the morning of 3 September confirmed the withdrawal opposite V, IV, and VI Corps. In response, Third Army ordered its corps to pursue the enemy "vigorously" with "properly constituted advanced guards" towards the stipulated near objectives as well as the more distant ones detailed by Byng on 29 August. Byng had specified that on his army's southern flank V Corps would go for Manacourt and Fins and then advance towards Vendhuille and Honnecourt; IV Corps in the centre was to take Ytres and Vélu and continue towards Banteux and Bantouzelle; VI Corps on the left was to secure Beaumetz and eventually Marcoing.

As the Canadian Corps of First Army and the cooperating three divisions of Third Army's XVII Corps advanced on the northern flank, the Guards Division occupied Lagnicourt and continued to advance south-eastwards. Villages to its front were in flames and, in anticipation of at least a few days of open warfare, Major General Fielding instructed his brigadiers and battalion commanders to be mounted. In accordance with corps orders an advanced guard of one infantry brigade, a brigade of RFA and one of heavy artillery, and sections of RE was formed. During 3 September this composite unit moved towards Boursies but was warned not to enter the village until it had gained touch with 2nd Division on its right. There was to be an assault at 0530 the next morning but patrols from the consolidated line to its north were to be allowed to reconnoitre inside the village during the night. Doignies was taken by 2nd Division in mid-afternoon and its advanced guard moved on towards Hermies and Demicourt. The accompanying whippets and Oxford Hussars were to attempt to gain a canal crossing north of the Arras – Cambrai road and a little south of Moeuvres. The infantry of 6 Brigade was to hold a line Hermies–Demicourt as an outpost position and to clear the ground west of the canal the following day. Patrols were then be pushed across to its east bank.

Also on 3 September, the advanced guard of 38th Division, V Corps, reached the high ground above the canal between Manancourt and Etricourt. The latter village was taken in the evening.

Companies of 13th and 14/Welch of 114 Brigade supported by 122 Brigade RFA, one troop of Carbineers, and a section of cyclists forced two passages across the canal in the afternoon of 4 September. They were then held up on the eastern bank by machine-gun fire coming from part of the Ytres-Equancourt Line running south from the Fins road west of Equancourt. The brigade spent a very uncomfortable period under gas and shell fire until relieved by 21st Division during the night 5-6 September.

In 17th Division's sector, once the trenches east of Rocquigny had been secured patrols went through an unoccupied Barastre; by the afternoon of 3 September, they were beyond Bus and close to the *sucrerie* on the crossroads north of Etricourt. Touch was gained with the Welch battalions of 114 Brigade on the right. From the hill above the canal, 7/East Yorks could see that both the railway and the road bridges over the canal were destroyed. Intense fire from the east bank forced them to dig in on the forward slope. A few hundred yards to the north, 10/West Yorks was halted by a troublesome machine gun firing from the copse south of Vallulart Wood. This was silenced when an 18 pdr was brought up and fired at the post from short range. Overnight, brigade HQ decided that the West Yorks would cross the canal tunnel above its southern portal; the East Yorks was to cross south of the tunnel entrance. Both had succeeded by late morning but were then confronted by the uncut wire of the Ytres – Equancourt Line which in this sector was known as the Mouettes Trench system. Little else of operational significance occurred during the rest of the day except for 6/Dorset's preparations for its projected morning assault on the trench system from the north. The Dorset battalion was, however, spared the fight when the brigade was relieved by 51 Brigade during the night.

Whilst it was deciding how the Mouettes Line should be attacked, 50 Brigade had sent patrols to locate 42nd Division on its left. Following its successful attack on Villers-au-Flos the East Lancashire Division, with 2 NZ Brigade on it left, had passed patrols of 8/Lancashire Fusiliers and Royal Scots Greys through the northern parts of Barastre, Haplincourt, and Ytres. Then, like 17th Division to the east of Ytres, it came up against the wire and machine guns of the Ytres-Equancourt Line. On 4 September, 125 Brigade fought its way into the enemy line and discovered Hayettes Wood to be empty. Patrols pushed on towards Neuville-Bourjonval. On the village's western approach, they were stopped by wire and hit by artillery and small arms fire. The right of the Lancashire Fusiliers was in contact with 17th Division, but the latter formation remained to the west of the Mouettes Line. It was clear that a coordinated attack by V and IV Corps was required if the defences protecting Fins and Metz were to be penetrated on a broad front.

At 0500 on 5 September, 38th Division attacked the line frontally north and south of the Fins road and was driven back. During the night, 51 Brigade, 17th Division had assembled with 10/Notts&Derby on the right and 7/Lincoln on the left. The Lincoln had marched around the north of Ytres and formed a one company east-west front facing south close to Hayettes Wood and the northern end of the occupied part of the Mouettes Line. The assembly had been spotted by the enemy but despite some incoming small arms fire the attack started as scheduled at 0930. At first the barrage worked but when it became ragged the company came under severe fire and was halted. It was decided to pause the attack until dusk when 7/Border was brought up and a new barrage fired. This was timed to coincide with a frontal demonstration by 38th Division. On this occasion the enemy was completely taken by surprise. The Borderers worked down the trenches, captured 13 machine guns and occupied the system as far as the outskirts of Equancourt. At the same time two companies of Lancashire Fusiliers of 125 Brigade fought their way into the southern part of Neuville- Bourjonval. They cleared the village together with a collection of nearby huts as far as the Metz road. The northern half of the village was taken by 1/Otago which had crossed the canal tunnel south of Ruyaulcourt in the face of some opposition.

Having carefully avoided a German minefield of 60lb trench mortar bombs, 3 Guards Brigade took Boursies on 4 September. Brigadier General Follett was told to push on and maintain pressure on the forward zone of the Hindenburg system west of the canal. Patrols were to reconnoitre possible crossing points, but Follett was ordered not to attempt any major operation. The area between a line Hermies–Demicourt and the canal was to be cleared by 2nd Division. The Spoil Heap on the canal's west bank north of the Havrincourt road yet again caused problems. On 4 and 5 September, 6 Brigade took the higher ground to the west of the canal and held the line of the railway but failed in two small scale efforts against the Spoil Heap. Patrols of 1/R. Berks and 1/KRRC working east from Demicourt tried to discover what might be the enemy's main line of resistance. Thick wire, machine guns, and forward 77 mm guns prevented the two battalions from penetrating the canal's outer defences. The Spoil Heap was finally taken on 7 September and further posts established to its north, but the Germans were not content to let the issue rest and counter-attacked several times.

The low ground lying between the south of Hermies and the north bank of the canal along where it travelled east-west close to the civilian cemetery was taken by 13/RF of 112 Brigade, 37th Division. The land on the south side of the canal was secured by 1/Hertfordshire. The fusiliers ran into heavy fire from the eastern bank when they tried to cross the open ground and the canal to the south of the railway and road bridges. The Hertfordshire had an easier task as they advanced into the northern part of Havrincourt Wood. The CO believed they had caught the Germans by surprise. The policy of what was termed "peaceful penetration" into the wood continued on 5 September, but the battalion had to withdraw from positions it had taken in Cheetham Switch when it came under enfilade fire from Yorkshire Spoil Bank and Banbury Hill.

During the night 5-6 September the New Zealand Division was withdrawn from the line without replacement; the corps' two remaining formations were thus required to extend their inner flanks by about 1,500 yards. On 8 September, 21st Division took Revelon Farm which lay almost due south of Gouzeaucourt, but it was clear that resistance was stiffening. The diarist of 17th Division acknowledged that fact and conceded that the Germans seemed determined to hold on to the area of higher ground crossed by Heather Trench and Heather Support. This system lay south of the Péronne – Cambrai road on the southern approaches to Gouzeaucourt. He bemoaned the reality that fighting patrols were now unable to make any progress and that if the advance was to continue thoroughly organized attacks would have to be planned and conducted.

The change to a two divisional corps front was part of a strategy whereby men and materiel were being rested as far as was operationally possible. GHQ was becoming increasingly concerned about the resources that would be available for the next stage of the campaign. Towards the end of August, the number of tanks made available for operations had been reduced and on 4 September all those machines in Third Army, with the exception of some gun carriers, were withdrawn into GHQ reserve. Orders had already been issued that the heavy artillery was to be rested and reorganised in preparation for the next moves forward. These would take place when the enemy's main line of resistance had been discovered. In the meantime, only mobile brigades of heavies at the rate of one per division would be available to support operations. Similarly, whenever possible one of the RFA brigades in every division was to be withdrawn from the line to rest. The infantry was instructed to keep in touch with the enemy with the intent of drawing in his rearguards, but men and resources were to be husbanded and communications improved.

In IV Corps' sector the pre-Cambrai and pre-21 March 1918 areas east of the canal facing the Hindenburg Line still needed to be re-retaken. The immediate objectives were thus Trescault and Beaucamp. In the adjoining V Corps area, the principal settlements north of the Péronne – Cambrai road which also needed to be recaptured were Gouzeaucourt and Villers-Plouich. The New Zealanders had tried on 9 September in coordination with V Corps to push forward from Havrincourt Wood towards Gouzeaucourt but had met with considerable resistance. In the same way as the staff of 17th Division had accepted that set-piece affairs had become necessary it was clear to the New Zealanders that resistance in African Trench and Support was hardening. This substantial trench system protected the western approaches to Gouzeaucourt. One of its most contested positions was a crossroads of two sunken lanes some 1,500 yards north-west of Gouzeaucourt known as Dead Man's Corner. This had become a particularly blood-soaked area.

Another major attempt along the front was to be made on 12 September. In the north, 62nd Division of VI Corps was to advance from the area immediately east of the canal to attack Havrincourt village. The West Riding Division had captured the same village on the opening day of the Cambrai operation 10 months earlier. In conjunction with the attack, 37th Division of IV Corps was tasked to take Trescault and what had been in April 1917 the contested position of Bilhem. The assault had been originally planned to coincide with the New Zealanders' effort on 9 September but had been postponed three times owing to the poor weather and other factors. Not least were the difficulties experienced in trying to bring up gas projectiles. In order to save the already over-tired infantry and pioneers, gun carrying tanks were employed to bring the firing apparatus and shells forward. The ground conditions and mechanical breakdowns caused problems, but they were eventually overcome, and infantry spared the labour and danger of hauling the equipment over low ground covered by enemy machine guns. Zero hour along the front was set at 0525.[14]

When 20th Division had taken Bilhem 16 months earlier the job had been done by one battalion of KRRC and one of RB. By coincidence battalions of the same two regiments, but on this occasion in 111 Brigade, were again to complete the task. Trescault village fell quite easily to 13/KRRC but as the lead companies pressed on towards Bilhem they came under severe small arms fire. A strong point positioned to the south-east of the ruined cottages and south-west of Bilhem posed a significant problem to the riflemen because there was no vestige of cover. Second Lieutenant Horace Wilding apparently knocked out one member of an enemy machine-gun team from 200 yards, but it was not until 13/RB on the right realised what was happening and poured fire into the position from the flank that Wilding and his men could again get forward. Forty prisoners were taken from the strong point, but the diarist makes the point that many Germans died at their posts rather than surrender. Similarly, the crews of two field guns continued firing over open sights until killed or wounded by Lewis gun teams who had approached within 200 yards of the guns. On the right, 13/RB had also had some difficulty advancing beyond strong points in the so-called Transvaal System of trenches; these lay 600 yards due south of Trescault. By 0730 the objectives were taken, and consolidation began. The

14 Over the same period, and owing to the poor ground and weather, the several tanks of No.1 Tank Gun Carrying Company tasked to assist 2nd Division by carrying gas projectors up to their intended firing positions had also experienced significant difficulties.

rest of the day was spent under fairly constant shell fire, with a company of 10/RF bringing up small arms ammunition and Mills bombs. At 1800,after a severe preliminary bombardment, a counter-attack fell on the junction of 13/KRRC and 13/RB. A protective barrage came down for 15 minutes which effectively trapped those Germans that had entered the British trenches. Hand-to-hand fighting followed but the Germans had nowhere to go. Some did escape from the trenches leaving over 20 of their dead and six who surrendered. The diarist of the Rifle Brigade credited the protective barrage as having contributed to "the fiasco in which [the enemy's] attacked culminated."

On the following day one company of 13/KRRC cooperated in an attack by 62nd Division close to the Trescault–Ribécourt road. The assault by 9/DLI (P) was halted and then thrown back. One platoon of 13/KRRC withdrew and sent up SOS flares when fire came into their left rear. The flares were not seen but fortunately a telephone connection remained intact with the guns. A protective barrage came down and was, in the words of one observer, "extraordinarily satisfactory." It did not, however, prevent an infantry assault with air support which again involved some very intense hand-to-hand trench fighting. An organised bombing attack finally solved the issue, and the enemy withdrew. Second Lieutenant Wilding was killed in the subsequent bombardment whilst firing a Lewis into the ranks of those of the retreating enemy who had not been hung up on the British wire. The enemy made one more rather half-hearted attempt on 14 September to regain Trescault but by the end of the day the trenches in that sector were back in the possession of those forces who had occupied them on the night of 19 November 1917.

The troops of 111 Brigade had lost heavily but had secured their objectives. In contrast, the New Zealanders opposite Gouzeaucourt had made little headway against African Trench. On 10 September the New Zealanders had reported the arrival of several salvoes of between 2-300 projectiles, each the size of an orange, which covered an area of up to three acres. It was clearly a gas, and one which burnt the grass where the small cannisters landed, but one which was not immediately identified. On 12 September, under the protection of six brigades of field artillery and three batteries of heavies, three battalions of 3 (NZ) Rifle Brigade assaulted the German positions and forced their entry into several of them. The enemy responded with fury and drove out 1 NZ Rifle Brigade from Snap Trench, north of Dead Man's Corner, and 2 NZ Rifle Brigade from African Trench on the right. This battalion had also been enfiladed from a German strong point south of Queen's Cross. This same strong point was also causing the left of 38th Division a very difficult time operating across and south of the Cambrai road. One company of 10/SWB tried to keep touch with the New Zealanders but was also thrown back to its start line. It tried four times during the afternoon to advance but was met on each occasion with resolute resistance.

The Welsh Division had only just come again into the line and was to stay there for more than another week. The New Zealand brigades began to be relieved by 5th Division on 14 September but not before the Germans had attacked some of the Kiwis' posts with *flammenwerfers*. The front line taken over by 5th Division immediately north of the Cambrai road was constituted by African Support; in the division's left sector it was Snap Trench until it joined with 37th Division about halfway between Trescault and Bilhem. This latter sector gave good observation over the Beaucamp ridge but in the southern half of the divisional line the crest between African Trench and Support meant that the enemy's and the British front trenches could not be seen by the other.

The next major attack by Fourth Army was scheduled for 18 September. It was not to involve IV Corps on any scale other than for 2/KOSB of 5th Division to protect the left flank of V Corps' 38th Division as the latter headed towards Gouzeaucourt. The corps' boundary was on the Gouzeaucourt – Metz road about 300 yards east of Queen's Cross. The KOSB went over at 0520 and, except on the extreme right, reached their limited objective of the sunken lane running south-east from Dead Man's Corner. Troops of 113 Brigade had not been able to get into African Trench and were forced back to their original line. When it became obvious the attack had failed both companies of the KOSB also withdrew to their start line. The defensive fire had been so intense and so immediate that the CO of the battalion believed the enemy was fully expecting the attack. A meeting was held involving staff officers of the brigades of both divisions and concluded that no more attacks should be attempted that day. The KOSB were relieved by 1/R.W.Kent durimg the night. The rest of the day was given over to patrolling and the steady arrival of gas and HE shelling.

The KOSB had suffered about 130 casualties; the unfortunate 38th Division was even more severely hit. In his report the diarist of 113 Brigade recorded the brigade had failed because 5th Division had been "unable to advance." The brigade's left battalion was 16/RWF and because it could not get forward the left flank of 14/RWF on its right became exposed. Companies of that battalion managed to fight their way into a trench which ran for about 300 yards north from the Cambrai road west of *Rue D'Enfer* until it joined African Trench. One report suggests that with their left exposed to enfilade fire, these troops held off "continuous" enemy counter-attacks for nearly 30 hours. When they ran out of bombs and ammunition the few survivors made their way back to their start line. Meanwhile another bombardment had preceded a further attack on the left which did secure a foothold in African Trench. The enemy counter-attacked a few hours later and, again, the fusiliers were forced back to African Support. South of the main road the division had pushed on a little way, but Gouzeaucourt's garrison of *Jaegers* was proving more committed than had been its defenders of April 1917.

With the failure of frontal attacks V Corps developed a plan to encircle Gouzeaucourt and pinch it out. This required the cooperation of IV Corps on the left because, until Beaucamp was taken any attempt to get around Gouzeaucourt to its west and north would be jeopardised by fire from the hamlet on the higher ground. Nothing of great importance happened 19 – 26 September save for artillery exchanges and inter-brigade reliefs. With an eye to future operations the British artillery put down various area shoots; these intensified as 27 September drew nearer. For the forthcoming operation 5th Division was to act as pivot for 42nd Division on its left. The East Lancashire Division was to advance south-eastwards from Trescault, pass to the east of Beaucamp, cross Highland ridge, and get onto Welsh ridge. If the division was to gain those objectives, Beaucamp would have to be taken by 5th Division. To the south of 5th Division, 21st Division of V Corps would by-pass Gouzeaucourt and gain position to attack Gonnelieu and the stretch of the Hindenburg to its east. The role of the southern brigade of 5th Division was thus to protect the left of 21st Division. Either 13 or 95 Brigade, which was at some stage to pass through, were to link with 21st Division close to Villers-Plouich. To achieve this African Trench would have again to be assaulted and secured.

The attack by 5th Division was to be against Beaucamp and Borderer ridges, and the southern section of Highland ridge. The two battalions of 15 Brigade chosen to lead the attack on the left of the divisional front were 1/Bedford on the left and 16/R.Warwick on the right. On the extreme left, one company of 1/Cheshire was tasked to take Beaucamp hamlet. The division was allocated six Mark V tanks and time was made available for some troops to train with them and live with their crews. The point was made in the division's diary that this was the first occasion its troops had been accorded such an opportunity. When the advance began the tanks were quickly knocked out or ditched but 1/Bedford crossed the Trescault – Gouzeaucourt road without too much difficulty. On their left the Cheshire also got forward, with the designated company supposedly having cleared Beaucamp. What precisely happened next, however, is unclear. The Cheshire's diary notes that its company mopped up the village twice; that of 1/Bedford claims it took part of the village but then had to evacuate it and did not return. The Cheshire's diary implies that as the 42nd Division could not get abreast of the hamlet, 15 Brigade had to withdraw. If the Cheshire company did ever clear the hamlet, either once or twice, the enemy quickly reoccupied it. Withering fire was unleashed from the buildings on the right of the Lancashire Fusiliers and Manchesters as they headed in the general direction of Boar Copse.

By late afternoon 1/Bedford had been forced back from most of its gains, and certainly from Beaucamp. On its right the Warwicks were also having a difficult time. They had fought their way into Dunraven Trench but had suffered heavy losses, particularly from one machine gun on the reverse slope of Beaucamp ridge which enjoyed an "extraordinary" field of fire. It was assisted in holding up the Warwicks' advance by others and by what were described as "good" snipers. A number of enemy prisoners had been taken and sent back towards the British lines, the reluctant amongst them being encouraged by the use of a stout stick wielded by Captain Izon. Enemy bombers, however, worked up a communication trench at the junction of the Bedford and the Warwick and systematically began clearing to right and left. The Warwick had exhausted their own bombs and, unusually, could not discover stocks of German stick grenades. Besides, it was quickly discovered that anyone who did try to get out of the trench to attack the bombing parties from above was quickly knocked over by the German machine gunners and snipers. One report suggests that the company of Cheshire which was still thought to be in the western end of Beaucamp was reinforced, although this seems unlikely. Other reserves assembled at Charing Cross. To the south, 13 Brigade had advanced behind the barrage but 1/R.W.Kent was brought abruptly to a halt in front of African Trench, south of Dead Man's Corner and only 200 yards from its start line. On its left 15/R.Warwick did little better. It was stopped by fire coming from trenches across Borderer ridge. With officer casualties heavy in all battalions except the Cheshire, NCOs and privates began taking the initiative. There are accounts of men organizing themselves into bombing groups, utilizing captured enemy bombs, forming rearguards while others withdrew, and of machine-gun teams bringing forward their guns to help stem the enemy counter-attacks. In spite of the bravery shown by many of the troops it was clear by nightfall that in terms of yardage the advance had been negligible.

During the night staff officers galloped about trying to ascertain what the situation was with regard to positions and unit strengths. Some sort of overall picture was obtained which included a realisation that 13 Brigade was unlikely to be of very much use and that 95 Brigade should be brought forward to continue the attack during the night. Liaison with 42nd Division confirmed that 125 and 127 Brigades had been hit badly by fire from Beaucamp and that the hamlet remained in enemy hands. Verbal orders were issued that two battalions of 95 Brigade would advance from about the junction of the sunken road running south-west from Beaucamp to the Trescault – Gouzeaucourt road and to link up with the East Lancashire Division on the approaches to Highland ridge. After a difficult march to their jumping off lines in the darkness which had necessitated a delayed zero, at 0240 1/Devon and 1/East Surrey moved forward against weak opposition. As the Surrey entered Beaucamp the enemy fled, discarding their rifles and machine guns; the Devon met rather stiffer resistance on the exposed ground to the south of the hamlet but outflanked the positions and pressed on. By about 1030 both battalions were on the lower slopes of Highland ridge and in touch with 42nd Division.

As the two battalions of 95 Brigade began their advance, the very weak 1/R.W.Kent managed to get two platoons into African Trench. Enemy resistance along the divisional front was clearly weakening and an aircraft reported that the enemy was seen evacuating the valley between Gouzeaucourt and Villers-Plouich. A cavalry patrol was pushed towards Villers-Plouich at about 1100 but reported that it had come under fire from positions on Welsh ridge to the east of the village. Nonetheless, reserve battalions were ordered forward partly in case of counter-attack but more in order to pass through and continue the pressure on Highland ridge and Villers-Plouich. In the early morning 1/East Surrey had moved down the slope and reached a trench running very close to the western and northern edges of the village. With 1/Norfolk and 1/Cheshire on their left, 1/East Surrey and 1/Devon were ordered to send patrols on to Surrey Road, west of la Vacquerie. Enemy opposition had not disintegrated but it had degenerated into one of isolated machine-gun posts rather than a coherent and definite line of resistance.

The situation became fluid and very confused as several battalions became concentrated in a confined area. It appears that 1/DCLI and 12/Gloucester made a difficult advance towards the sunken lane linking La Vacquerie and Gonnelieu. It is also likely that when 15 Brigade received orders for three battalions to pass through 95 Brigade and continue the advance eastwards astride the Cambrai road, rather than wait for the appointed time and supposed place, GOC 15 Brigade opted to send two battalions through immediately he could get orders to them. In what was a chilly and wet night the decision and the general confusion caused immense problems for the staffs and ration parties. The diarist of 16/R.Warwick noted with obvious satisfaction that the drummers who comprised the ration party were able, unlike those of other battalions, to locate their companies. The left of the division was in touch with the New Zealanders (who had leap-frogged 42nd Division) at the south-east corner of La Vacquerie; the advance by 1/Norfolk and 1/Cheshire met with little opposition as they moved in the direction of Banteux. During the following night 5th Division was relieved by 37th Division.

On the other side of the corps' boundary, 21st Division of V Corps had come into the line on the south-western and southern approaches to Gouzeaucourt on 26-27 September. Its left brigade attacked on 27 September astride the Cambrai road with 1/R.W.Kent of 5th Division to its left. Companies of 12/13th Northumberland Fusiliers fought their way into African Trench and held it until a ferocious counter-attack in the evening forced them out. South of the main road 1/Lincoln had edged across Heather Trench and thus closer to the southern exits of Gouzeaucourt. Early on the morning of 28 September an aircraft reported the village to be empty. Patrols moved into it from the western side and worked their way eastwards until they reached the railway. An attack was prepared for the following night, with 110 Brigade having moved up on the right and 2/Lincoln joining 1/Lincoln on the left. In the expectation of another assault during the night the enemy gassed and shelled the forming up positions north and south of the Cambrai road. When the attacking battalions showed themselves in the moon-light at 0330 to follow the barrage they were raked by machine guns sited on the higher ground of Fusilier ridge. The attack ground to a halt with battalions mixed up and disorganised. Some sort of order was re-established by dawn and 1/Wiltshire was somewhat optimistically ordered to pass through the forward battalions, followed by 12/13th NF and 1/Lincoln, and continue onto the Gonnelieu ridge to take Gonnelieu village from the north. The plan collapsed because the Germans continued to occupy and resist from trenches directly in the path of the proposed advance. Accounts vary as to whether it was actually 16/R.Warwick of 5th Division or one of 21st Division's battalions which was the first into an evacuated Gonnelieu early in the morning of 30 September.

12

Regaining the Wastelands: Conclusion

By 30 September, therefore, units of VI, IV, and V Corps were again occupying the villages and positions in the northern devastated zone that British and Australian units had taken by the early days of April 1917. In several areas some units were even a little further east. The advance had been conducted by troops many of whom had never before been in action. By this stage of the war the BEF was comprised largely of 18-19 year old boys and men in their 30s. Many of the enemy units were similarly composed and they, too, in the main had fought well until their position seemed untenable. Then, many were content to surrender. The machine-gun teams had, however, often fought to the end and had inflicted severe losses on the attacking battalions. The morale of these enemy troops remained largely unbroken and staged their rearguard actions on grounds of their own choosing. They had fought their actions with what today would be described as excellent economy of force. In the face of this often resilient defence, British post-battle reports understandably praised the attitude, endurance, adaptability, and courage of the troops in what had developed into more-or-less open warfare. The operations since mid-August had been almost continuous, with the enemy being given no rest, but the British troops were themselves exhausted. In order to maintain morale, the divisional AA&QMGs and staff had done what they could to ensure rations were delivered regularly together with such additional extras such as lemons and chewing gum. Divisional canteens were kept supplied and, together with the cookers, travelled with the B Echelon. So that the troops could have as many comforts as possible when out of the line their packs and greatcoats closely followed the advance. The field cashiers were also at hand to provide money for purchasing comforts at the canteens and rest ares under divisional control were adequately supplied with water for washing

According to 5th Division's AA&QMG water supply was "the great and outstanding trouble" of the advance across the uplands. The supply of three Garfield lorries by corps to the division was "absolutely invaluable" for the maintenance of its supply. Before the operations began the division had received 550 water crates and every brigade held four 100 gallon water tanks for emergencies. These proved largely sufficient, although double the number would have been preferred. To supplement the reserves field companies searched endlessly for uncontaminated wells or positions for new bores. They were handicapped by a shortage of pumps and requests were submitted for the provision of chain-helice petrol operated pumps and windlasses with ropes and buckets. These could be erected quickly and resulted in, for example, 93 Field Company of 17th Division opening 32 wells in addition to erecting numerous water troughs and tanks in about one week.

The period of the advance had been what 3rd Division described as "instructive and interesting." It had provided the troops and staffs with "valuable" preparation and opportunities to experiment with the process and tactics of open warfare. The widely employed advanced guard system was generally thought to have worked well. Most divisions had one infantry brigade leading and the other two following in support and reserve. The brigades spent two days in each role before alternating. The usual formation was for two battalions to be the van, each with two companies up. If the division was working on a narrower front, or if the enemy rearguard withdrew before being attacked, one battalion was considered sufficient as the lead. In 42nd Division sometimes only one strong patrol of platoon strength would lead the advance. When it met opposition it would be supported by a creeping barrage and, if that was insufficient to eliminate the machine-gun nest or nests, a rather more set-piece assault would be organised. GOC 38th Division advocated attacks on a narrow front of only about 500 yards per battalion. He believed that as the Germans were utilising defence in depth the advance should also be made in depth. A narrow front meant that the artillery could concentrate on a smaller area and if companies advanced in echelon on the flanks of the principal thrust they would be expected to deal with the expected counter-attacks.

The essential problem confronting all senior divisional officers was the lack of training opportunities for troops to learn the new tactics required for this type of warfare. With some justification, GOC 5th Division complained that his division had had no real time for training since its arrival from Italy in mid-April. Despite that, Major General Ponsonby believed that the initiative of his subalterns and NCOs in handling their men was "remarkable" and applauded the regularity by which NCOs assumed command when their officer was killed. The fine fighting spirit of the men was thought to have been behind the successes during August and early September. By the end of the month, however, one brigadier in the division considered that the initiative shown by NCOs in dealing with machine-gun positions "was not good." There was widespread concern about the apparent inability of subalterns and NCOs to advance by compass bearing and there were regular complaints about a lack of maps. In what little time was available for training too much of it was apparently spent on PT and bayonet work rather than on practising how to use rifle grenades and coordinating the use of trench mortars. Four light Stokes were usually attached to each brigade and were widely considered to have been very useful. The gun was slung on the back of a man and a helmet replaced the heavy and bulky base plate. Each man of the detachment carried two rounds and fought as infantry once the ammunition was exhausted. The practice of attaching two mobile 6 inch Newtons to the lead battalions was also thought to have worked well because they offered almost immediate support against machine-gun positions. If sufficient rounds had been carried up they could provide a form of close artillery support to the infantry who, it was thought in some quarters, had been insufficiently trained in how to fight their own way forward. They were too prone to go to ground and wait for the artillery to provide cover. This was a problem that one senior officer believed, "Will have to continue to be faced."

Too little attention was also paid to learning how to use ground effectively, scouting activity, and in practising how to mop up concealed or over-run machine-gun posts. Sometimes attacks were so hastily organised that men were forced to abandon prepared hot meals at the assembly positions and move forward so quickly that they arrived at jumping off points in an uncoordinated and unaligned jumble of platoons and sections. As they were sorted out into coherent sections and platoons the men assumed batteries of machine guns grouped in pairs, fours or even eights were already in position to fire an overhead barrage and protect their flanks. But there did remain some dispute as to how machine guns should be deployed in support of attacks. Some senior officers argued they should come under the command of the CO of the battalion they were assisting; others that the COs had too many other things to think about and should leave the issue of the machine guns to the batteries' own commanders. There was a fairly widespread consensus, however, that sections should be allotted a definite area and a definite task instead of simply being "tied to the battalion." The "task" could include guarding valleys and approaches to dead ground and providing fire to break up counter-attacks.

In the same way as the machine guns were vital as a support arm to the infantry, the artillery continued to play a similarly crucial role. Artillery group commanders were described as living "cheek by jowl" with infantry brigadiers and claimed to have adapted swiftly to the tactics of open warfare. They even tried to find time to train numbers of gunners in the use of captured German 77mm field pieces and trench mortars. There were demands for all guns to carry at least eight rounds of smoke on their limbers because attempts to lay a smoke barrage were sometimes delayed by having to bring up shells from the rear. They had to be ready at short notice to fire creeping barrages of smoke and shrapnel, but the urgency of the shoot often meant that the guns could fire only what were known as straight line affairs. This was in part because the infantry's forward positions were often speculative. This problem was addressed in 17th Division by allocating the infantry a series of definite short bounds. Each bound had to be completely gained and the news reported back to the guns before the troops could resume the advance. The brigades were not, however, always able quickly to concentrate their guns and thus their fire. Given the sometimes congested roads the guns of individual batteries could often not advance at the same speed or as a coherent unit. This prompted demands that the bulk of the available guns, which often included a brigade of heavy artillery operating under divisional orders, should come under divisional command rather than the advanced guard commander. But in order to provide immediate supporting fire for the van it was suggested that the leading battalion should have the services of a single, or occasionally a section, of 18 pdrs. These forward guns were considered to be good for morale and useful for knocking out machine-gun posts and halting possible enemy counter-attacks. A balance had to be kept as to how far forward these were to operate and what degree of infantry protection they should enjoy. There were instances, for example, of their crews being felled by snipers and machine-gun fire.

The artillery usually won the praise and appreciation of the infantry during the advance but one component of the all-arms battle which did not receive such universal acclamation was the Tank Corps. GHQ's attempt to withdraw as many tanks as possible in order for them to be serviced and regrouped in preparation for the anticipated set-piece battles against the *Siegfried Stellung* meant that only a small number of Mark IVs remained available for use. These machines were very unreliable and slow and, as one officer noted, had been "adequately countered" by the enemy forces. Whippets were considered to be a better option but there were generally too few of them available. At different times during the August and September operations Major General Deverell had described the tanks as being a "complete failure," a "disappointment" because they did not even cross the start line, and of being "of no value." Major General Ponsonby considered tank-infantry cooperation had been "not entirely satisfactory" and that their worth was questionable. He believed that they would have been more use if they followed, rather than led, the infantry. He also wanted the machines to be under his command when operating with his division but as well as remarking that there was often no time for the tanks to liaise with the infantry commanders he accepted that tank personnel were often exhausted by their almost continuous activity and that they did whatever they could to assist.

Supply tanks were, however, of great value. In particular they carried forward ammunition and engineering stores which saved the weary infantry from having to perform the tasks. They "helped enormously" in the consolidation process of newly-won positions and prompted Major General Solly-Flood to comment, "They should always be available if possible." Assistance in re-supply was also provided by 59 Squadron RFC. Its aircraft could drop boxes of SAA often within 25 minutes of a request being submitted by divisional staff. This swift response gave troops confidence and boosted their fighting spirit. Requests for re-supply could also be made directly to DHQ by pigeon although, as with the case of aircraft, this did not always work well in stormy weather. There were occasional reports of troops running short of SAA, but this was usually owing to the heavy expenditure by Lewis guns on low flying enemy aircraft and on enemy counter-attacks. Overall, it seems as that Q Branch and its staff and personnel did manage to keep the forward troops adequately supplied with the necessities.

This also included the engineers' and pioneers' stores. During offensive operations GOsC divisions wanted at least some of the pioneers to come under their direct command rather than being hived off to corps. The usual compromise was for two companies of pioneers to be attached to the attacking infantry brigade so that they could immediately work on consolidation. The other company (or two others in the case of 14/R.Warwick) worked on roads in the rear.[1] With the tactical situation rapidly changing, the necessity of the OC field company section and OC pioneer companies to keep in constant touch with the GOC brigade to whom they were attached was considered to be paramount. Sometimes engineering dumps hastily abandoned by the enemy proved useful for the supply of timber, picks, shovels, and wire cutters. Sections of RE usually accompanied the pioneers to search for booby traps but this work was also done, when it was available, by personnel of tunnelling companies.

As in all offensive operations during the war one of the greatest of the many difficulties was how to maintain open communication between division, brigade, and the forward troops. Divisional cavalry proved "invaluable" in assisting in this and there were calls for a full squadron rather than the usual couple of troops to be attached to every DHQ. Because they were in almost continual contact with the enemy they could not do what were described as their "legitimate tasks" but they were particularly useful in maintaining lateral communication with flanking divisions. Cyclists, too, proved adept at this but were handicapped when riding across country. Valuable as they were, however, the mounted troops could not always ensure that their own division's creeping barrages were coordinated with those of the flanking divisions. The part answer seemed to be to have the artillery group HQ relocate to the DHQ. This helped but an OC of one divisional signal company believed the difficulties would be diminished if DHQ were more prepared to make use of the wireless. He blamed their neglect of their use on a lack of confidence in their reliability, inadequate training on the part of signal personnel, and the time it took for the barely trained signallers to encode and decipher messages. He also criticised the limited use of power buzzers during open operations but believed the construction of a new and

1 Pioneer battalions had been reduced from four to three companies in February-March 1918. This was a sensible move because it aligned with the number of infantry brigades and field companies within a division.

more practical hand cart designed by the wireless officer of 25th Division would allow them to be transported far more readily and easily.

Another major difficulty in establishing and maintaining communications was a lack of cable. In trench warfare availability had not been much of a problem but as the advance continued, additional cable had to be found. Teams recovered and re-used that which had been previously laid between DHQ and brigade HQ but as the battles moved forward more had to be found to keep corps HQ in touch with its several DHQ and also with army HQ. A system evolved which employed only one telephone line for all three battalions of a brigade and its attached batteries back to brigade HQ. Further lines were then added between DHQ and its various report centres. The limited number of lines meant that follow-on brigade HQ were obliged to establish themselves along the line already laid. Wherever possible lines were laid on higher ground and kept clear of roads, villages, and valleys. Ideally, dumps of light hop poles were kept at the divisional report centre to lift lines over roads and tracks. As if their task was not already sufficiently difficult, signallers worked with the handicap of a cable wagon which was poorly designed and inadequate for the task. The system of report centres was, however, thought to work well and there was some thought given towards establishing battalion report centres in addition to the brigade and divisional ones. Because this would have involved yet more lines, signal companies urged battalion HQ, and especially FOOs, to make more use of Lucas lamps and other visual means of communication. The common complaint was that FOOs had become far too used to telephones during trench warfare and were unprepared for the current operations.

Signallers also advocated more regular use of pigeons by the infantry. Baskets were sent up daily by despatch riders or mounted orderlies but "for no very comprehensive reason" OC companies were accused of "hardly thinking of them." They tended instead to use runners, especially if the company commander was not close to his pigeon basket. However, runners were vulnerable whereas pigeons were simply unpredictable. The cost in runners in the period of open warfare was substantial. Battalion COs tended to move about during operations which meant that runners often had difficulty in locating them and spent more time than necessary under fire. Furthermore, too often runners were sent forward with the attacking companies and became casualties even before they had attempted to deliver a message. Whenever possible the "excellent and valuable" motorcycle despatch riders were used by DHQ, but signallers were frequently bewildered as to why the infantry did not make more use of contact aircraft. The troops carried Popham Panels, were supposedly aware of the set times the aircraft would be overhead to receive signals and had ground sheets to spread as additional indicators. It was generally accepted, however, that cable communications were sometimes already in place by the time the aircraft appeared and that troops were reluctant to disclose their position to enemy observers by signalling to the aircraft. The main advantage gained from air cooperation was thus the intelligence collected by the aircrew from observation rather than by information received from signallers on the ground.

The flow of open operations meant that divisions were often unable to bury their own dead; the job was often done by corps although divisional burial officers could remain behind to clear the fallen once their formation had moved on. Casualties were heavy but the medical facilities were sufficient and never overwhelmed. The usual practice was for one field ambulance to clear the left attacking battalion or brigade and another, the right. The dry weather meant that tracks were usually firm enough for motor ambulances to work close to the front and offer speedy evacuation. In preparation for its attacks on Ervillers, Sapignies and Béhagnies between 23-25

August, for example, 2nd Division despatched its RAMC bearers from No.6 and No.100 Field Ambulances to 5 and 6 Brigades respectively. An advanced dressing station was established about 300 yards west of Courcelles on the Courcelles – Ayette road; a main dressing station lay between Ayette and Douchy; a casualty clearing station was, in the words of one OC field ambulance, "rumoured!!!" to be opening at Bac-Du-Sud. Motor ambulances could get as far forward as Béhagnies and these, together with wheeled carts cleared the wounded to the ADS. Here they were re-dressed and sorted into walking and lying cases. The walking wounded were transferred by six lorries lent by 3rd Division and two by corps to the collecting post at the crossing of the light railway 500 yards north-west of Ransart. There was a YMCA hut at the collecting post to provide sandwiches and tea. The post-battle report stated that casualties were slight, and the wounded easily cleared.

Divisions had been relieved whenever possible to allow of short rests but the opportunities for such periods were extremely limited. GHQ estimated the enemy still had 40 fresh divisions to put into the line but how close to establishment they were was speculative. The enemy divisions that had faced the British advance had certainly been massively worn down, but so, too, had the British formations. During the approximately almost six weeks between 21 August and 29 September some divisions in IV, V, and VI Corps had suffered well over 1,000 fatalities. Battalions had been re-filled by inexperienced troops who, if they were lucky enough, had acquired survival and battle skills on the job. Many others had not survived their first engagement. Reports of their behaviour and morale on the often intensely hot and frequently featureless battlefields are almost unerringly positive. They possessed "fine fighting qualities", displayed "an excellent spirit," and were "well handled in difficult circumstances." The cooperation between unit commanders and staffs was described as "entirely whole-hearted." The German machine-gun rearguards had continued to show equally determined resolution and bravery but the ways and means by which they had been pressured relentlessly by the advancing brigades, supported by seemingly bottomless reserves of artillery and air power, had proved that bravery was not in itself sufficient. The war had evolved into one of a series of well-coordinated and executed all-arms operations maintained by a logistics system which could keep the forward arms supplied with the tons of ordnance arriving daily at the Channel ports. Against this overwhelming tide of materiél the Germans would ultimately be unable to sustain a defence. The Northern Wastelands had been retaken by the British and Dominion divisions but in front of them once again loomed the still formidable obstacle of the Hindenburg Line.

Tour 1: Le Transloy (43 miles)

The village of Le Transloy lies on what was about the eastern limits of the final attacks of the Somme offensive. As late as 27 January 1917, 1/Border was involved in an operation intended to take the western part of the village. On 17 March 1917, 5th (Aust) Division found it deserted and the village quickly became used as a rest and assembly area for troops and artillery. On 23 March 1918, 23/RF of 99 Brigade withdrew through it after the CO realised his battalion was on its own in the Green Line to the east. The following day, 51 Brigade of 17th Division acted as rearguard on the main road as 52 Brigade moved through Le Transloy towards Flers. The London battalions of 140 Brigade fell back through it on 24 March but when those of 141 Brigade, intermingled with troops of 17th Division, approached the village they spotted German patrols had beaten them to it. The British troops were marshalled around to its north. On 2 September 1918, 17th Division conducted an operation to envelop the village. Two battalions of 52 Brigade, 9/Duke's and 12/Manchester, were to work around from the south while 7/East Yorks circled from the north. By the time the two pincers closed to the east of the village the enemy had withdrawn. Having eventually overcome some stout resistance from the enemy in the civilian cemetery to the west of the village two companies of 6/Dorset moved unopposed through the ruins. The view from the civilian cemetery on the D19 to Lesboeufs looks across the motorway and the old Somme battlefields to the west (**1**).

Drive south on the N17 and turn left onto the D19 towards Rocquigny. There were many transport lines and dumps either side of the main road. Knightsbridge Camp was on the south side of the D19 soon after the turn from the N17 (**2**). The village defences constituted a part of the Rocquigny–Bapaume Line in 1917; in 1918 it had a strong major trench running from the north, round its western side, and covering the southern approaches. On 19 March 1917, 20th Division passed through the village and incorporated some of the German defences into the temporary line of resistance. Until the March Offensive the village and its fields housed many heavy batteries and their horse lines. In the early morning of 24 March 1918, 142 Brigade arrived at the village following its circuitous march from Vallulart Wood. It was about at the same time that 51 Brigade, having failed to find any troops of the London Division, was ordered to fill the gap between the village and Sailly-Saillisel and make contact with 9th (Scottish) Division. A line was taken up from 600 yards due south of Rocquigny to run south-westwards to the Bapaume – Péronne road, and to about 800 yards from the northern end of Sailly-Saillisel. It gained touch with 52 Brigade in the village itself and briefly with some troops of the Scottish Division. The right of 51 Brigade was then pulled back to the Bapaume road about halfway between Le Transloy and Sailly-Saillisel. The village also witnessed the withdrawal of troops of the detached 99 Brigade and the RND. What remained of 4/Bedford and the Artists after they had fought their way out of an almost complete envelopment to the east of the village passed through, as did

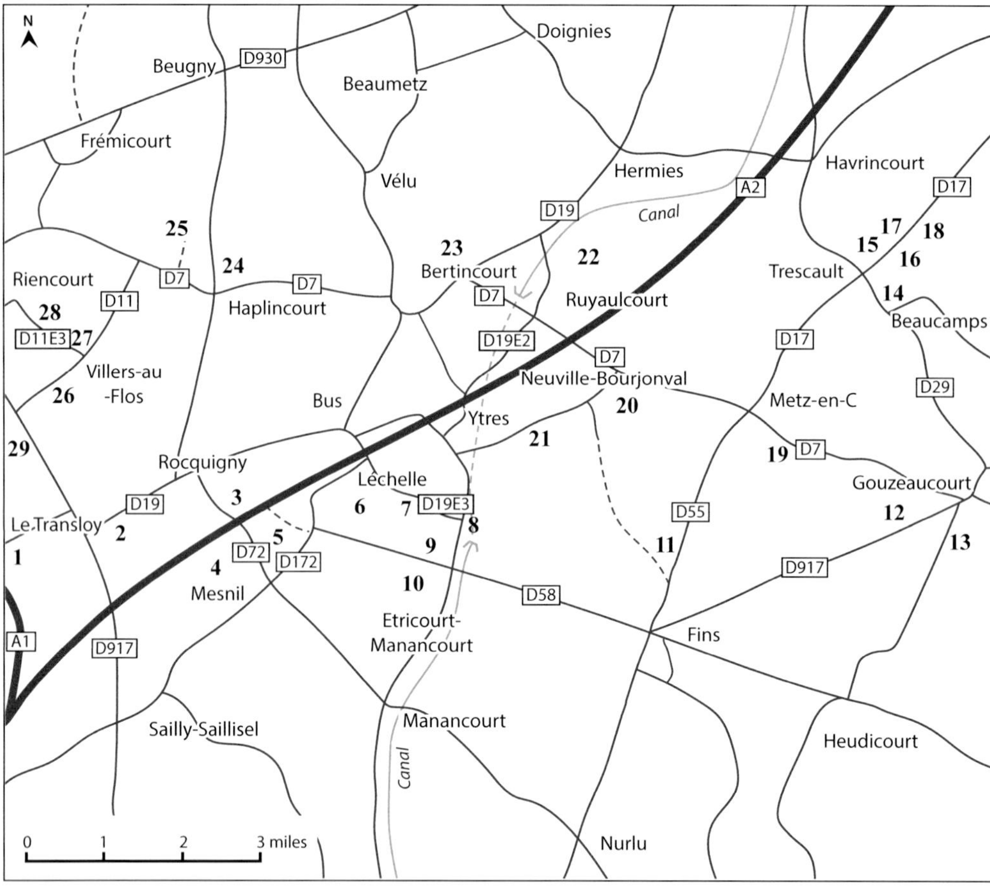

Tour Map 1 Le Transloy.

two battalions of 50 Brigade, 6/Dorset and 7/East Yorkshire, These battalions were accompanied by several supporting tanks. On 2 September 1918, 50 Brigade re-took Rocquigny and pressed on to take the trenches to its east between about the motorway and the D19.

Take the D20 towards Mesnil-en-Arrouaise. On the left of the road and just before the motorway was the site of Lonely House (**3**). This lay on what was the original road which ran down to Equancourt and Fins. There is now a farm complex on the site. In the early morning of 24 March, two battalions of 140 Brigade held a trench of about 200 yards in length across the old road. The brigade's third battalion was a little to the west where it was in touch with 141 Brigade. One company of 1/R.Berks of 99 Brigade was also in the area. The initial enemy attacks from Mesnil were repulsed but around midday the flank of 10/Sherwood of 51 Brigade in Loon Wood was turned (**4**). (The wood can be seen due west of Mesnil, south of the motorway) This attack confirmed the suspicion that 51 Brigade was, in fact, the right of Third Army. Under intense enfilade fire 18th and 19/London were compelled to withdraw to the edge of the village. The brigade's left battalion, 20/London, was in touch with 12/Manchester of 52 Brigade and three tanks deployed in support.

Leave Mesnil on the D172, and head north-east. Bear right to keep on the D172 towards Equancourt. The area towards the motorway was heavily fought over by the London Division (**5**). Turn left after about 800 yards onto the D19E3 to Léchelle. The trees of Four Winds Farm (**6**) are across the fields on the right. Those of Léchelle Wood were closer to the lane but the copse no longer exists. In the village follow the D19E to the right. Five Points Cemetery (**7**) is in the fields on the right as the road drops down to the D43/D18. By September 1918, field ambulances and a CCS had returned to the area around the station. (The station area and adjoining sidings is signed now simply as 'Gare'). The cemetery was made by those units. There is a spread of casualties from, among others, 7th, 17th, 21st, 33rd, and 38th Divisions. Three of the graves are those of: Brigadier General Sanders, DSO and Bar, GOC 50 Brigade, 17th Division; 27 year-old Major Edward McCosh, 9/HLI, and 22 year-old Captain Arthur Williams of 15/RWF.

Continue to the T junction and park at Gare (**8**). Before the enemy offensive three CCS were stationed close to the railway in this area. Walk up and over the southern portal of the canal tunnel. Vallulart Wood is on the left; the remaining section of Hayettes Wood is a little further on to the north-east. There is now no real gap between the two woods. This position offers good views across an area of intense activity by elements of 47th and 63rd Divisions and 1/KRR during the retreat of March. In early September battalions of 17th Division fought their way across the canal and towards the Mouettes System of trenches less than a mile to the east.

Return to the car and drive down the D43. At the crossroads turn right and visit Equancourt – Rocquigny Road British Cemetery (**9**).

On the southern side of the D172 and about opposite of the cemetery was Léchelle aerodrome (**10**). The hangers almost abutted the road a little further to the west. The area was crossed by 20th Division in March 1917. Machine guns of 2nd Division were positioned on the slopes facing east and were then joined by the remnants 47th Division and those of 1/R.Berks, 23/RF, and 1/KRR of the detached 99 Brigade. On 23 March they temporarily held a line running roughly north-south across the airfield and the road, east of Four Winds Farm, and on to the D19E.

From the cemetery, return to the crossroads. Go straight over. The *sucrerie* defended by elements of 2 Bn MGC and 1/R.Berks was where the engineering works is now located on the south side of the crossroads. Continue towards Equancourt. Two hundred yards after a track joins the road from the left, another a few yards further on joins from the right. This was where the Mouettes System ran cross the road. Continue towards Fins. Turn left onto the main D917 and take the D55 towards Metz-en-Couture. Fins village was taken by 20th Division on 4 April 1917. Drive up the slope and park at the civilian cemetery just beyond a fork in the road (**11**). This site offers an excellent panorama of the area crossed by the Dessart Ridge and Metz Switches. This was the Battle Zone of 47th Division in March 1918 and the terrain crossed by 20th Division in April 1917 as it moved towards the capture of Metz. Return to Fins and take the D917 towards Gouzeaucourt. What today constitutes the remains of the once much larger Dessart Wood are passed on the left. About 300 yards south of Gouzeaucourt a slight rise on the left of the road marks the position of the mill attacked by 2/RB of 8th Division on 4 April (**12**).

Sitting on top of the ridge away to the right is Gauche Wood. When 8th Division launched its well-planned attack against Gouzeaucourt and the wood on 12 April, 2/West Yorks was to the east of the wood, 2/Scottish Rifles and 1/East Lancs advanced northwards up the railway and the land between it and the main road. To the left of the road 1/Notts&Derby approached the village from the west. On 22 March 1918, Gauche Wood was eventually lost by the South Africans of 9th Division and the village was evacuated. In September the area on both sides of the main road witnessed the several attacks on the African and Heather Trench systems by the New Zealanders, 5th, 21st, 17th, and 38th Divisions' attacks. The fighting was ferocious but by the end of September Gouzeaucourt had been taken.

Gouzeaucourt New British Cemetery (**13**) is 200 yards down the D29 which join the D917 from the right soon after the first line of houses. Continue through the village in the direction of Cambrai and at a fairly sharp right hand bend 300 yards past the church, go straight over onto the D29 signed, amongst other places, to Trescault and Hermes. After another 800 yards, turn left, still on the D29 towards Trescault and Hermes.

(If you have time, continue straight on to visit Villers-Plouich. The road is now the D56. The village contains the large Fifteen Ravine Cemetery in the lower ground to the right (which was actually Farm, rather than Fifteen, Ravine) and the communal cemetery, which contains a row of graves largely of RND men, towards the northern end of the housing on the D56. The track at the northern end of the cemetery leads up to the ravine where Corporal Foster of 13/East Surrey won his VC in April 1917. Drive back into the village and in front of the *Mairie* take the small *rue de Beaucamps*. Sunken Road Cemetery is sited about 300 yards up the lane on the right. Continue into the hamlet of Beaucamp. This provides excellent views in all directions and underlines how tactically important the hamlet's position was to both attackers and defenders. To the east are Welsh and Highland Ridges; the clump of trees to the north-west encloses Bilhem; and Ribécourt lies in the valley to the north-east. Leave the hamlet by the northern route and join the D29 at what was known as Charing Cross (**14**).

If you did not take the detour through Villers-Plouich, continue on the D29. Beaucamps hamlet (NB: the modern spelling has a 's') appears in a clump of trees on the right after about a mile. The signed road into the hamlet leaves the D29 at Charing Cross (**14**). Park on the verge at the junction and look north, west, and south. Several attacks against Beaucamp in 1917 and September 1918 were launched from about the line of the road. A small clump of trees in the fields to the south-west marks Dead Man's Corner; the eastern face of Gouzeaucourt Wood is on the slope in front of you. Winchester Valley and Metz village can be seen to the north of west.

Drive north into Trescault and turn right onto the D17 towards Ribécourt. Trescault communal cemetery (**15**) with its small number of British burials, including that of Lieutenant Pearce, 4/Grenadier Guards in the bottom right corner, is 100 yards along the left fork *rue de l'Egalité*. On the D17 the trees around the now-abandoned Bilhm, taken in a sharp operation by 12/KRR on 25 April 1917, are soon seen on the right (**16**); a memorial to 42nd (East Lancashire) Division is on the left (**17**); Ribécourt Road Cemetery is a few yards further on (**18**). From this position Boar Copse and Highland and Welsh ridges can be seen to the east, as can much of the Forward and Battle Zones within the Flesquieries Salient. Although the defences within the salient were largely substantial the weakness was, as always, the fact that it was a *salient* and thus easily threatened on its flanks.

Return through Trescault and follow the D17 towards Metz-en-Couture. Metz was taken on 4 April 1917 by the well-coordinated attack of the KRR and RB battalions of 59 Brigade approaching from the south. In March 1918, 47th Division and some elements of the RND withdrew through it; on 6 September it was re-taken by 1/Otago Regiment. Turn left towards Gouzeaucourt on the D7 at the village crossroads and call in to the British extension of the civilian cemetery (**19**) before the road begins to pass to the south of Gouzeaucourt Wood. This is a good position to appreciate the extent of the Metz Switch in which the brigades of 47th Division fought following their initial withdrawal from the Forward Zone. The switch ran north-south almost through the cemetery, with New Switch branching off eastwards about 250 yards to the north. The main switch continued north, crossed the D17, and ran into Havrincourt Wood. To the south the switch followed Dessart Ridge and joined with Dessart Switch to run to the west of Fins.

Return through Metz village and follow the D7. Pass along the southern face of Havrincourt Wood and turn left onto the D7E1 to Neuville-Bourjonval. Visit the British cemetery in the field on the left (**20**). This cemetery contains 206 soldiers, almost all of whom are identified. There are many of 59th and 42nd Divisions from the summer months of 1917. A young 21 year-old captain of 7/Manchester, Robert Grant, was killed in May 1917, and Sergeant Harold Seville, 10/Manchester, a piecer in an Oldham cotton mill, died a month later. When out at rest in the village some of the Oldham territorials had witnessed an evacuated French farmer under escort being allowed to dig in what had been his back garden. To their astonishment the troops saw the man dig up a bag of coins and valuables. From then on, if the Oldhamers had any spare time they had spent it digging furiously in the former gardens of the cottages in the hope of finding buried treasure.

Continue towards Ytres on the D17E1 but once clear of Neuville-Bourjonval park where you can and look south (**21**). On the right is the area of Hayettes and Vallulart Woods; in the centre distance is Equancourt; slightly left is the area crossed by Neuville Switch and the Green Line which ran down to pass east of Equancourt. The Lancashire Fusiliers of 125 Brigade approached Neuville-Bourjonval across this open land from the south-west in September 1918

Drive to Ytres. The village was taken by 61 Brigade, 20th Division on 27 March 1917. With the broad gauge running through it the village became an area of dumps and camps. Elements of 142 Brigade fell back through it during the withdrawal. It was with the assistance of plundered alcohol from one of its dumps that a battalion of Germans made a very noisy and apparently happy attack towards Bertincourt during the night of 23-24 March 1918. In the September advance, battalions of 17th Division, including 10/Notts&Derby, either passed through or close by the village without encountering any significant opposition.

Pass through the eastern side of the village on the D18 towards Bertincourt. Immediately after crossing the motorway, turn right onto the D19E2 to Ruyaulcourt. On the same day as 12/KRR cleared Neuville-Bonjonval, 7/DCLI attacked but failed to secure Ruyaulcourt. The Germans evacuated the village on 28 March 1917, and it was consolidated by 7/SLI of 61 Brigade, 20th Division. The RND withdrew through it on 23 March, and it was retaken on 4 September as 1/Otago made its way towards Neuville-Bourjonval. The village's main feature is the northern portal of the canal tunnel. The waterway continues in the direction of Hermes, passing Hebburn and Garforth Spoil Tips a few hundred years further north. The large Ruyaulcourt Military Cemetery (**22**) is found along an unmarked lane running north-east from the village and which heads towards some fairly dubious canal bridges to the south of Hermes. The lane is narrow and there is not a great deal of parking space in front of the cemetery or room to turn the car around. Return to the village and at its western end turn right onto the D7 to Bertincourt. About half a mile before Bertincourt, and just 400 yards before the junction with the D19 on the right, the road crosses the former broad gauge railway and what became part of the Green Line during the March retreat. Four companies of 2/RMLI dug themselves in close to the railway embankment on 23 March. As Surgeon Lieutenant Gould, attached to the RMLI established his aid post here he bemoaned the fact that only a month before he had been sniping partridges at the very spot. Follow the D7 into Bertincourt.

Bertincourt was another of the villages taken in late March by 20th Division. The Light Horse is thought to have passed through it or close to its northern edge soon after the infantry had taken it. In the morning of 23 March 1918 two brigades of 2nd Division had been deployed to protect what became known as the Bertincourt Salient. By the morning of 24 March, the position was impossible to maintain so 5 and 6 Brigades, and the RND to the south, began to withdraw. About two companies of 2/RMLI were cut off and eventually surrendered but Surgeon Lieutenant Gould managed to escape capture and re-joined the division. The battalions of 142 Brigade also passed very close to the south of the village, with some reports indicating that elements passed through it. Their passage was lit by the light of burning dumps. In September 1918 it was re-occupied by 1/Canterbury. Bertincourt Chateau Cemetery (**23**) is in the north-eastern outskirts of the village, on the north side of the D7. Almost opposite the cemetery on the southern side of the road was the village *sucrerie*. This was used as an assembly area to reorganise troops as they withdrew from the so-called salient.

The cemetery is small, with just under 50 burials. There are nine men from 9/North Stafford, pioneers to 37th Division, and men of 42nd Division. There are also three gunners of 145 Heavy Battery and four from 123 Brigade RFA of September 1918.

Continue on the D7 towards Haplincourt. The Green Line ran parallel to the road, about 200 yards to its north until it turned north soon after a track running between Barastre and Lebucquière crosses the road about half away between Haplincourt and Bertincourt. Haplincourt village was far enough behind the front systems to be used as a camping and training area until March 1918. During the withdrawal in March the route of the D7 was under almost continual shell fire. Large numbers of British troops were also caught in enfilade, especially from the north, as they pulled back towards the Red Line. On the higher ground (**24**) to the east and north of the crossroads at the northern end of the village where the D20 leads up towards Delsaux Farm, Lieutenant Armstrong of 1/King's with 30 men and two Lewis guns joined with two Vickers to inflict "appalling casualties" on the enemy. A quarter of a mile further east in the Green Line two machine guns of 6 Brigade had also halted the advance for a time of enemy troops debouching from Vélu Wood. Haplincourt Wood was on the south-west side of the village. Little of it is left now but for a time in 1918 it served as a tankodrome. During the retreat eight tanks brought up SAA ammunition as well as providing cover to 2nd Division's two brigades of withdrawing infantry. In September 1918 troops of either 2 (NZ) Brigade or a patrol of Royal Scots Greys working with 42nd Division passed through the abandoned village.

Follow the D7 towards Bancourt. As the road climbs, and a little to its north, 2/South Stafford managed to establish a HQ on a slightly sunken track as the battalion withdrew from the Green Line (**25**) The battalion retired in four groups, the last of which was led by the CO, Lieutenant Colonel Alban. He was badly wounded as he crossed the 700 yards of open ground but with the assistance of Captain Williams, the MO, Second Lieutenant Bona, and a stretcher bearer the party succeeded in reaching the temporary HQ. The survivors continued on towards Beaulencourt. At the crossroads, turn left onto the D11 and drive towards Villers-au-Flos. On 2 September 1918 a party of New Zealanders attacked some troublesome Germans housed in a collection of huts on the southern side of the crossroads. The enemy had been pouring fire into 6/Manchester as it worked towards Villers-au-Flos but were silenced by the Kiwis.

Against no opposition Australians of their 5th Division marched through Villers-au-Flos on 18 March 1917. On 23 March 1918, remnants of 152 and 153 Brigades, together with pioneers and sappers of 51st Division fell back to the Red Line a few hundred yards to the east of the village. The survivors of the attached 57 Brigade, 19th Division also joined them there and again came under command of their own division. Since the German withdrawal in March 1917 the village had become one of dumps, camps, and heavy artillery batteries. There seems to have been only token fighting in it during the British withdrawal and on 2 September, 42nd Division had a reasonably straightforward task in clearing it. The assault by 127 Brigade was part of a coordination operation between IV and V Corps. With the support of four tanks, a mobile 18 pdr, and LTMs, 5th and 6/Manchester advanced south-eastwards from Riencourt. The layout of several of the farm tracks and former sunken lanes around the village has altered to a degree but the axis of advance was essentially north and south of the current D11E. The main opposition came from a series of machine-gun posts in a sunken lane which crossed the road to Beaulencourt to the south-west (**26**). The lane ran down to Lubda Copse, which was taken by 1/East Yorks as the Manchester attacked on its left. Both the copse and the lane have since disappeared. The German cemetery (**27**) in the village is a little difficult to find but can be reached from *rue Lecomte* which used to be the main street running through the housing. The former site of the chateau is about opposite the access path to the cemetery.

Leave the village on the D11E towards Riencourt-les-Bapaume. Manchester Cemetery (**28**) is on the right a little before Riencourt. As its name suggests, the cemetery has the graves of Manchesters of 42nd Division. Many of them were members of the 5th and 8th Battalions, the Wigan and Ardwick units, respectively. There are graves of four officers attached to the battalions from 18/Manchester (3rd City Battalion), and one from 13/London (Kensington) Battalion,

Riencourt was, and is, little more than a hamlet. It was of no real tactical importance and was abandoned on 24 March. On 30 August 1918 it was protected by two strong trenches and several machine-gun nests. An initial attack by 5/East Lancs and 8/Manchester on 30 August failed against strong resistance. On the following day, two companies of 10/Manchester advanced due east from about the line of the Bapaume – Péronne road. They followed a heavy barrage but were immediately hit by a counter-barrage and intense small arms fire. Skilful section manoeuvre and firm leadership by the company commanders and NCOs managed to clear the defenders after a costly fight. The text-book action earned the gratitude of the ever hard to please divisional GOC, Solly-Flood. He acknowledged that the battalion had "gone one better."

Drive to the D917 and turn left towards Beaulencourt. The village was entered on 17 March 1917 by troops of 5th (Aust) Division, who then continued on to Riencourt. The fairly extensive cellars below the village were put to good use as divisional and brigade HQ, as well as those of the supporting arms. During March 1918 the village witnessed the withdrawal of many units and formations, not least several battalions of the RND who attempted to reorganise before moving further back. During the advance at the end of August the garrison of the *sucrerie* (**29**) between Beaulencourt and Le Transloy on the main Bapaume – Péronne road put up a resolute defence. The ruins were taken, lost, and retaken several times by 21st Division. The site, which lies on the west side of the main road immediately before the northern end of the village, is now occupied by a small residential and light industrial estate. The route is now back where it started at Le Transloy.

Tour 2: Bapaume (36 miles)

Bapaume was a first day objective for the cavalry on 1 July 1916. The Germans evacuated it on 17 March 1917 and re-entered it on 24 March 1918. It was taken by the New Zealand Division on 29 August the same year. There are about 20 principally Australian and New Zealand graves in the communal cemetery at the north end of the town on the east side of the D917 (**1**).

From the centre of Bapaume head south. The D917 comes in from the left immediately after the town centre. It continues as the D917 towards Péronne. The compact Bapaume Australian Cemetery (**2**) is found on *rue Chemin Blanc* almost immediately on the left after the D917 has begun its turn to the south. Continue on the D917 for about 400 yards and turn left onto the D7 signed towards Bancourt. The motorway and its toll booths have disrupted to some extent the land to the north of the D7 but there remain plenty of open areas as in 1917-18. The land between the motorway and the west of Bancourt was held for a short time by 56 and 58 Brigades of 19th Division on 24 March following their withdrawal from the Green Line. Because there were no existing trenches, and as pressure continued all along the front, the battalions were ordered to pass through Bapaume and take up new positions to its west. Follow the D7 to pass south of Bancourt. Turn left at the crossroads to visit the large Bancourt British Cemetery (**3**).

Drive north and then turn right into Frémicourt. The village was entered by the advanced guard of 5th (Aust) Division on 18 March 1917. On 21 March 1918, 7 Brigade of 25th Division was held in reserve in the village before being called forward. On 30 August the New Zealand Division took Bancourt, went through Frémicourt and consolidated a line about 200 yards to its east. On entering the village take the first left in the centre which takes you up to the Bapaume-Cambrai road. There is a small track immediately opposite but turn right onto the main road. Another track joins from the left but, cautiously, turn left onto another small track after another 50 yards. This lane is surfaced but can in winter become very muddy. It is used by local traffic and in reasonable weather should not cause any difficulties.

The lane leads up to Vaulx-Vraucourt and crosses land heavily fought over in March 1918 and August-September 1918. On 24 March, 19th Division ordered 56 and 58 Brigades to withdraw fighting to a line roughly Bancourt-Frémicourt-400 yards north of the main road. Although a combination of a motor machine-gun section and the guns of 19 Bn MGC did manage to break up some of the German masses forming to the east of the lane and close to the old railway embankment, the attacks continued. Drive on and cross the line of the old railway. There was a great confusion and inter-mixing of units in the area. In the Green Line on the slopes to the right were troops of 58 Brigade, especially 9/RWF. Elements of 123 Brigade of 41st Division formed a line on the lane itself for about 200 yards and connected with 7 Brigade of 25th Division. Drive past a lone mast on the left and continue for about 400 yards. It was in this area where the Green Line crossed the lane that Captain Hayward of 1/Wiltshire won his Victoria

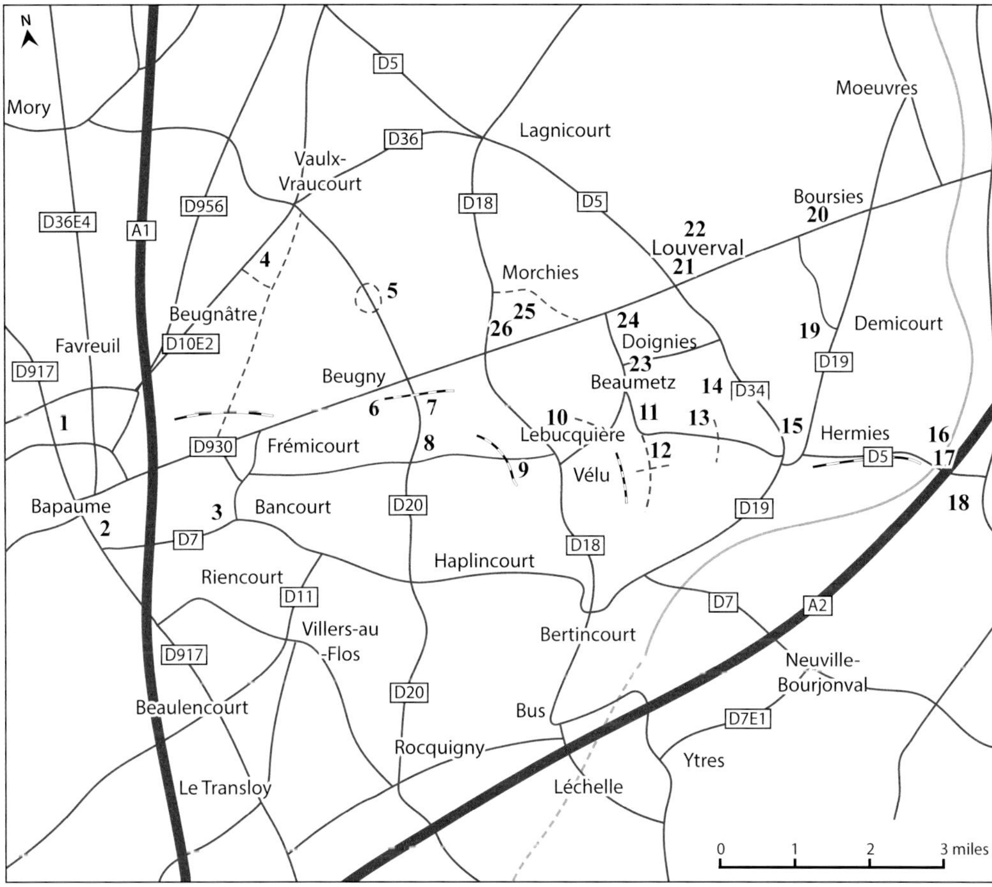

Tour Map 2 Bapaume.

Cross. The left of the Wiltshire was in touch with 124 Brigade a little north of where a track runs off to the left. Take this track and join the D10E2, Turn right towards Vaulx-Vraucourt and after 400 yards on the right visit Vaulx Australian Field Ambulance Cemetery (**4**).

This is one of the very few CWGC cemeteries that contains more German than British and Dominion dead. There are 61 Germans and 52 British and Australian identified remains. The Germans are very largely those killed in March 1918. Among the Allied troops are Major A Geddes MC, of 17th Kite Balloon Company and the 18 year-old Second Lieutenant Kenneth Wendt of 10/Battalion AIF. There are also several soldiers of 4/South Stafford. Following the 1908 Haldane reforms twelve English line regiments formed a 4th (Extra Reserve) Battalion; five of them eventually went to France. The South Stafford deployed in October 1917. It was posted to 7 Brigade, 25th Division until June 1918.

Continue towards Vaulx-Vraucourt and, as the housing begins, turn right onto *rue du Pont*. Turn left and then right onto *rue Brice*. At the T junction turn right and after 100 yards take the left fork. Continue until coming to a diamond crossroads of lanes. Take the left fork and head south-east. The Green Line followed the lane a few yards to its right. You can see the lane in the valley on the right on which you drove north from Frémicourt; the trees surrounding Australian Field Ambulance cemetery on the ridge further over. On 23 March this part of the Green Line, which incorporated Hill 120 (**5**), was held by 9/RWF of 19th Division. It seems likely that there were also some 10/Cheshire of 7 Brigade in the vicinity.

On 29 August 1918, 15/R.Warwick of 5th Division had been tasked with maintaining contact with the New Zealanders advancing on Frémicourt and also to secure this high ground north of the village. The Warwick, and 1/R.West Kent on its left, ran into heavy fire coming from the former Green Line. Little progress had been made when 95 Brigade arrived to relieve 13 Brigade in the evening of 29 August. The next morning 1/DCLI on the right was to cover the New Zealanders' attack on Frémicourt and gain Hill 120. On the left, 1/Devon was to attack the former Green Line in touch with 62nd Division on its left close to Vaulx-Vraucourt. Four tanks were available for the assault. Following a creeping barrage the DCLI came under severe fire from the right but once Frémicourt had been taken by the New Zealanders, the Cornwall, supported by 1/East Surrey, pushed on to Hill 120. On the morning of 31 August, the enemy counter-attacked. Three tanks supported by infantry penetrated the inter-divisional boundary north-east of Frémicourt. This assault was beaten off and the retreating Germans ran into the British protective barrage being fired by the very active and mobile guns of D/15 Battery, 27 Brigade RFA. Turn right onto the D930 in Beugny. Red Cross Corner Cemetery (**6**) is 150 yards towards Bapaume on the south side of the road and north of the old railway embankment. The front row of 25 graves (Row K) are those of men killed or died on 21 March. They were buried by the Germans. There are also others of that date, for example three gunners of 47 Battery (How) 41 Brigade RFA, 2nd Division (II.B) scattered amongst the August burials.

Turn around and go back into Beugny. Turn right towards Haplincourt on the D20. The road crosses the line of the railway, with the old station house on the left (**7**). Stop at Delsaux Farm Cemetery (**8**). The Light Horse took the strong point here on 18 March 1917 and discovered the details of the German withdrawal on the body of a dead German officer. On 22 March 1918, 9/Welch of 41st Division occupied Beugny and fought a fine defensive engagement which allowed 9/RWF and 6/Wiltshire to withdrawal through it. Later, the sector of the Green Line which ran through the farm and the crossroads at the cemetery was allotted briefly to 6 Brigade of 2nd Division. It next came under the command of 56 Brigade, 19th Division. On the morning of 24 March, 9/Cheshire, and 8/North Stafford on its right, were attacked very strongly. Counter-attacks restored the positions temporarily but as the main pressure continued to be on V Corps to their right, 19th Division was compelled to withdraw. On 2 September 1918, Beugny was to be assaulted by 1/Cheshire and the farm by 1/Norfolk. Tanks were also involved. The objective was Chapel Spur to the east of the village. It proved to be a difficult operation with the Cheshire becoming trapped for a time in the southern part of the sunken lane you drove down from Hill 120. Another attempt under a stronger barrage was tried the next day but 16/R.Warwick found Beugny had been abandoned during the night.

Turn left at the crossroads by the cemetery and drive towards Lebucquière. Just before reaching the village, and where the railway once crossed the road (**9**), park and look south. This gives a good panorama of the area. On the left is the dark mass of the west face of Vélu Wood. Germans poured in their hundreds from the wood and were mown down by a combination of fire from machine guns, Lewis guns, rifles, and the artillery of various units as they debouched. The defenders were on the slopes and enfiladed the enemy that made it as far as the valley immediately to your south. Eventually numbers told and the troops withdrew to the Green

Line. North of the railway, although the view is not as clear, was the area where the Germans massed before attacking Delsaux Farm and Beugny from the south-east. The counter-attack led by Captain Palmer of 9/Cheshire, assisted by two platoons of 2/South Stafford, reached about as far as this point.

Drive into Lebucquière and visit the communal cemetery extension (**10**). This lies on the south-eastern side of the village and involves joining a dead end lane which winds between some farm buildings. This medium sized cemetery with just under 800 burials was begun in March 1917. It was used again in September 1918 and, post-war there was considerable concentration. Of the total burials a little over 260 are unidentified. There are men from a wide variety of units and divisions. George Summers of 5/Gloucester probably died of wounds in German hands on 27 July 1916. That month his battalion was fighting on the Somme. There is a headstone in II.B.4 for an unidentified sergeant of the London Rifle Brigade. It has a date of death of 24 March 1918. If the date was correct there was only one sergeant of the LRB killed that day. He was James Gration DCM. When 2/5th London (LRB) was disbanded in February 1918 Gration and many others of the battalion were posted, much to their annoyance, to 28/London (Artists Rifles) of 63rd RND. Gration was originally remembered on the Arras Memorial to the Missing, but the grave has now been identified as his. At the time of this writing, he awaits his own named headstone. Two others from the battalion in the cemetery who were also posted to the Artists are Rfm Frank Tucker in III.B.11 and Second Lieutenant Francis Newell in I.A.11. Newell had been wounded as a rifleman in October 1916 with 1/LRB and on recovery was commissioned and sent to 2/LRB in October 1917. Captain William Thomson in I.E.4 of 41 Squadron RFC was killed on 17 July 1917 while flying either a F.E.8 or a D.H.5. His squadron, which boasted no fewer than 17 'aces' was converting from the former to the latter type of aircraft in July 1917;

Rejoin the D18 and head south towards Vélu. In the hamlet, and by the former station, take the D18E1 to Beaumetz. The road crosses land occupied largely by 51st Division but, for example, 57 Brigade formed a defensive flank at about the railway embankment just north of the hamlet. A little further north of the railway 6/Gordon was held in reserve on 22 March and 300 of 10/Worcester were placed between 5th and 6/Seaforth Highlanders in a line formed on 23 March. Take the first right in Beaumetz and drive down to Beaumetz Crossroads Cemetery (**11**). This has 184 identified remains of the 254 buried here. The cemetery was established in March 1917 and used again in September and October 1918. There was a good deal of concentration after the war, including many of the Gloucesters and Worcesters killed during their counter-attack on 21 March. There are five gunners of 293 Battery lying together, all killed on 21 March, and Brigadier General Gilbert Follett, GOC 3 Guards Brigade killed on 27 September 1918. Most of Beaumetz had been taken on 21 March 1917 by the Australians of 60/ Battalion but it was not completely abandoned by the enemy until several counter-attacks had been repelled on 23-24 March.

Take the road south from the cemetery, cross the old railway, and drive straight across the crossroads which appear immediately. Park and look at the views (**12**). The track on which you are parked goes south to what was very much contested land. Two hundred yards down it there is a junction of tracks. Dugouts in the banks of the cross tracks were used in turn by several brigade HQ. The eastern face of Vélu Wood is on the right, with evidence of the other railway passing close to its edge. The embankment was the site of the rearguard action by two companies of 7/A&SH supported by the machine guns commanded by Major Harcourt. The land drops away to a shallow valley before gently climbing again to a crest which carries the Bertincourt

– Hermies D19 road immediately north of the canal. On a clear day Ruyaulcourt church spire can be seen in the far distance about due south. In the course of the fighting of 21-24 March battalions and batteries of 2nd, 17th, 19th, and 51st Divisions fought in this area east and north-east of Vélu Wood. Captains James of 8/Gloucester and Gribble of 10/R.Warwick both won their Victoria Crosses in this sector; battalions of 58 Brigade fought here before withdrawing on Beugny. In the valley to the south, 2/Ox&Bucks set up bivvies in the evening of 22 March. They had marched up from Vallulart Wood Camp during the day and arrived to find rations, but no rum. Return to the car and drive towards Hermies.

About a mile further on the road is crossed by a north-south track. Park here off the road and walk to the north (**13**). After 50 yards, cross the old railway and look at the view. Doignies is to the north-east and Beaumetz to the north-west. Running roughly parallel to the track which goes towards Beaumetz and about 150-200 yards to its right was Hermies Switch. Units of 19th and 51st Divisions manned this series of trenches as the enemy debouched from Hermies. Bruno Mill was on the track leading up to Doignies (**14**). Two machine guns of 25 Bn MGC poured sustained fire into massed ranks of Germans as they advanced west from Demicourt and Hermies. The guns were supported by another pair belonging to 51 Bn MGC firing from the Doignies – Beaumetz road to the north-west of the mill site.

Drive to Hermies and turn left onto *rue Saint Michel*. Hermies Hill and Hermies British Cemeteries are on the right and left of the road respectively about 200 yards on (**15**). The town was taken by 1 (Aust) Brigade on 9 April after some heavy fighting. Private Kenny won the Victoria Cross for his work, but the enemy was determined to force the Australians from the town and launched several very strong counter-attacks from the direction of the canal. The town was lost on 23 March 1918 and re-taken in early September by 2nd Division.

Hermies British Cemetery was used between April-December 1917. It has a total of 107 burials, including eight graves identified as a group rather than individually. There are members of 36th Division, 8/Dukes, many of which were killed on 29 April 1917, and Australians of 2/ Battalion killed on 9 April. Grave F.10 is that of Brigadier General Roland Boys Bradford VC, MC, the 25 year-old GOC of 186 Brigade. He was killed on 30 November 1917 during the German counter-attack in the Cambrai battle.

Hermies Hill has the graves of over 1,000 Allied soldiers. Over 70 of them are of 62nd Division who were exhumed from their first cemetery in Havrincourt Wood, many 2/Australians from 9 April 1917, and 10/Sherwood of March 1918. There are also many from the RND and 47th Division. There are two relatively elderly second lieutenants: Edward Scott of 7/East Yorks and Lucius Crane of 14/Worcester (P). Scott had been commissioned from the ranks and had a Long Service and Good Conduct Medal. He was 39 and was killed in February 1918. Crane was 36 and died in August 1918.

Drive into the centre of Hermies and take the D5 towards Havrincourt. The trees covering the Spoil Heap (**16**), whose garrisons caused so much trouble to the Australians in April, 17th Division on 22 March, and 2nd Division in September, are on the left. This open ground to the north of the road was riven by trenches and witnessed some ferociously intense fighting. Following one attack there were something like 150 German dead in front of one company of 3/Battalion's wire; 7/Lincoln and 10/Sherwood beat of attacks here in March 1918; 1/R.Berks and 1/KRRC found the area heavy going in September.

The line of the old railway ran parallel to the right of the road, with the civilian cemetery and canal further on to the south. Further on the road crosses the motorway and canal. Park off the road and, being wary of the traffic, walk onto the bridge (**17**). Below is the canal cutting. Unfortunately, there is no easy way down to the towpath from this position. The village of Havrincourt and its huge wood are seen clearly to the east and south. The site of Yorkshire Bank (**18**) can be discerned at the wood's northern edge abutting the towpath on the east side. A large mine crater known as Versuvius was blown in the road ahead. If you have time for a walk the towpath can be reached by following the track which leaves the D5 soon after the town's football ground and heads across the fields towards the Spoil Heap.

Return to Hermies and take the D19 heading north towards Demicourt. The road crosses the land over which the enemy swarmed once they had broken into the Battle Zone of 51st and 17th Divisions. The major Juniper Trench, which became Logan Switch further east, crossed the road soon after the built up area has ended. There are 10 British and Dominion graves of September and October in Demicourt Communal Cemetery (**19**) which is found on the small road to Boursies. Continue on the D19 and park about 1,000 yards north of Demicourt. This is about where the British front trenches crossed the road. They system ran north-west to cross the Cambrai road just to the east of Boursies; to the right it ran south-east across the open ground towards the canal and the Spoil Heap which lie over the crest of the slightly higher ground.

Drive to the Cambrai road and turn left towards Bapaume. Boursies straggles along the main road. It was taken by 12/Battalion on 9 April 1917 following a deceptive ruse on the night of 7-8 April. The Germans launched one major counter-attack, but the village remained in British hands until 21 March 1918 when 152 Brigade was forced from it. It was re-taken by the Guards Division on 3 September. There is an interesting village war memorial on the north side of the road (**20**). Continue along the D930 until the Cambrai Memorial on the right (**21**). Turn up the small road on the east side of the memorial into Louverval and stop at the T junction 300 yards to the north. The chateau and its wood were on the north side of the junction (**22**). The wood has all but disappeared and there is a modern complex now hidden by the hedge where the chateau used to sit. On 2 April 1917, 56/Battalion ran into difficulties in its attack on the hamlet, but the wood and chateau were finally taken. At the same time, 55/Battalion attacked Doignies but, again, the attack initially miscarried. The area was lost by 153 Brigade of the Highland Division during the first surges of the German offensive on 21 March

Return to the Cambrai road, turn right and then at the second left, turn left at the crossroads onto the D34 towards Doignies. At the T junction in the village turn right towards Beaumetz. The road offers good views to the north and south. To the right and as the road begins to climb, the two Vickers which fired in support of those at Bruno Mill were dug into the road bank. Further along a forward 18 pdr of A/256 Battery gave covering fire as troops of 153 Brigade withdrew from Doignies. So, too, did two Lewis guns housed in the trench HQ of D Company of 51 Bn MGC on the road. To the south of the road the length of Hermies Switch stretched to the south on the forward slope in front of Beaumetz. This is the area across which 8/Gloucester and 10/Worcester of 57 Brigade supported by 10 tanks attempted their counter-attack towards Doignies in the evening of 21 March 1918. Take the first left past some farm buildings and drive down to the open ground (**23**). There are good views of the approaches to Hermies Switch; the site of Bruno Mill is due east. Hermies can be seen in the centre right distance.

Return to the village and go straight over the crossroads to climb gently up towards the Cambrai road. This was the sunken lane down which a column of Germans was marching when machine guns and artillery were turned on them. Unable easily to escape up the lane-side banks, scores were killed. Immediately opposite where the lane joins the main road was the site of the farm which was fought over several times by the Australians and Germans in April 1917. Turn right and 150 yards on visit Beaumetz-les-Cambrai Military Cemetery No.1 (**24**). This was originally a German cemetery. Post-war the German graves were removed and some of the known British remains re-interred in collective graves. There is only one officer, Second Lieutenant Kay of 6/Gordon, among the 75 identified graves. The men are mainly from 51st, 6th, and 25th Divisions killed on 21 March. One headstone marks the resting place of 14 unidentified British soldiers. Rather strangely there is one headstone for another unidentified man only three yards away,

Opposite the cemetery on the north side of the main road tracks lead off to the north and east towards Lagnicourt and Louverval. Machine guns of 51 Bn MGC on the right hand track took a heavy toll of Germans advancing down the main road. Enemy cavalry were spotted to the north of the guns' positions during the morning of 22 March. The position marks about the rear of 51st Division's Battle Zone and was the scene of very heavy fighting between the advancing enemy and units of the Highland and 19th Divisions, and 9/LNL and 11/LF of 25th Division.

Drive west along the main road and take the second turning on the right at a small crossroads after about 800 yards. There is a lone tree on the right about 20 yards before the crossroads. This small-surfaced lane runs into Morchies and passes Chaufours Wood on the left (**25**). The wood is not large as it was in 1918 but remains in the same place. The fierce and confused fighting during 22 March continued in the area. In 51st Division, 6/Black Watch and 7/Gordon fought a rearguard here and in their support Colonel Hugh Craigie-Halkett, CO of 9/LNL, won a bar to his DSO. By using a Vickers dug in at his battalion HQ just north of the crossroads he reportedly wiped out a battalion of enemy infantry and its transport on the main road. Further along the lane two companies of 11/Cheshire of 75 Brigade were engaged and elements of the much dispersed 19th Division were also active.

Continue to Morchies and turn left in the village onto the D18. The main action in and around Morchies is covered in Tour 3. Just south of the village is the small Morchies Australian Cemetery (**26**). There are some Australian dead of March and April 1917, a few 11/Queens of March 1918, and considerable numbers of 2/Royal Scots and 7/SLI who suffered here in September 1918.

Drive south, with Chaufours Wood now seen on the left. This road crosses the land held by 58 Brigade, 19th Division on 22 March. The brigade's two forward battalions were in fairly good touch with 123 Brigade on its left across the fields towards Maricourt Wood. One company of 4/KSLI was also north of the *sucrerie* which lay at the junction of the D18 and the D930. Turn right and follow the D930 back to Bapaume.

Tour 3: Favreuil (45 miles)

There is a particularly attractive and well maintained war memorial in front of Favreuil's *Mairie* (**1**). The village was entered by 2nd (Aust) Division on 18 March 1917 and quickly developing into an area of camps for supporting arms. In the early morning of 21 March 1918 two brigades of 25th Division were ordered to assemble in Favreuil and to be prepared to move forward in support of 6th and 51st Divisions. Additional artillery brigades and field companies were also sent to the east of the village, close to the Beugnâtre road. When the withdrawal began the Red Line ran through Monument Wood to the south-west of the village and about opposite to where the memorial to the Franco-Prussian War now stands on the D917. On 25 August 1918 the village was taken by 111 Brigade of 37th Division, with 2 (NZ) Brigade on its right.

Take the D10E3 towards Beugnâtre and visit Favreuil British Cemetery set back on the right (**2**). This is a slightly concentrated cemetery. An interesting group of graves can be seen in Plot II.E. Six men of 36th Coy Labour Corps were buried together, all of whom were killed on 21 March 1918. They may well have been victims of a German shell on their billet. Four had been transferred, probably for health reasons, from line infantry battalions, and two posted from battalions of the Training Reserve. Those who had previously served in a line regiment before being transferred to a Labour Corps unit have that regimental badge on their headstone.

Beugnâtre was taken on the same day as Favreuil in March 1917. There is a communal cemetery on its east side which contains 10 Allied graves (**3**). Two of the graves are of young second lieutenants, the crew of a BE2e of 4 Squadron RFC shot down on 24 March 1917. The village and its surrounds were used extensively by the field artillery and sappers of divisions in the line. On 21 March 1918, 7 Brigade of 25th Division garrisoned the Army Line to the east of the village and on 24 March exhausted remnants of 120 Brigade passed through on their way towards Biefvillers. To the south-east, 19/Middlesex (P) and 23/Middlesex were attempting to reorganise and dig something of a line but they, and what was left of the other battalions of 123 Brigade and the attached 7 Brigade, were soon driven back. On 25 August, 2/KOSB of 5th Division retook the village.

Continue on the D956 to Vraucourt. During the night of 21-22 March 1918, 10/11th and 14/HLI of 120 Brigade, 40th Division, formed a defensive flank along the road (**4**). They were in touch with 6/7th RSF (P) of 59th Division on the left but had no contact with 6th Division on the right.

Units of 2nd (Aust) Division pressed on from Beugnâtre and occupied Vraucourt and Vaulx-Vraucourt during the afternoon of 18 March 1917. The villages are far from attractive, with some considerable industrial and agricultural complexes to the west, north, and south. The villages were lost by 6th Division on 22 March 1918 and were again much fought over in August and early September 1918. The 2nd West Riding Division made several failed attempts to clear

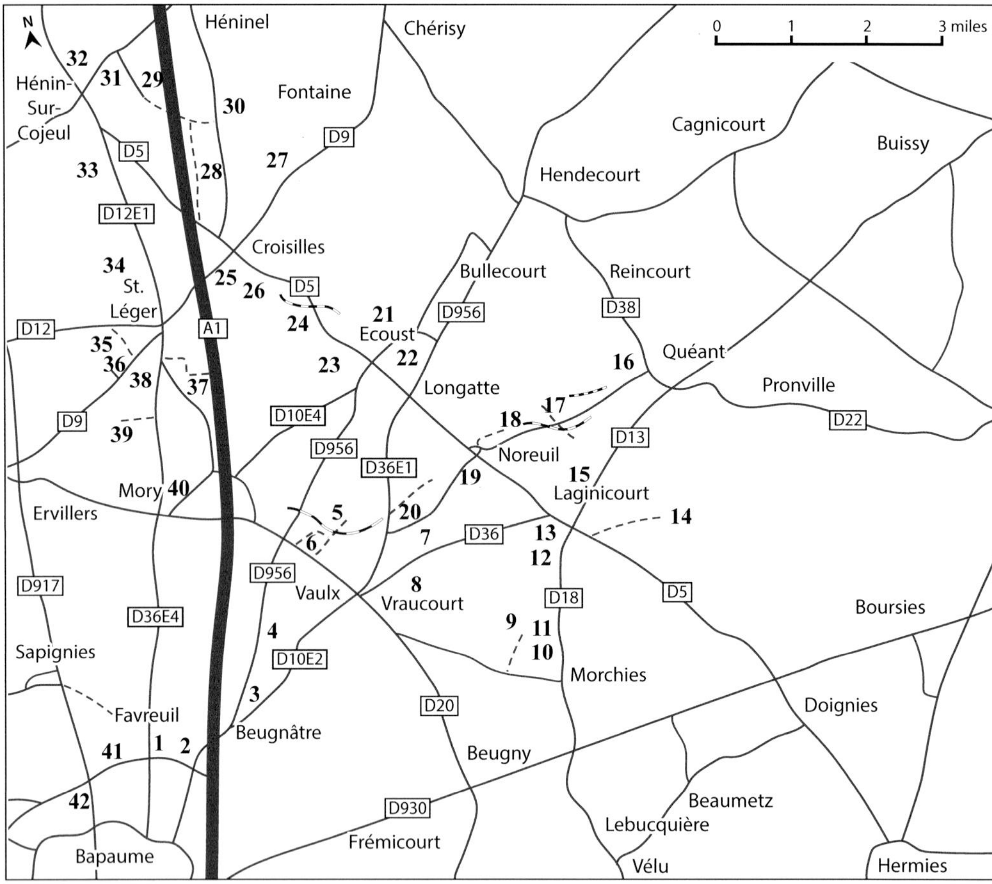

Tour Map 3 Favreuil.

the villages and the open land to their immediate south and east. It was not until 2 September that they finally succeeded in getting through and beyond the ruins.

The road layout has altered marginally since 1918 and there is little evidence of the hard fighting within the built up area. The railway to its north has gone leaving little real trace, and what was the German cemetery close to the broad gauge is now under the plough (**5**). There is an interesting memorial on the road from Vraucourt to a member of the Bachele family, who were the principal land holders in Vaulx-Vraucourt, and an art deco church on the lane leading to the site of the former German cemetery (**6**). Vaulx Hill Cemetery lies about half a mile out of the village on the D36 road to Lagnicourt (**7**). The cemetery lies on the position of Vaulx Trench, the front line of 6th Division's Third System of 21 March. To the north it became Vraucourt Trench in 59th Division's sector; to the south it ran down in front of Vaulx and Maricourt Woods to Morchies. Five hundred yards ahead of the cemetery was the strong point that was finally taken by whippets, 2/Suffolk and 7/KSLI on 2 September.

The track which leads south at the side of the civilian cemetery crosses the position of the former Vaulx Wood (**8**) but can be difficult walking in wet weather. It is easier to return to

Vaulx-Vraucourt and turn left onto the D20 towards Beugny. After about 1,500 yards a lane comes in from the left just as a line of trees begins on the right side of the road. Take the lane. This crosses the area attacked by the York&Lancs and KOYLI battalions of 62nd Division in August 1918. In March 1918 there was a huge confusion of battalions and brigades either side of the lane. Vaulx Wood was on the left; this was lost and regained several times, with 8/ Border and 2/South Lancashire being particularly active here in its defence. Vaulx Trench, which formed part the Vaulx-Morchies Line, ran parallel to the lane about 20 yards to its left. It was manned by 2/York&Lancs and 1/KSLI of 16 Brigade and also by the company of 1/ Buffs which won the "race" to enter the trench before the advancing Germans arrived. At least one company of 3/Worcester was also in a stretch of the line near Maricourt Wood. It was here that 9/Norfolk and 2/Sherwood attempted to re-group and where a counter-attack supported by tanks and the artillery of 256 Brigade RFA was attempted. On the right of the lane in the fields between it and the D20, battalions of 19th Division assembled and dug in as batteries of 18 pdrs moved to the rear.

The lane passes the southern face of Maricourt Wood. The lane on the wood's eastern face gives access to the memorial to Major Wingate RE (**9**). The lane is quite well surfaced and from the memorial there is a good view of the land crossed by the Germans debouching from Lagnicourt towards the former position of Vaulx Wood and the Vaulx-Morchies Line. Return to the lane and turn left towards Morchies. The village was taken by 59/Battalion on 20 March 1917. The banks either side of the road obscure the view but as the village is approached look south over the land occupied and fought over by 19th and 41st Divisions in March 1918. Turn left in the village and head north on the D18 towards Lagnicourt. Stop at Morchies Military Cemetery (**10**). The register here also contains the details of those buried in Morchies Australian, and Lagnicourt Hedge Cemeteries. There are five identified and three unknown British and Canadian soldiers who probably died as prisoners of war buried in the nearby civilian cemetery (**11**).

In the afternoon of 21 March, 11/Cheshire moved to the south-east of the village in support because a major German thrust came down the road which follows a shallow valley from Lagnicourt. Remnants of 2/DLI, 1/West Yorks, and 11/Essex rallied for a short time close to this point before being driven back through the village. The track that passes the civilian cemetery, which also previously formed part of a large German military cemetery, goes north-westwards across the fields to meet another track in a small copse. Within the latter, a sunken track running past the Wingate Memorial branches to the left; to the right a lane leads past Lagnicourt Hedge Cemetery; straight over a track goes across the valley and the higher ground west of Lagnicourt to link up with the D36. The loss of Morchies and the penetrations of the Vaulx-Morchies Line by the evening of 22 March meant that the British line could be marginally straightened. Morchies and the higher ground to its east, which had been the objectives of 62nd Division's several thrusts from Vaulx-Vraucourt, were re-taken by 2nd Division on 3 September 1918.

Continue into Lagnicourt-Marcel. There was a German airfield, the home of *Jasta 2,* in 1916 in the fields on the left (**12**). Lagnicourt Hedge Cemetery (**13**) is located 300 yards along the first turning to the left, *rue de Beugny.* There are five soldiers of 7/SLI, the battalion which began the cemetery, four from 4th Field Ambulance and two from 9th Field Ambulance. Both of the ambulances served the Guards Division. There are nine London Scots of September-October 1917 and also a number of Germans buried here.

The village was taken by 7 (Aust) Brigade on 26 March 1917 after a hard and costly fight. Outposts were established about 200 yards to the east and gradually extended as the weeks passed towards Quéant. It was lost by 6th Division on 21 March 1918 and re-taken by the Guards Division on 3 September after 8 Brigade of 3rd Division had fought a difficult operation to prepare the ground. Drive through the village past the church and take the D5 to the right towards Louverval. As you climb out of the village turn left at the small shrine onto *rue de Doignies*. The lane crosses an area of several important trenches: Skipton Post was on the right; Bradford Reserve crossed the lane where the red barns have since been constructed; Bradford Trench, 6th Division's front line of this sector in March 1918, crossed the lane after a further 600 yards. Drive on about this distance and park (**14**).

To the north-east beyond the windmills are Quéant and Pronville. This ground was the Forward Zone of 6th and 51st Divisions, an area filled with trench systems, dugouts and wire. Travel Trench ran parallel to the D5 on its east side behind you. Communication trenches ran from it to the left and right. Further towards the windmills the British front trenches were not exactly parallel to the road but vaguely mirrored its route. Close to Louverval Wood the front line lay about 2,000 yards to the road's north-east, but it gradually grew closer to the road as it curled back in a north-westerly direction to pass north-east of Lagnicourt about where you are standing. To the south is the main Cambrai–Bapaume road near Louverval; to the far south-west, and beyond the D5, are Chaufours Wood and Beugny.

Return to Lagnicourt and at the staggered crossroads in the village take the right turn onto the D14 to Quéant. The road follows Cornhill valley along which enemy troops poured in the fog of 21 March. On the wall opposite the entrance to the civilian cemetery (**15**) on the left there is a unusual memorial to the village's fire fighters who died on active duty. Bradford Reserve crossed the road through the cemetery, while the front line, Bradford Trench, crossed it after another 600 yards to the east. The German front system to the south-west of Quéant was another 700 yards further on. Drive into Quéant and take the D38 towards Riencourt-les-Cagnicourt. Quéant Communal Cemetery British Extension is on the left as the road climbs out of the village (**16**).

Turn round and head back towards the village. Take the right turn immediately after the communal cemetery and then the left fork after 150 yards. This is the Hirondelle valley, and you are following the route of those enemy forces which on 21 March turned the left of 6th Division and the right of the 2nd North Midland. The British front line, Bradford Trench which in this sector had become Leeds Trench, crossed the road just as the road draws close to the stream on the left; Leeds Reserve, which north of the road here became Halifax Reserve, crossed it 500 yards further on just before tracks join the road from both left and right. The broad gauge railway crossed to the south side of the road at about the same spot and Dewsbury Trench joined the road from the north at about the cross tracks (**17**). Macaulay Avenue ran south of and parallel to the road from where the track joins the valley at the cross tracks. It became Vraucourt Switch after crossing the D5 south of Noreuil. It then followed the valley down towards Vaulx-Vraucourt.

At the junction with the D5 in Noreuil turn right off the main road to climb past the church and onto *rue de Bullecourt*. At the first junction, known to the troops as Iggaree Corner, turn right and drive onto the higher ground for views across to the railway embankment, Bullecourt, and the approaches to Longatte and Ecoust (**18**). This was the right boundary of 59th Division and the Forward Zone garrisoned by the Notts&Derby battalions of 178 Brigade on 21 March.

It is also the area where 2/R.Scots and 1/RSF of 8 Brigade encountered very stiff opposition on 2 September. Return to the village and visit Noreuil Australian Cemetery on its south-western edge (**19**). Vraucourt Switch crossed the track which runs south past the cemetery as the lane climbs. The track crosses the D36 at the Dunelm strong point and then continues across the fields to the sunken cross tracks west of Lagnicourt. It was down this track that the tanks in support of 3rd Division waddled in September.

Take the left at the northern end of the cemetery. This small road which, although sometimes muddy is usually passable, follows the Hirondelle. The lengthy Vraucourt Switch followed it on its southern side. On the other side of the valley is Vraucourt Copse. On joining the D36E1 a slight diversion can be made to visit Vraucourt Copse Cemetery (**20**). Turn right onto the main road and take a track on the right after 250 yards indicated by a CWGC sign. This is where the old railway crossed the road, and the lane can be wet and broken. The lane, known as *rue de l'Hermitage*, degenerates into a path that runs alongside the stream to Noreuil. Do not take the car any further than the cemetery, which is on the right 120 yards from the main road. Private Hugh McIvor VC, whose public memorial is in Courcelles-le-Compte, is buried here. Return to the D36E1, left and drive through Valux-Vraucourt on the D36. At the crossroads north-west of Vraucourt take the D956 towards Ecoust.

The area crossed by the D956 witnessed ferocious fighting in both 1917 and 1918. To the east the land drops away to the Hirondelle valley; to the west is the shallow valley known as Maida Vale. The D10E4 from Mory follows this depression. The land then rises to the plateau nicknamed the Hog's Back. Three hundred yards along the D956 from the junction with the D36, Vraucourt Trench on the right crossed the road and became Banks Trench on the left. After another 300 yards Vraucourt Reserve became Banks Reserve on the western side. These were the rear trenches of the March 1918 Battle Zone of 59th Division. It was in Vraucourt Trench that the pioneers of 6/7th RSF (P) fought their rearguard when most of their division had become casualties. It was also from about this position that 2/5th Lincoln launched its ill-fated counter-attack in the afternoon of 21 March. Towards Maida Vale and the Hog's Back hundreds, if not thousands of advancing Germans had been shot down by some of the surviving machine guns of 59 Bn MGC and divisional 18 pdrs. Further north along the road and about where the H.A.C. Cemetery now lies, was the series of enemy posts which caused so much difficulty to 2/Border, 8/Devon, 2/Gordon, and 2/1st HAC of 7th Division in March 1917. Ecoust and the adjoining Longatte were finally taken by 8th and 9/Devon, and 2/Gordon in a blinding snowstorm on 2 April 1917.

In Ecoust, turn left at the roundabout towards Croisilles and park at the civilian cemetery on the right (**21**). This was the area of higher ground that Major Keating and his few survivors of 176 Brigade were making for when they were finally surrounded and captured. The culvert under the railway was used as a battalion HQ and an aid post. Walk to Ecoust-St-Mein British Cemetery and follow the track towards the railway embankment. The view beyond is across the fields west of Bullecourt and what had been the Forward Zone of 176 Brigade. The communication trench called Pelican Avenue ran north to Stanhope Redoubt. Tiger Trench and then Valley Support joined it from the left, with the front line, Joy Ride Trench, running mainly east-west about 1,500 yards north of the embankment. Walk eastwards along the embankment until reaching the road. The buildings which now lie on the former Station Redoubt (**22**) are 200 yards to the left. Follow the road south for a few yards and use the grass path that leads to Ecoust Military Cemetery (**23**). At the roundabout turn right and return to the car.

Follow the D5 to Croisilles. The rising land to the left of the road was heavily contested in the attempts to take the town in the advance of 1917, to prevent its capture in March 1918, and then to re-take it during the Hundred Days. The railway embankment on the left was assaulted by 22/ Manchester (**24**). Many of their dead lie in the cemetery tucked away on the other side of the railway line. There is a small supermarket on the D5 and a couple of cafés in the centre. The town has grown in recent years and the construction of the motorway to its west has altered some, and obliterated others of the sunken lanes where much of the fighting took place in both 1917 and 1918. There are two British cemeteries, both on the southern side of the town: Croisilles British (**25**), and Croisilles Railway (**26**). There are tracks which lead to the higher ground south of the town running past both of the cemeteries. They are best walked rather than driven and offer some good vistas of the area over which the 7th, 18th, and 21st Divisions operated in March and April 1917, and 34th Division in March 1918. The sunken one from Croisilles British (right fork after crossing the bed of the old railway) winds up to the plateau and the *péage* cutting between the village and St-Léger Wood. A short drive along the D9 towards Fontaine offers views of the ground to the north-east of Croisilles (**27**). The Hindenburg Line crossed the road from left to right about halfway to Fontaine.

The most direct route north from the centre of Croisilles is to take the *rue d'Héninel* to the right soon after the *Mairie*. It runs close to the position of Hill Switch where 25/NF and 16/R. Scots were "blown" from their trenches on 22 March. The road climbs up to a plateau and then drops down Hénin Hill, past Héninel-Croisilles Road Cemetery, to the village of Héninel. If the weather is good rather than take the *rue d'Héninel* it is worth continuing on the D5 and turning up the track to the right immediately before the road goes under the motorway. This lane runs parallel to the motorway to reach Summit Trench Cemetery (**28**). This is very much a cemetery of Royal Fusiliers, largely of 167 Brigade, 56th Division. Most of them died on either 24th or 27 August when the division tried yet more attacks on Croisilles. One of the graves is that of Second Lieutenant George Merrikin. At 40 years of age Merrikin, who had originally enlisted in the RAMC and was a priest or deacon in the Church of England, was a relatively aged officer for his rank.

There are good views from the cemetery across the land attacked by 56th and 52nd Divisions in late August 1918. The track can be followed and then joins with a tarmac lane coming up on the left which drops under the railway and motorway. Take this lane and on the right soon after the bridges is Cojeul British Cemetery (**29**). The cemetery contains the grave of Private Horace Waller, 10/KOYLI. He was awarded a VC for his gallantry near Héninel on 10 April 1917.

This section of Hénin Hill was attacked by two HLI battalions of 157 Brigade of 52nd Division on 24 August. They spent two hours being barraged by their own artillery before then being held up by uncut wire. Two days later three battalions of 155 Brigade advanced south-east across the hill and penetrated the Hindenburg line between Croisilles and Fontaine.

At the cemetery turn round and go back under the motorway and follow the cinder tracks towards the windmills. After passing a still substantial bunker on the left of the track you will join *rue d'Héninel* close to where Héninel-Croisilles Road Cemetery lies in the valley below (**30**). Turn left, visit the cemetery and drive into Héninel village. There are several cemeteries close to the village but most of those who lie in them were killed during the Battle of Arras.

At the junction in the village turn left onto the D33 and drive towards Hénin. Pass under the railway and motorway and take the second left in the village to go up to Saint Martin Calvaire British Cemetery (**31**). Hénin was taken by 2/Green Howards and 19/Manchester on 2 April 1917. Most of the fighting took place at its western end close to the *Mairie* beyond the crossroads on the D35. Hénin Crucifix Cemetery is 200 yards north of the crossroads on the right of the D5 (**32**). Drive south on the D5 and take the right fork onto the D12ED1 towards St-Léger. Hénin Communal Cemetery Extension is set back on the right soon after the residential area ends (**33**).

The wide open space between Hénin and St-Léger was crossed by 58th and 18th Divisions in March 1917. The village of St-Léger was occupied by 6/Northants of 54 Brigade on 19 March. The village and its surrounding sectors were also quickly filled by elements of 7th and 2nd Divisions. The fields to the north and south of the village were the scene of rearguard actions by, in particular, 34th and 40th Divisions on 21-22 March 1918. These formations were joined shortly by 31st Division. It was from the south-east of the village that the three companies of 25/NF counter-attacked on 21 March and were not seen again. Battalions of 103, 119, and 121 Brigades fell back through the village towards Judas Farm and the Sensée valley on 22 March. On 23 August Judas Farm and the site of the mill were recaptured by the Guards Division.

On entering the village from the north turn right onto the D12. The second track on the right led up to the site of the village mill and Mill Copse (**34**). Continue on the D12 heading west. The large farm complex on the left as the road bends to the right is the site of Judas Farm (**35**). As the road turns left, the trees lining the old railway embankment can be seen across the fields to the right. The line runs up towards Boyelles. The area between the railway and the lane which runs parallel to it from the main road was used by the enemy as a shell dump in the summer of 1918. Return to St-Léger and turn right. At the main crossroads at the bottom of the slope turn right and then fork right after 80 yards. Turn right between two barns by the CWGC sign and park where you do not block access to the gardens and parking areas of the houses. The beautiful St-Léger British Cemetery is a short walk along the edge of the field and then the wood which covers part of the railway embankment (**36**).

Return to the crossroads in the village and turn right onto the D36E2 towards Mory. On the climb out of the village a track comes in from the left. This has a surface but can get quite muddy in wet weather. Follow it around to the right, past a large barn and then look around (**37**). To the east beyond the motorway and the TGV is Croisilles; Hally Copse was to the north-east but is now under the motorway; to the north is St-Léger Wood. The area from just east of the wood down across the lane on which you are standing and some way to the south was where 9/NF and 10/Lincoln fought their rearguard and where Second Lieutenant Ernest Beal of 13/Yorkshire won his Victoria Cross. Beal is commemorated on the Arras Memorial to the Missing

Return along the track and turn left onto the D36E2. Mory Street Military Cemetery is 100 yards up the hill on the right (**38**). This contains the graves of 66 soldiers, of whom five are unidentified. Thirty-five of the graves are those of 2/Coldstream of 27 August 1918, and several Scots Guards of three days earlier. There are also four gunners of 261 Brigade RFA in a joint grave. Two of the Coldstream Guards officers, Captain Edward Watson-Smyth aged 21, and Second Lieutenant G.C.Brassey, aged 19 years, were sons of well-known long-established English families.

Take the right fork further south onto the D36E3 towards Mory. The site of the regrown Mory Copse is on the left just as the road begins to bend slightly to the left. Turn onto a track on the right 150 yards south of the copse and park (**39**). The view to the west is across the valley to Ervillers; to the north-west is the Sensée valley running up to St-Léger. This area was the scene of several particularly ferocious attacks and counter-attacks by the Guards, 31st and 40th

Divisions in March 1918. For example, on 23 March, 21/Middlesex advanced up the slope from almost directly in front of where you are standing, and 13/East Surrey a little further to the left.

Drive into the village and turn left at the crossroads. Mory Abbey Military Cemetery is 300 yards along the road on the left (**40**). Continue to the junction and fork in the road to the east and park. There is not a great deal to see other than wide open spaces. Ecoust and Vaulx-Vraucourt are about three miles to the east and south-east. In March 1917, the cavalry and advanced guards of 2nd, 7th, and 18th Divisions were all working across this sector as they approached the outpost villages. On 22-23 March 1918, units of 34th and 40th Divisions withdrew across this open area to Mory. The village was retaken in August by the Guards and 5/KOYLI of 2nd West Riding Divisions,

Return to the village crossroads and turn left towards Favreuil on the D36E4. Once clear of the village and heading south, Sapignies church can be seen in the far right distance. In March 1918, 40th and 41st Divisions were very active in this area. On 24 March, and with the assistance of what was left of 13/East Surrey after its counter-attack at Mory, 120 Brigade managed to establish a line parallel to the west side of the road. The stand was short-lived because the enemy was through to the north and south. Closer to Favreuil the three field companies of 41st Division had been attempting to dig a trench to link with that held by 120 Brigade, but the enemy soon compelled a withdrawal. Drive into the village, past the *Mairie* and turn right onto the D10E3 towards Sapignies. Drive past the water tower and pull off the road just before the crossroads (**41**). Look to the north. A sparse line of trees in the distance marks a lane between Sapignies and Favreuil. Between that lane and the road on which you are standing was the area across which 123 Brigade and the attached 7 Brigade withdrew with the support of tanks on 24 March. Favreuil was thought to be still held by 124 Brigade, but this proved to be an erroneous assumption. In late August, with the New Zealand Division on its right, 111 Brigade of 37th Division attacked across the same area. There was some confusion as to whether 2/4 Dukes of 62nd Division advanced down the small lane linking Sapignies and Favreuil but 12/RB and 13/KRRC had to work through a heavy German barrage to assault a strongly defended trench to the west of the houses. The village was cleared during the night of 25-26 August. The two attacking battalions were supported by 10/RF and, less actively by 1/Essex. It had been a difficult and costly operation.

Return to your car. The memorial to the 1870-71 war is immediately opposite when you reach the crossroads 50 yards ahead (**42**). Bapaume is to the left and Ervillers to the right on the D917.

Tour 4: Ervillers (33 miles)

Ervillers (**1**) was entered on 18 March 1918 by 29/Lancers of the Lucknow Brigade. The cavalry quickly handed it over to what were probably troops of 62nd Division. By the following day elements of 22 Brigade, 7th Division, were in the village. On 25 March 1918, after a determined defence by 10/Manchester of 42nd Division and 92 Brigade of 31st Division the village was evacuated. It was re-taken by 2/South Stafford and 1/King's of 2nd Division on 23 August 1918.

From the northern end of the village on the D917 turn right towards St-Léger on the D9. On 23-24 March 1918 these fields were occupied by disorganised elements of 34th and 40th Divisions. Whilst trying to establish some sort of order from the chaos, 10th and 11/East Yorks of 92 Brigade moved into the area with 4 Guards Brigade on their left in the Sensée valley (**2**). After 900 yards, turn right at a crossroads where tracks join from either side. This lane has a surface and is usually passable. It crosses the area where 13/East Surrey formed up for its attempt to regain Mory and also where 13/Yorkshire and 21/Manchester held the line. On their left 4 Guards Brigade had advanced up the slopes from the valley. At a crosstracks 250 yards on, turn right. This surfaced track soon connects with the D36 coming in from Mory. Drive into Ervillers and turn left onto the D917. After about 200 yards, turn right onto the small *Rue du Moulin*. Follow this narrow but surfaced road down to Béhagnies.

The road runs more or less parallel to the D917 and crosses the ground which saw intense activity in March 1918. Ervillers Trench (**3**) cut the lane about 100 yards after the first dog-leg to the left at its northern end. This was the trench that was so crowded with troops from a variety of different units that 5/East Lancs and 10/Manchester, who had been sent to hold it, could not get in. Bee Wood Trench and Wood Support ran close to the lane on the left. In the fields to the west the small site of Bee Wood is no more, but the trees on the slight rise of Gomiécourt ridge in the distance can be discerned. Keep straight on after passing the civilian cemetery and turn right onto the D917.

Turn right into Sapignies. In the middle of the village take *rue de Biefvillers* and visit the German cemetery on the right hand side of the lane (**4**). After a strong defence by 14/A&SH the village fell on 25 March. It was recaptured shortly afterwards by 8/Lancashire Fusiliers but was quickly lost again. It was re-taken on 25 August by 2/Ox&Bucks after a stiff fight. The Lancashire Fusiliers of 125 Brigade withdrew across the open ground towards the Gomiécourt ridge. Continue south on the *rue de Biefvillers*. In August 1918 a German strong point was in a shrine on the left about 100 yards from the cemetery. Its commander was captured by a patrol of 1/KRR. When later the KRRC moved on towards Favreuil, 1/Essex assembled at the shrine in support. In the fields further west machine guns took a heavy toll of the advancing Germans debouching from the village in March 1918. When it had been relieved by 41st Division, 75 Brigade plus the divisional sappers and pioneers crossed the land to dig in on Gomiécourt ridge.

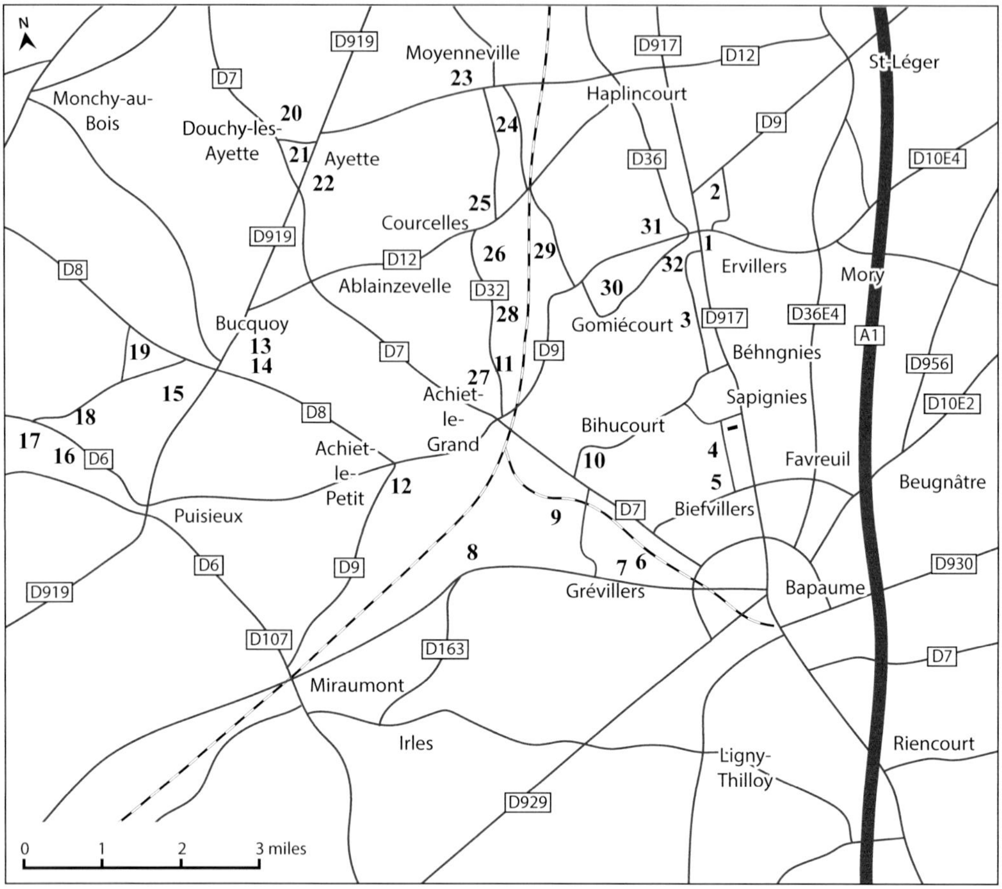

Tour Map 4 Ervillers.

Follow the lane down, keep left at a small fork, pass a quarry on the left (**5**) which was used as a brigade HQ and turn right onto the D10E3 towards Biefvillers.

The village was taken by 6 (Aust) Brigade on 17 March 1917. In March 1918, the road and adjoining fields were crossed by trenches manned by exhausted troops from several brigades. The Germans reached the D917 south of Sapignies and advanced towards the garrisons, some of which were certainly 41st Division, attempting to hold the approaches to the village. It was evacuated on 25 March 1918 and retaken without a fight by 8/SLI of 37th Division on 25 August 1918. Go through the village and turn left onto the D7 towards Bapaume.

When clear of the village, an intermittent row of trees to the right marks the line of the old railway (**6**). In March 1918 three field companies of 41st Division manned what had been part of the substantial R.1 and R.2 German defences of March 1917. The sappers were close to the railway and were just about in touch with 124 Brigade on their left. Enemy debouching from Bapaume on 25 March 1918 were stopped by the sappers but at considerable cost to the defenders. The left of 19th Division was a little south of the railway. Take the first exit at the roundabout onto the D9. The road crosses the line of the railway almost immediately. Elements of 41st Division joined those of 19th Division in the fields between the road and the railway on 25 March 1918. Visit Grevillers British Cemetery (**7**). This is a large cemetery and also contains a memorial to those New Zealanders with no known grave who were killed between March and August 1918.

Grevillers was taken on 14 March 1917. Three CCS were quickly ensconced close to the village. In March 1918, 57 Brigade and remnants of 51st Divisions fought a rearguard close to it before withdrawing. On 24 August the village was re-taken by the New Zealand Division from the rear. If you have time, drive west through the village and onto *Grand Rue*, This roads heads towards the south-east corner of Loupart Wood (**8**). The wood was occupied and lost several times during the course of 1918. It was also used as an assembly and re-grouping area. Several divisions such as 51st, the RND, and 62nd Divisions saw action close to or inside the wood. Park where you can before reaching the wood. Look south across the open ground towards Ligny-Tilloy and north to Bihucourt. Return to Grevillers and turn left onto the D29 and then shortly right towards Bihucourt.

The road leads towards the strongly wired and protected Bihucourt Trench. This ran diagonally north-west – south-east across the road a few score yards in front of the old railway line (**9**). On 16 March 1917 troops of 12/Middlesex and 7/Bedford were held up in front of the trench, particularly by enfilade fire from the slightly higher ground to the left. The following day 17/Middlesex found the trench and the village deserted. Savoy Camp was established north of the junction where the small road joins the D7. There are two British soldiers buried in the communal cemetery on the east side of the village (**10).** One is an unidentified New Zealander, the other is Rfm Ward of 12/London. Ward probably died of wounds received during the 1 July 1916 attack at Gommecourt. During the fighting of 25 March 1918, 122 Brigade was put into reserve to rest and regroup at Bihucourt. Two of its battalions were withdrawn shortly afterwards and when the enemy attacked, 15/Hampshire and a company of 6/Manchester attempted to defend the village. They were both quickly forced to withdraw. On 23 August 1918, 10/RF of 111 Brigade took the village from a fairly determined German rearguard. Continue into and carefully through Achiet-le-Grand. The large British cemetery is on the north-western outskirts of the town to the west of the railway (**11**).

On 18 March 1917 a German machine gun in the civilian cemetery that lies next to the British plots held up 2/5th Dukes for a while as the lead companies approached the town. The Lucknow Brigade entered and passed through the residential area followed by 7/Bedford. Two CCS were established close to the present cemetery and, by 28 March, with the repair of the broad gauge as far as the town it became a railhead. On 23 March 1918 what was left of 6th Division withdrew to the town. Two days later there was a huge traffic jam as guns, transport, and stragglers tried to clear the town, The exhausted remnants of 41st Division passed through it and despite a stubborn resistance by 6/Manchester and 17/NF (P), it was lost later that same day. On 23 August a machine gun once again inside the cemetery this time halted the advance of the RND for a time, but the town was later taken by 13/RB and 13/KRRC of 111 Brigade assisted by 8/SLI and tanks

Leave the cemetery, turn right onto *Rue Jacques Brel* and then left onto the D7. Turn right onto the D9 at the crossroads. This was the site of the brickworks whose garrison, together with that of a trench to its south, caused problems to 112 Brigade as its three battalions approached the railway line in August. Drive down the D9 towards Achiet-le-Petit. On the outskirts of the village take the left fork onto *Rue du Cimetiere*. There is the crew of a Lancaster shot down in

April 1944 in the communal cemetery (**12**) and a relatively small German cemetery close by. In the same way as in the larger Achiet-le-Grand further up the D9, there was a massive traffic blockage in the village on 25 March 1918. Two brigades of 62nd Division reached the village later that day, 52 weeks after they had passed through it unopposed in March 1917. Brigades of 19th Division withdrew to its vicinity and sent officers into the village to collect stragglers and shepherd them into the line. What little was left of 51st Division also passed to its south as its troops withdrew towards Puisieux; 124 Brigade of 41st Division extended a line to its south. On 23 August 1918 it was taken by battalions of 5 Brigade, 2nd Division. Take the D8 from the north-west of the village towards Bucquoy.

At the small crossroads at the edge of the village turn right onto *Chemin des Rouliers*. At the crossroads after 100 yards go straight over on to a narrow surfaced lane (**13**). Drive along this for 400 yards and stop. On 14 March 1917 rushed and ill-prepared attacks on the village by 46th and 7th Divisions resulted in disaster. Three days later 7th Division discovered the village to have been evacuated. Late on 25 March 1918, a brigade of 62nd Division manned trenches on this ridge roughly along the line of the lane. Elements of 41st Division managed to pass through to the rear. The 2nd West Riding Division was eventually forced back and parts of the village were lost. In April, a major enemy attack pushed 8/Lancashire Fusiliers of 42nd Division and 13/RF of 37th Division from the central parts of the village. On 23 August, 37th Division, with the help of a well-planned barrage and tanks re-took the ruins and the higher ground across which the lane runs.

Turn around and turn right at the small crossroads. There are some Allied graves in the communal cemetery and the British Communal Extension is beyond the north-west side of the communal cemetery (**14**). The register in the extension cemetery has details of the eight identified burials in the communal cemetery. Follow the *Rues des Prés* down to the D8, turn right and then left onto the D919 in the centre of the village. Queen's Cemetery is on the right at the southern end of the village (**15**). Drive down to Puisieux, passing Fork Wood on the right just as the road climbs gently about mid-way between the two villages. The wood has changed its shape and is now larger than it was when defended by troops of 186 Brigade on 26 March. Puisieux was cleared on 26 February 1917. In March of the following year stragglers were collected by officers of 19th Division and sent into the line do defend the village with some of their own battalions and those of 25th Divisions. Brigades of 62nd Division also became heavily involved as the enemy pushed through the village and along the valley towards Hébuterne.

At the northern end of the village turn right onto the D6 towards Gommecourt. The open rolling countryside leads on past Owl Trench (**16**) and Rossignol Wood Cemeteries (**17**), both on the left of the road. Rossignol Wood itself sits alongside the road opposite Owl Trench Cemetery and then spreads back to the north. It is about the same size now as it had been in 1914. On 27 February 1917, 16/West Yorks of 31st Division made a disjointed attack on the wood which ended in badly. In March 1918 heavy pressure was brought to bear on 62nd Division whose brigades were attempting to stop the enemy's north-westwards advance from Puisieux. It was here that Lieutenant Colonel Ironside and his 100 machine gunners arrived to offer their services, and a counter-attack involving 11 tanks was made. On 27 March, 2/4th York&Lancs was forced out of the wood but a counter-attack by 5/KOYLI and tanks recaptured it. The KOYLI was forced out of it the following day and then came the confused episode in which Lieutenant Colonel Watson won his Victoria Cross. The later attack by 8/West Yorks was an equally torrid affair. On 5 April, 63 Brigade of 37th Division's attack on the wood went badly wrong and caused heavy casualties. It was during this attack that Chaplain Bayley Hardy won his VC. The padre crawled across the open ground to help and comfort wounded men who had been hit by enemy machine guns firing from inside the wood.

Rossignol Wood Cemetery, like Vaulx Australian Field Ambulance visited in Tour 2, is another of the rare CWGC cemeteries which has more German remains than British. The cemetery was begun by 46th Division and contains the graves of 19 identified men of 5/North Stafford and 14 of 5/South Stafford. These are some of the men killed on 14 March during the division's ill-timed and inadequately prepared attack on Bucquoy. The cemetery holds the remains of 41 British and 70 German soldiers.

At the diagonal crossroads after the cemetery turn right. Part of the wood's north-western face butts onto the road 200 yards from the crossroads. There are the mouldering remains of several bunkers amongst the trees (**18**). Park and looked behind you to the south-west. The mass of Gommecourt Wood is on the right and Gommecourt No.2 Cemetery in the slight valley directly in front. Hébuterne church steeple can be seen in the far distance. You are looking over the land attacked on 1 July 1916 by 56th Division. Drive along the narrow road, passing the large Bois du Biez on the left, until reaching Bucquoy. Shrine Cemetery is on the north-west side of the village on the left of the D8 just as the houses finish (**19**). It contains another 27 identified men of the North and South Stafford killed on 14 March 1917. Join the D919 in the centre of the village and head north towards Douchy-les-Ayette.

On joining the D7 bear left to Douchy-les-Ayette. The British cemetery is on the right a little before the village (**20**). Private Thomas Woodcock VC, 2/Irish Guards, is buried here. The village was occupied by 4/Lincoln on 18 March 1917; its close neighbour, Ayette was entered by 5/Lincoln the same day. The twin villages were attacked in March 1918, with the Germans eventually being halted about where the British Cemetery east of Douchy now lies. Ayette had been defended by 93 Brigade of 31st Division while 4 Guards Brigade of the same division acted as the reserve around the villages. The Guards Division was to the north. On 27 March, much to Lieutenant General Haldane's annoyance, 93 Brigade abandoned Ayette. The following day the Germans attacked towards Douchy from the north but were held up by 2/Grenadier Guards. On 3 April 15/HLI mounted what turned out to be a costly but effective assault to recapture Ayette. Ayette British Cemetery (**21**) is beside a farm track running off *Rue du 11 Novembre* on the west side of the D919. Park carefully to avoid blocking access to what is both a dump of discarded farm equipment and a barn yard. In the same way as Mory Street Cemetery, Ayette British is also very much a cemetery of guardsmen. One of the graves is that of Captain Edward Budd, Irish Guards. Budd was awarded the MC and two bars. The Indian and Chinese Cemetery (**22**) is up an often muddy track on the left of *Rue de Courcelles* on the east side of the D919.

From the centre of the village, turn off the D919 onto the 10 ton limited *Rue de Moyenneville.* This small road was crossed 500 yards west of Moyennevelle by the long Aerodrome Trench which started at the airfield on the higher ground to the south. The hamlet was entered by squadrons of the Lucknow Brigade on 18 March 1917. Owing to the confusion created by the shell shocked brigade major, on 26 March 1918 two battalions of 93 Brigade had withdrawn beyond Moyenneville. At least one company of 18/DLI was in the area where Aerodrome Trench crossed the small road from Ayette; 15/17th West Yorks was just west of Moyenneville; 13/York&Lancs was further to the west, largely south of the road.

At the T junction beyond the civilian cemetery, turn right and then fork right onto *Chemin du Bois.* This leads to Two Trees Cemetery (**23**) which is well worth a visit but whose access in wet weather can cause problems for vehicles. It can also be difficult turning the vehicle round at the cemetery. It is probably best to park before the road loses its surface and walk 450 yards down the track to the cemetery. The cemetery has a little under 50 burials, of which 14 are identified men of 15/17th West Yorks, and another eight known to have belonged to that battalion. There are also four of 18/DLI of the same 93 Brigade. Most of the remainder are from 3/Grenadier Guards who died in August.

Return to the car, turn round and drive back towards the hamlet. Forty yards after *Chemin du Bois* joins the main road turn right onto a small road heading south towards Courcelles. This crosses the ground counter-attacked by 15/17th West Yorks on 26 March and it was in this area that Sergeant Mountain won his Victoria Cross (**24**). Drive south. The Allied aerodrome was on the right with Coffee Work and Ridge Work, two former British but later German strong points in August 1918, a little closer to the road across the open fields. To the left and north-east is the village of Hamelincourt. This village, with its small quarries and Hamel Work to its south-west, and Moyenneville, were retaken by the Guards Division on 23 August. The main line railway passes between them.

Courcelles was entered by mounted troops of V Corps on 17 March. The infantry of 7th Division followed and took possession of the village the following day. The railway passing to its east, with its cutting and crossing points, was a rallying point for withdrawing troops in March 1918. Two brigades of 42nd Division regrouped here before withdrawing further west. On 23 August, 1/RSF of 8 Brigade cleared the village with some difficulty; 7/KSLI worked on its left flank. Once the village had been taken, 13/King's and 1/NF pressed on to the railway.

On reaching the start of the housing on the northern edge of Courcelles, turn right onto *Rue de Verdun*. Follow it down past the church. On the right of the downward slope is the memorial to Private Hugh McIvor VC, 2/R.Scots (**25**). Go straight over the crossroads shortly after and then turn right at the T junction further on. This is now the D32 signed towards Achiet-le-Grand. Follow this round and soon after the houses finish on the left is an interesting necropolis of French troops (**26**). The mass grave contains the remains of 275 soldiers killed in October 1914; around its edges are 39 crosses remembering others who died. Continue towards Achiet-le-Grand. Logeast Wood, which saw some particularly severe fighting in March 1918 and from where tank-supported assaults towards the railway began in August, is on the right. On 28 March an estimated three battalions of Germans were destroyed on the west side of the road by artillery fire as they massed in preparation for an attack towards Ayette (**27**).

Avoid going into the town by turning left 200 yards after crossing under the railway and left again onto the D9 towards Gomiécourt. After about half a mile the road takes a 90 degree right. Turn left here in front of the civilian cemetery and carefully cross the railway. The embankment to the south and the cutting to the north of the crossing point were used extensively by units moving up and back from the front. The line was reached by 7th and 62nd Divisions on 18 March 1917; during the withdrawal a year later it was defended by battalions of 125 and 126 Brigades of 42nd Divisions. Trench mortar batteries of 31st Division and battalions of its 92 Brigade were dug in a little further north around the level crossing. In August 1918, 13/King's and 1/NF had some difficulty in securing the cutting and the crossing point partly because their supporting tanks were hit from the flank as they approached the line. Walk up the grass path to visit Railway Cutting Cemetery (**28**). It holds many of the Northumberland Fusiliers and other troops of the 2nd and 3rd Divisions who died in August.

Drive back across the railway and turn left onto the main road. As the road turns to the right, take the track on the left. After 500 yards turn left towards Warry Copse Cemetery (**29**). This compact little site sits above the railway cutting and is very much a cemetery of men of the 3rd Division who died in August 1918. Drive back along the track and rather than turn right onto the lane you came up, keep straight on until you hit the small road. Turn right onto it and into Gomiécourt village. At the T junction in the village turn right and then immediately left. This heads south for 600 yards. At the T junction turn left. A lane comes in from the right after 60 yards. This leads to, and over, the slight rise of the Gomiécourt ridge to join the D31 west of Sapignies. This was the lane across which 5/East Lancs counter-attacked on 25 March. It covers interesting ground but is not really suitable for cars. Keep on the original lane. Gomiécourt South Cemetery is set back from the lane on the left (**30**). Triangle Wood was 150 yards to its north-east.

The cemetery has 206 burials, very largely of men killed in August 1918. They come from 62nd Division, especially 187 Brigade, 2nd, and 37th Divisions, and reflect the action which took place in the approach to the recapture of Ervillers and Sapignies. One of the few graves which is not from this later period of the war is RSM William Douglas. He was killed on 21 March 1918 whilst serving with 2/4th Ox&Bucks. This battalion was part of 61st (2nd South Midland) Division which manned Enghein Redoubt and other defences in the Battle Zone west of St Quentin. As RSM, the South African War veteran Douglas was more likely to have been in battalion HQ than in the forward defences. Wherever he actually was at the time of the German offensive, his body was removed a substantial distance to be buried at Gomiécourt. Many of his battalion and division lie in Chapelle British Cemetery, Holnon.

Gomiécourt was more a hamlet than a village in 1917. The withdrawing Germans set fire to what was left of it and it was entered by patrols of 2/5th Dukes on 18 March. On 25 March 1918 it was shelled by the guns of both sides; this disrupted the plans of 126 Brigade to withdraw through it. In August, it was taken by 8/KORL and 2/Suffolk of 76 Brigade, 3rd Division. Once the hamlet had been taken, battalions of 2nd Division moved through supported by whippets to continue the advance across the open ground towards Ervillers, Sapignies and Béhagnies. Close to the cemetery, 2/Ox&Bucks assembled in support as 2/HLI and 24/RF moved forward. The attack was opposed and held up. Troops caught in the open sought shelter in the area of Bee Wood.

Drive on towards Ervillers. On 23 August 1918 2/South Stafford and 1/King's of 6 Brigade advanced astride the road to take Ervillers. At the crossroads soon after the civilian cemetery, turn left, cross the D9 onto *Rue de Courcelles* and park off the road. This is the area where 10/Manchester beat off eight major attacks on 25 March and where Henry Lawson had his meeting with the smart young officer of the Coldstream Guards (**31**). Return to the crossroads behind the civilian cemetery and turn left. Follow the road round to visit Ervillers Military Cemetery (**32**).

This is a neat little cemetery with the graves of 67 soldiers, 15 of which were prisoners who died of wounds and were buried by the Germans among their own dead. The German remains were later removed. Most of the British dead are from 62nd and 7th Divisions. Close to the bottom of the gentle slope and under four headstones are eight soldiers of 2/R.Warwick. Their battalion was not in the line on 21 March 1917, so they were possibly all killed by random shelling as they rested or worked behind the forward positions.

Rejoin the D917. Right towards Bapaume; left towards Arras.

Appendix

Corps Order of Battle[1]

German Retreat to the Hindenburg Line

14 March-5 April 1917
Fifth Army (Gen. Sir H.Gough)
II Corps (Lt.Gen.C.W.Jacob): 2nd, 18th Divisions
V Corps (Lt.Gen.E.A.Fanshawe): 7th, 46th, 62nd Divisions
XVIII Corps (Lt.Gen.Sir F.I.Maxe): 58th Division
I ANZAC (Lt.Gen.Sir W.Birdwood): 2nd, 4th, 5th Australian Divisions.

German Offensive in Picardy

Battle of St Quentin 21-23 March: First Battle of Bapaume 24-25 March: First Battle of Arras, 28 March 1918
First Army (Gen.Sir H.S.Horne)
XIII Corps (Lt.Gen.Sir.H.de B.de Lisle): 56th Division
Third Army (Gen.Hon.Sir J.H.G.Byng)
IV Corps (Lt.Gen.Sir G.M.Harper): 6th, 19th, 25th, 41st, 42nd, 51st 62nd, NZ Divisions, 4 (Aust) Brigade, 4th (Aust) Division
V Corps (Lt.Gen.E.A.Fanshawe): 2nd, 12th, 17th, 47th, 63rd Divisions
VI Corps (Lt.Gen.J.A.L.Haldane): Guards, 3rd, 31st, 34th, 40th, 59th, 2nd Canadian (2 brigades) Divisions, 97 Brigade, 32nd Division
XVII Corps (Lt.Gen.Sir C.Fergusson): 4th, 15th Divisions

1 NB. Not all of the divisions listed served with the corps concerned for all of the periods of the specified battles. Those listed fought with the corps given for at least part of the official duration of those battles.

Advance to Victory

21 August-30 September 1918

Third Army (Gen,Hon.Sir J.H.G.Byng)
Battle of Albert, Second Battle of Bapaume, Battle of Havrincourt, Battle of Épehy, Battle of the Canal Du Nord
IV Corps ((Lt.Gen.Sir G.M.Harper): 5th, 37th, 42nd, 63rd, NZ Divisions
V Corps (Lt.Gen.C.D.Shute): 17th, 21st, 38th Divisions
VI Corps (Lt.Gen.J.A.L.Haldane): Guards, 2nd, 3rd, 52nd, 56th, 59th, 62nd Division

Maps

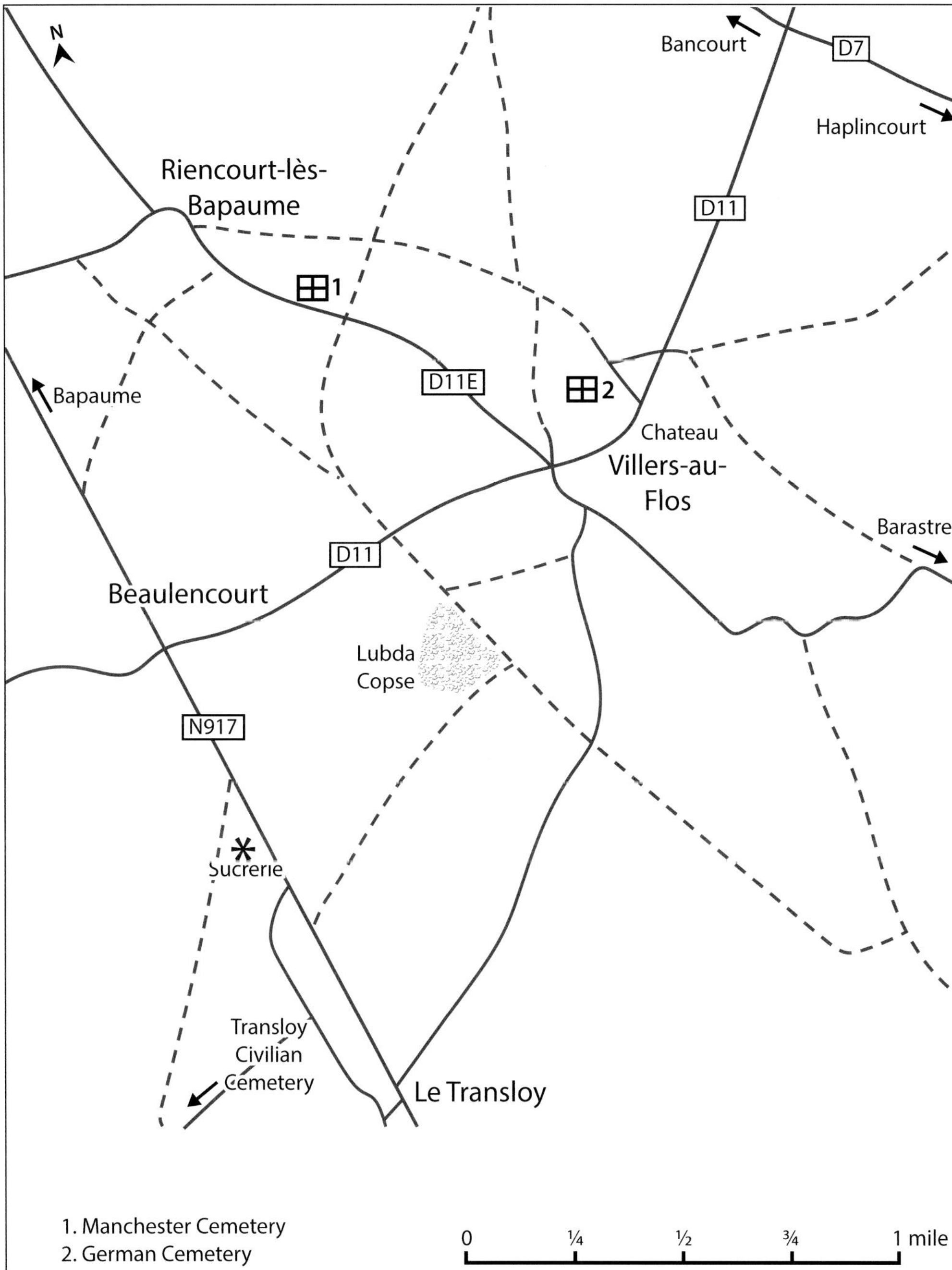

Map 2 Le Transloy–Villers-au-Flos–Reincourt-les-Bapaume.

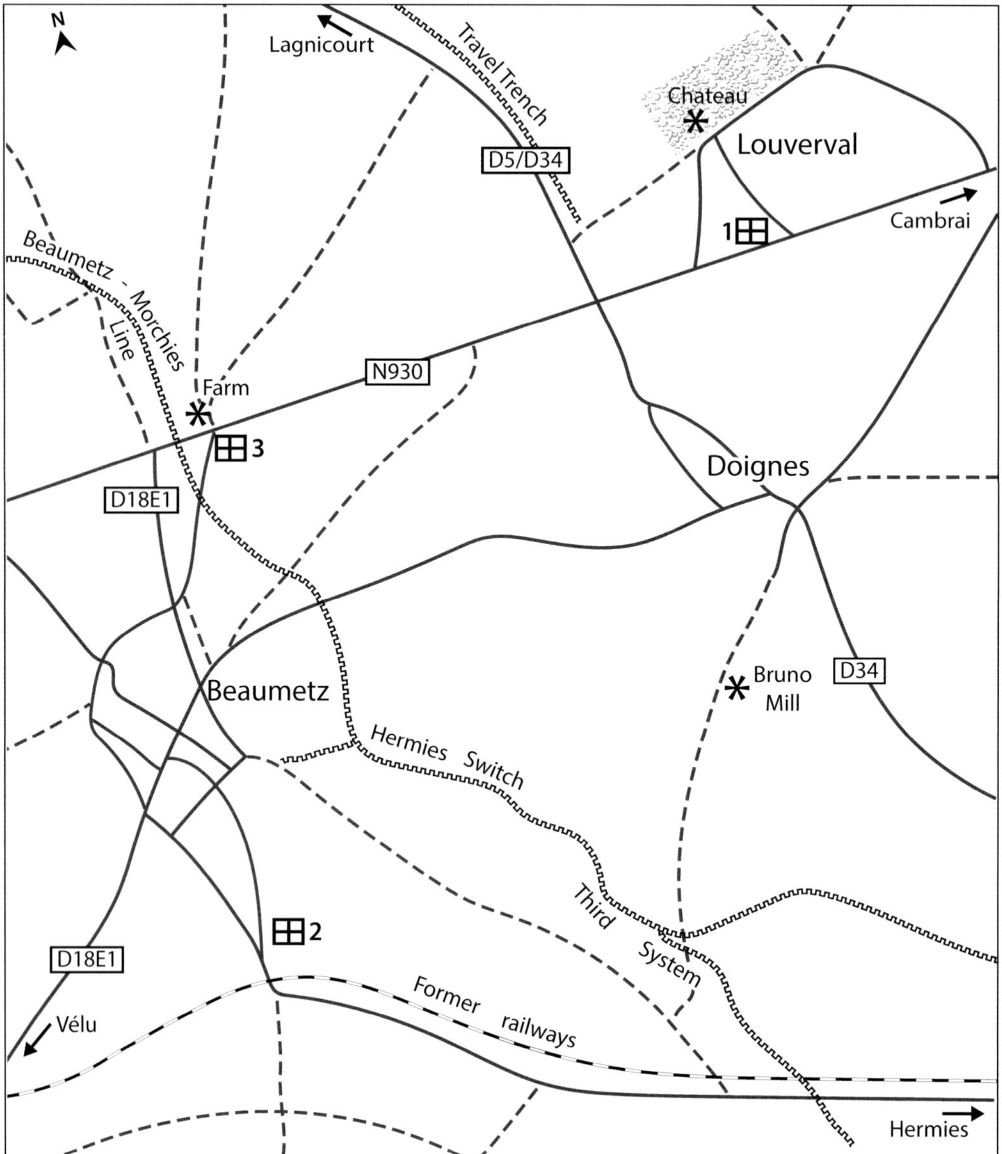

Map 3 Beaumetz–Louverval.

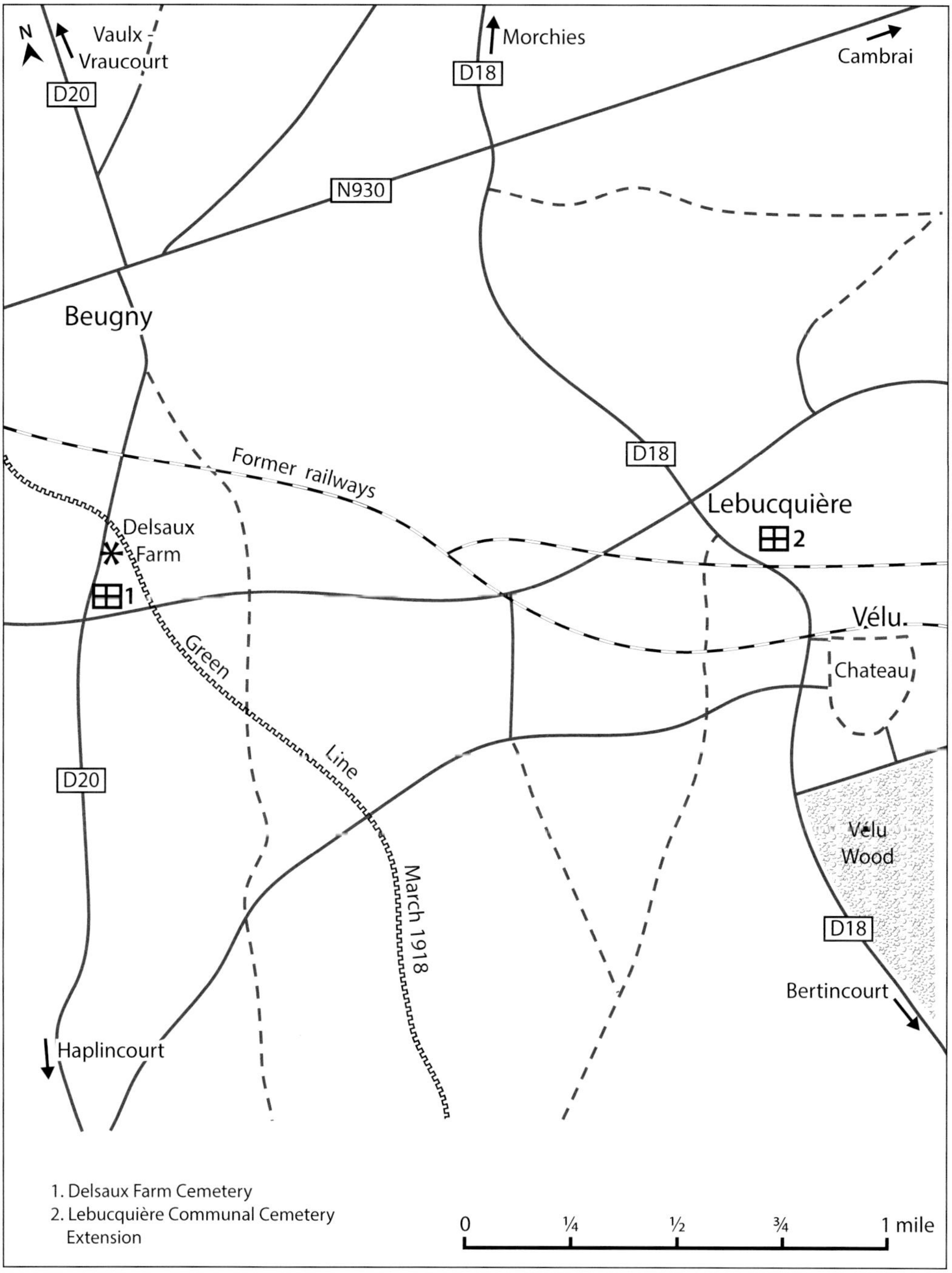

Map 4 Beugny–Vélu.

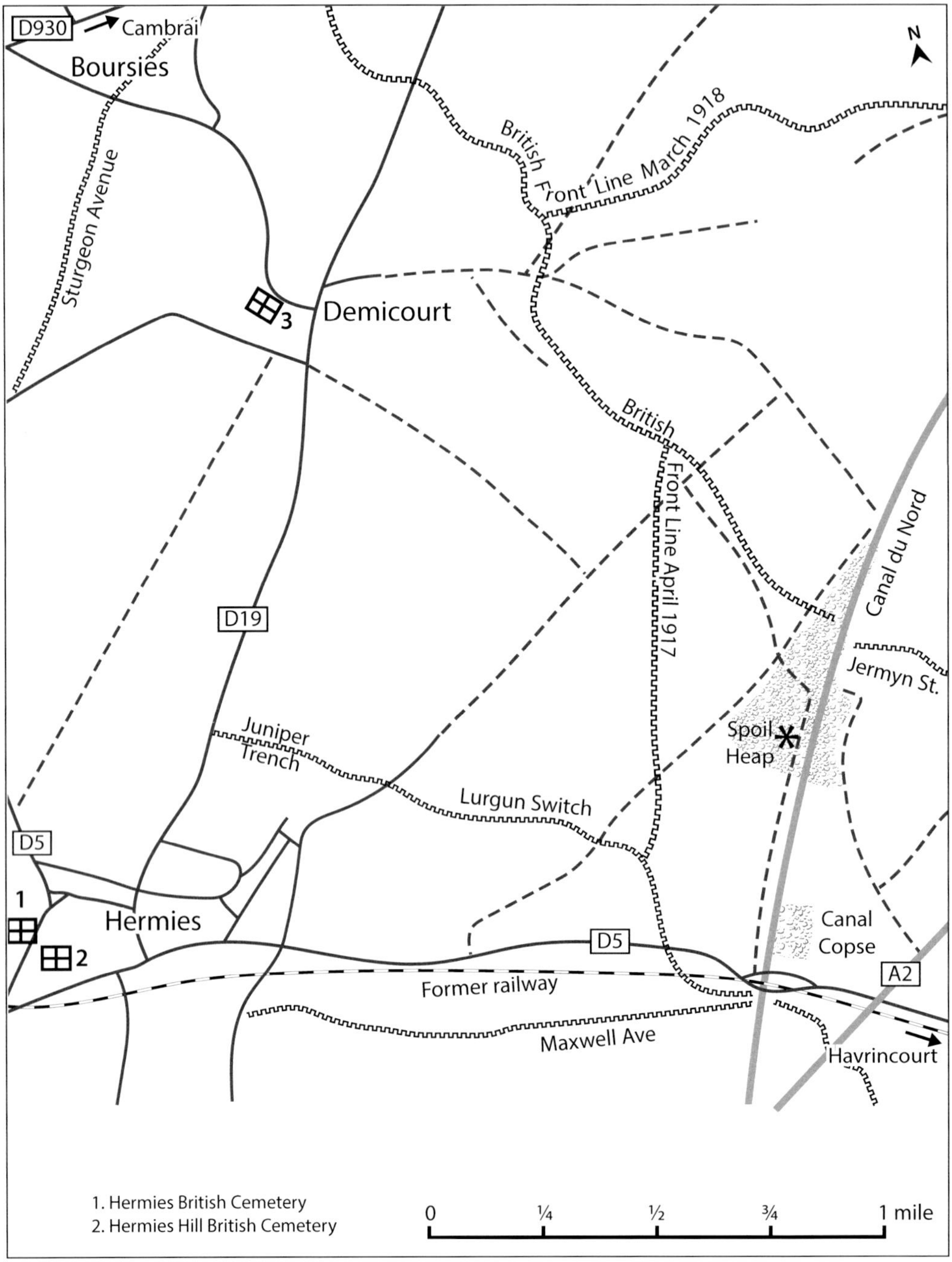

Map 5 Boursies–Havrincourt.

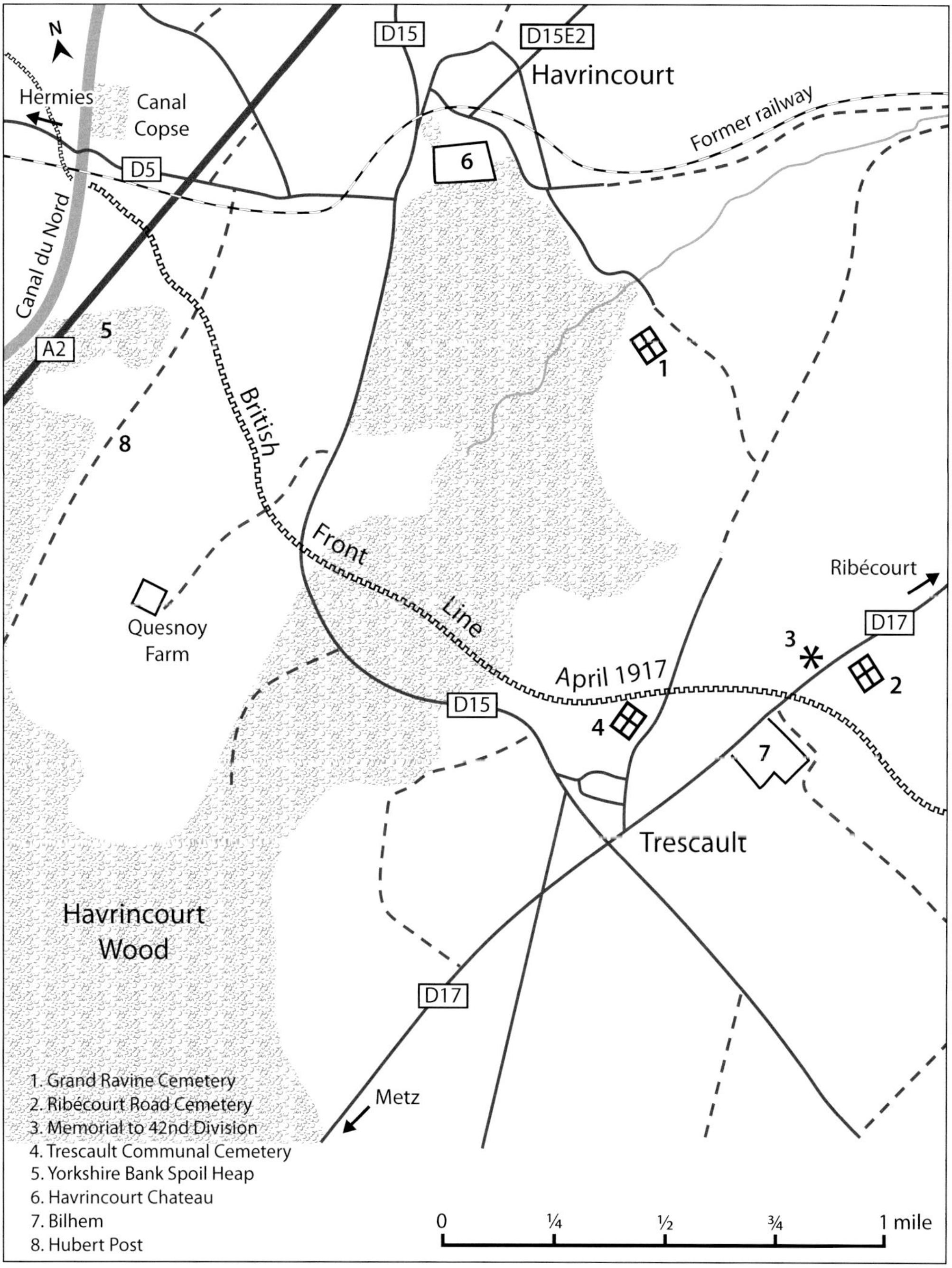

Map 6 Havrincourt–Trescault.

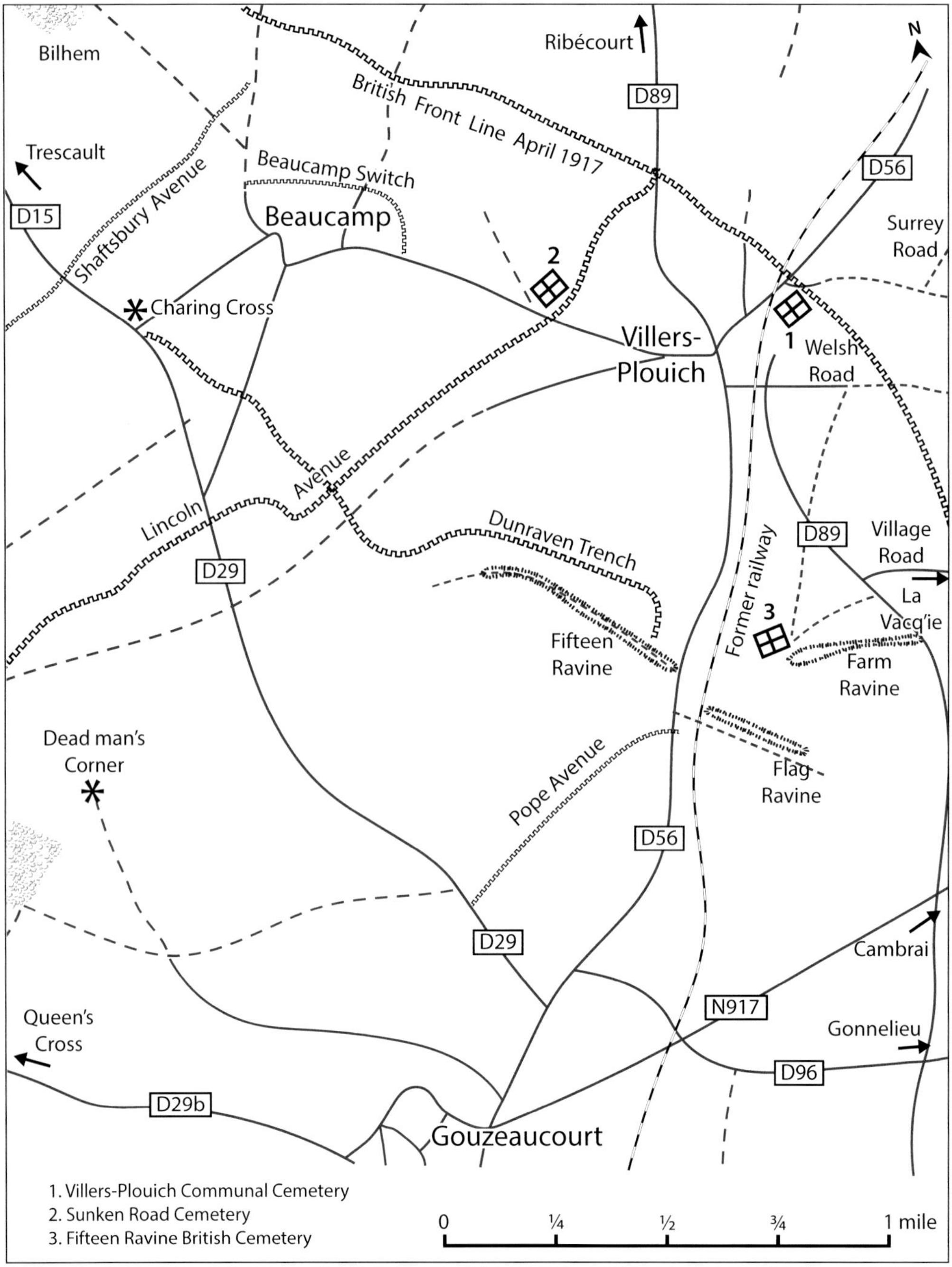

Map 7 Beaucamp–Gouzeaucourt.

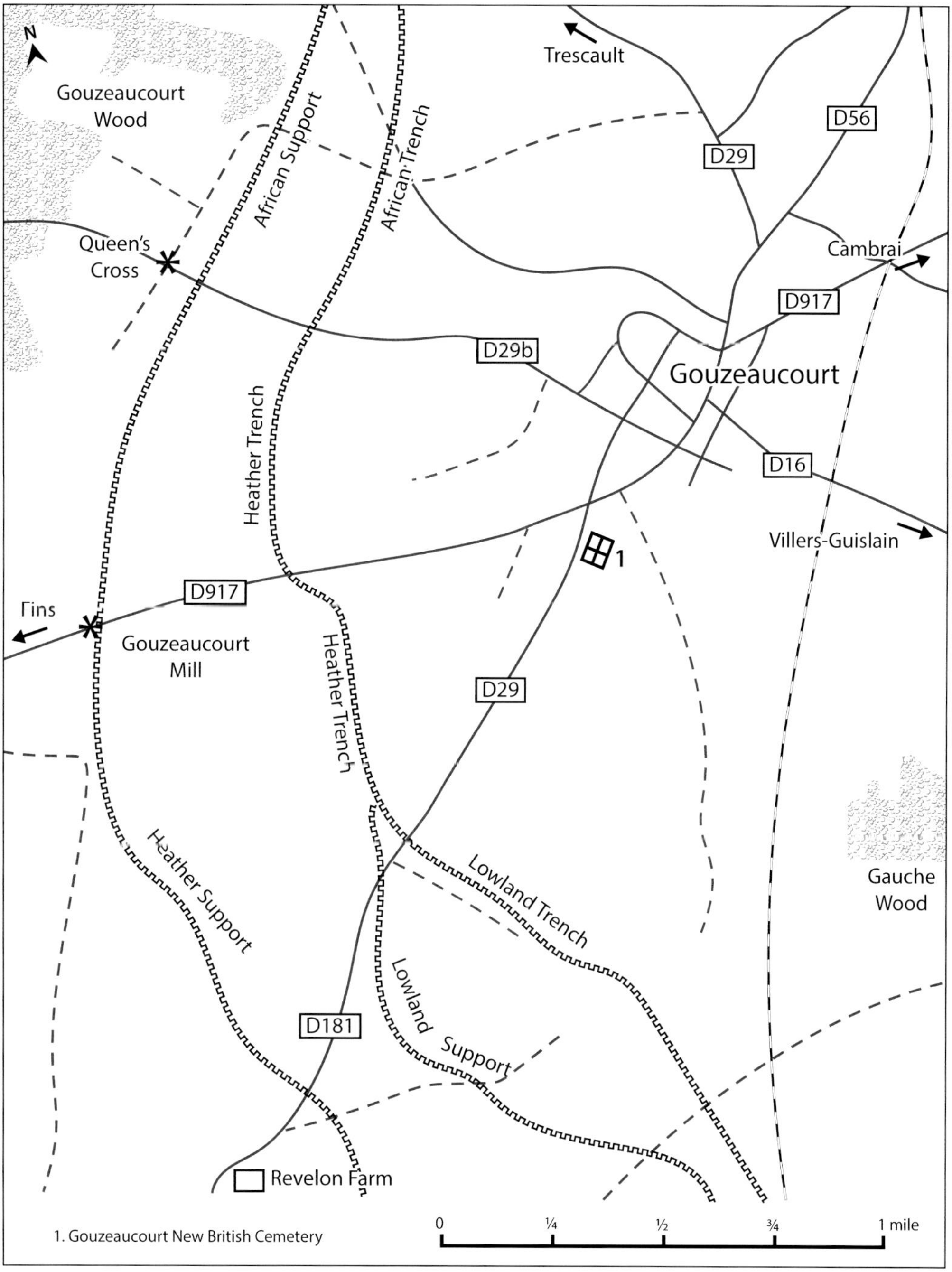

Map 8 Gouzeaucourt.

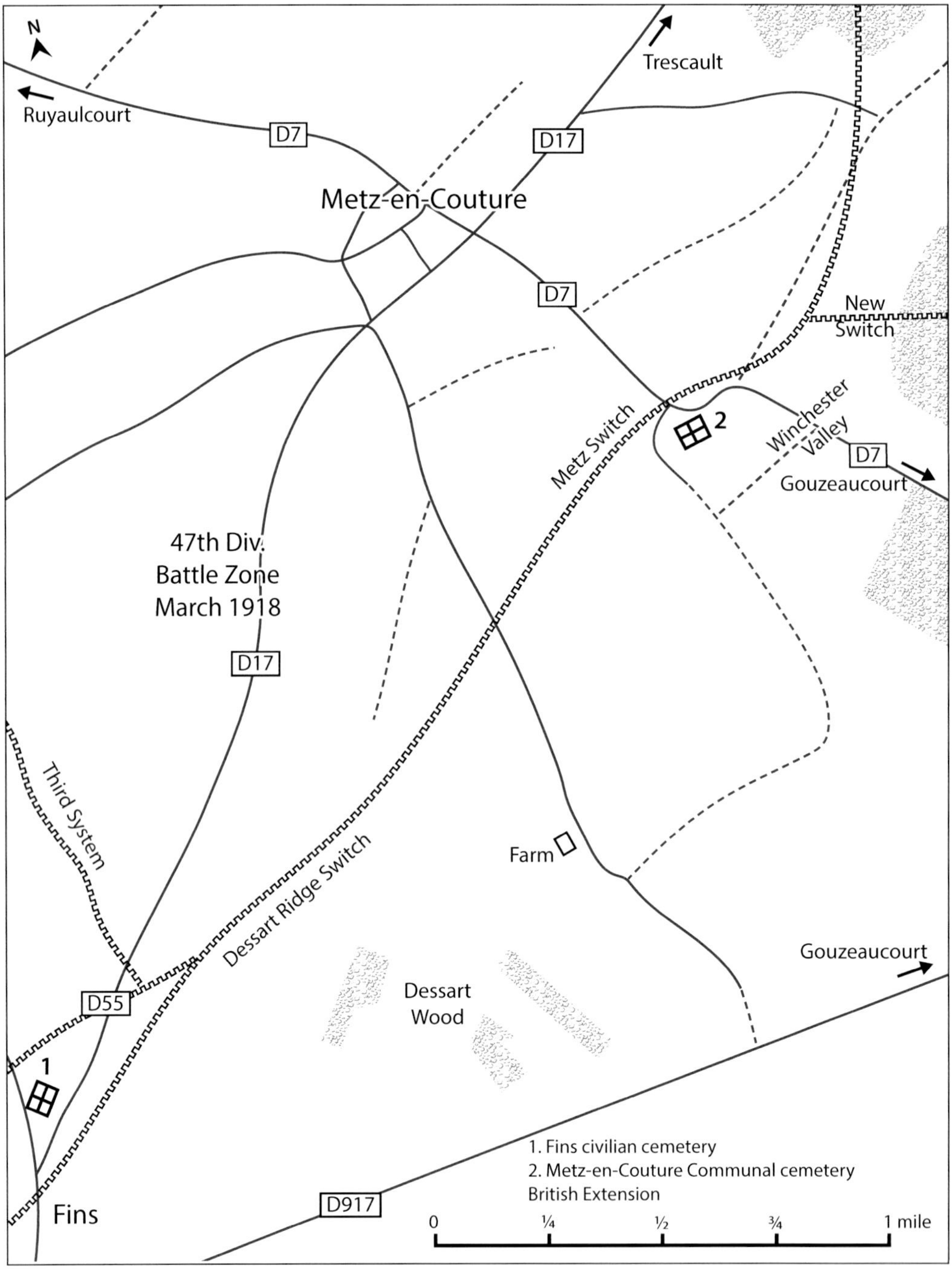

Map 9 Metz-en-Couture – Fins.

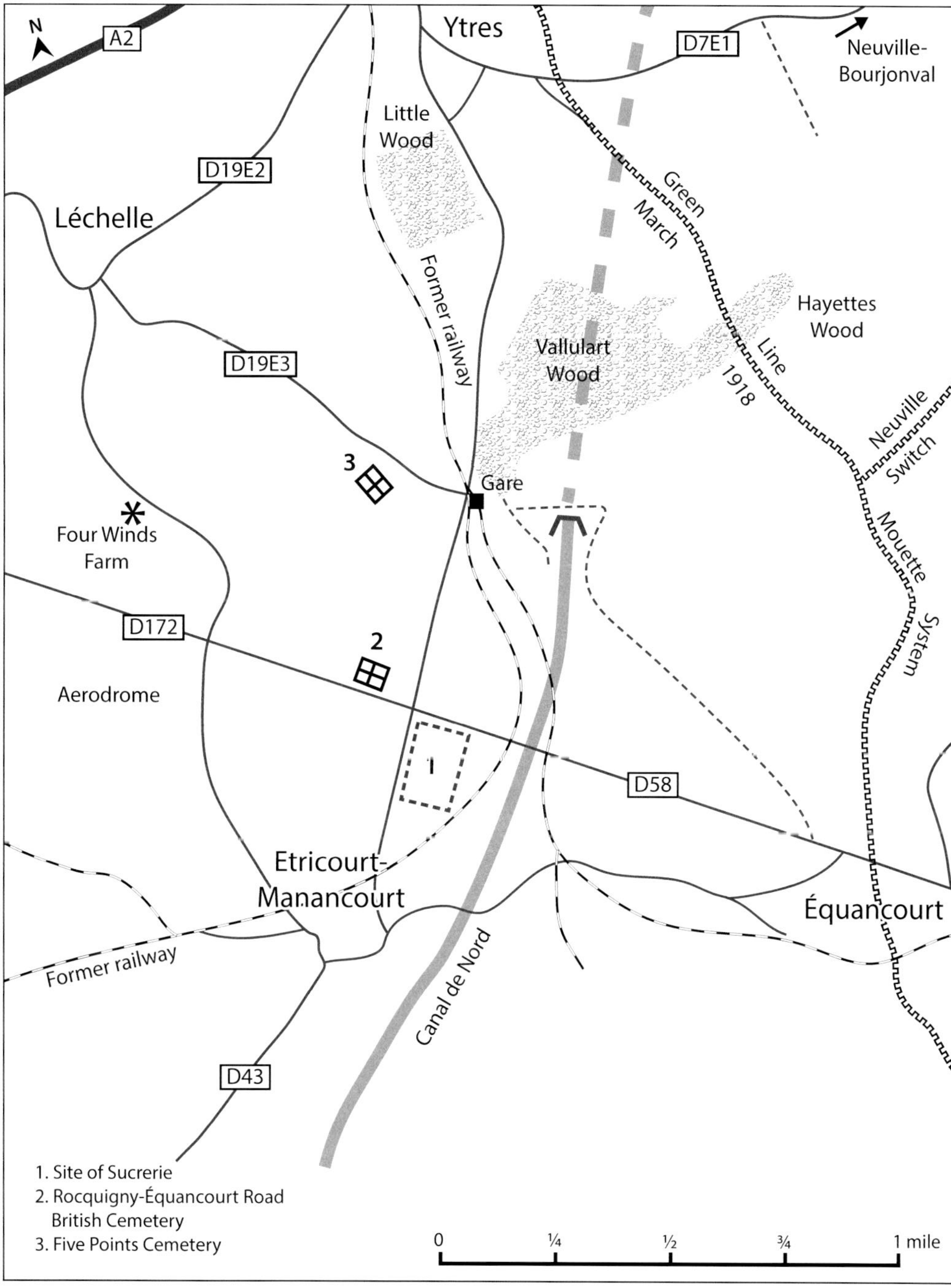

Map 10 Équancourt – Léchelle.

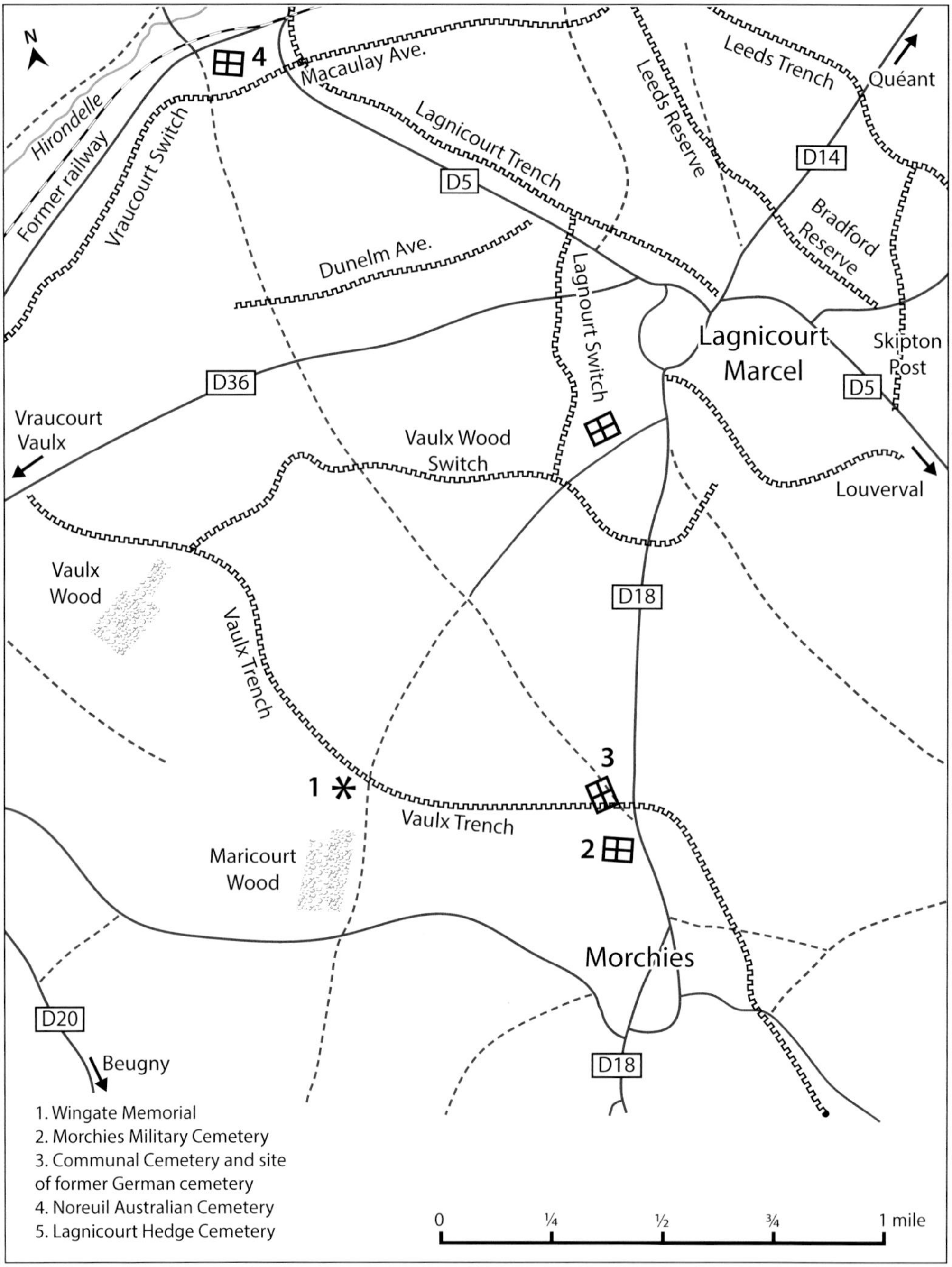

Map 11 Lagnicourt-Marcel.

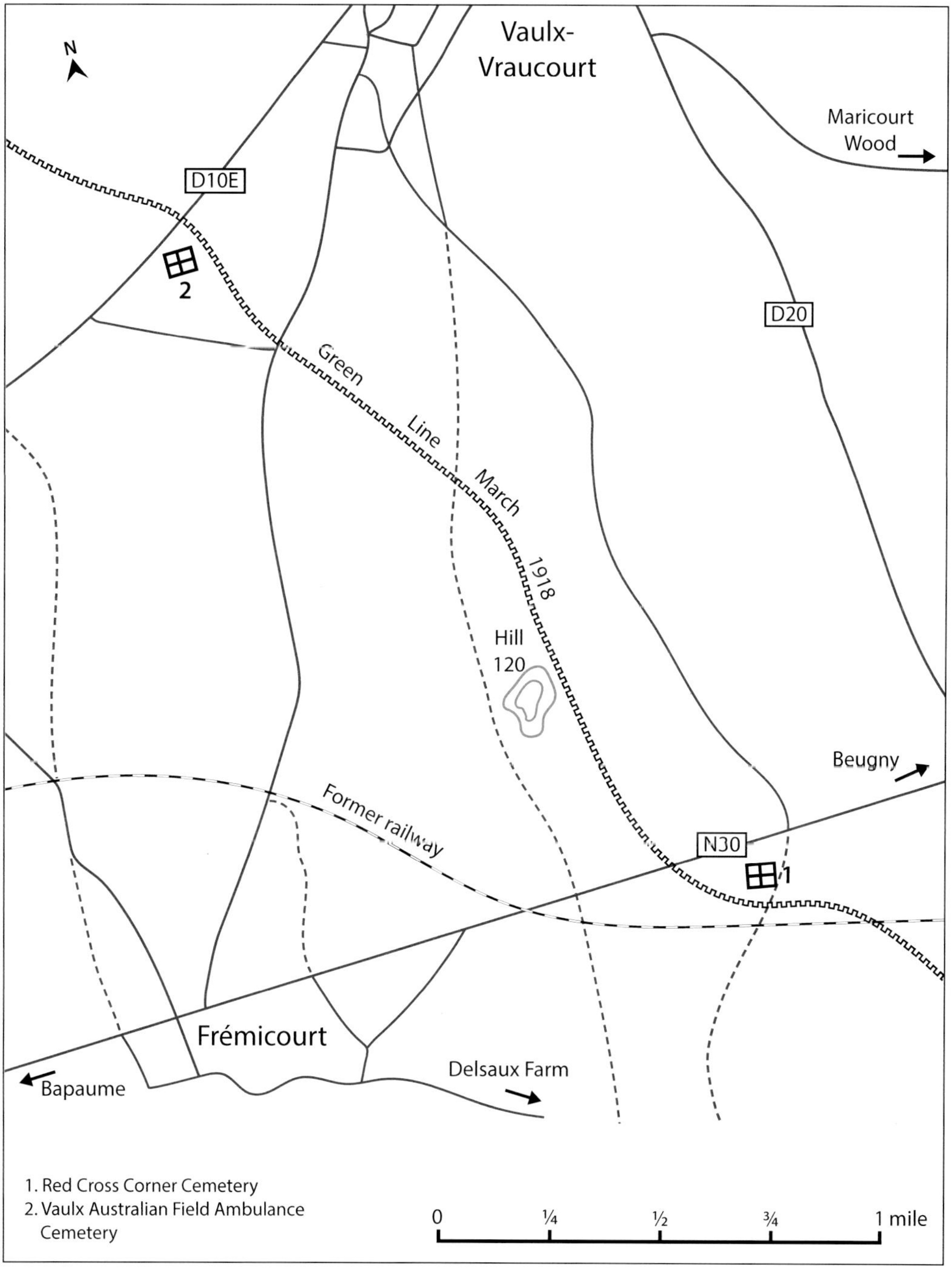

Map 12 Vaulx-Vraucourt – Frémicourt.

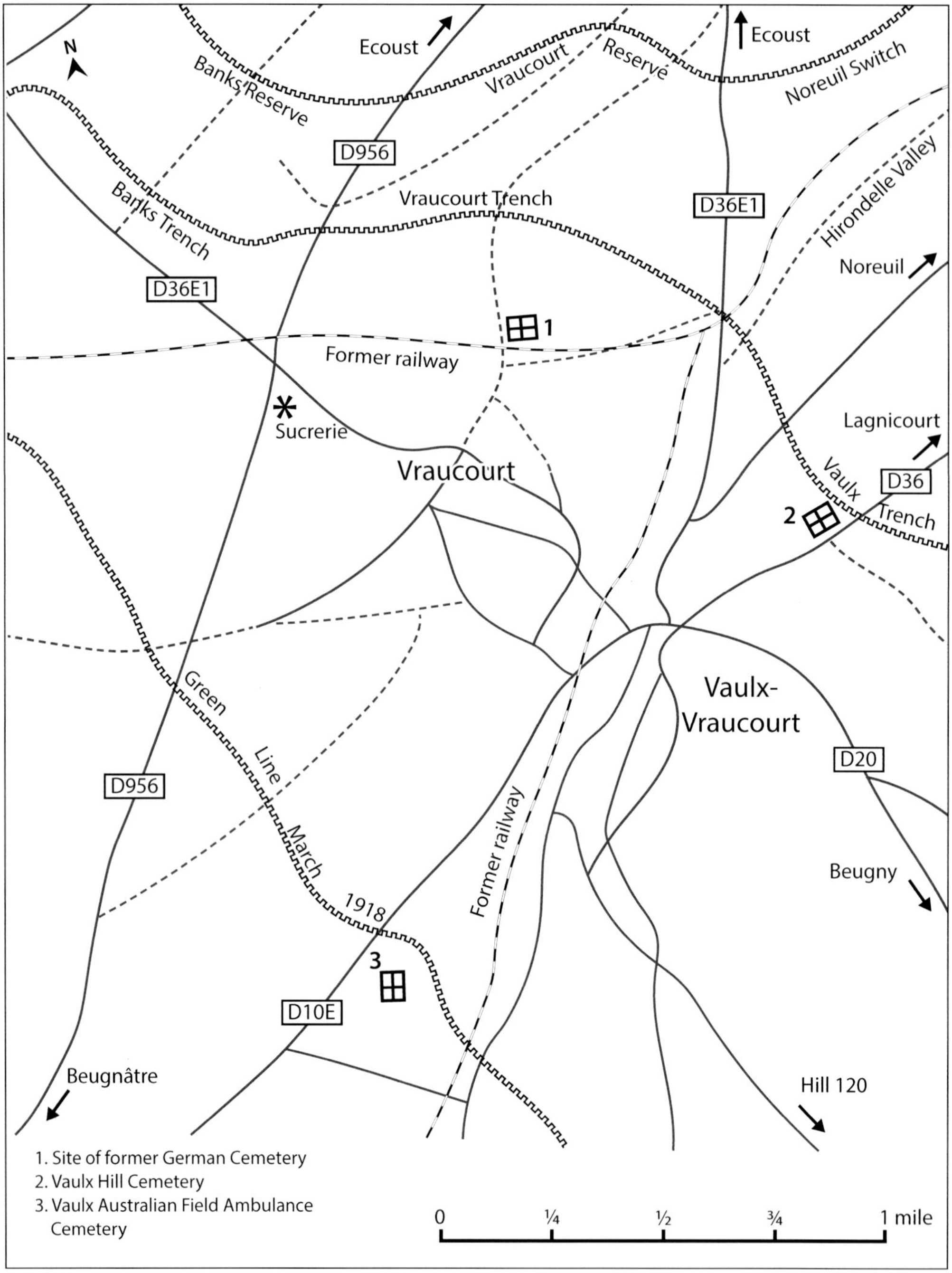

Map 13 Vaulx-Vraucourt.

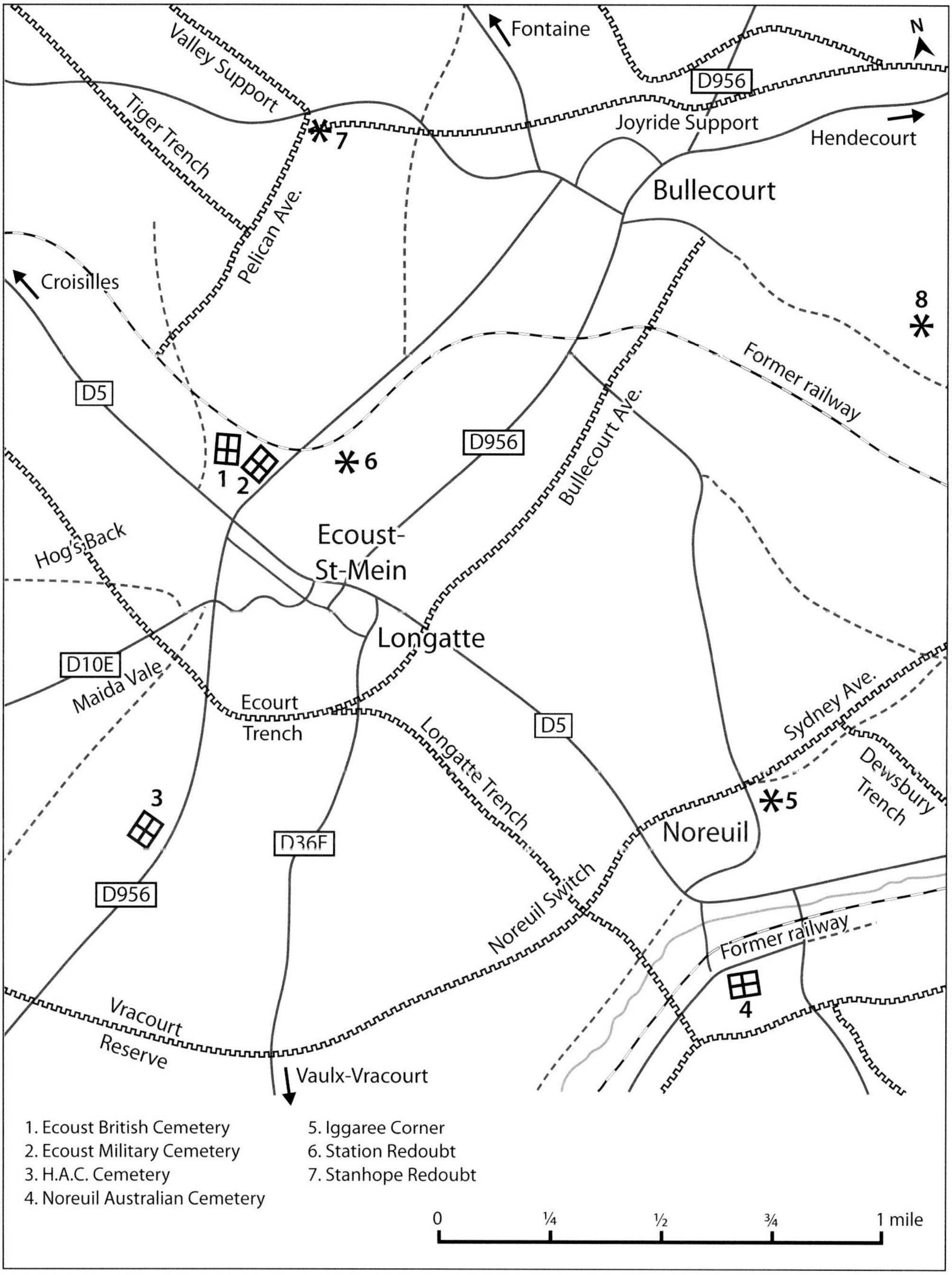

Map 14 Écoust-St-Mein – Noreuil.

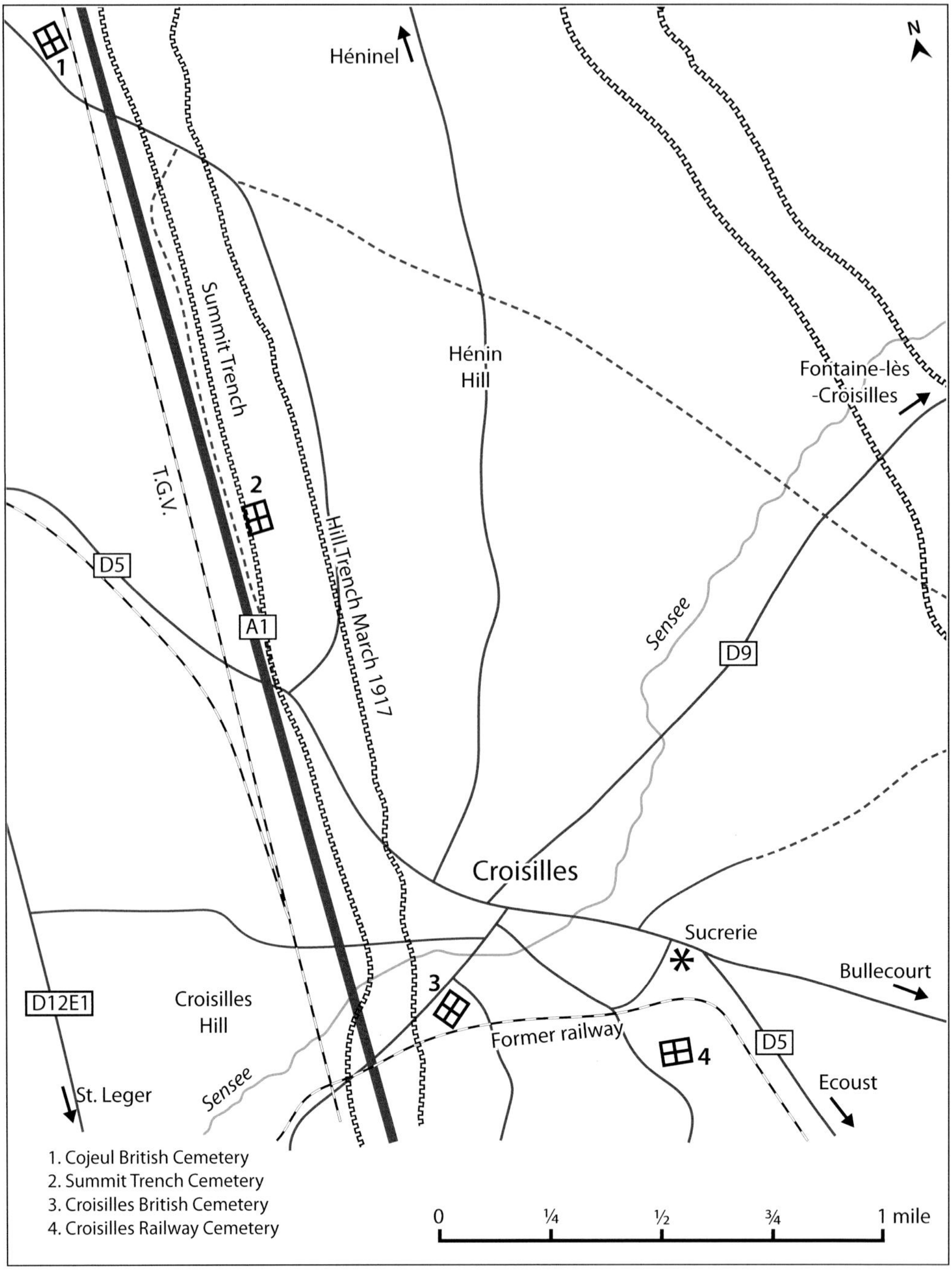

Map 15 Croisilles.

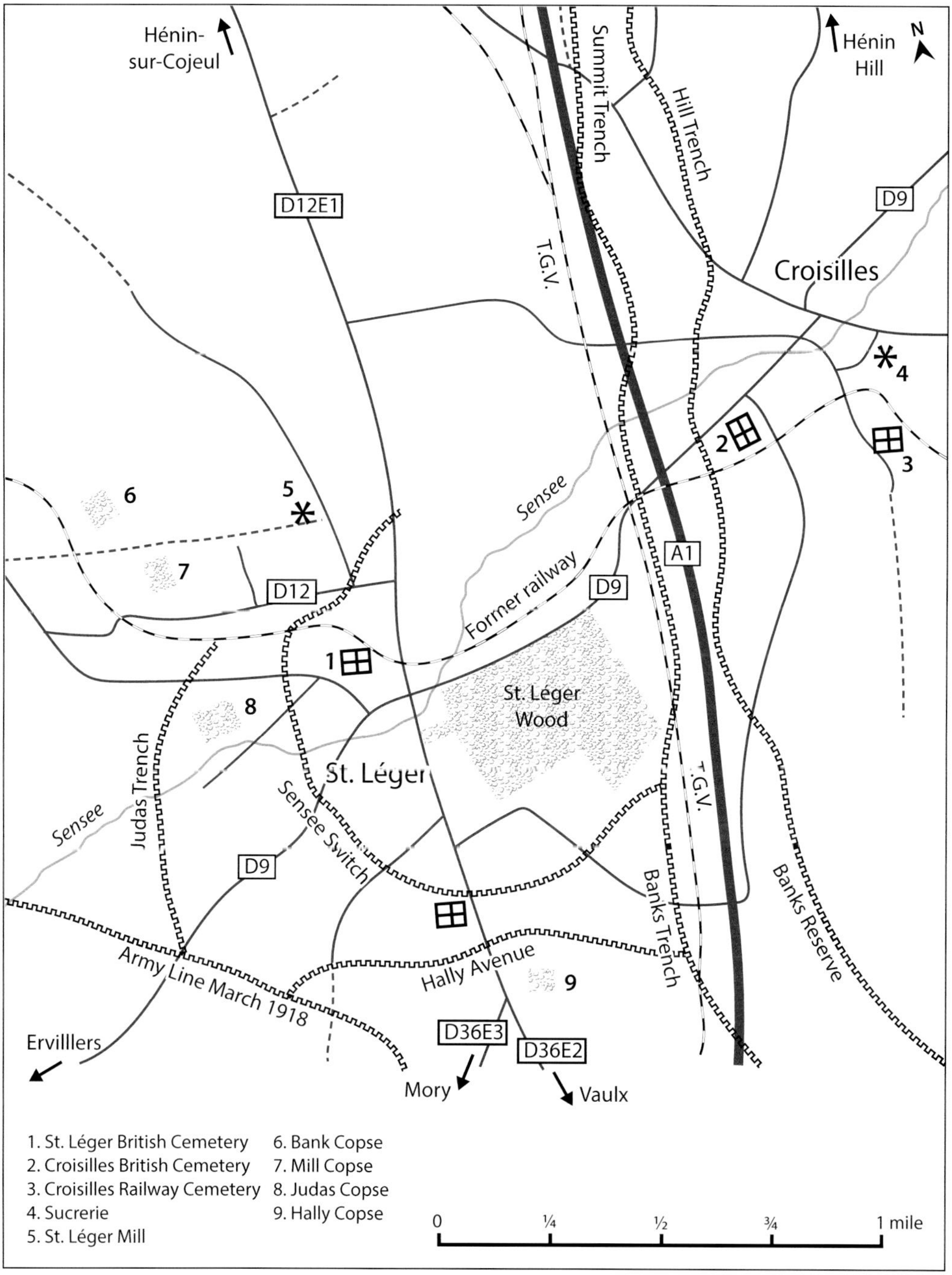

Map 16 Croisilles–St.Léger.

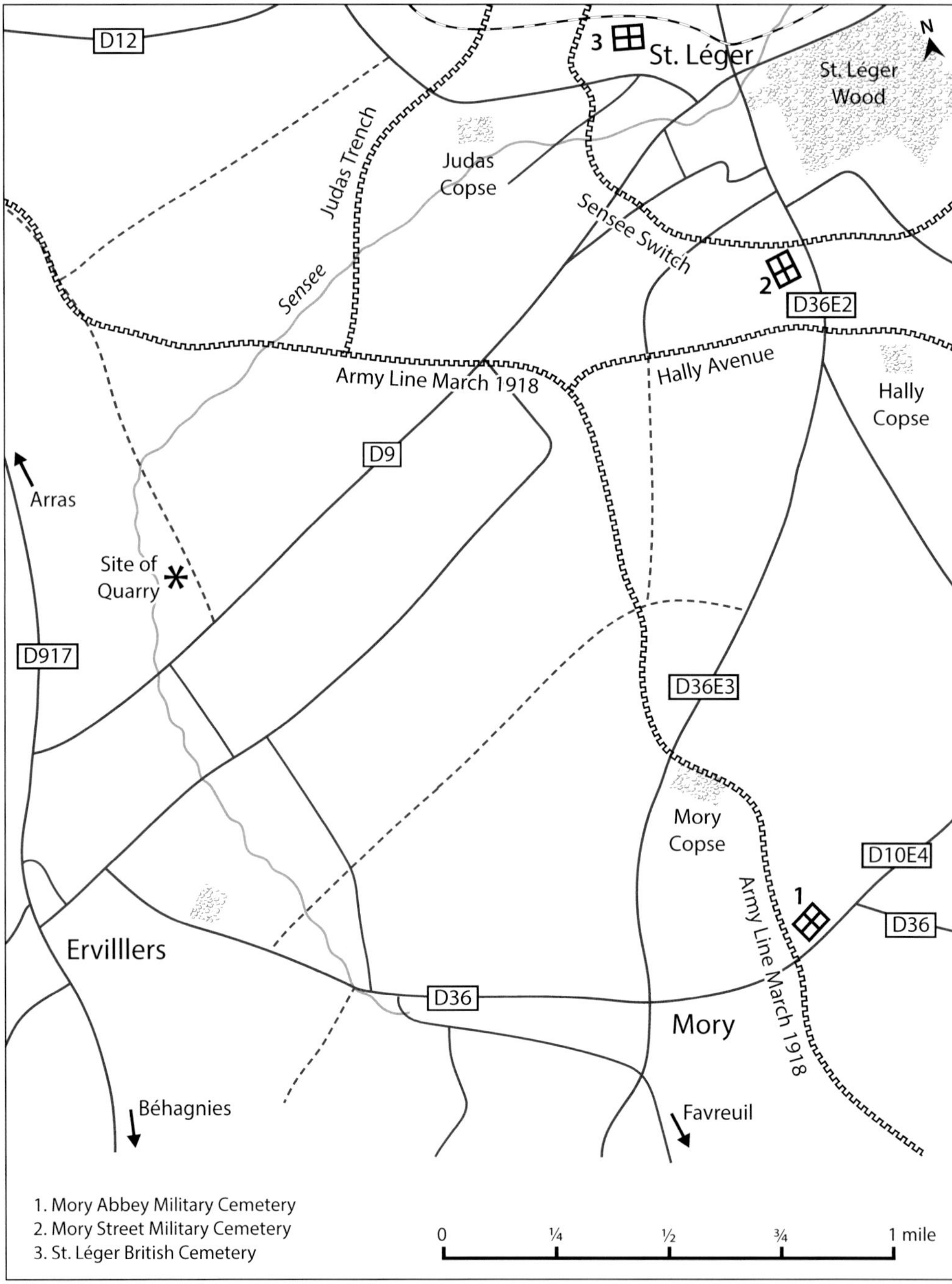

Map 17 St.Léger–Mory.

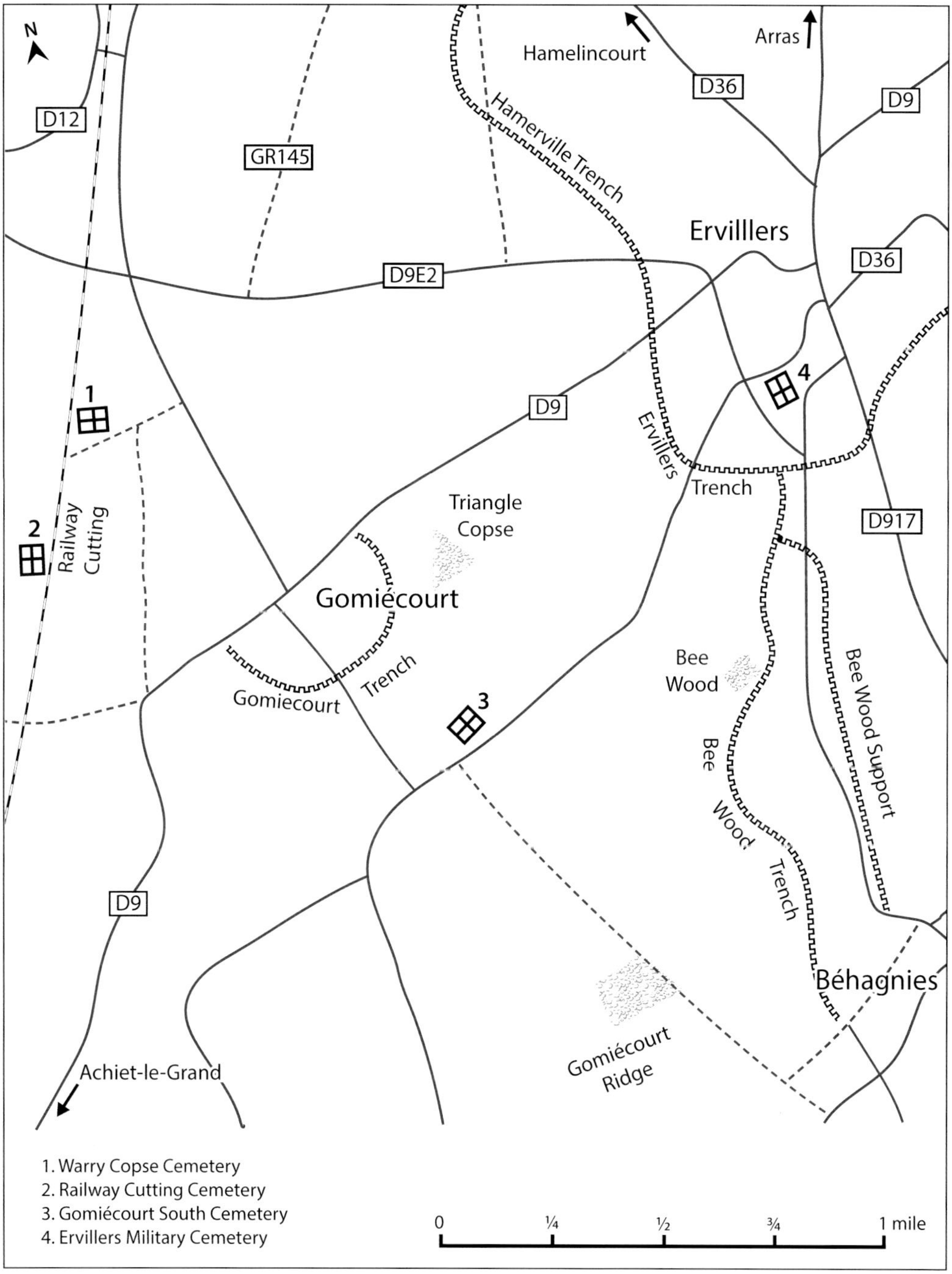

1. Warry Copse Cemetery
2. Railway Cutting Cemetery
3. Gomiécourt South Cemetery
4. Ervillers Military Cemetery

Map 18 Ervillers–Béhagnies.

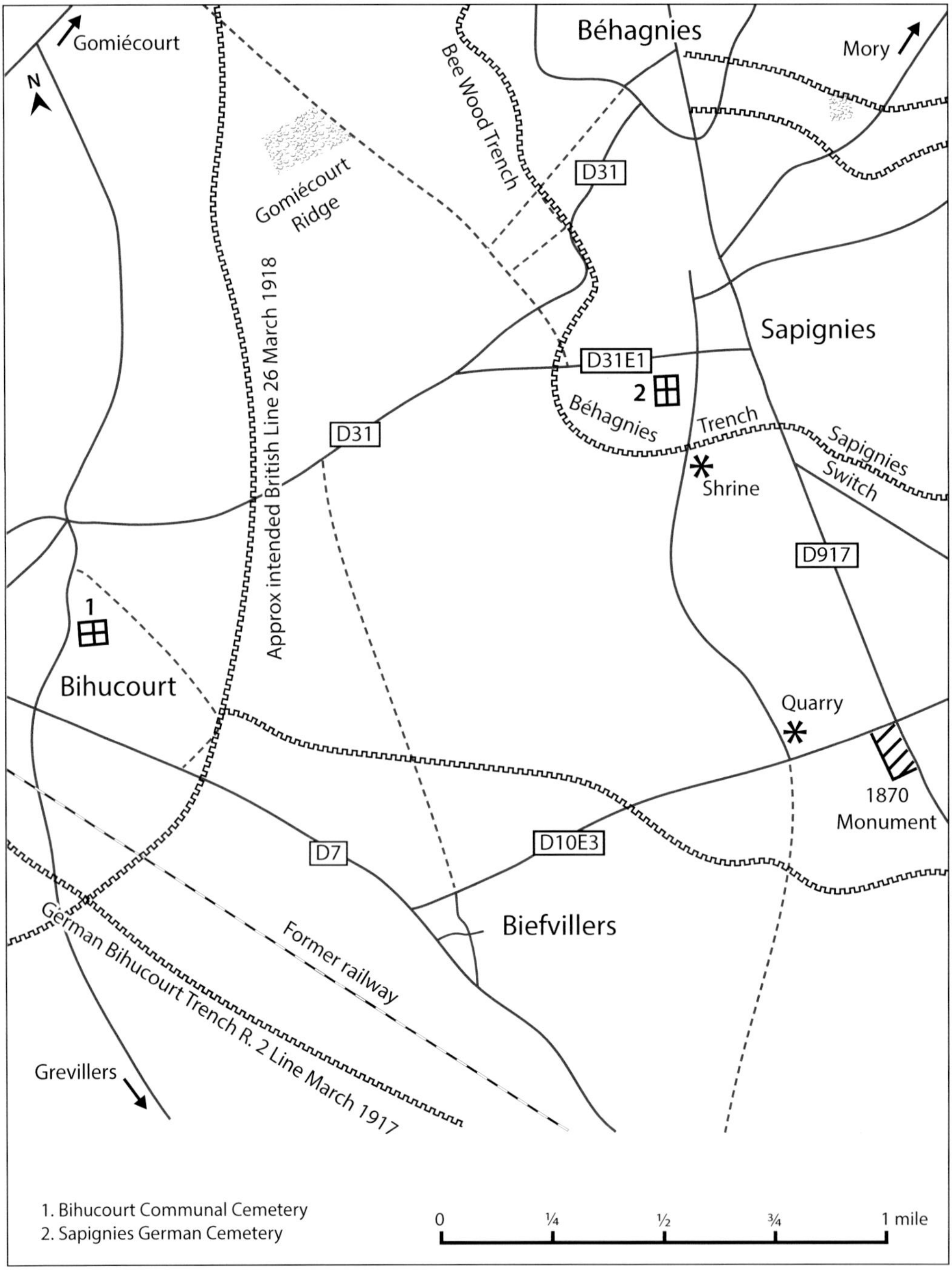

Map 19 Béhagnies–Bihucourt.

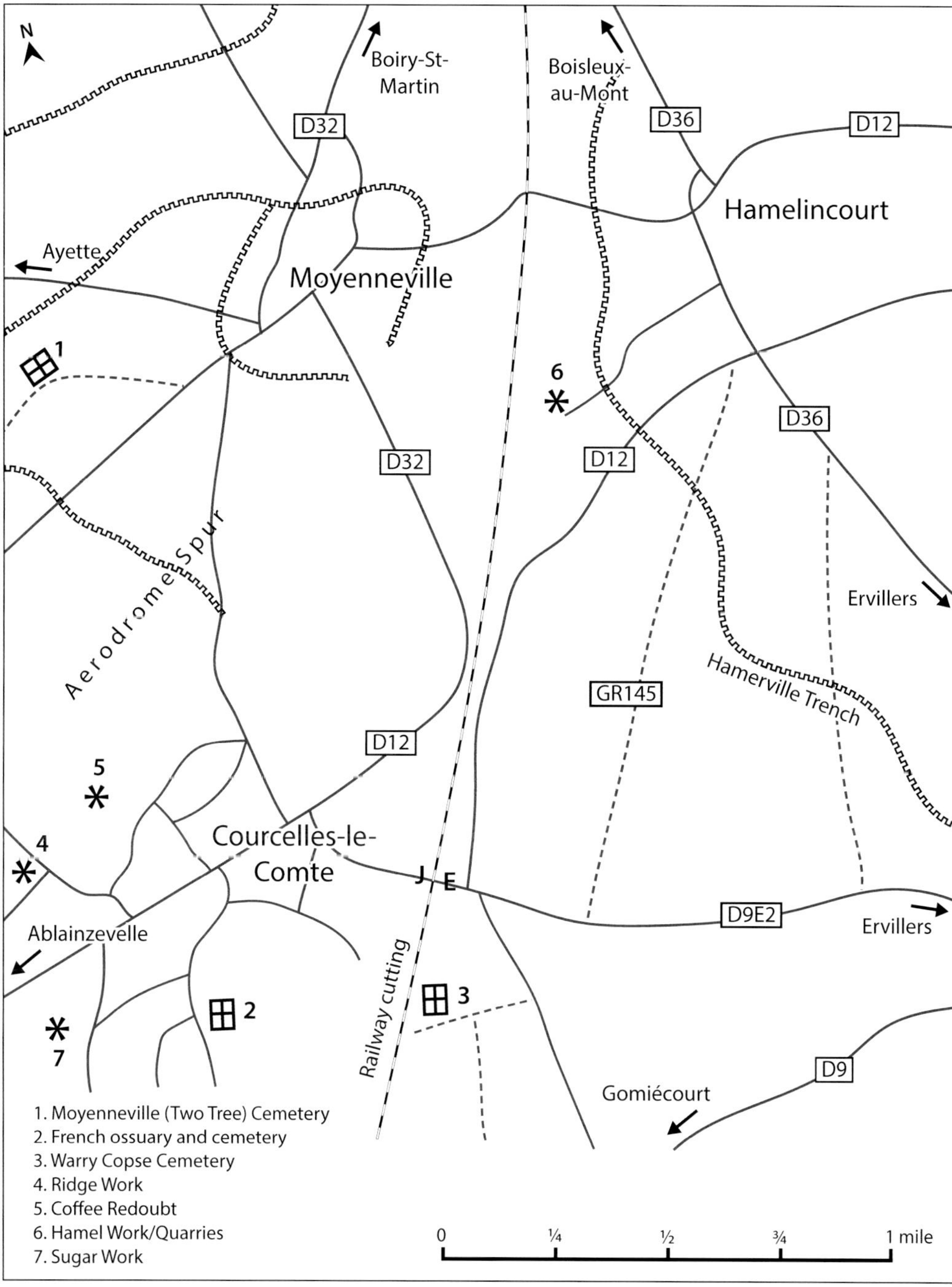

Map 20 Hamelincourt–Courcelles-le-Comte.

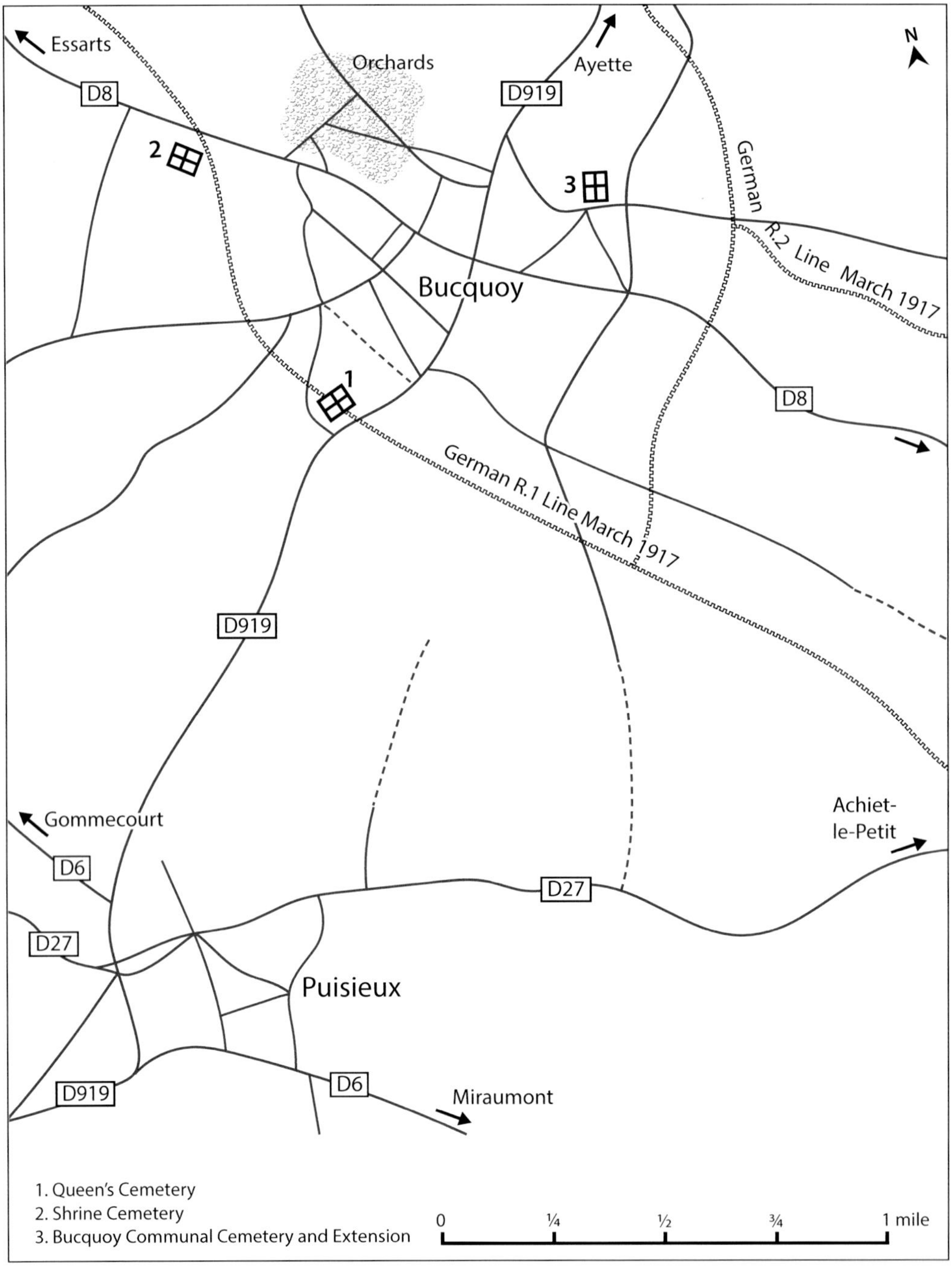

Map 21 Bucquoy–Puisieux.

Index: People and Places

Ablainzevelle, 16, 54-56, 79-82, 190, 217
Achiet-le-Grand, 16, 20, 64, 69, 70, 72, 73, 76-79, 131-33, 140, 191, 192, 194, 215
Achiet-le-Petit, x, 13, 15, 16, 21, 59, 73-75, 78, 79, 132
Adinfer, 52, 56
Alberich, Operation, 14
Anderson, Lt.Col, 136
Arras, x, 13, 14, 16, 19, 20, 34, 36, 41, 50, 54, 57, 72, 73, 83, 131, 135, 152, 177, 187, 195
Arras, Battle of, x, xi, 13, 16, 20, 28, 33, 41, 57
Avesnes, 15, 70, 72, 139
Ayette, 16, 54-57, 81, 114, 131, 166, 190, 193, 194, 217, 218

Bailey, Brig.Gen.V, 98, 99, 137
Bainbridge, Maj.Gen.G, 120
Bancourt, 68-71, 139, 144, 172, 174, 175
Bapaume, x, xi, 13-15, 69-71, 75, 76, 96, 122, 130, 138, 139, 142-44, 174, 176, 179, 180, 190
Barastre, 18, 85, 90-95, 97, 153, 172
Barnett-Barker, Brig.Gen.R, 89, 94
Barrow, Maj.Gen.G, 23, 23, 41, 119
Bazentin, 71, 96, 97, 99
Beal, 2Lt.E, 50, 187
Beaucamp, 37-40, 155-59, 170, 204
Beaulencourt, 71, 92, 94, 96, 97, 144, 151, 152, 172, 173, 175, 219
Beaumetz-les-Cambrai, x, 17, 30, 35, 64-69, 85, 125, 149, 152, 168, 175, 177-80, 182, 200
Béhagnies, 14, 51, 53, 73, 76, 78, 112, 133, 134, 137, 139, 149, 165, 166, 189, 195, 214-16
Bell, Lt, 61
Bell, Capt.E, 94
Bently, 2Lt, 65
Bertincourt, 17, 18, 66, 69, 86, 90, 92-94, 97, 98, 123, 151, 168, 171, 172, 175, 177, 201
Bethell, Brig.Gen.H, 124, 126
Beugnâtre, 17, 51, 60, 63, 64, 72, 139, 142, 143, 175, 181, 182, 190, 210
Beugny, 17, 61, 64, 65, 67-71, 149, 150, 168, 175-78, 182-84, 201, 208-10
Biefvillers, 15, 16,72, 73, 75, 76, 113, 133, 138, 144, 181, 189, 190, 216
Bihucourt, 15, 16, 53, 64, 72-79, 133, 134, 138, 139, 190, 191, 216
Bilhem, 37-40, 155, 156, 170, 203, 204
Blackall, Lt.Col, 73
Boiry-Becquerelle, 20, 54, 135
Boiry St-Martin, 217
Boiry-Sainte-Rictrude, 20
Boisleux-Saint-Marc, 56
Bond, Brig,Gen.C, 95
Boursies, 32-35, 59, 65, 66, 86, 107, 150, 152, 154, 175, 179, 182, 202
Boyall, Lt.Col, 63
Boyelles, 20, 49, 50, 56, 135, 187
Braithwaite, Maj.Gen.W, 79, 80, 120,
Bridgford, Maj.Gen.R, 53 56
Brodie, Lt.Col,W, 134
Bucquoy, x, 14-16, 24, 54, 73, 78-81, 83, 114, 132, 190, 192, 193, 218
Beugnâtre, 17, 51, 60, 63, 64, 72, 139, 142, 143, 181, 182
Bullecourt, 14, 24, 26, 28, 31, 32, 34-36, 41, 44-46, 49, 57; Battle of, x, xi, 130
Bullen-Smith, Brig.Gen.W, 91
Burn, Brig.Gen.H, 125
Bus, 18, 90-93, 95, 97, 153, 168, 175
Byng, Gen.J, 14, 28, 41, 44, 48, 67, 84, 128, 131

Canal du Nord, x, 18, 34, 37, 202, 203
Carter-Campbell, Maj.Gen.G, 59, 60, 68, 125
Cemeteries
  Achiet-le-Grand Comm.Ext, 191
  Achiet-le-Petit German, 191
  Australian Field Ambulance, 175, 176, 193, 209, 210

Ayette group, 193
Bancourt British, 174
Bapaume Communal, 174
Bapaume Australian, 174
Beaumetz group, 177, 180
Bertincourt Château, 172
Beugnâtre Communal, 181
Bihucourt Communal, 191, 216
Bucquoy group, 192
Cojuel British, 186, 212
Courcelles French, 194
Croisilles British, 186, 212, 213
Croisilles Railway, 186, 212, 213
Delsaux Farm, 176, 201
Ecoust group, 185
Ervillers Military, 195
Favreuil British, 181
Fifteen Ravine, 170
Five Points, 101, 169, 207
Gomiécourt South, 195, 215
Gouzeaucourt British, 170
Grevillers British, 191
H.A.C, 185
Hénin group, 185-86
Héninel-Croisilles Road, 186
Hermies Hill & British, 178
Lagnicourt Hedge, 183
Lebucquière Comm.Ext.
Louverval Memorial, 179
Manchester, 173
Metz Comm.Extension, 170
Morchies group, 183
Mory Abbey Military, 187
Mory Street Military, 187
Neuville-Bourjonval British, 171
Noreuil Australian, 185
Owl Trench, 192
Quéant Comm.British Ext, 184
Queen's, 192
Railway Cutting, 194
Red Cross Corner, 176
Ribécourt Road, 170
Rocquigny-Equancourt Road, 169
Rossignol Wood, 192
Ruyaulcourt Military, 171
Shrine, 193
St Léger British, 187
St Martin Calvaire British, 186
Sapignies German, 189
Summit Trench, 186, 212
Sunken Road, 170
Two Trees, 193
Vaulx Hill, 182
Villers-au-Flos German, 173
Villers Plouich Communal 170
Vraucourt Copse, 185
Warry Copse, 195
Cherry, P, Capt, 31
Clive, Lt.Col.P, 83
Coke, de E, Brig.Gen.E, 143
Contalmaison, 99
Cope, Brig.Gen.T, 46
Cormack, 2Lt, 144
Courcelette, 93, 94,96, 124
Courcelles-le-Comte, 16, 52, 54-56, 76, 78, 79, 115, 131, 136, 166, 190, 193-95, 217
Craigie-Halkett, Col.H, 10
Croisilles, x, 15, 17, 21-28, 31, 32, 48, 49, 110, 135, 136, 141-42, 182, 185-87
Crouch, Lt.Col, 150
Cubbitt, Maj.Gen.T, 120
Cumming, Brig.Gen.H.14, 27

Davies, Lt.Col.O, 83
Delsaux Farm, 17, 69, 70, 93, 104, 150, 172, 176, 177, 201, 209
Demicourt, 32-34, 59, 65, 67, 152, 154, 175, 178, 179, 202
De Pree, Brig.Gen.H, 138
Deverell, Maj.Gen.C, 58, 133, 145, 119, 132, 146, 163
Dierville Farm, 16
Dobbin, Brig.Gen,H, 48
Doignies, 31-33, 35, 65-67, 69, 86, 87, 105, 152, 168, 175, 178, 179, 182, 184
Douchy, 16, 81, 114, 166, 190, 193
Douglas, RSM.W,195

Ecoust-Saint-Mein, 17, 22-28, 31, 32, 45-47, 49, 50, 109, 136, 140, 144-47, 182, 184, 185, 188, 210, 211
Eden, Brig.Gen.A, 96
Elles, Brig.Gen.H, 95
Ervillers, x, 15, 16, 50-53, 57, 73, 76-79, 111, 112, 116, 131, 133-35, 137
Etricourt18, 70, 152, 153, 168, 207
Equancourt, 18, 70, 85, 88-91, 98, 102, 103

Fanshawe, Lt.Gen.E.A, 14, 15, 44, 96, 117, 128, 196
Favreuil, 14, 15, 17, 51, 60, 61, 63, 69, 72, 111, 113, 138, 139, 142, 175, 181-83, 185, 187-90, 214
Fielding, Maj.Gen.G, 54, 55, 58, 119, 152

Fins, 18, 70, 88, 89, 102, 152, 153, 168, 169, 171, 205, 206, 219
Flesquières, 44, 65, 67, 85, 95
Follett, Brig.Gen.G, 141, 154, 177
Fontaine-les-Croisilles, 24, 26, 27, 143, 182, 186, 211, 212
Foster, Cpl.E, 39, 170
Four Winds Farm, 18, 89, 90, 101, 169, 207
Francis, Brig.Gen,S, 14
Frederick Karl, Prince, 30
Frémicourt, x, 14, 17, 63, 68, 70, 72, 144, 149, 168, 174-76, 182, 209

Gadd, Lt.Col, 45, 46, 48
Gomiécourt, x, 15, 16, 54, 76-78, 115, 116, 131, 133-35
Gommecourt, 78-82, 191-193, 219
Gonnelieu, 37, 38, 157, 159, 160, 204
Goodman, Brig.Gen.G, 25, 26
Gorringe, Maj.Gen.G, 88, 100, 118
Gort, Lt.Col,J, 137
Gough, Gen.H, 13, 14, 15, 24, 30, 31, 34, 41, 43
Gouzeaucourt, x, 18, 19, 37, 38, 87, 103, 154-59, 168-70, 204-06
Gration, Sgt,J, 177
Grevillers, 13, 71, 76, 76, 138, 190, 191, 216
Gribble, Capt.J, 69, 104, 178
Gueudecourt, 94, 96, 98, 151

Haldane, Lt.Gen,J.A, 44, 52-58, 77, 116, 128, 131, 133, 135, 175, 193
Hamel, 97, 132
Hamelincourt, 16, 54, 56, 135, 215, 217
Haplincourt, 66, 86, 93, 151, 153, 168, 172, 175, 176, 190, 199, 201
Harcourt, Maj, 69, 177
Hardyman, Lt.Col.J, 138
Harper, Lt.Gen.G.M, 44, 53, 57, 59, 70, 73, 75, 76, 77, 78, 79, 82, 84,117, 131
Havrincourt, 18, 33, 34, 44, 86-88, 92, 154, 155, 168, 171, 177-79, 202, 203
Hayward, Capt.R, 68, 174
Hébuterne, 54, 74, 80, 81, 192, 193
Héninel, 27, 49, 141, 182, 186
Hénin Hill, 49, 126, 135, 136, 141, 186, 212, 213
Hénin-sur-Cojeul, x, 20, 45, 52, 136, 182, 186, 187
Hermies, x, 17, 30, 32-34, 36, 59, 65-67, 69, 85-87, 105, 150, 152, 154, 168, 175, 178, 179, 182, 200, 202, 203
Hindenburg Line, x, 13, 19-22, 27-29, 31, 34, 36, 37, 40, 41, 105, 107, 130, 135, 136, 141, 143, 152, 155, 166, 186
Hirondelle valley, 31, 35, 45-48, 59-61, 63, 107-09, 147, 148, 184, 185, 208, 210
Hopcroft, RSM, 69
Hull, Maj.Gen.C, 141
Hutchison, Brig.Gen.A, 91, 96

Iggaree Corner, 47, 211
Irles, 13, 74, 75, 76, 133, 128
Ironside, Lt.Col.E, 80, 134, 192

Jacob, Lt.Gen.c, 120
James, Lt.Col.A.H, 80
James, Capt.M, 104, 69, 178
Jeffreys, Maj.Gen.G, 70, 85
Jenson, Pte.J, 32
Judas Farm, 10, 20, 50, 110, 187, 213, 214

Keating, Major, 46
Kennedy, Brig.Gen.H, 89, 121
Kenny, Pte.T, 33, 178

Lagnicourt-Marcel, 17, 22, 30-36, 59-65, 106-08, 147-50, 152, 175, 180, 182-85, 200, 208, 210
La Vacquerie, 159
Lawford, Maj.Gen.C. 70, 72, 73
Lawrie, Maj.Gen.C, 97, 118, 138, 139, 142
Lebucquière, x, 17, 59, 65-68, 70, 85, 93, 104, 151, 172, 172-77, 182, 201
Léchelle, 68, 89-94, 168, 169, 175, 207
Lesboeufs, 71, 94, 96-99, 151, 167
Le Transloy, x, 15, 90, 94-99, 144, 151, 152, 167-69, 171, 173, 175, 199
Ligny-Thilloy, 94, 190, 191
Loch, Brig.Gen.G, 136
Longatte, 17, 22-24, 27, 31, 34, 45-47, 49, 145-47, 182, 184, 185, 211
Louverval, 31-33, 59-66, 86, 123, 147, 175, 179, 180, 184, 200, 208

Manancourt, 89, 152, 168, 207
Marden, Maj.Gen.T, 48,59, 60, 64
McDonald, Lt.Col, 75
McIvor, H, Pte, 185, 194
Mars, Operation, 56, 57, 83
Martinpuich, 71, 96, 97, 139
Maxe, Lt.Gen.I, 22
Mayne, Capt, 144
Merrikin, 2Lt.G, 186

Mesnil-en-Arrouaise, 90, 95, 97, 98, 101, 152, 168, 169
Metz-en-Couture, x, 18, 37, 70, 85, 88=90, 103, 153, 154, 157, 168-71, 203, 206
Meunier House, 19
Mildren, Brig.Gen.W, 98
Miraumont, 13, 75, 80, 131, 132, 138, 190, 218
Morchies, 17, 35, 60-68, 93, 148-50, 175, 180-83, 200, 201, 208
Morval, 71, 96, 97, 151
Mory, x, 16, 17, 20, 23, 24, 47, 50-52, 70, 71, 111, 112, 134, 135, 137, 140, 141, 146, 175, 182, 185, 187-90, 193, 213, 214, 216
Moser, Lt.Gen.von O, 34
Mountain, Sgt.A, 55, 194
Moyenneville, 16, 54, 55, 115, 131, 190, 193, 194, 217

Neilson, Lt.Col, 136
Neuville-Bourjonval, 18, 70, 88, 90, 103, 153, 154, 168, 171, 175, 207
Neuville-Vitasses, 20, 28, 141
Newland, Capt.J, 35
Nicholson, Maj.Gen.C, 49
Noreuil, 17, 27, 28, 30-36, 45-47, 49, 59, 61-63, 107-09, 145-48, 182, 184, 185, 208, 210, 211
Norris, Lt.Col, 22
Nurlu, 18, 70, 168

Palmer, Capt, 70, 177
Pereira, Maj.Gen.C, 90, 92
Péronne, 18, 19, 37, 38, 71, 94, 95, 97, 98, 144, 151, 152, 154, 155, 167, 173, 174
Peel, Lt.Col, 78
PonONSBY, Maj.Gen.J, 120, 162, 163
Potter, Lt, 65, 131
Pronville, 34, 60, 107, 150, 182, 184
Puisieux, x, 13, 74, 75, 79, 80
Pys, 74, 75, 94

Quéant, 28, 31, 32, 59, 148, 149, 151, 152, 182, 184, 208

Rawling, Brig.Gen.C, 25
Reed, Cpl, 39
Ribécourt, 37, 39, 156, 170, 203, 204
Riencourt-les-Bapaume, 34, 71, 142, 144, 151, 168, 173, 175, 184, 190, 199
Robertson, Maj.Gen.P, 91, 92, 95
Rocquigny, 14, 18, 89-99, 152, 153, 167-69, 175, 207
Romer, Maj.Gen.C, 47, 48, 58, 118

Ruyaulcourt, 18, 154, 168, 171, 178, 206

St-Léger, 15-17, 20, 22-24, 45, 48-52, 110, 111, 135, 137, 140-43
Sailly-au-Bois, 53, 75
Sailly-Saillisel, 92, 95, 96, 98, 99, 167
Saint-Martin-sur-Cojeul, 20, 26, 141
Shaw, Lt.Col, 135
Shoubridge, Maj.Gen.T, 24, 26, 27
Shute, Lt.Gen.C, 116, 131
Siegried Stellung, see Hindenburg Line
Simner, Lt.Col, 96
Smith, Lt.Col, 83
Solly-Flood, Maj.Gen.A, 52, 53, 78-81, 151, 164, 173
Stafford, Lt.Col, 90-94
Stubbs, Lt.Col, 134

Thilloy, 13, 94, 138, 139, 142-44, 190
Thornton-Smith, 2Lt, 37
Towsey, Brig.Gen.F, 72
Trenches/redoubts/defence lines/HQ
  Aerodrome Trench, 193
  African Trench/Support, 155, 156, 157, 158, 159, 205
  Army Line, 50, 51, 63, 67, 137, 144, 181, 213, 214
  Banks Trench/Reserve, 45, 50, 141, 143, 143, 185, 210, 213
  Beaumetz-Morchies Line, 64-67, 125
  Beauregard Dovecote, 13, 131, 132
  Bullecourt Avenue, 146, 211
  Butte de Warlencourt, 71, 74
  Dead Man's Corner, 155-58, 170, 204
  Dessart Ridge/Switch, 87, 88, 103, 169, 171, 206
  Dewsbury Trench, 45, 148, 184, 211
  Dunelm Avenue/Redoubt, 60, 107, 108, 148, 185, 208
  Ervillers Trench, 52, 189, 215
  Garforth Soil Tip, 171
  Green Line, 68-70, 86-93, 95, 102-04, 127, 167, 171, 172, 174-76, 201, 207, 209, 210,
  Grevillers Trench, 13
  Hebburn Spoil Tip, 86, 87, 92, 171
  Heather Trench/Support, 154, 159, 170, 205
  Hermies Switch, 65-67, 86, 105, 178, 179, 200,
  Hill Trench/Switch, 186, 212, 213
  Hindenburg Line,
  Horseshoe Redoubt, 45
  Jermyn Street, 86,

Joyride Trench, 45, 57, 211
Lagnicourt Trench, 60, 62, 108, 148
Leech Avenue, 62
Leeds Trench/Reserve, 59, 60, 184, 208
Longatte Trench, 147, 211
Macaulay Trench/Avenue, 60, 148, 149, 184, 208
Metz Switch, 87, 88, 89, 90, 92, 98, 102, 103, 170, 206
Pelican Avenue, 185, 211
Pontefract Trench, 45, 147
Purple Line, 54, 56, 82
Queen's Cross, 156, 157, 205
Quentin Mill, 19
R.1, R.2, R.3, 13, 15, 20
Red Line, 68, 69, 70, 92-97, 172, 173, 181,
Rocquigny-Bapaume Line, 167
Skipton Post, 61, 62, 184, 208
Spoil Heap (Hermies), 34, 86, 105, 154, 178, 179, 202
Stanhope Redoubt, 46, 185, 211
Station Redoubt, 46, 146, 185, 211
Sturgeon Avenue/Support, 65, 202
Summit Trench, 135, 136, 137, 141, 142, 143, 212, 213
Sydney Avenue, 147, 211
Travel Trench, 60, 62, 184, 200
Vaulx Trench, 48, 106, 148-50, 182, 183, 208
Vaulx-Morchies Line, 60-64, 125, 183
Vraucourt Trench, 47, 48, 145, 149, 182, 185, 210
Yorkshire Bank, 92, 106, 179, 203
Ytres-Equancourt Line, 153
Trescault, 37-39, 155-158, 168, 170, 203-06

Vaulx-Vraucourt, 30, 35, 45, 47, 48, 50, 60, 61, 63, 64, 71, 72, 106, 108, 109, 136, 140, 145, 148-50, 174-76
Vélu, 17, 144, 152, 168, 175, 177, 182, 201
Villers-au-Flos, 15, 69, 92-95, 97, 151-53, 168, 172, 175, 199
Villers-Guislain, 19, 37
Villers-Plouich, x, 37-39, 68, 155, 157, 159, 170, 204

Walker, Brig.Gen.H, 60, 125
Warlencourt, 71, 73, 138
Watson, Lt.Col.O, 82, 192
Whittle, Sgt.J, 35
Wingate, Maj.R, 62
Winter, Lt.Col, 94
Woodcock, Pte.T, 193
Wood/copse
Adinfer, 20
Banks, 141
Bee, 52, 76, 112, 116, 134, 189, 195, 215, 216
Chaufours, 64, 67, 180, 184
Dessart, 18, 102, 169, 206
Fork, 80, 81, 192
Gauche, 19, 169, 205
Gouzeaucourt, 18, 87, 103, 170, 205
Hailly, 135, 141, 187, 213, 214
Haplincourt, 93, 172
Havrincourt, 18, 88, 92,154, 155, 171, 178, 203
Hayettes, 90, 101, 103, 153, 169, 171, 207
High, 94, 97, 99, 142
Judas, 135, 213, 214
Léchelle, 90, 169
Logeast, 15, 16, 52, 73, 79, 80, 81-82, 114, 194, 219
Loon, 95, 168
Loupart, 14, 71, 74, 133, 138
Louverval, 32, 65, 86, 123, 184
Maricourt, 17, 60-64, 106, 180, 183, 208
Monument, 69, 140, 181
Mory, 50-52, 137, 140, 141, 187, 214,
Rossignol, 14, 80, 81, 83, 192
Vallulart, 89, 90, 101, 102, 153, 167, 169, 171, 178, 207
Vaulx, 17, 35, 60-63, 66, 106, 149, 150, 182, 183, 208
Vélu, 17, 30, 66-69, 85, 86, 92, 93, 104, 172, 176-78
Vraucourt, 17, 47, 108, 185

Yatman, Brig.Gen.C, 96
Ytres, x, 18, 70, 90, 91, 93, 97, 102, 103, 144, 152, 153, 168, 171, 175

Index: Formations and Units

Armies
First: 132, 151, 152, 196
Third: 14, 16, 19, 28, 41, 43, 53, 71, 81, 83, 85, 88, 95, 121, 124, 128, 129, 131, 132, 137, 138, 144, 147, 149, 152, 154, 168, 196, 197
Fourth: 14, 18, 132, 157
Fifth: 13, 14, 17, 21, 43, 57, 70, 84, 89, 124, 152, 196

Artillery brigades – *27th*, 144, 176; *34th*, 99; 36, 93; *78th*, 92; 79, 92; *104th*, 69; *122th*, 71-73, 75, 78, 79, 82, 153, 191; *160th*, 49; *256*, 64, 183; *296th*, 46; *310th*, 21

Cavalry brigades/regiments – *King's Dragoons*, 22; *29/Lancers*, 16, 189; *Lucknow Bde*, 15, 16, 21, 22, 189, 191, 193; *Oxford Hussars*, 150, 152; *R.Scots Greys*, 153; *Yorkshire Dragoons*, 16

Corps
II: 22-29
IV: x, 45, 53, 57, 59-84 *passim*, 85, 108, 130-160 *passim*
V: x, 13, 14, 15, 16, 17, 20, 22-29, 65, 66, 67, 69, 70, 71, 73, 74, 76, 79, 80, 84, 85-120 *passim*, 125, 130-160 *passim*, 161, 173, 176, 194
VI: x, 19, 45-58, 71, 73, 77, 79, 130-160 *passim*, 166
VII: 19, 20, 21, 23, 85, 87, 95, 102
VIII: 22-29
XV: 37-40
XVII: 141
XVIII, 19, 20, 117
I ANZAC: 30-36

Divisions
Guards, ix, 52, 54-56, 119, 135-37, 140-42, 144, 145, 148, 152, 179, 183, 184, 187, 189, 194
2nd, 41, 57, 69-71, 74, 75, 85-90, 92-96, 131, 133-40, 150, 152, 154, 155, 166, 169, 172, 176, 178, 183, 189, 192, 195
3rd, ix, 54, 56-58, 116, 119, 131-136, 142, 145-48, 162, 166, 184, 185, 195
5th, 132, 133, 138, 140, 142, 144, 145, 149-51, 156, 157, 159, 160, 162, 172, 176, 181
6th, vii, 48, 50, 59, 60, 63-65, 67, 109, 123-25, 127
7th, ix, 14-17, 20-26, 119, 185, 189, 192, 194
8th, 18, 19, 37, 38, 169
9th, 85, 87-89, 92. 95, 98, 169
17th, 65, 66, 69, 85, 87, 90-96, 99, 125, 126, 151-55, 161, 163, 167, 169, 171, 178
18th, 13, 15-17, 20, 22, 23
19th, ix, 44, 64, 66, 67, 69-74, 85, 86, 93, 119173, 174, 176, 180, 183, 190, 192
20th, 18, 19, 36, 37, 40, 155, 167, 169, 171, 172
21st, 23-26, 139, 151-54, 157, 159, 173
25th, ix, 59, 60, 63-65, 67, 70-72, 76, 120, 124, 165, 174, 175, 180, 181
30th, 19, 20, 23, 29
31st, 14, 50-57, 81, 114, 123, 127,
34th, 46-50, 52, 63, 126, 186
38th, vi, ix, 103, 120, 152, 153, 156, 157, 162
39th, 38
40th, ix, 19, 37, 38, 47-50, 52, 53, 61, 72, 73, 75, 120, 181
41st, viii, 57, 63, 64, 67, 68, 70, 71, 73, 79-80, 82, 174, 176, 188-92
42nd, 52-57, 73, 75-82, 112, 116, 132, 138, 144, 150, 151, 153, 157-59, 170, 162, 172, 173, 189, 192, 194
46th, 16, 20, 193
47th, 86-92, 95-100, 103, 118, 169, 170, 178
51st, 59, 60, 63, 65-67, 69, 70, 74, 75, 79, 86, 87, 94, 122, 123, 127, 173, 177, 180, 192
52nd, 135, 136, 141, 143, 147, 148, 186
56th, 28, 135, 136, 141-43, 146, 147, 183, 193, 196

58th, 20
59th, vii, ix, 45, 47, 48, 49, 53, 57, 58, 61, 63, 109, 118, 184, 185
62nd, ix, 15, 16, 25, 34, 36, 74, 78-81, 113, 114, 120, 136, 137, 139-50, 155, 156, 176, 178, 183, 188, 189, 192, 195, 197
63rd (RND), 85. 87-93, 95-100, 122, 124, 127, 132, 138, 139, 142-44, 167, 170, 171-73, 177, 178, 191

Australian: *1st*, 34, 36; *2nd*, 17, 31, 34, 36, 181; *4th*, 34, 196; *5th*, 15, 17, 30, 32, 167, 173, 174

New Zealand: 80, 132, 138, 139, 142-44, 151, 154, 174, 188

Field Companies RE: *93*, 161; *130*, 66; *469*, 62

Field Ambulances
4th, 183
9th, 183

Infantry Brigades
1st (Gds), 137, 141
2nd (Gds), 49, 50, 131, 135
3rd (Gds), 135, 137, 141, 154
4th (Gds), viii, 51-54, 56, 81, 111, 114, 189, 193
5, 87, 91-93, 134, 137, 139, 192
6, 16, 93, 94, 134, 137, 152, 154
7, 63, 67, 68, 70-73
8, 15, 131, 147-49, 184, 185, 194
16, 60, 61, 64, 125, 183
18, 60, 62, 65
20, 26
22, 20, 26, 189
25, 18
50, 86, 92, 95, 96, 98, 153, 167, 168
51, 86, 92, 95-98, 152, 167, 168
52, 86, 87, 92, 95-98, 152, 167, 168
54, 23
56, 69
57, 66, 67, 69, 70, 72, 74, 173, 177, 179, 191
58, 67-69, 70, 72, 86, 174, 178, 180
59, 18, 170
61, 18, 171
62, 25-27
63, 83, 139, 192
64, 152
71, 60-62, 64
74, 63-67, 72, 124
75, 60, 61, 64, 67, 70, 180, 189
76, 132, 133, 142, 146, 195
91, 14, 24, 26, 27
92, 52-54, 56, 81, 189, 194
93, 53-56, 193, 194
95, 132, 144, 145, 157-59, 176
97, 56, 196
99, 85, 88-90, 92-94, 98, 134, 137, 167, 168
101, 48, 49
102, 48, 49
103, 48, 49
113, 152, 157
114, 153
115, 138, 152
119, 38, 51, 52
120, 50, 51, 73, 181, 188
121, 38, 121
122, 71-73, 75, 78, 79, 82, 191
123, 68, 70, 72, 78, 174, 180, 181, 188
124, 72, 73, 78, 175, 188, 190, 192
125, 76-78, 81, 83, 153, 171, 189
126, 52, 57, 76-78, 81, 144, 195
127, 76-78, 151, 152, 173
140, 87-90, 98, 121, 167, 168
141, 88-90, 98, 99, 101, 167, 168
142, 87-90, 98, 99, 167, 171, 172
152, 65, 66, 68, 71, 74, 125, 179
153, 65, 70, 71, 75, 179
154, 65-68, 74, 75
155, 141, 143, 186
156, 135, 136, 141, 148
157, 136, 143, 186
167, 135-37, 141, 143, 146. 186
168, 135, 136, 143, 146
169, 141, 143
176, 46, 48, 185
177, 46-48, 50-53, 73, 109
178, 45, 48, 184
185, 79, 80, 82, 145, 149, 150
186, 15, 79-81, 140, 144, 145
187, 80-82, 140, 149, 150
188, 90, 91, 97, 138
189, 87, 90, 97, 132, 138
190, 90, 91, 96

Infantry Regiments and Battalions
Coldstream: *2nd*, 187; *3rd*, 77
Grenadier: *1st*, 135, 137, 141; *2nd*, 56, 83, 114; *3rd*, 135, 194; 141; *4th*, 170
Scots: *1st*, 135, 141, 187; *2nd*, 137
Welsh: *1st*, 13 Irish: *2nd*, 55, 93
Argyll & Sutherland Highlanders: ; *6/7th*, 127; *7th*, 73, 65-67, 69, 73, 104, 177; *12th*, 38-40; *14th*, 50, 73, 189

Bedfordshire: *1st*, 151, 157, 158; *4th*, 91, 97, 167; *6th, 83*; *7th*, 15, 191
Berkshire, R: *1st*, 89, 90, 98, 123, 131, 134, 137, 154, 168, 169, 178; *2nd*, 18
Black Watch: *6th*, 65, 189; *7th*, 65, 71
Border: *1st,* 167; *2nd*, 25, 185; *7th*, 87, 96, 153; *8th*, 60, 61, 64, 183
Buffs: *1st*, 60, 61, 126, 183
Cheshire:*1st,* 150, 157-59, 176; *9th*, 70, 74, 93, 176, 177; *10th,* 63, 68, 72, 73, 176; *11th,* 61, 63-65, 180, 183
Devonshire: *1st* 132, 144, 145, 159, 176; *5th,* 145; *8th*, 23, 27, 28, 185; *9th*, 27, 28, 185
Dorsetshire: *6th*, 92, 96, 152, 153, 167, 168
Duke of Wellington's: *2/4th*, 80, 111, 139, 188; *5th*, 15, 16, 80, 81, 191, 195; *8th*, 178; *9th*, 96, 167
Durham L.I: *2nd,* 62-64, 183; *9th*, 73, 79, 80, 149, 150, 156; *18th*, 55, 56, 193, 194; *20th*, 73
East Lancashire: *1st*, 46, 48, 49, 169; *2nd*, 19; *5th*, 52, 76, 78, 144, 173, 189, 195; *11th,* 53
East Surrey: *1st*, 144, 159, 176; *12th*, 72, 73, 78; *13th*, 38, 39, 50-53, 111, 170, 188, 189
East Yorkshire: *1st*, 152, 173; *7th,* 86, 96, 152, 167, 178; *10th*, 27, 53; *11th*, 52, 56, 189
Essex: *1st*, 133, 140, 188, 189; *11th*, 62-65, 183
Gloucestershire: *8th*, 66-69, 178, 179; *12th*, 133, 159
Gordon Highlanders:*1st*, 133, 146-48; *2nd*, 23, 27, 185; *4th*, 65-67; *5th*, 177; *6th*, 65, 66, 177, 180; *1/7th*, 65, 180
Hampshire: *2/4th*, 145; *15th,* 73, 78, 82, 191
Hertfordshire, *1/1st,* 133, 154
Highland L.I: *2nd*, 93, 94, 134, 139, 195; *5th*, 136; *6th*, 136, 169; *10/11th,* 50; *14th*, 50, 181; *15th*, 57, 193
Honourable Artillery Company: *2/1st*, 25,
Kent, R.West: *1st*, 133, 144, 157-59, 176; *10th*, 72
King's (Liverpool): *1st,* 93, 128, 134, 137, 172, 189, 195; *11th*, 131; *12th,* 18, 38; *13th*, 131, 132, 146, 147, 194
King's Own Royal Lancaster: *8th,* 195; *11th*, 38, 40
King's Own Scottish Borderers: *2nd*, 142, 157, 181; *4th*, 141
King's Own Yorkshire L.I: *2/4th*, 81, 82, 140, 149, 183; *5th*, 81, 82, 140, 149, 150, 183, 188, 192; *10th*, 186
King's Royal Rifle Corps: *1st*, 85, 89-91, 94, 123, 134, 137, 154, 169, 178, 189; *12th*, 37, 40, 170, 171; *13th*, 133, 139, 140, 155, 156, 188, 191; *18th*, 70, 72
King's Shropshire.L.I: *1st*, 60, 61, 183; *4th*, 67, 68; *7th*, 131, 148, 149, 150, 182
Lancashire Fusiliers: *5th*, 83; *7th*, 83; *8th*, 76, 81, 83, 132, 153, 189, 192; *10th*, 85, 96; *11th,* 65-68, 180
Leicestershire: *1st,* 61, 62; *2/4th,* 46, 50-53; *11th*, 61
Lincolnshire: *1st*, 159, 160; 2nd, 159; *4th*, 16, 50, 51, 193; *2/5th*. 16, 50, 51, 53, 185, 193; *7th*, 86, 87, 92, 153, 178; *8th*, 138, 139; *10th*, 48-50, 187
London: *1st*, 28, 135; *1/2nd*, 143; *4th*, 135; *5th (LRB),* 143; *2/5th*, 177; *12th (Rangers),* 191; *13th (Kensington),* 173; *14th (Scottish),* 135, 146, 183; *15th (CSR),* 88; *16th (Queen's Westminsters)*, 143; *18th (Irish),* 88, 98, 168; *19th (St.Pancras),* 89, 98, 168; *20th*, 168; *2/20th*, 145; *21st*, 88, 89; *22nd*, 89; 23rd, 88, 89; *24th*, 90, 99; *28th (Artists),* 91, 97, 167, 177
Loyal North Lancashire: *9th*, 65, 66, 100, 180
Manchester: *5th,* 151, 173; *6th*, 76-78, 82, 151, 152, 172, 173, 191; *7th*, 152, 171; *8th*, 76, 78, 82, 144, 173; *10th*, 52, 56, 57, 77-79, 132, 144, 171, 173, 189, 195; *12th*, 86, 87, 92, 96, 98, 152, 167, 168; *18th*, 173; *19th*, 26, 186; *20th*, 98; *21st*, 24, 26, 27 189; *22nd*, 14, 24, 26, 27, 186
Middlesex: *4th*, 139; *7th*, 141, 146; *8th*, 136, 141, 143; *12th*, 15, 191; *17th*, 16, 191; *19th*, 70, 72, 181; *20th*, 50, 51; *21st*, 188; *23rd*, 72, 73, 181
Norfolk: *1st*, 145, 150, 159, 176; *9th*, 61, 63, 64, 183
Northamptonshire: *6th*, 20, 23, 187
North Staffordshire: *5th*, 14, 193; *2/6th*, 46; *8th*, 70, 74, 176; *9th*, 172
Northumberland Fusiliers: *1st*, 131, 133, 147, 148, 194; *7th*, 76, 77; *9th*, 48-50; *12/13th*, 159, 160; *13th*, 25, 27; *17th*, 191; *22nd*, 48; *23rd*, 48, 49; *25th*, 48, 49, 186, 187
Oxford & Bucks L.I: *2nd*, 134, 139, 178, 189, 195; *2/4th*, 195; 6th, 37
Queen's: *2nd*, 14, 24, 26, 27; *11th*, 72, 79
Rifle Brigade: *2nd,* 18, 19, 169 ; *12th*, 37, 170, 188; *13th*, 133, 139, 140, 155, 156, 170, 191
Royal Fusiliers: *4th*, 146, 147; *7th*, 97; *10th*, 133, 139, 140, 156, 188, 191; *13th*, 83, 133, 138, 154, 192 ; *17th*, 93, 94, 134, 137; *23rd,* 89, 90, 94, 131, 134, 137, 167; *24th*, 91, 93, 134, 139, 195

Royal Scots: *2nd*, 107, 148, 180, 185, 194; *4th*, 135; *5/6th*, 57; *7th*, 135; *15th*, 48, 49, 186; *8th*, 68; *16th*, 48, 49
Scots Fusiliers, R: *1st*, 107, 131, 148, 185, 194; *2nd*, 148; *4th*, 141; *5th*, 141; *6/7th*, 47, 50, 53, 181, 185
Scottish Rifles: *2nd*, 19, 169; *7th*, 135
Seaforth Highlanders: *4th*, 65, 66, 69 ; *5th*, 65, 177; *6th*, 65, 75, 125, 129, 177
Sherwood Foresters: *1st*, 19, 169; *2nd*, 62, 64, 183; *2/5th*, 45, 46, 48; *2/6th*, 48; *7th*, 46, 48; *10th*, 86, 87, 92, 98, 168, 178, 153, 171
Somerset L.I: *8th*, 133, 138, 190
South Lancashire: *2nd*, 60, 62, 64, 183
South Staffordshire: *1st*, 24, 26, 27; *2nd*, 15, 93, 134, 172, 177, 189, 195; *4th*, 72, 73, 175; *5th*, 14, 193; *2/6th*, 46
South Wales Borderers: *4th*, 99; *5th*, 69; *6th*, 66, 76, 78; *10th*, 156; *12th*, 38
Suffolk: *2nd*, 132, 133, 146, 148, 182, 195; *11th*, 48, 49; *12th*, 50, 53
Warwickshire, R: *2nd*, 195; *10th*, 67, 69, 70, 74, 178; *14th*, 133, 142, 164; 1*5th*, 133, 144, 158, 176; *16th*, 150, 151, 157, 159, 160, 176
Welch: *9th*, 68, 176; *13th*, 153; *14th*, 153; *17th*, 38, 39; *18th*, 38, 39, 50-52
Welsh Fusiliers, R: *1st*, 25; *4th*, 85, 87, 88; *9th*, 68, 70, 174, 176; *14th*, 157; *15th*, 169; *16th*, 157; *19th*, 38
West Yorkshire: *1st*, 62-64, 183; *2nd*, 19, 169; *2/7th*, 81; *8th*, 80, 82, 145, 153, 192; *10th*, 85, 96; *15/17th*, 55, 56, 193, 194; *16th*, 14, 192
Wiltshire: *1st*, 63, 68, 72, 73, 159, 174, 175; *6th*, 67, 68, 70, 176
Worcestershire: *3rd*, 65, 66, 183; *10th*, 66-69, 74, 93, 177, 179; *14th*, 178
York & Lancaster: *2nd*, 60, 61, 63, 183; *2/4th*, 81, 140, 149, 150, 192; *13th*, 55, 56, 193
Yorkshire (Green Howards): *2nd*, 25, 26, 186

Naval Battalions – Royal Marines L.I: *1st*, 97; *2nd*, 97, 171, 172; *Anson*: 97; *Drake*: 87, 91, 97; *Hawke*, 85, 91, 97, 139; *Hood*, 97, 138

Australian: *1st*, 33; *2nd*, 33, 178; *3rd*, 33, 34; *4th*, 34; *9th*, 36; *10th*, 175; *11th*, 34; *12th*, 33-35, 179; *17th*, 35; *19th*, 35, 36; *20th*, 35, 35; *50th*, 31, 32; *51st*, 31; *52nd*, 32; *55th*, 32, 179; *56th*, 32, 179; *59th*, 17, 183; *60th*, 17, 177

New Zealand: *1/Canterbury*, 172; *1/Otago*, 154, 170, 171; *NZ Rifle Bde*, 132, 156

Labour units: *36th* Company, 181

Machine Gun Bns: *2nd*, 169; *5th*, 142; *6th*, 60, 63; *17th*, 92, 94; *19th*, 70, 86, 170; *25th*, 65, 105, 178; *31st*, 76; *34th*, 49; *51st*, 65, 69, 178-80; *59th*, 47, 185; *62nd*, 80, 140

RAF/RFC: *4 Squadron*, 181; *15 Squadron*, 22; *41 Squadron*, 177; *59 Squadron*, 164

Tank Units: *No.1* Tank Gun Carrying Coy, 155; Tank Corps, 95, 163; *2nd* Tank Bn, 64; *8th* Tank Bn, 66, 93; *10th* Tank Bn, 72